PARALLEL TRACKS

PARALLEL TRACKS

The Railroad and Silent Cinema

Lynne Kirby

DUKE UNIVERSITY PRESS DURHAM

Acknowledgments

I began writing about trains and cinema in Paris in 1984 at La Sorbonne nouvelle (Censier/Daubenton). The first person to encourage me to pursue the topic was Jacques Aumont, to whom I am immensely grateful for early inspiration and invaluable critical insights. I must also thank Raymond Bellour, whose equally invaluable insights were crucial to the development of the study while I was at the Centre américain. Thanks are owed also to Roger Odin, who nurtured this work at Censier as my thesis director, and all the others at Censier who influenced the work, most notably Frank Kessler, Michel Marie, and the late Christian Metz. The late Sarah Kofman of the Sorbonne also had a significant impact on my approach to the subject. I dedicate this book to her and Christian.

To Janet Bergstrom I owe a giant debt of gratitude. As my dissertation advisor, she encouraged, supported, and inspired me in ways too numerous to mention. I am also indebted to my superb dissertation committee; Steve Mamber, Kathryn Montgomery, Anne Mellor, and David Kunzle all made writing the dissertation both stimulating and fun.

Through a predoctoral grant, the Smithsonian Institution made it possible for me to conduct historical research at the National Museum of American History (NMAH) in 1986–87. I could not begin to thank railroad historian William Withuhn, my advisor at NMAH, for the opportunity to profit from his considerable expertise and wisdom. Carlene Stephens of NMAH generously shared a wealth of material and insights on time and the railroads. Thanks go as well to the other Smithsonian fellows who inspired and sustained me during that time, in particular Charlie McGovern, Colleen Dunlavy, Wayne Durrell, and Grace Palladino (who merits extra-special thanks for photo support).

Thanks are owed the excellent staff at the Motion Picture Division of the Library of Congress who helped me identify and interpret dozens of early films that form the backbone of this study. I am grateful in particular to Patrick Loughney, Katharine Loughney, Pat Sheehan, Paul Spehr, Barbara Humphrys, Rosemary Hanes, and Joseph Balian. Charles Silver, Mary Corliss, Terry Geesken, and Mary Lea Bandy of the Museum of Modern Art also made my research there on silent railroad films both enjoyable and engaging.

I credit both Tom Gunning and Miriam Hansen with much of the historical and theoretical grounding of this book, and I thank them for incomparable close readings of the manuscript and suggestions for improving it. Tom's groundbreaking work on early cinema is evident throughout these pages, as are Miriam's pioneering revisions of silent film history. Both Tom and Miriam have provided me with wonderful friendship and crucial intellectual support over the years, as well as sterling examples of scholarship.

Others have contributed in different ways to this study. Erika Suderburg literally made it possible for me to complete the original study, and gave untold support and inspiration. Nataša Durovičová has been an invaluable sounding board and source of arcane train postcards for more than a decade. To Anne Friedberg I owe shared insights into nineteenth-century proto-cinematic culture, and my favorite toy train. Michael Jackson provided critical support during the writing of the first draft of the manuscript. Mme Madeleine Malthête-Méliès allowed me to see important, little-known films made by her grandfather. A reading of my work on *The Iron Horse* at Harvard University in 1989 was improved by suggestions from Stanley Cavell, Alfred Guzzetti, Suzan Pitt, and Rob Moss, while work presented on *The Crowd* in Frankfurt and Bern as part of the 1990 Feminismus und Medien Symposium benefited from feedback by Heide Schlüpmann, Gertrud Koch, and G. J. Lischka. In addition, André Gaudreault, Jean-Pierre Criqui, Christine Lapostolle, Ed Dimenburg, Chuck Wolfe, Paolo Cherchi-Usai, Donald Crafton, John Tagg, Faruk Tabak, Garrett Stewart, Murray Smith, Maria LaPlace, Fran Gleitman, Betsy Bilger, Bruce Jenkins, Rob Silberman, Joss Marsh, Suzanne Stenson, and Thomas Elsaesser all challenged me to think of my material in interesting and provocative ways. I also wish to acknowledge the long-standing influence of Maureen Turim, whose intellectual example first drew me to the study of film.

I am grateful to Constance Penley and Jane Gaines for bringing my work to the attention of Duke University Press, and to Connie for her early support of my work in *Camera Obscura*. Ken Wissoker at Duke deserves a medal for encouragement, patience, and editorial intelligence, all of which have made a difficult job pleasurable.

Finally, I thank my parents, Robert and Jackie Kirby, who have helped me in so many ways; and Neil Sieling, whose love and support took me all the way to the finish line.

Portions of this book have appeared in the following publications: "Geschlecht und Werbung," *Feminismus und Medien*, ed. G. J. Lischka (Bern: Benteli Verlag, 1991), *Um 9* series; "Gender and Advertising in American Silent Film: From Early Cinema to the Crowd," *Discourse* 13 (Spring/Summer 1991); "The Urban Spectator and the Crowd in Early American Train Films," *Iris*, no. 11 (Summer 1990); "From Marinetti to Vertov: Woman on the Track of Avant-Garde Representation," *Quarterly Review of Film and Television* 10, no. 4 (1989); "Male Hysteria and Early Cinema," *Camera Obscura*, no. 17 (Dec. 1988); "Da Marinetti a Vertov: La donna nel tema reppresentativo dell avanguardia," *Segnocinema*, no. 30 (Nov. 1987); "Temporality, Sexuality and Narrative in *The General*," *Wide Angle* 9, no. 1 (1987); "La femme et le train dans le cinéma primitif, classique et expérimental (1895–1929)," *L'Ecrit-voir* (les Publications de la Sorbonne, le Collectif pour l'Histoire de l'Art), no. 7 (1985–86).

Any errors or omissions in this manuscript are mine alone.

Lynne Kirby
New York
April 1996

PARALLEL TRACKS

1. *The Arrival of a Train at Le Ciotat Station*, Lumière Brothers, 1895.
Museum of Modern Art.

In 1925, British film critic Caroline Lejeune wrote in a review of John Ford's *The Iron Horse:* "Ever since the first producer sent his hero westward behind the first film engine it has been certain that the road to adventure lies along the track of those gleaming rails. Horses may be clean-limbed and fleet. The slim racing-car may be lovely in its pride. But for the kinema only the steel trail runs right into the heart of adventure. . . . Of all the machines that have turned and throbbed their way across the kinema screen none is more potent, none has moved to a finer measure, than the railway engine on the track."[1] It would be hard to dispute Lejeune's claims for cinema's love affair with the railroad. Since 1895, when the Lumière brothers showed *L'Arrivée d'un train en gare de La Ciotat* — one of the very first films projected publicly — the railroad has occupied an important place in cinematic representation (photo 1). Film might be said to owe one of its hallmark techniques, the tracking shot, to the train, and certainly one of its most enduring images in the countless views of arrivals and departures from train stations. And many a film has made use of the train as a ready-made site of crime, disaster, and romance — in a word, drama.

French film critic Dominique Noguez suggests that perhaps no form of transport has haunted the history of cinema as much as the train.[2] The railroad is in fact so omnipresent in the history of film as to be invisible, taken for granted. Yet hundreds of silent films either seized on the train as an image or integrated the train into their shooting strategy. The Lumières' first "arrival" film gave rise to a fascination with the train that persists to this day, and one that was overwhelming in the silent period. From George Méliès, Edwin S. Porter, and D. W. Griffith to Abel Gance, Dziga Vertov, Buster Keaton, John Ford, and King Vidor, silent film history has seemed to accord a special status to the railroad.

How can we explain this fascination the railroad holds for cinema? Why does silent film seem to privilege the train — including the trolley, elevated railway, and subway — over other forms of transportation, both older (the horse, the coach) and newer (the automobile, the airplane)? Some would see the cinema's interest in the train as that of the double: the cinema finds an apt metaphor in the train, in its framed, moving image, its construction of a journey as an optical experience, the radical juxtaposition of different places, the "annihilation of space and time." As a machine of vision and an instrument for conquering space and time, the train is a mechanical double for the cinema and for the transport of the spectator into fiction, fantasy, and dream. It is a metaphor in the Greek sense of the word: movement, the conveyance of meaning. Like film's illusion of movement, the experience of the railroad is based on a fundamental paradox: simultaneous motion and stillness. In both cases, passengers sit still as they rush through space and time, whether physically and visually, as on the train, or merely visually, as in the cinema. The train would then be cinema's mirror image in the sequential unfolding of a chain of essentially still images and the rapid shifts of point of view that the train and cinema experiences entail.

These compelling overlaps, however, are embedded in a myriad of cultural, social, and historical relations linking these two modern institutions. While the mechanical and visual similarities between the train and the cinema have certainly been exploited throughout film history and up to the present day in feature films and television, cinema's fascination with its double has deeper motivations rooted in the histories of technology, mass entertainment, and perception.

The railroad should be seen as an important *protocinematic* phenomenon, a significant cultural force influencing the emergence and development of the cinema during the silent period in both the United States and Europe. A primary objective of this book is to show that the railroad was, first of all, a social, perceptual, and ideological paradigm providing early film spectators with a familiar experience and familiar stories, with an established mode of perception that assisted in instituting the new medium and in constituting its public and its subjects. An equally important objective is to illuminate what the railroad offered cinema as a highly charged cultural image, a potent legend that informed the development of narrative as well as nonnarrative film. As I will show, the railroad was a contested figure in various struggles to establish film as an instrument of power versus an arena of experimentation and freedom.

At two basic levels — as a machine for producing and consuming images, and as the films themselves — the cinema developed images, myths, and perceptions of the train as much as the train informed cinema's own ways of conceiving of itself. Discourses on the train's representation in film might be said to reflect a fundamental instability common to both technologies. The instability of the railroad lies first of all in the very experience of mobility, of a passenger's being at once immobile and in rapid transit, lulled to sleep and yet capable of being shocked awake. It also lies in bringing together for a brief period individuals from all walks of life, while dynamizing and hence destabilizing relations among them, within a culture profoundly uprooted by the intrusion of the iron horse.

In cinema, instability is built into the basis of the filmgoing experience: the perceptual illusion of movement is tied to the physical immobility of the spectator and to the sequential unfolding of a chain of still images that constitute the basis of every film. The degree to which that instability was either controlled or exploited is a central issue for both the railroad and the cinema during the silent film era. This issue recurs across the themes of this book, themes that stem from the multiple ways in which the railroad forms a paradigm for cinema and defines a context for the figure in which the railroad and the cinema meet most profoundly: the spectator-passenger.

Laying the Tracks for the Movies

Cinema was born in 1895, during the golden age of railway travel in the United States.[3] The movies arrived at the end of a century defined mechanically and temporally by the railroad, a preeminently nineteenth-century institution. The railroad was originally a British invention that appeared in the late eighteenth century in Newcastle in the form of coal cars pulled over iron tracks by horses.[4] The first true railway locomotive did not arrive until 1804, and the first commercial railway line, the Stockton and Darlington, until

1825.[5] The first American railroad, the Baltimore and Ohio, was chartered in 1827, while the French and Russians started later, and until well in the 1840s were slow to lay track.[6] With the help of a French engineer and an English locomotive, Germany (still not a unified nation at the time) opened its first line in 1835, but construction was begun in earnest only after 1848.[7] In all countries, early lines were privately owned, but they had to obtain land grants, as well as permission to build, from the state.

English railways developed in a particularly laissez-faire fashion, with Parliament refusing to take charge of the railways. In the United States a similar situation occurred, but with government mediating the interests of canal owners and shippers — whom the railroad would ultimately replace — and the growing demands of the railroad companies.[8] In the United States, for example, the 1862 Pacific Railroad Act signed into law by President Lincoln authorized the Central Pacific and Union Pacific Railroads with capital and generous land grants that, in retrospect, were not exactly Lincoln's or Congress's to give.[9] The trend everywhere was toward increased consolidation, to the point of control by a few wealthy interests by the end of the nineteenth century. Even the French government's early intervention was designed to benefit the French railroad companies.[10] Ultimately, in part because of the experience of World War I, all systems were nationalized: the French in the early 1920s, the British in the 1940s (though heavy regulation had been instituted since the twenties), and the American in the 1970s.[11]

Established in the prime of industrial capitalism, the railways were Western culture's prime mover in stimulating the growth and creation of the coal, steel, and iron industries on which the railroads and the various industries served by them depended: lumber, livestock, ore, food, and manufactured goods.[12] By introducing fast, mass transportation capable of shrinking the time and distance between the point of production and the point of consumption, the railroads stimulated both ends of the economy to unprecedented degrees, carving entire towns out of raw landscape and contributing to the growth of cities. The great stations that sprang up at key points in cities and towns from the 1840s on were merely the monumental, aesthetic crowns of the economic and social power the railroads held in society, trumpeting an era, a century that belonged to the steam locomotive.

The major lines of the present English system were in place by 1852, while in the United States, railroad construction peaked much later (1916), nearly half a century after the completion of the first transcontinental railroad and roughly parallel to the Russian system, which dates back to the late 1830s, but experienced a boom in the last three decades of the nineteenth century.[13] Passenger traffic in the United States was originally a secondary concern, but it quickly developed as a form of revenue by the early 1840s.[14] The golden age of railway travel in the United Kingdom during the 1870s and 1880s resulted in part from lower fares, greater comforts, and higher speeds ("workingmen's trains" had been added in the 1860s as excursions for third-class travel).[15] European trains reflected social divisions in car design and in providing individual cars for individual classes, while American trains were theoretically classless — i.e., without rigid division into first/second/third-class cars — until the appearance of luxury trains in the 1880s, which followed on the preceding decade's invention and refinement of the Pullman sleeping car.[16] Meanwhile, the Pullman cars depended on the use of newly freed slaves as low-paid porters, thus continuing an overt master-servant practice rooted in whites' perceptions of their own status — perceptions encouraged by the railroads (at first, Pullman porters were paid no wages at all, only tips).[17]

Created in an era of British empire, railways outside the West appeared initially as an extension of Western imperialism. Indeed, it has been said that imperialism itself was a function of the railroad, so important was the train to expanding European and American economic and political interests.[18] The British were responsible for railway construction in India, Canada, Asia, Africa, and Latin America in the second half of the nineteenth century as a means of extending empire and controlling access to natural resources.[19] The process was one of both coercion and collaboration — in Argentina there was nationalist sentiment for building a railway system before the appearance of the British capital they needed to carry out the plan — but designed fundamentally to serve the Western-controlled world economy and developed nations.[20] This was true of American "railway imperialism" as well. The development of a railroad system in Mexico between 1876 and 1910 was utterly dependent on foreign investment, primarily American, and oriented the national economy toward export production and the international economy dominated by Western nations (many lines ran into Mexico directly from the United States via railway concessions).[21] Germany, France, and Japan also joined in making use of the railroad as a tool of imperialist expansion around the world, whether through direct governmental investment or through private financiers.[22]

Railway travel throughout Western nations declined in relation to the rise of the automobile in the 1910s and the car's mass acceptance in the twenties. In Russia, World War I and the Revolution devastated the railway system, which would not recover until after World War II. And though railway passenger traffic began to shrink in European countries, it plummeted dramatically in the United States, whose railroad system was effectively defeated as the dominant form of mass transportation at the end of the twenties.[23]

Training Audiences for Film

Since the railroad as a social, technological, and cultural institution was at its maturity when cinema arrived as a mass spectacle, the notion of paradigm must be taken in both a historical and theoretical sense. As a *social* paradigm, we find reception of the technology and the institution of the railroad in society repeated in early responses to the cinema: both were seen as a blessing and a curse. The social paradigm entails a discursive paradigm: discourses produced in response to the arrival of the railroad in the nineteenth century and split between embrace and resentment are paralleled in remarkably similar rhetoric by those produced around the arrival of the cinema. We find in both discourses the same ambivalence, the same fears about the eradication of tradition, and the same concerns about the social benefits and moral corruption embodied in each technology.

As a key agent of incorporating outlying regions into the orbit of the city, the centers of the First World, the train was a force of integration, of linkage, of coherence; it tried to make the world readable. At the same time, the force of such integration was profoundly dislocating. In its global rampage, the train literally uprooted and destroyed both Native American and European-American communities in the United States and preexisting communities in all parts of the world where colonialism and imperialism held sway. It redefined boundaries and accentuated differences, which it tried to smooth out in its imposition of hegemonic homogeneity.[24] Literature and popular imagery from the nineteenth and early twentieth centuries emphasized both aspects of the train.

The ambivalent attitude toward the train found a parallel in the ambivalence that greeted the early cinema. It is a commonplace that the cinema in both the United States and Europe had to legitimate itself socially.[25] While film was seen as a medium of enormous creative and economic potential, it was also seen as a site of immorality, both in practices of exhibition ("dens of iniquity") and in the kinds of images proffered for public consumption. Like the train, the cinema was obliged to clean up its image. Both sets of discourses emphasize the perceptual and aesthetic dimensions of the machines in question as well as their educational and moral dimensions. Each technology was also seen as a promising terrain for integrating the masses into a social whole, for leveling differences in a "democratic" space, a melting pot, all the while taking for granted the institutionalized racism that depended on African Americans and imported Chinese workers for lowly railroad labor while barring them from riding the rails and watching the movies with white passenger-spectators.

As a *perceptual* paradigm, the railroad established a new, specifically modern mode of perception that the cinema absorbed naturally.[26] In other words, the kind of perception that came to characterize the experience of the passenger on the train became that of the spectator in the cinema. Cultural historian Wolfgang Schivelbusch calls this "panoramic perception" to underscore the sense in which what early train travelers referred to as "the annihilation of space and time" owed something to the effect of the panorama, an eighteenth-century invention that was the virtual reality experience of its day.[27] The perceptual paradigm of cinematic spectatorship includes a changed temporal consciousness — an orientation to synchronicity and simultaneity embodied in the railroads' institutionalization of standard time in 1883. Simultaneity as a mode of consciousness infected cinematic spectatorship from the beginning and became institutionalized in the classical system of alternation and parallel editing.

Both panoramic perception and the radically new time consciousness were premised on a fundamental discontinuity and instability: the experience of shock.[28] Besides the shock of temporal disorientation in relation to speed, acceleration, and simultaneity, the spectator-passenger was susceptible to the shock of surprise during the train journey (as emblematized by the accident) and the film journey (exemplified by rapid point-of-view shifts within the frame and across different shots). An unstable western subject, embodied concretely in passengers and spectators, was created — one anticipating, yet immune, to shock. This was the modern urban subject jostled by forces that destabilized and unnerved the individual, creating a hysterical or, in nineteenth-century terms, "neurasthenic" subject. In the urban railway films of early, classical, and avant-garde cinema, the power of disruption and discontinuity as expressed doubly by the train and cinema contributed either directly or indirectly to the creation and re-creation of such an unstable subject.

The unstable subject of both the railroad and the cinema was a suggestible subject.[29] The obverse of the hysterical, neurasthenic individual was the hypnotized, or hypnotizable, subject, one in whom shock had opened up a space of vulnerability to the image, one in whom the vulnerability to a dream-like, fantasy state relaxed inhibitions and allowed for the possibility of sugges-tion. The suggestion might be rooted in sexuality and gender, but it served the ends of the consumer culture that anchored, and was anchored by, both the railroad and the cinema. "Accept this truth, these images, these values," each institution implored its ideal consumer-subject.

Perceptual, temporal, and metaphorical logic was also a technologic that linked the two nineteenth-century machines of economy and leisure in prac-tices of tourism, the spectacle, and the amusement park ride.[30] Thus, as an *ideological* paradigm, the railroad created a subject invested in the consumption of images and motion — that is, physical displacement — for entertainment. The railroad's subject was a tourist, a subject of leisure. The early cinema's status as an entertainment medium partly defined by the railroad was clearest in exhibition practices like Hale's Tours (1904–11), where the cinema merged literally with the train. Here, films shot from moving trains were projected inside converted railroad cars, thus advancing film's appeal to a mass spectator-ship common to both the train and the cinema and joining the tourism of the passenger to that of the spectator.

In terms of the impact of the railroad on filmic representation, we must consider not only the image, but the ways in which train films address their spectator-passenger. The ambivalence toward the railroad is interiorized by early cinema, but interiorized in such a way as to ignore the good or ill that the railroad represented. What mattered most in early train films was the shock effect in and of itself, the thrill of instability, which addressed a new subject cut loose from its moorings in traditional culture and thus potentially open to anything. Many early films exploited the train image for its shock potential, often at the expense of narrative coherence. The fear of accidents as com-monly reported in newspapers and magazines informed cinema's representa-tion of the train as a terroristic creature as well as the allegedly terrified response of the first spectators of *L'Arrivée d'un train*.

In the 1920s many experimental European films returned to the train as a terrifying vehicle of speed and a dynamic technology capable of representing film's own power. By incorporating the perceptual disorientation associated with the rapid rush of movement bound up with the train, these films cele-brated modernity as a liberating force and aimed to free film from its status as an instrument of bourgeois domination. In *Berlin: Symphony of a City, Entr'acte, La Roue,* and *Man with a Movie Camera* the freedom and playfulness of the train fuel the aesthetic experimentation of the films themselves. In *Man with a Movie Camera* particularly, the disruptive force of the train and its aesthetic potential are the revelation of a new vision, a revolutionary vision, both cinematically and ideologically.

From a middle-class, European-American perspective, the train as a "good object" appeared most often in mainstream, Hollywood-defined cinema. Stabilization was a priority of classical cinema as it emerged and distinguished itself from early cinema. A relation of what might be called mutual legitimation was formed. Railroad companies in the United States were early patrons of train films, often using film as a means of advertising their lines and legitimating their cultural pretensions — for example, in Edison/Porter's *Romance of the Rail* (1903). In simple journey narrative films like these, the train is relatively stable compared to its representation in early and avant-garde film. Even here, however, we can read against the grain of the text through traces of the anarchic early film: the film contains its own parody, which thus unbalances it as a fictitiously "whole," narratively resolved text.

The question of how instability was treated revolves around a particular aspect of the type of subject created by both the railroad and the cinema — that of gender. For the debates over the healthy or ill effects of each institution were phrased in gendered terms, whether literally (the train and the cinema as bad influences and places of license or danger with respect to female sexuality), or figuratively (the perception of the railroad as a demon whose destructive effects weakened culture and masculinity and feminized the male individual). The gender issue is crucial for my treatment of the subject, since most train films, from the beginning to the end of the silent period, are about gender and its relation to the machine. Set up as bracketed experiences where anything could happen between departure and arrival, many train films stage a recurrent scenario of coupling, uncoupling, and perversion with respect to the romantic, heterosexual couple. Often the unstable subject of the train and film is a subject of uncertain or variable sexual identity — an uncertainty given free and comic reign in early cinema and in certain avant-garde films, but coded and channeled, though not repressed, in classical American film.

The "subject" I am referring to is a European-American spectator embodied in a myriad of concrete individuals who come together and share subjectivity through the cinema while maintaining the differences they bring with them into the theater.[31] This group includes spectators of color, who though kept from sharing literal theater space with white spectators, were addressed in many of the same ways and through many of the same films as were European-American spectators. In so many films where images of African Americans, Asian Americans, and Native Americans appear, the films are addressing all spectators as European-Americans, since, especially in train films, people of color appear rarely and, when they do, are seen mainly as background figures, comic buffoons, or evil menaces. This does not mean, of course, that audiences of color received and responded to these images in the ways that white culture might have dictated. For example, as Mary Carbine has shown in her important study of black moviegoing in Chicago during the silent period, African Americans had their own contexts — and theaters — for consuming movies, contexts that allowed for different forms of expression and response.[32] Yet, while not a dominant theme in this book, in large part because of the dearth of people of color in the films considered, race will play an important part in this narrative, whether considering the Chinese who helped build the railroad, the Native Americans victimized by the railroad's progress, or African Americans enlisted as porters to smooth the journeys of white passengers and spectators.

The question of cinema's subject, along with the representation of the train, became a question of national cinema in the twenties. In classical narrative cinema the train was generally given the role of integration and linkage, of stabilization, especially in terms of American national identity: the mythology of assimilation to a "universal" American identity. This was an ideology that supported a stable white male subject by controlling the instability that was associated with femininity and "foreign-ness" or "otherness" in the broadest sense, including, crucially, a racial sense. Whether by incorporating African Americans or by demonizing Native Americans, the move to respectability, in both American and European cinema, was a move to control the spectator, particularly white, working- and middle-class women, by instituting a universal American male identity with its imagery and narratives.[33] This effort meant that to "moralize" itself — to become respectable — cinema had to address a white, middle-class spectator. In the United States this development heralded the birth of classical cinema — the institutionalization of a mode of production and a cultural practice that distanced itself from the "wild youth" of early cinema. For the white female spectator this change was at first both a repression and a liberation. In the teens, we see "good" women characters who are extremely active and represent a displaced masculinity — before being "disci-plined," unsuccessfully, in films of the twenties, when the Hollywood system became much more stable. As regards the train, such a change was also a move toward stabilizing the image of the railroad, primarily through genres, a cate-gorizing framework that developed as a major stabilizing force of the Holly-wood system in the twenties.

In early films the train appeared as a site for the instability of sexuality and of identity in general. In avant-garde cinema this disruptive power of the train was unleashed, both to positive and negative effect, and as a statement about the power of cinema; in Soviet avant-garde cinema it was progressive, a part of the hope of the future; in French avant-garde cinema it was tragic, making victims of modernity. Yet even the classical Hollywood film was incapable of fully repressing the fundamental instability specific to film. Thus, a major sense in which the train and the cinema are doubles for each other is the sense in which each has historically represented its own instability as the opposite — a "smooth ride" on a constantly shifting vehicle — by integrating the modern, primarily urban subject into a larger, mechanically defined world.

Tracking the Vehicle from Departure to Arrival

To chart the relations between two such complex and enormous institutions as the train and the cinema requires an expansive spirit of inquiry, one open to many methods of analysis, criticism, and historical investigation. My aim is an illumination of the relations between the railroad and the cinema through several prisms, not a comprehensive theory that will account for all aspects of the phenomenon in all historical contexts, which would be impossible in any case. Thus, while history and theory are important tools for understanding these relations across many contexts, my narrative is heavily influenced both by the available primary source material and by my own theoretical predilec-tions. Starting from a historical and analytical perspective, I place theoretical speculation within a cultural network of references that will ultimately help us make sense of the representation of the railroad in specific films. This book represents an attempt to see a huge and elusive phenomenon as a changing, dynamic relation among several different kinds of "texts."

My objective, broadly speaking, is to understand the emergence and growth of cinema as part of a larger social and cultural picture in which we can see cinema in relation to other apparatuses of modernity — specifically, the railroad — and to explore the various links between two technologies that profoundly influenced the ways in which we perceive and use the modern world. As an apparatus for the production and consumption of moving images, the cinema has been compared to dreams, memory, and hypnosis — in short, to the psyche.[34] Drawing in part on these comparisons, I aim to locate the cinematic apparatus between theories of the subject and historically specific cultural practices that informed the creation of passengers and spectators.

This study is strongly inspired by the work of Walter Benjamin and Roland Barthes. Benjamin's nonlinear history of perception and cultural forms emphasizes the social relations bound up with cultural representations and practices as well as the importance of technique and technology in the history of modernity.[35] Wolfgang Schivelbusch, whose study *The Railway Journey* has laid an important foundation for this book, demonstrates that Benjamin's theory of shock is useful for understanding the train as a perceptual paradigm for modern life as it came to be in the nineteenth and early twentieth centuries.[36] The railroad created its masses of subjects in relation to physical, visual, and social shock, and the rail industry tried to manage that relation — to control shock — throughout its history. Benjamin related the experience of shock to the factory and to urban life in general, especially traffic in the streets, and he saw film as a logical extension of the technology of shock in its incorporation of discontinuity and juxtaposition as formal principles, particularly of montage.[37] I will extend the argument to consider the specific conjuncture of train and cinema, while drawing on his general approach to cultural objects for my own analyses.

Roland Barthes's criticism applies semiological principles to the analysis of both high art and popular culture. Barthes's *Mythologies* and *S/Z* provide useful theoretical paradigms for understanding cultural objects.[38] *Mythologies* analyzes cultural practices and representations as diverse as the face of Garbo, the wrestling match, and the cultural distinction between wine and milk in French culture in terms of how they create meaning and how such meanings serve particular socioeconomic interests in society. *S/Z* is a detailed analysis of a Balzac novella that looks at the text through its own specific codes and in light of wider contexts like the culture in which it was produced. Barthes invokes a number of intertexts that together "create a kind of network, a topos through which the entire text passes (or rather, in passing, becomes text)."[39] What is important for my purposes is that Barthes does not purport to explain the text, or pin it down in any classical, structuralist manner; he preserves the basic sense in which a text as a dynamic process always eludes the grid of a structure.

My approach also owes much to Michel Foucault, whose notions of discourse as practice, and as effects and supports of power, are useful in mapping a set of social relations across two separate institutions.[40] I "read" events and experiences, as well as texts and images, to understand the train and the cinema as parts of a discursive field, that is, a field of culturally determined meanings suffused with power relations. The relations that arise among specific practices around both the railroad and the cinema can be seen in light of Foucault's concept of discursive formation: "Whenever, between objects, types of statement, concepts, or thematic choices, one can define a regularity (an order, correlations, positions and functionings, transformations), we will say, for the sake of convenience, that we are dealing with a discursive formation. . . . "[41] Discursive formations very much concern relations between different cultural phenomena that bespeak common sets of rules about how these phenomena are thought of, approached, and experienced.

Foucault's *Discipline and Punish* is a particularly compelling model of how to approach linkages among various institutions concerned with the management of bodies and subjects in a particular social formation. In this work, Foucault demonstrates how a paradigm of changing concepts of discipline from the seventeenth through the nineteenth centuries links a number of different institutions, such as the military, schools, and factories.[42] This is useful insofar as I see the railroad as a preexisting and coexisting paradigm that affects cinema's self-conception, sometimes directly, but more often indirectly — i.e., paradigmatically. As much as possible, I want to tie the train's representation in the cinema to the train's historical and ideological functions, to national differences, and to social-sexual factors bearing on an understanding of the train's popular representation.

My study owes a tremendous amount to the work of Tom Gunning and Miriam Hansen, who along with Anne Friedberg have done much to advance research and analysis of the kinds of intersections that film history occupies in relation to the modern world — leisure practices, technology, the city, consumerism, the modern emphasis on the visual, and how the subject of cinema emerges from an encounter with various forces affecting urban life in particular.[43] Giuliana Bruno's 1993 work on the city films of Elvira Notari also makes an important contribution in these areas.[44]

In addition to these thinkers, this book draws on various theoretical perspectives rooted in a number of disciplines, from psychoanalysis and textual analysis to social history, film history, and the history of the railroad. Psychoanalytic theory provides a useful guidepost in analyzing gender and sexuality in cultural, historical, and textual terms. Besides posing its own reading as an erotically charged public icon, the train appears in many films as a stage for sexual encounters, often of a perverse nature. When my analysis does turn to a psychoanalytic reading, the main axis of orientation in understanding the nature of this perversity is revisionist Freudian theory, strongly informed by feminist thought. The work of Sarah Kofman and Jean-François Lyotard, as well as feminist literature on psychoanalysis and film, are important to my analysis.[45]

It would be impossible to ignore narrative theory in studying narrative films, and I find the work of Tzvetan Todorov, Barthes, Stephen Heath, and Laura Mulvey particularly useful.[46] Other perspectives that inform my analysis in important ways can be found in social histories of leisure and/or perception (e.g., works by Jackson Lears, Kathy Peiss, Lary May, Jonathan Crary),[47] film history and theory (the work of Hansen, Gunning, Judith Mayne, Robert Allen, André Gaudreault, and Charles Musser, among others),[48] railroad history (studies by Leo Marx, Jeffrey Richards and John H. MacKenzie, James A. Ward, and others),[49] and textual analysis of film (most notably the writings of Raymond Bellour, Thierry Kuntzel, and Janet Bergstrom).[50]

It is important to note an existing body of writing on the train and the cinema, much of which has directly benefited this book (see below). However, important differences exist between much of this work and what I am attempting to do. The work I am presenting in these pages aims to extend and deepen many of the initial insights made about train and cinema by placing them into larger, social-historical contexts, drawing attention to the crucial relation of gender to both, and offering detailed analyses of both little-known and well-known films, in many cases offering new conclusions about them.

In 1989, when I finished the dissertation that is the basis of this book, little scholarly writing on the subject paid any attention to these issues. The literature on relations between the railroad and the cinema began for me with Robert Allen, whose article on "The Archeology of Film History" still provides a good orientation to considering film in relation to nineteenth-century technology.[51] Others dealing directly with the train-film connection included Dominique Noguez and Mary Anne Doane, who each dealt with metaphorical connections between the train and cinema in provocative and useful ways.[52]

Charles Musser's study of the travel genre of early cinema and the tourism common to both film and train laid an important foundation for my consideration of these phenomena,[53] while Raymond Fielding's detailed account of Hale's Tours proved useful as well.[54] The work of Frank Kessler and Gabriele Jutz on perceptual and metaphorical relations between the train and the panorama and diorama was and is extremely suggestive with regard to the cinema.[55] By contrast, John Huntley's book *Railways in Cinema*, while the most comprehensive on the subject to date, is largely a descriptive, annotated catalog of train films from 1895 to the present.[56]

The 1990s have seen the appearance of many important and exciting publications dealing with early and silent cinema, including seminal books by Tom Gunning, Miriam Hansen, Charles Musser, Eileen Bowser, and Richard Koszarski.[57] Work that is closer to my own has also appeared, most notably in articles by Ben Singer and Lauren Rabinovitz, in Sumiko Higashi's work on Cecil B. DeMille, and in Michael O'Malley's important history of American time, which encompasses both the railroad and the cinema.[58] This newer material is reflected in updates I have made to the original dissertation.

From 1984 until 1989 primary research of documents and images of railroad and film history was conducted at the Smithsonian Institution's National Museum of American History, the Library of Congress, the British Film Institute, the George Eastman House in Rochester, New York, the Museum of Modern Art, the University of California-Los Angeles Film and Television Archive, and in various private collections in France and Italy. Besides viewing hundreds of prints of films, I looked at a vast array of railroad documents (guidebooks, schedules, brochures, special publications, advertisements, catalogs), stereographic images, photographs, and both high art and popular images in illustrated trade and mass magazines. I also consulted literary sources, contemporary writings on both the railroad and the cinema, film magazines, film criticism, and early histories of the cinema.

The overwhelming majority of films I viewed were American, because of their much greater availability to me. As a result, the book is heavily skewed to American examples. Although my generalizations are indicated in most instances, it should be clear from the outset that my assumptions and conclusions are informed to a great extent by the primary material at hand.

It should also be clear that I am limiting this study on purpose to silent cinema. The train does in fact continue to be an important, recurrent figure in sound cinema, from *Shanghai Express* to many Alfred Hitchcock films from the

1930s on. I choose to focus on silent film primarily in order to be able to manage the corpus — the subject and number of films covered are huge. And shifts in representation owing to sound — the train whistle, for example, adds a new significance narratively and symbolically — make the end of the silent era a natural stopping point.

A Note on the Route Taken

This book breaks down into four main chapters that trace the themes and arguments outlined above in a loosely chronological and thematic fashion. Although each chapter represents a different topical emphasis, taken together they define a chronological trajectory leading from the prehistory of cinema (concurrent with the nineteenth-century history of the railroad), through early cinema and the 1910s and finally to the 1920s, the focus of the last two chapters. Each chapter also includes detailed analyses of specific films, which weave together the larger thematic threads of gender, culture, and perception.

Chapter 1 concerns the prehistory of cinema in relation to the emergence and institutionalization of the railroad and the impact of the railroad paradigm on modes of spectatorship specific to early film. It focuses on perceptual and ideological overlaps between the train and the cinema in discourses that include the panorama, tourism, and photography. The unstable subject that links these discourses and institutions is considered in relation to gender, and an argument is made for an early film spectator whose gender orientation is destabilized in early train films and early film exhibition practices.

Chapter 2 continues the analysis begun in chapter 1 of the railroad and its relation to gender and race. This chapter considers shifts in film form during the silent era as they relate to white women in particular and the institutionalization of regulated modes of spectatorship. After looking chronologically at all of these relations in silent film history, I go on to consider the survival of early film form within the classical film text of the twenties in terms of textual instability and gender.

Chapter 3 articulates the thematic of the unstable subject of the railroad and film with respect to an urban point of view and an urban spectatorship. The urban point of view is placed within the context of the "culture of consumption" — specifically, advertising and its relation as an optical practice of modern society to the kind of subject created by the railroad and cinema. Varying perspectives on the "modern" as expressed through the train and the cinema, seen as doubles for each other, are considered in detailed analysis of two films: *The Crowd* (King Vidor, United States, 1928) and *Man with a Movie Camera* (Dziga Vertov, USSR, 1929).

Chapter 4 takes into account the significance of national orientation as it influenced the representation of the train in silent film. The concerns of earlier chapters, primarily the romantic couple, and the notion of integration versus disintegration with respect to both the train and the cinema, are reprised in relation to the distinction between classical Hollywood and avant-garde film. Textual analysis is the primary mode of inquiry posed with respect to two films that provide an instructive contrast in national modes of representation: *The Iron Horse* (John Ford, United States, 1924) and *La Roue* (Abel Gance, France, 1923).

ONE

*Inventors and Hysterics: The Train in the Prehistory
and Early History of Cinema*

Beginning in 1895, cinema established itself first and foremost as a window on
the world, a dazzling new source of visual information in the form of short
films called actualities. Taken from the French term *actualités*, which, roughly
translated, means "things happening now," "actualities" referred to documentary, newsreel-type footage of current events, famous people, entertainments,
disasters, cities, expositions, novelties, and landmarks.

Early film production up to about 1904 was overwhelmingly dominated
by actualities. Most actualities were travel and scenic films, meaning everything from train journeys through various parts of the world to sights of all
kinds photographed in exotic or remote locales.[1] Travel subjects constitute
roughly half the titles in the Vitagraph Company's 1903 catalog, while the
earliest catalogs of Biograph productions (when the company was still called
AM&B — the American Mutoscope & Biograph Company) reveal that out of
some 2,500 films produced from 1896 until 1902, several hundred were travel
and scenic films, of which most involved a train or some aspect of the railroad.[2]
These include titles like *Taken from a Trolley* (ca. 1896), *Train Coming Out of
Station* (ca. 1897), and *View on Niagara Div., Michigan Central* (1899), as well as
scores of "arrival" and "departure" train films paralleling those produced by
French and English filmmakers.[3]

In a most elementary sense, shooting a moving train, the fastest vehicle in the world in 1895, gave filmmakers an opportunity to show off film's powers of registration, its ability to *capture* movement and speed. Many titles offer clues to the in medias res approach to filming trains, the idea being that the vehicle must be in motion to be properly represented: *Entering and Issuing from Tunnel from Pilot of Engine* (AM&B, 1903), *Down Exeter Incline* (Warwick, 1896), *Through Three-Mile Cascade Tunnel* (AM&B, 1903). Edison's production is comparable for the same period, and to both we may add the Miles' Brothers' railroad crashes, Selig's and the Vitagraph Company's Far West train trips, Lumière's "arrivals" from around the world, and a similar output in England.[4]

Fiction film, which came increasingly to dominate film production after 1902, also early on made great use of the railroad, including the elevated train and the subway. The train might be featured as an actor in its own right, as an important dramatic vehicle, or as the actual ground of vision, the thing that almost ontologically makes possible the view before the spectator. In *The Photographer's Mishap* (Edison/Porter, 1901), *The Ghost Train* (AM&B, 1903), *The Tramp's Miraculous Escape* (Edison, 1901), *Uncle Josh at the Moving Picture Show* (Edison/Porter, 1902), *A Railway Tragedy* (Gaumont, 1904) and *Rube and Fender* (Edison, 1903), the train is an antagonist, a threatening opponent to a human subject. *Le Voyage à travers l'impossible* (Méliès, 1904), *The Deadwood Sleeper* (AM&B, 1905), *What Happened in the Tunnel* (Edison/Porter, 1903), *Grand Hotel to Big Indian* (AM&B, 1906), *Streetcar Chivalry* (Edison/Porter, 1903), *Nervy Nat Kisses the Bride* (Edison/Porter, 1904), and *A Romance of the Rail* (Edison/Porter, 1903), all use the train as a highly motivated setting that determines much of the narrative action. *A Trip to Berkeley, California* (Biograph, 1906), *The Hold-Up of the Rocky Mountain Express* (Biograph, 1906), and *A Trip on the Catskill Mountain Railway* (Biograph, 1906) combine documentary with fiction to produce hybrid journey narratives that exploit various aspects of the movement of the train. And films like *Catching an Early Train* (Edison/Porter, 1901), *Five Minutes to Train Time* (AM&B, 1902), *The Bewitched Traveller* (AM&B, 1904), and *The Suburbanite* (AM&B, 1904) merely assume the train as a symbol of rationalized time, such that off-screen train time, and in some cases on-screen train time as well, determine the action on-screen.

One explanation for the fascination with the railroad seems obvious: many early filmmakers were inventors, men with vested interests in machines, technology, and progress. Thomas Edison himself had experimented with electrical locomotive power in the early 1880s.[5] William Kennedy Laurie Dickson, who with two others founded the American Mutoscope Company in

1895 (before it became AM&B), up to then had been Edison's assistant.[6] And William Selig of Chicago, another early filmmaker, was also an inventor, while the Lumière brothers came to cinema as manufacturers of photographic supplies.[7] Thus, it seems natural that the interests of the railroad were, at least in part, those of early film. In a sense, even Edison's will-to-monopoly, forged in the numerous patent wars fought over the phonograph, the Vitascope (his first film projector, actually the invention of Thomas Armat), and other machines, might owe something to his railroad magnate peers and the corporate spirit that would eventually lead him to form the Motion Picture Patents Company in 1908.[8]

If film was interested in the railroad, the railroad was just as interested in film. Perhaps the most legendary railroad patron in film history was Leland Stanford, the former governor of California and coowner of the Central Pacific Railroad, who in 1872 commissioned Eadweard James Muybridge to make his photographic series analyzing the sequence of movements of a horse in motion, the series that would inspire both Etienne-Jules Marey and Edison in their cinematic experiments.[9] American railroad companies had in fact been avid patrons of the fine arts and photography from the mid-nineteenth century on. In 1858, for example, the B&O Railroad sponsored a famous Artists' Excursion, "an event epitomizing the rapport established at mid-century between the artistic community and the railroad interests."[10] More than fifty artists, photographers and literati traveled at the invitation of the B&O from Baltimore, Maryland, to Wheeling, West Virginia, with several stops along the way for sketching and photographing the views (photo 2). The widely reported event is the first known instance of a railroad using art to publicize itself.[11] The B&O wanted to be known to the public as the "Picturesque Line of America" and thereby increase its revenues, which had fallen in relation to passenger traffic.[12] By the 1890s, like most major lines in the late nineteenth century, the B&O had an official staff photographer, who authored an article, "The Wonder of the Age," in the first issue of the *Book of the Royal Blue* (1897), the B&O magazine named after its luxury limited rail line.[13] The "wonder" referred to in the article is not, however, the locomotive, but cinema. The article announces future company plans to produce and exhibit more films showing such scenes as two Royal Blue trains passing each other at scenic points. (photo 3).[14] Film here was extending a function fulfilled by photographers like William Henry Jackson and Andrew Joseph Russell, the two greatest photographic documentarians of the westward expansion of the railroads.

2. *B&O Artists' Excursion, West of Piedmont*, 1858.
National Museum of American History.

Early film catalogs in turn took pains to thank the various railroad lines
that allowed them to shoot on or from trains.[15] In the 1901 Edison catalog, its
Northern Pacific Railway series is preceded by a paragraph expressing indebt-
edness to the line's officials. The item further notes: "Many of the scenes . . .
show the resources of this company for handling large numbers of people,
baggage, freight and excursion parties, and give to prospective tourists and
merchants an idea of the facilities with which this road handles traffic of all
kinds."[16] Billy Bitzer, who would go on to become D. W. Griffith's celebrated
cameraman, recounts in his autobiography that this mutual promotion was
widespread when he was starting out at Biograph in the late 1890s:

> The New York Central appreciated the advertising value of the movie we
> had taken of the Empire State Express. Our picture-taking equipment,
> which was very heavy and cumbersome . . . was transported over their
> lines free of charge. The camera operators received courtesy-free passage
> anywhere they wished to go. We were invited to avail ourselves of special

3. *Film Crew Shooting B&O Royal Blue, Thomas Viaduct,* c. 1897.
National Museum of American History.

engines, or cars, for the purpose of taking movies of the scenery along the
way. This led to other railroads making similar offers. The advertising
was then put on a commercial basis — first by the Union Pacific, whose
crack train, the Overland Limited, we photographed. . . . Next came the
Canadian Pacific, contracting with us for movies. I started on one trip for
them which covered thirty thousand miles from the time I started until I
returned, about two months. On these combined railroads, my trip took
me from New York to California, photographing the New York Central,
Michigan Central, Chicago Northwestern, Union Pacific, and on lines
from Montreal to Nova Scotia. During this time I was always supplied
with my own special car.[17]

These promotional films, which were not marketed as such by the filmmakers,
form a complement to the voluminous travel literature put out by the railroads
in the United States from the 1880s until the 1920s.

But neither of these models — what we might call the "author" model in the case of individual filmmakers, and the "patronage" model in the case of the railroad companies — explains the fact that train films appear in other national cinemas and in the United States without links to an "inventor consciousness" or railroad patronage. And neither can account for the diversity of production, and the vastly different points of view on the train. The extremely antiunion Edison might show a docile labor force of section hands cheering the passing of the Black Diamond Express, but he could also mine a head-on collision for all it was worth, or exploit popular images of the danger of train travel in both comic and dramatic films.

To form a fuller picture of the forces affecting film's representation of the train in early cinema, we need to focus first on the controversial integration of the railroad into American and European societies and on how it appears in other media and representational practices that preceded and coexisted with cinema. The unstable position of the railroad, its social and cultural complexity, brought forth a range of responses that included celebratory embrace and critical hostility, as well as sheer ambivalence. The reception of cinema in its first thirty years followed a strikingly similar path. Insofar as the cinema emerged in relation to the railroad as a great technology of its age, we have to be aware of what it owes to both the positive and negative reception of the train and how the image of the train in various media influenced the relations between the railroad and the cinema.

Early filmmakers drew on a wide range of representations of the train in a number of cultural practices, from photography to amusement parks, and thereby appealed to an audience that straddled the immigrant populations and the working class, as well as vaudeville's more middle-class patrons. To understand the broader context of this diversity, I will focus on the "legitimation crisis" of the railroad, primarily the American railroad, and its parallels in cinema, and then look at some of the representational practices that influenced the image of the train in film.[18] These practices will be considered with a view toward a spectator who could be said to bridge the railroad and the cinema at a certain moment in the history of each. For the discursive comparison alone cannot fully explain the extent to which the cinema can be said to be heir to the railroad. The "paradigm" of the railroad prepared a path for the institutionalization of a certain kind of subject or spectator that cinema would claim as its own, a subject molded in relation to new forms of perception, leisure, temporality, and modern technology.

A Controversial Machine — 1

It is no surprise that the B&O, the Lackawanna, the Lehigh, the New York Central, the Northern Pacific, and other lines would be so interested in cinematic and other forms of advertising. From the beginning, the railroads had to be vigilant in legitimating their cultural and economic place in American society, despite the literary, artistic, and self-promotional paeans they inspired or themselves created. Everywhere the railroad went, its arrival precipitated an avalanche of debate about its potential for both evil and good. Such was particularly the case in Europe where the public perception of the train's destruction of tradition was understandably much greater than in the United States. But in both places, the railroads had to steer a course through an ambivalent and unresolved public opinion.

On the one hand, the arrival of the railroad in Western industrial nations was greeted by a chorus of approval. In a nod to spokesmen for the railroads in the nineteenth and early twentieth centuries, some contemporary views of the train as a socioeconomic object accent the linking function of the railroads, their value as forces of cohesion and creation of the social body.[19] Jean-Luc Evard notes that "the train is the first great social machine: it cements all spaces in its homogenizing rings, thus bringing together the four instances of political economy — production, distribution, circulation, consumption — and continually intermingles them. It creates original landscapes with proto-filmic qualities, it brings together merchandise, individuals, classes, animals, and this conjunction is the often magical manifestation of its rigorously egalitarian, unitary and divisive principle. . . . "[20]

The railroad's "original landscapes" feature prominently in Leo Marx's classic study of "the machine in the garden," which looks at nineteenth-century American thought and literature in light of the cultural conflict between the "machine" (technology, especially the train) and the "garden" (America as the new Eden). Defenders of the machine emphasized the integration of the train into the landscape, and the crossing of regional and social barriers entailed by the standard-bearer of progress.[21] Marx quotes Charles Caldwell, whose "Thoughts on the Moral and other Indirect Influences of Rail-Roads" appeared in *New England Magazine* in 1832: " 'Alpine scenery and an embattled ocean deepen contemplation, and give their own sublimity to the conceptions of beholders. The same will be true of our system of Rail-roads.

Its vastness and magnificence will prove communicable, and add to the standing of the intellect of our country.' "[22] Another writer in 1853 saw the locomotive as a kind of fulfillment of mythic prophecy, the building of "an empire
and an epic" on land to be crossed by the iron horse: " 'Shall not solitudes
and waste places cry for gladness at his coming?' "[23] This rhetoric of progress found many adherents outside the railroad, steamship, and industrial-
technological community, most notably in Daniel Webster and John Stuart
Mill.[24]

One need consider only *The Lackawanna Valley* (1854) by George Inness
to realize the utopian vision of the integration of technology and nature that is
implied in such a view. This well-known painting, a commission from the
president of the Delaware, Lackawanna and Western Railroad, was, in the
words of Leo Marx, "a fulfillment of Emerson's prescription for achieving
harmony between the new technology and nature."[25] Inness's work shows a
pastoral idyll, with the railroad integrated gently into the background, its
steam clouds echoing the cloud puffs behind the church, whose steeple could
almost pass for a factory stack in the perfect marriage of the spiritual and the
industrial. The point of view is clearly from above, that of the shepherd boy
who, perched on the hillside, gazes lazily and benevolently upon the docile,
man-made scene below.[26]

Wolfgang Schivelbusch notes that for adherents of progressive thought
in the first half of the nineteenth century "the railroad appears as the technical
guarantor of democracy, harmony between nations, peace, and progress,"
adding that "according to them, the railroad brings people together both
spatially and socially."[27] In France, the greatest champions of the railroads
were the Saint-Simonists, who held a utopian socialist view of the potential for
good embodied by the railroad.[28] In the United States, representatives of the
railroad early on touted it as a vehicle of national unity. Even Emerson privileged the railroad as an instrument of unification for the nation.[29] For some
railroad defenders, the vision of the train as a democratizing force marked the
train as a specifically American machine, especially insofar as the United States
embraced technology and mechanization in an intense and rapid manner compared to other nations (photo 4). Walt Whitman is only the most famous
literary representative of this enthusiastic acceptance.[30]

The railroads in the United States from their beginnings until the 1970s
remained private companies that linked up regions primarily for economic
gain.[31] In France, by contrast, the function of linking, of joining two disparate

4. *Across the Continent: Westward the Course of Empire Takes Its Way*, lithograph, Currier & Ives, 1868. Metropolitan Museum of Art, gift of George S. Amory in memory of Renee Carhart Amory, 1966.

geographical points, soon became an economic and political obligation heavily managed by the state.[32] But whether in the name of public or private interests, the train represented order and rationality — after all, it is the railroads that demanded the global standardization of time according to their schedules.[33]

Insofar as the train has always been a physical extension of an imperialist vision, of the hegemonic expansion of an economic and cultural power, a principle of incorporation and arrangement, and of the discipline of heterogeneous territories, its function has been that of coherence, order, and regularity. In general, the train is a vehicle that imposes sense on what modern Western culture sees as irrational: nature and tradition. It enforces a kind of readability or understanding according to the authority of *its* codes and *its* master — the white male entrepreneur. The conquest — indeed, creation — of a market is inscribed in the work of circulation and communication that is the economic motive of the railroad, its very raison d'être.

One could, however, insist equally on the effect of delirium and dislocation in the literature that addresses the role of the train in history. For, if the train links and associates, it does so at the price of undoing everything in its path. Opposition to the railroad appeared in all countries building railroads in the nineteenth century, including the United States, though it was stronger in Britain, France, and other European countries where "progress" had a much narrower berth.[34] The "annihilation of space and time" that the first riders of the rails experienced spoke to the destruction and disintegration of the old space-time, of tradition linked to nature, and of a moral economy.[35] Victor Hugo's oft-quoted description of a train trip taken between Brussels and Antwerp in 1837 is a curious mixture of impressionistic amazement at the visual blending of objects and colors along the way and an aesthetic orientation opposed to the machine: "Such is the sad infirmity of our time; the dryly useful, never the beautiful. . . . As for me, given Watt naked, I would gladly clothe him in Benvenuto Cellini. . . . "[36] As Schivelbusch notes, it is a question of two contradictory sides of the same process: "on the one hand, the railroad opens up new spaces that were not as easily accessible before; on the other, it does so by destroying space, namely the space between points."[37] This is realized and articulated as the loss of local autonomy or, as Walter Benjamin might have said, the loss of "aura."[38]

For Native Americans, the railroad represented a brutal invasion of their lands and the destruction of traditional ways of life. Following the literal and metaphorical trails blazed by decades of white trappers, traders, miners, and settlers from the seventeenth through nineteenth centuries, the railroads in the 1860s and 1870s cinched the intrusive influence and presence of European-Americans in the West and led the way for exploitation and development of the land.[39] Kansas, Nebraska, Colorado, Wyoming, and South Dakota became major battlegrounds over Indian resistance to white claims on the land, with the Union Pacific Railroad, and its "right" to cross Cheyenne and Lakota hunting grounds, acting as a potent symbol of Manifest Destiny.[40] In addition to bringing ever more white people, the railroads furthered the damage to nature by driving away buffalo, antelope, and other wild game hunted by the Indians.[41] The railroads also contributed to the wholesale slaughter and near-extinction of the buffalo, both by hiring people like Buffalo Bill Cody to supply railroad construction crews with meat, and by encouraging white passengers to shoot buffalo indiscriminately for sport from train windows as they plowed through the West.[42] As befitted their status and power in the European-American economy, the railroads were able to count on the federal government to advance their interests with military protection and overt congressional and judicial sabotage of treaties meant to protect Indian rights.[43] Needless to say, the iron horse was not warmly embraced by Native Westerners.

Although they did not draw attention to the destruction of the Native people that occupied the land, Eastern-based European-American critics of the railroad, including artists, writers, and poets, emphasized the destruction of the landscape, both rural and urban.[44] Similar to the ways in which modern freeways have been allowed to blast through long-standing neighborhoods and communities, the railroad physically altered towns and the countryside, while erecting stations in the most economically suitable or convenient sites. In the United States, in particular, the railroads came to constitute a paradoxical form of urban planning, with the tracks defining the right of the train to charge straight through towns and woods, streams, fields, even mountains, and divide social classes once physically much closer.

As a white critic of the railroad, Henry David Thoreau held an essentially ambivalent view: the railroad was an inevitable and ultimately necessary link in the chain of progress, but also a "devilish Iron Horse" whose intrusive presence in the forest produced a "Deep Cut" in the land (see chapter 2, below).[45] And as Marx notes, even Ralph Waldo Emerson, whose essays in the early 1840s had come to reconcile the machine, particularly the locomotive, with the transcendental American garden, later came to doubt the compatibility of the pastoral and the industrial.[46]

The new order of the railroads entailed the disorder of the old European-American world in moral terms as well. The social body it created hardly resembled the society of yore, much as the railroad landscape stood apart from a more traditional landscape. In the words of Jean-Luc Evard, "Iron transportation was thus an ambiguous machinery: even as it hypostasized its objective qualities of rapidity, punctuality and irradiation, it came to symbolize the desire for deracination and the kind of accelerated movement proper to a mass culture."[47] Schivelbusch, citing Georg Simmel, notes that a particular type of alienating experience became typical for second- and first-class passengers. For the first time, he observes, total strangers were forced to stare at each other silently, thus reducing social relations between people in public to mere sight.[48] In contrast to the conversationless upper-class experience, which was marked by deep fear of being embarrassed by one's compartment companions, the carriages of third- and fourth-class travel were lively, noisy, and heterogeneous. (This is not to say, however, that lower-class train travel did not entail its own form of alienation as depicted, for example, in Honoré Daumier's famous *Third-Class Carriage* caricatures, which capture the empty expressions of women and men exhausted by hours of work.)[49]

In addition to contributing to a breakdown of traditional social relations and a traditional public sphere, the train carried the threat of a literal, physical disintegration, that of the accident.[50] For the train traveler, the fear of the accident was inscribed in the journey itself. From the beginning, the train and its apparatus, especially tunnels, represented a dangerous gamble. Daumier caricatured this sense of risk in his drawings devoted to the railroads. And not only the railroad periodicals, but a popular review like the French *Illustration* published in each edition the statistics on railroad accidents, while English magazines like *Punch* ritually ridiculed the uncaring and often dangerous intrusion of railroads into the life of society — the accidents, the unsafe riding conditions, the threats to the safety of women, the noise.[51]

But if the beginnings of the railroad were marked by a certain lack of precaution vis-à-vis the security of passengers, the risk of accident, especially in the United States, only grew as the nineteenth century wore on. Historian Robert Reed demonstrates that railroad accidents began to occur with alarming regularity only after 1853.[52] This was registered with fear and outrage in the United States and elsewhere.[53] According to an English observer in 1912, American railroads were the most dangerous in the world, particularly for nonpassengers: "If a cart or human being persists in occupying the track again — so much the worse for it or him. . . . Generally speaking, 'taking one's chance' is the lot of anybody or anything crossing the track, and the list of killed and wounded becomes appalling to English ideas. In 1901, for instance, 4,135 people other than passengers were killed and 3,995 wounded."[54]

The position of the railroads in Western nations continued to be one of constantly negotiating legitimacy, whether public or political. In France, the struggle between the six *grandes compagnies* and the state-owned networks was complemented by public complaint over the power of the railroads and, from the 1860s to the turn of the century, by the threat of an underground railroad in Paris.[55] In the United States, railroads were faced by 1895 with not only accidents, but a series of social and political crises that attracted the glare of public scrutiny — notably, the robber baron scandals. Through the use of "water stock" — some of it issued to members of Congress — in the late 1860s and 1870s, Jay Gould, Daniel Drew, Jim Fisk, and Commodore Cornelius Vanderbilt, to name only the most famous robber barons, swindled control of the major railroads, made enormous profits, caused intermittent panic in the stock markets, and blazed a wide trail of corruption, including the bribery of major politicians — until regulation caught up with them in the 1890s.[56]

Government regulation had begun to have an impact on the industry only in the 1890s. Regulation was initially the result of the Grange Wars of the 1870s and 1880s, a conflict that pitted Grangers (farmers), whose crops were hostage to whatever rates the railroads wished to charge them, against, in the Grangers' view, the "greed and tyranny of the railroad corporations" that were "carrying out a systematic warfare upon the people of the United States."[57] The Grangers numbered in the hundreds of thousands, and they organized to end the rebates given in secret by railroads to preferred corporate customers; they also opposed the exorbitant rates charged by railroad-controlled grain elevators where farmers had to store their surplus. The farmers were first organized in 1867 by Oliver Kelley, a clerk at the Bureau of Agriculture in Washington, D.C., and the first regulatory legislation was passed in Illinois in 1871.[58] The railroads ensured the reversal of some of the legislation passed in the 1880s, and they continued to abuse regulation well into the twentieth century. With the establishment of the ICC (Interstate Commerce Commission) in 1887, however, the government, backed by public opinion, advanced the struggle to control the runaway railroad monopolies.[59]

Violent labor unrest marked the late 1870s, 1880s, and 1890s, beginning with the 1877 railroad strike that catalyzed the first U.S. government labor policy in response to the near-paralysis of the national transportation system and the troubled public debate it inspired.[60] The unrest culminated in the famous 1894 Chicago railroad strike led by Eugene Debs.[61] The strike marshaled 100,000 men to boycott the Pullman Company, whose near-feudal tyranny over its workers (long hours, low wages, and no alternatives to the company-owned housing, stores, etc.) had initially resulted in the 3,000 Pullman shop employees walking out.[62] The refusal of the Pullman management to negotiate infuriated the railway union led by Debs, whose cautious approach to strikes and violence — and sympathetic attitude toward black railway workers, often enlisted by the company as strikebreakers — was outvoted by the rank and file.[63] Debs's success in soliciting so many sympathy strikers to cripple the nation's railway traffic in turn resulted in Federal troops rushing in to crush what the press called "Debs' Rebellion," so warlike was the conflict. Debs was jailed, but for hundreds of thousands of workingmen, he became the first true American labor martyr in standing up to the monolithic power of the railroads.[64]

In light of this unstable social and political context, the self-promotional efforts of the railroads in the late nineteenth century were in effect a renegotiation of legitimacy.[65] At the height of railroad travel, fully into its golden age, when the railroads were virtually the only game in town for mass transportation, lack of public confidence translated into pressure on politicians to control rates, schedules, and safety features.[66] In other words, even with a corner on public transportation, the railroad powers had to contend with regulatory challenges to their enormous profitability well into the twentieth century. Nothing demonstrates the response to this challenge more vividly perhaps than the literature churned out by the industry itself. In 1913, for example, the *Railway Age Gazette* published *Sayings and Writings About the Railway — By Those Who Have Managed Them and Those Who Have Studied Their Problems.* The book is a sort of Bible of railroad virtues and includes articles on "Civilization's Largest Factor" and "An Industry Necessary to Life." According to one of the book's authors, "It is not an exaggeration to say that in the past history of this country, the railway, next after the Christian religion and the public school, has been the largest single contributing factor to the welfare and happiness of the people."[67] Another railroad defender appealed to Western art history to justify the image of the railroad engineer as both an artist and the most competent, capable man of his day — in short, as a "Renaissance man." The author compares the train engineer to Michelangelo and Leonardo, also "great engineers" of their epoch.[68] The following year, *Railway Age Gazette* offered a clear statement of the situation: "the railroads should have the cooperation of the public. . . . The great trouble today is everybody has some kick coming that is unwarranted. Many people wish to start legislation against railroads when they do not really know what they are doing."[69]

The renegotiation was largely successful, of course, and as John Stilgoe emphasizes, the "romance of the rails" found eager adherents in the popular railroad mythology cultivated after 1880 — cultivated in large part, of course, by the railroads and their massive culture industry.[70]

A Controversial Machine — 2

The early history of cinema uncannily repeats that of the railroad in the polarization of discourses into "for" and "against," using similar lines of argumentation. The first American film historians praised the cinema as an art of democratic expansion and integration. Robert Allen has shown how early critics like Robert Grau (1914) and Terry Ramsaye (1926) constructed the birth of cinema as the arrival of a truly democratic art in the line of technological advances, notably the train, toward the resolution of social and economic problems. "Their view of cinema technology as democratic art is but a late expression of a dominant technological aesthetic which emerges in popular discourse on technology as early as the mid-nineteenth century. The machine is not merely regarded as utilitarian problem-solver and means of social and economic salvation, but quite literally as a wonder to behold, as an aesthetic experience."[71] The term "democratic art" was used in 1913 by the *Nation*, which judged film's mass appeal in a positive light, but this term no doubt derived from earlier journalistic descriptions of the nickelodeon as " 'democracy's theater.' "[72]

Hugo Munsterberg continued the discourse of democracy and aesthetics in his 1916 study of the photoplay, considered one of the earliest works in film theory. *The Film: A Psychological Study* treats film as a great democratic *art*, taking pains to situate it within the Kantian terms of unity and autonomy.[73] Munsterberg sees the ability of film to "annihilate space and time" as liberating for the subject of cinema: "One actor is now able to entertain many thousand audiences at the same time, one stage setting is sufficient to give pleasure to millions. The theater can thus be democratized. Everybody's purse allows him to see the greatest artists and in every village a stage can be set up and the joy of a true theater performance can be spread to the remotest corner of the lands."[74]

But above and beyond, and before, these aesthetic legitimations of the cinema was the fact of film's enormous popularity, beginning with its debut in 1895 as projected cinema. As an entertainment thriving in both a vaudeville, middle-class milieu and an arcade, working-class context, film in the United States found a mass audience that only grew with the advent of nickelodeons in 1905. Though, as Musser notes, audiences for early films are difficult to describe with accuracy, it is fairly certain that the earliest audiences included patrons of all classes.[75] The audience depended on the venue: vaudeville and local opera houses drew a range of classes stratified by price; working-class spectators went to storefront theaters and dime museums; and middle- and upper-class patrons attended lectures or church events that included films.[76]

Audiences mushroomed with the nickelodeons and their rapid proliferation (reaching a peak of 8,000 in 1908).[77] According to Russell Merritt, "If we may believe the most conservative estimates, by 1910 nickelodeons were attracting some 26 million Americans every week, a little less than 20 percent of the national population."[78] In New York alone, the weekly figure was 25 percent of the city's population, while in Chicago the figure was more like 43 percent and, Merritt adds, "the lion's share of that audience came from the ghetto."[79] With the nickelodeons, what had been primarily a vaudeville and arcade entertainment became accessible to a much wider audience.[80]

In Great Britain nickelodeon viewers were until 1904 predominantly music hall audiences, that is, patrons of "the dominant form of popular urban entertainment in Britain in the second half of the nineteenth century."[81] As such, these patrons were largely working-class. In France, the Lumières premiered cinema in the Grand Café, and it flourished among middle-class audiences in Parisian café concerts, wax museums, and dedicated *salles*, but its popularity grew even more as it moved on to fairgrounds, traveling circuses, and other established popular venues where it found its primary audience.[82]

Contemporary film historians see early cinema as one of many social institutions that served to homogenize the public and to integrate the heterogeneous masses (notably immigrants) into American society.[83] In this scenario, the cinema accomplished through the moving image what the train achieved by physical and geographical movement designed to introduce people to the social world of "Americans" and their values and to dissolve class distinctions among the public by creating an indistinct mass. This attempted transformation borrows, of course, from the railroad's rhetoric of incorporation and acculturation. The "democracy of the movie theater" was doubly, paradoxically about training the newly arrived masses in the ways of American consumerism and providing them with a space that "kept alive fantasies of resistance to that culture."[84]

It is precisely the "democratic" character of the movies that disturbed various representatives of middle-class morality in the early 1900s.[85] The corollary in the cinema to the kinds of social disintegration precipitated by the railroad is the moral destruction engendered by the cinema's mingling of classes and genders in the viewing space as well as by the "liberal" cinematographic subjects disrespectful of Victorian morality. While many hailed the cinema's technological and potentially pedagogical wonders, moral and social reform groups, often religious, saw it as the corruption of middle-class values and, in the United States, of the virtues of the "good citizen."[86] Church groups of every denomination, reformers like Jane Addams, and anti-vice organizations like New York's Committee of Fourteen denounced the movies for their ill effects, especially on women.[87] "To these guardians of public morality the movie theaters were one more example of corrupt institutions and practices that had grown up in the poor and immigrant districts of the new industrial city; they belonged in the same class as brothels, gambling dens and the hangouts of criminal gangs."[88] Jacobs and Sklar insist on the economic motive of the moral protest: the cinema represented a form of competition for the church and other institutions.[89] In a famous incident, reformist pressure forced the mayor of New York to close down the city's 550 nickelodeons on Christmas day of 1908.[90] Out of this act came a board of censorship, formed initially in 1909 by several leading civic groups in New York (becoming the National Board of Review of Motion Pictures in 1915). The National Board of Censorship, which grew out of the People's Institute when the New York Exhibitors Association approached that organization following the Christmas incident, was formed in March 1909 with the approval of the Motion Picture Patents Company, which Edison had just put together, and which agreed henceforth to submit its films to the board for inspection, vowing to cut any objectionable footage.[91]

Heeding the demands of censorship, filmmakers ended up incorporating critical voices into the imagery of cinema, "cleaning up" its output and making it respectable, much as the Film d'Art in France had responded to aesthetic criticism by incorporating "art" into its visual and narrative repertoire.[92] The Film d'Art arose as a "high art" answer to the perceived frivolity, commercialism, and even danger of the cinema, which was still principally a fairground amusement in France until around 1906.[93] Moreover, the incorporation of "honorable" subjects like stage plays was correctly perceived as having the potential to turn a handsome profit from the class of patrons it could attract.[94]

In both the United States and Germany, debates over the "health" of the cinema, its influence for bad as well as good, occurred around the same time. From 1907, educational groups in particular, and religious and medical reformers, turned the cinema into an object of public health discourse. These groups drew direct cause-effect lines between film and alcoholism, nervous disorders, social unrest, and sexual perversion.[95] "Warning against the moral dangers of the entertainment film — humorous sketches and, in particular, the mushrooming genre of melodramatic narrative — the proponents of *Kinoreform* emphasized the educational potential of the new medium, prescribing a fare of scientific and geographical documentaries and other teaching films."[96] Miriam Hansen links this initial wave of outcry at the cinema in Germany with a second wave of reformist tendencies that revolve around aesthetic issues and the cultural status of the film, tendencies that came to a head from 1912 until 1914.[97]

By attuning themselves to the demands of respectability, both the first true mass transportation and the first true mass entertainment came to conquer the public in equally massive and irreversible ways, until newer technologies arose to challenge the dominance of each. The remarkably similar physical marks each left, however, have not yet been superseded: the railroad station and the film theater. Again, we find a similar discourse on the "temples" each were said to have created. Indeed, the great Neo-classical and Gothic stations, like their Greco-Roman, Gothic, and Babylonian equivalents in the cinema, were designed to signify "art" and "culture" to the millions they accommodated, to aestheticize their crude economic function, the profit motive, with icons of legitimate culture and respectability.[98] In other words, both the train and the cinema were designed to seduce the public, the patron, the customer.

The cinema's concern as it transformed into an industry was indeed to mold the souls of its audience, to create a subject suited to visual consumption. While cinema's discourses of morality and immorality parallel the earlier ones of the railroad, the links between them run deeper than perceived similarity of discourse, or paradigms of reception; those links have to do with the creation of a subject, an ideal consumer of what each had to offer. The railroad and the cinema, in short, meet in representational practices that produce a spectator-passenger drawn from a dynamic public.

Cinema's spectators were recruited from the railroad in a number of both literal and figurative senses. Beyond the question of whether each institution was "good" or "bad" for the public and the nation, each revolutionized the ways in which people perceived their world, and each created a new kind of subject.[99] The senses in which I am referring to a subject — social, technological, perceptual, and psychoanalytic — can be illuminated in three basic paradigms: Tourism and Photography, Panoramic Perception, and Time and the Railroad. These areas will serve as a basis for analyzing an early cinematic spectator whom I will suggest is the outcome of trends and forces represented by the three.

Tourism and Photography

The accomplishment of "democracy" in cinema meant turning the audience into tourists, something the railroad had begun to do in concert with forms of visual representation in the 1840s. The travel or tourism function fulfilled by numberless early films was rooted in various representational practices of the nineteenth century, photography being one of the best-known. Most early filmmakers came out of a technical tradition, and many of these were experienced first in photography — for example, the Lumière brothers, who owned a photographic film factory, the English filmmaker Birt Acres, a photographer, and the American Sigmund Lubin, owner of a photography business.[100] Photography gave to early cinema a number of its cinematographers as well. Like many of his colleagues, Lubin, a still photographer, shifted to *moving* photography in 1895.[101] He took with him an interest in the train as a subject, one that was already established in the canon of photographic genres popular among the mass public. In stereography especially, the train was both object and agent of a wealth of "views" that circulated in the culture as surrogates of travel (photo 5).[102] Both photographic companies and the railroad companies, as well as amateurs, made and distributed photographs, stereographs, postcards, and, in a few cases, *cartes de visite* in the waiting rooms of railroad stations and nearby newsstands.[103] Like the railroad itself, these were objects that rarely were found outside the purview of the increasingly urbanized U.S. population in the late nineteenth century.

From the beginning of the 1880s, improvements in the speed of the photographic process and the portability of the camera spurred the spread of photography both professionally and nonprofessionally.[104] The new dry plates, which had a far more rapid exposure time than their collodion predecessors, were immediately put to use to satisfy obsessions with the capture of movement, meaning the train — the fastest-moving vehicle of the day. "A photograph taken from the back of a train moving at forty miles an hour was exhibited by Joshua Smith of Chicago at the 1881 meeting of the Photographers' Association and was regarded as one of the seven wonders of the world. . . . "[105] This convention of advertising the speed of train travel with a still photograph seems to date no earlier than the 1880s and certainly seems to be related to the progress of photographic technology (photo 6).[106] Such views were important in establishing the image of the train as a subject, and not merely an agent, of the new perception. Combined with an iconographic tradition in art that seized on the iron horse as an aesthetic object supported by railroad money or sponsorship, these photographic views set up an iconography of technofetishism complemented by an obsession with speed. Again, it cannot be emphasized enough the extent to which the "beauty" of the machine and its landscape was in part a self-conscious advertising creation by the rail-

5. *B&O. Track Scene Near Grafton*, stereograph, c. 1900. National Museum of American History.

6. *Empire State Express*, photograph by A. P. Yates, Syracuse, N.Y., May 10, 1893. National Museum of American History.

roads designed to legitimate their presence in the wilderness and aestheticize or cover over the destruction of nature (photo 7).[107]

With the invention and mass marketing of a portable camera that used transparent film and a compact method of rolling the film, Eastman's Kodak camera was instrumental in creating a new and vast public of amateur photographers from 1889 on.[108] As Patricia Zimmerman demonstrates, the introduction of the "You push the button, we do the rest" Kodak increased the participation of a broad middle-class public in the consumption of images as a leisure activity, fostering the perception that amateur photography was a democratic art available to everyone.[109] And this perception was encouraged by the growth of travel as a leisure pursuit promoted by the railroads and spreading to the middle classes.[110]

The purposes to which Kodaks were put created a new class of patrons: tourists. "As photographs give people an imaginary possession of a past that is unreal, they also help people to take possession of space in which they are insecure," writes Susan Sontag. "Thus, photography develops in tandem with one of the most characteristic of modern activities: tourism. For the first time in history, large numbers of people regularly travel out of their habitual environments for short periods of time. It seems positively unnatural to travel for pleasure without taking a camera along."[111]

For Sontag, the camera fundamentally turns people into tourists of reality. In the United States the pact between photography and tourism appeared earlier than elsewhere, and encouraged a predatory seizure and consequent transformation of foreign places linked closely to the railroad: "After the opening of the West in 1869 by the completion of the transcontinental railroad," notes Sontag, "came the colonization through photography."[112] This colonization can be seen in the famous views of the West taken by photographers like A. J. Russell and William Henry Jackson, who accompanied the building of the railroads westward and documented, as paid employees, the transformation of the sublime American landscape into an ordered world in which the white man held pride of place.[113] As Gunning points out, film played a vital role in legitimating through travel views the colonial wars occurring from that time on, and we may add that the same holds true for naturalizing the conquest of the West and the displacement and extermination of Native peoples.[114] This practice abetted the railroad's project of setting the agenda for late-nineteenth-century leisure and popular aesthetics through its rigorous publicity campaign in the 1880s and 1890s.

7. *B&O Photographic Corps*, c. 1858. National Museum of American History.

The "democratization of tourism," its ever-widening availability in the late nineteenth and early twentieth centuries for white middle-class travelers, and somewhat later for the working class, was accomplished not only in the production of images of faraway places on a mass scale, but in their consumption.[115] Those who could not actually travel could seize on the tokens, the surrogates, of travel in published photographs and stereographs. And what could not be purchased, possessed, and accumulated as an object could be experienced through purchase as spectacle in the form of the travel lecture and/or the travel film.

Illustrated travel lectures were a popular entertainment featured either autonomously in such venues as churches or cultural institutes for "refined" genteel folk, for example, or as part of a vaudeville program. The most famous representative of this genre was Burton Holmes, successor to the equally renowned John Stoddard.[116] Like Stoddard, Holmes built his career on travel lectures illustrated with hand-colored slides of exotic sites from around the world. Holmes reigned in the late 1890s and early 1900s, touring the country with his sidekick and projectionist Oscar de Pue. In many pre-nickelodeon venues the travel film found ready-made audiences already accustomed to travel as entertainment.

What makes Holmes interesting for my purposes is that the kind of continuity which can be identified from the projection of static scenic views, including those of trains, to that of moving images of the same genre was made by Holmes and de Pue themselves. Their tour began to incorporate projected moving pictures in addition to colored stereographs as early as 1897, and they included, significantly, their own version of the *Empire State Express* — to compete, one can only assume, with Biograph's extremely popular film of the same title.[117] Holmes thus contributed to producing one of the great genres of early film, the travel genre.

One of the most popular genres until about 1904, travel films continued to be narrated by a lecturer, who ranged over everything from collections of sites "edited" and arranged by the exhibitor to hybrid narratives such as *The Hold-Up of the Rocky Mountain Express* (Biograph, 1906) and *The Great Train Robbery* (Edison/Porter, 1903).[118] A line can in fact be traced from the travel lecture to *The Great Train Robbery*, considering the fact that Porter's film was often introduced first by railway panoramas that put the viewers in the position of the soon-to-be-held-up passengers in the story.[119] Indeed, the fact that *The Great Train Robbery* involves a train journey codes it as a travel film as much as a western or a melodrama (photo 8). As Charles Musser points out, in addition to the fact that the railway film was considered a subgenre of the travel film, *The Great Train Robbery* was advertised either as a travel or a crime film, depending on the desires of the exhibitor.[120] *The Hold-Up of the Rocky Mountain Express* is basically two films in one: a travel/panoramic stricto senso and a fictional scenario that unites interior and exterior. Both *Hold-Up* and *The Great Train Robbery* are hybrid narratives that show an unproblematic mixture of genres in early film.[121] To Musser's analysis, we would add an emphasis on the motivating force of the train journey in the shift from documentary to fiction, the sense in which an already-determined narrative is inscribed in the journey. These are narratives in which things happen to tourists in an otherwise documentary mode, one in which exoticism was coupled with danger, and the thrill of travel and sheer motion with that of event and desire.

Thus did the touristic subject of photography become the touristic subject of cinema, a subject conditioned to desire the token possession of an inaccessible place and experience through vision — through the imaginary. The touristic subject is the railroad's contribution to the voyeur of both photography and film.[122] And if the gala, cross-country railroad journey marking

8. *The Great Train Robbery*, Edison/Porter, 1903. Museum of Modern Art.

the opening of Universal City in 1915 tells us anything, it is that the early film industry itself took this relation seriously.[123]

Panoramic Perception

It is conventional wisdom that while the photograph forms the material basis of film, the development of the *cinema* — projected moving images — owes more to the history of projected images and large-scale visual spectacle than to photography. The marriage of the photo and the projector, itself inconceivable without Marey's chronophotographic gun (the prototype of the film camera), represents the convergence of various forms of public and private visual spectacle, the representation of movement in images, and an apparatus for recording reality: the magic lantern, the Zoetrope, the camera.[124]

As noted, a similar phenomenon underlies the relation of photography to the railroad and the cinema: a spectacle-oriented "touristic consciousness" that preexisted all three technologies but that came to be defined and refined in relation to each. This consciousness was embodied from an early stage in the panorama and diorama, two monumental ancestors of Burton Holmes's travel shows. Anne Friedberg succinctly links a number of nineteenth-century cultural phenomena: "The same impulse that sent flaneurs through the arcades . . . sent shoppers into the department stores, tourists to exhibitions, spectators into the panorama, diorama, wax museum, and cinema."[125]

Throughout the nineteenth century, first the panorama and then the diorama provided audiences with scenic views that at an early date became linked with the experience of railroad travel and can be seen as protocinematic entertainments. The first panorama was created in 1787 in Edinburgh, and the phenomenon soon spread to France and Germany (1800) and to North America.[126] By the 1820s, panoramas had conquered a large mass public and were to remain a popular entertainment until the 1870s in England and until the end of the century in some places.

The panorama consisted of a large, 360-degree, realistic painting of a scene from nature or history, usually a famous battle or a view — a city, a harbor, a battlefield. The spectator would stand at the center of the circular painting, which was lighted in such a way that the lower parts remained dim. For early spectators, the illusion was powerful in its realism: "Placed in semi-darkness, and at the centre of a circular painting illuminated from above and embracing a continuous view of an entire region, the spectator lost all judgment of distance and space, for the different parts of the picture were painted so realistically and in such perfect perspective and scale that, in the absence of any means of comparison with real objects, a perfect illusion was given."[127]

Frank Kessler and Gabriele Jutz see the panorama as an entertainment that not only influenced the way in which railroad perception was described (as "panoramic perception"), but that itself profited from its similarity to the railroad as a form of ersatz tourism. "The panorama is simultaneously complementary to and dependent on phenomena like the press, organized tourism, the railroad, etc. Complementary because it adds illustrations; with its 'You-are-there' effect, it even produces the illusion of replacing these phenomena. Dependent, because it assumes a foreknowledge on the part of the spectator, an already-existing interest that permits him to appreciate the verisimilitude of what is shown."[128]

The diorama took the trompe l'oeil of the panorama a step further by providing spectators with shifting scenes that created an impression of movement. In their study of the diorama and the daguerreotype (the diorama is acknowledged to be the invention of Louis Daguerre, the inventor of photography), Helmut and Alison Gernsheim cite an 1859 source describing the succession of views made available to the first patrons of Daguerre's Diorama at the Place du Château d'Eau (now Place de la République). The huge, 22 by 14 meter transparencies were modified by manipulated light and shadow; to alter the scene, the auditorium containing the seated spectators was rotated as lighting effects shifted attention from one scene to another. Spectators passed subtly from the interior of Canterbury Cathedral to a Swiss valley surrounded by snow-capped mountains.[129] On a visit to the Diorama in 1823, a reporter for *The Times* (London) remarked on the striking lighting effects: "From a calm, soft, delicious, serene day in summer, the horizon gradually changes, becoming more and more overcast, until a darkness of approaching storm, discolours every object. . . ."[130]

Kessler and Jutz compare the diorama to the cinema; both involve a dark space (*la salle obscure*), the superimposition of two temporal levels (the diegetic and the real time of the presentation), and the use of light in the apparatus that presents the spectacle.[131] The diorama's significance with respect to both the railroad and the cinema lies in its advance of the "panoramic effect" in the representation of time and history: "the panorama appears as a substitute, an ersatz for the train journey, and it is not coincidental that panoramas die out as the railroads rise in importance."[132] In the United States, railroad companies often produced their own dioramas — for example, the Santa Fe Railroad's electric Diorama of the Grand Canyon, made for the 1915 Pan Pacific Exposition.[133]

For my purposes, the link between both the panorama and diorama and the railroad, as well as with later photography and cinema, appears most clearly in the kinds of discourse generated around the "panoramic perception" of train travel. Schivelbusch has described in detail how the nineteenth-century experience of train travel involved an extraordinary transformation of the relation between the passenger and the landscape. As noted, the total reorganization of time and space effected by the coming of the train was commonly referred to in the mid-nineteenth century as "the annihilation of space and time."[134] The speed of train travel created a temporal and spatial shrinkage and a perceptual disorientation that tore the traveler out of the traditional space-time continuum and thrust him/her into a new world of speed, velocity, and diminishing intervals between geographical points. Hurtling through space in the body of the train (conceived as a projectile), as if being shot through the landscape, travelers experienced the loss of the foreground, and thus the homogeneity of space between them and the view outside the window. This was experienced as a loss of depth perception and a loss of aura, in Benjamin's sense of the distance that endows things with uniqueness.[135] With his/her view mediated by a framed glass screen, the passenger's visual perceptions multiplied and became mobile, dynamic, panoramic. Panoramic perception, in contrast to traditional perception, no longer belongs to the same space as perceived objects; the traveler sees the objects, landscapes, etc., through the apparatus which moves him/her through the world.[136] Using a somewhat different route than Schivelbusch, Jonathan Crary arrives at a similar conclusion: "What takes place from around 1810 to 1840 is an uprooting of vision from the stable and fixed relations incarnated in the camera obscura. . . . In a sense, what occurs is a new valuation of visual experience; it is given an unprecedented mobility and exchangeability, abstracted from any founding site or referent."[137]

The importance of the frame as a condition of this vision links the train with photography and cinema. Schivelbusch even refers to this kind of perception as "filmic," emphasizing in addition to the frame the character of montage, of juxtaposition integral to the "new reality of annihilated in-between spaces."[138] An 1861 text by Benjamin Gastineau, cited by Schivelbusch, gives perhaps the clearest expression of the protocinematic quality of train travel. In *La Vie en chemin de fer*, he wrote: " 'Devouring distance at the rate of fifteen leagues an hour, the steam engine, that powerful stage manager, throws the switches, changes the decor, and shifts the point of view every moment; in quick succession it presents the astonished traveler with happy scenes, sad scenes, burlesque interludes, brilliant fireworks, all visions that disappear as soon as they are seen. . . . ' "[139] For Schivelbusch, this is the essential character of the panorama, though we might more accurately label it *dioramic* perception, where the concept of editing is more applicable. For that sense of juxtaposition of disjunct scenes that constitutes film editing can be found first in the diorama — and the train.

It is in panoramic perception that the railroad as a perceptual paradigm for the cinema is located by contemporary scholars. Mary Anne Doane extends Schivelbusch's analysis: "The train, and the cinema as well, thus contribute to the detachment or dissociation of the subject from the space of perception—what might be termed a despatialization of subjectivity effected by modern technology. . . . The classical cinema, though a regularization of vision and the subject's relation to the screen, reasserts and institutionalizes the despatialization of subjectivity."[140] Friedberg sees the panorama and diorama specifically as early foundations for what she calls the "mobilized virtual gaze" of the flaneur and the contemporary spectator. Unlike the panopticon, she maintains, the panorama and diorama were "designed to *transport*—rather than *confine*—the spectator-subject. . . . These devices produced a spatial and temporal mobility—if only a 'virtual' one."[141] She also notes that both depended on the spectator's immobility and highlighted the visual function, much as in cinematic spectatorship.[142]

There is evidence, however, that the link between railroad and cinema formed in panoramic perception was not lost on early observers and makers of film. As Gunning notes, the early film genre of "panoramic views" often overlapped with travel films, particularly railroad films that were shot with the camera mounted on the front of a train.[143] "Panoramic views" formed part of the perceptual marriage of the railroad and the cinema that was strikingly consummated in early film exhibition practices like Hale's Tours. Hale's Tours, a nickelodeon amusement introduced in 1905 at K.C.'s Electric Park in Kansas City, used actual train cars for its "thrill" effect.[144] The apparatus was modeled on turn-of-the-century fairground and amusement park entertainments that seated "passengers" in railway cars while painted scenery rolled past the windows.[145] Hale's Tours used filmed panoramic views shot from the fronts of locomotives, which gave the viewer the illusion of being on a train—an illusion reinforced by the rocking back and forth of the train car and often by the blowing of a whistle.[146]

At its most popular moment in 1906–7, Hale's Tours theaters numbered more than five hundred around the United States. This directly analogous relation between train and cinema—a relation contingent on proximity as much as resemblance—could also be found in many of the French traveling fairs where cinema was projected during its first decade. Around the turn of the century many traveling showmen in France depended on a locomotive-like generator to power their projectors and generate light. Fascinated by images of apparatuses that for us uncannily recall Hale's Tours, Jacques Deslandes and Jacques Richard describe these strange "locomobiles" that often burned coke and produced a dramatic spectacle: "These sorts of locomotives with very tall smokestacks emitting great white clouds in fact often constituted, in the first years of the century, the main attraction of the traveling cinema parade. Back then, when nighttime in those little French villages was still quite dark, the milky glass globes and electric light garlands that burned on the facade of the 'theater' were already a festival for the eyes."[147] Apparently a similar type of steam engine-generator that also resembled a locomotive occupied an equally important place in the traveling cinemas of England at roughly the same time.[148]

Beyond these literal marriages of the train and the cinema, the railroad as an analogy can be glimpsed in the writings of Terry Ramsaye, who recounts in his *A Million and One Nights* (1926) an anecdote that is remarkable for how literally it pertains to the paradigmatic argument. Albert E. Smith, founder with J. Stuart Blackton of Vitagraph, is said to have solved the problem of flicker in film images while riding a train. Peering out the window while riding through the New Jersey landscape, Smith saw an analogy to screen flicker in the repetition of telegraph poles the train swept past. He remarked a similar effect in that produced by looking through a picket fence as the train passed through a station. "This gave him the notion of dividing up the flicker of the motion picture by adding blades to the then single-bladed shutter. He tried this out and found that by multiplying the flicker he in fact eliminated it in effect. The resulting betterment of projection was extraordinary."[149] Ramsaye draws the obvious conclusion: "So the movie shutter is related to the Pennsylvania Railroad's picket fence at Manhattan Transfer."[150] Though Ramsaye was not self-consciously invoking the railroad to point to a paradigmatic relation, the reference serves as symptom of a larger paradigm and frame of reference at work.

Hugo Munsterberg in his 1916 study of the photoplay engages the discursive paradigm of the railroad in describing the relation of film to its spectator. *The Film: A Psychological Study* makes frequent reference to the expansion of the world made possible by film's contraction of time and space. Both are effected through a montage of different views, but also through the length of individual shots, and, of course, the choice of subject. Munsterberg describes the freeing of representation — and the spectator — from the dictates of time and space in films that take the viewer touristically around the world in a matter of minutes or even seconds.[151] Though he does not draw direct comparisons between the railroad and the cinema, Munsterberg does make references to the railroad. In one case the railroad is cited for playing a direct role in the production and consumption of the filmic experience, when footage of the investiture of the Prince of Wales was shot in Carnarvon at 4 P.M., developed and edited on a train, and projected in London at 10 P.M. that same day.[152]

Medical discourse also registered the train/cinema analogy. In a 1907 issue of *Moving Picture World*, an article reports that St. Louis oculists agreed with then-current German research on the damage that watching moving pictures can cause to the eyes, but they "say there is no necessity here to declare war on the kinematograph shows, as they are doing in the German capital." A Dr. Campbell is quoted: "Looking at moving pictures is like reading a book on a train. Where the focus changes all the time, it is a strain on the eye to follow the object it is looking at. Particularly is this the case if the eye is defective. Even a perfect eye cannot stand looking too long at a moving picture or watching too many telegraph poles flash by a moving train." Dr. Campbell's advice is simply "not to visit moving picture shows if your eyes are weak. They will not permanently destroy the eyesight, but they produce an irritation of the retina caused by a confusion of images. All moving pictures are not equally difficult to watch. In some, the quivering motion is reduced to a minimum. In others, it is violent."[153]

What all of these theories of vision have in common is the assumption of a modern world whose objects refuse to stay still for the observer/spectator. Or, in Crary's terms: "The very absence of referentiality is the ground on which new instrumental techniques will construct for an observer a new 'real' world. It is a question, in the early 1830s, of a perceiver whose very empirical nature renders identities unstable and mobile, and for whom sensations are interchangeable."[154] This radically different concept of perception posited an essentially arbitrary relation between sensations and referents. It also assumed a radically new sense of time for which the railroad bore great responsibility.

Time and the Railroad

The "annihilation of space and time": the notion that conceptually links the railroad and the cinema as well as the telegraph, telephone, and other machines of communication, was not merely an abstract response to the compressive effects of mechanical speed. In a literal sense both the railroad and the cinema wiped out preexisting ideas and experiences of time and space and substituted their own as new sociocultural norms (photo 9). The perceptual reorientation of both the railroad and the cinema entailed a new temporal reorientation as well. The effect of the shrinkage of space was to convert space

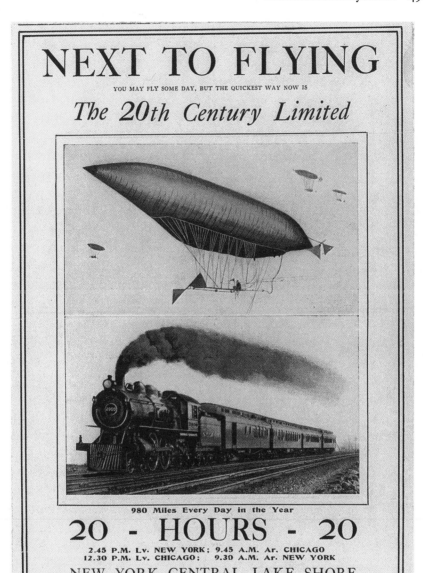

9. *The 20th Century Limited*, New York Central Railroad flyer, 1902.
National Museum of American History.

into time, to turn the distance between two cities into a matter of days or hours and, in film, to turn the visual passage from Tokyo to Lyons into a matter of seconds. Both the railroad and the cinema demanded obedience to a new authority of movement and scheduling. For Vachel Lindsay, writing in 1915, the new authority of the cinema was indeed temporal. Referring to the differences between the theater and the cinema, he noted: "The keywords of the stage are *passion* and *character*, of the photoplay, *splendor* and *speed*."[155]

The railroad provided the paradigm of a radically new time consciousness, for it is the railroads that gave rise to, indeed mandated, standard time the world over. Until 1883, the year railroad managers met in St. Louis and then Chicago to call a time convention on standard time, Americans measured their lives by a huge variety of local standard times. The local time of a town or city was typically determined according to noontime — the sun — and set by town clocks. So variable was the concept of local time in 1880 that 115 local times were in use across just the four states of Michigan, Illinois, Wisconsin, and Indiana.[156] Local times were not necessarily coordinated with each other; that task devolved to intercity interests, notably the railroad system.

The railroads themselves were using fifty-three different standards (the Union Pacific alone used six).[157] Railroad stations servicing more than one line thus displayed different clocks with times corresponding to the standards of individual lines.[158] While punctuality and precise timekeeping were important to each line, as the early use of timetables indicates, coordinating and scheduling for passengers and cross-country freight were a nightmare of confusion and irritation.[159]

Since the 1850s, many had proposed standard times, as well as a meridian, in the United States (to be coordinated with Greenwich). Britain had been united into one time zone since 1848 — the first national standard time system.[160] But various business, scientific, and governmental interests in the United States failed to agree on the issue of a meridian in relation to which time zones might be divided. The problems of reconciling local with national and international time were also considered, though the scope of these problems could scarcely be imagined at the time (in fact, standard time became federal law only in 1918, with the controversial passage of daylight saving time).[161] Finally, in 1883, the general time convention voted to adopt the standards proposed by William Frederick Allen, editor of the *Official Railway Guide*. In Allen's Greenwich-based division of the United States into four zones, local time would be abolished and each zone would vary from the next by one hour.[162] On Sunday, November 18, 1883, at noon, most of the United States converted to standard time.[163] A truly national railroad network and national market were now in place — with local opposition to "railroad time" only beginning.

Two technological developments were crucial in bringing the railroads to the 1883 landmark event: improvements in pocket watches and their mass marketing, as well as the use of the telegraph to coordinate time. With the introduction in 1880 of the Waterbury, the first truly cheap watch, the early 1880s witnessed an unprecedented permeation of watch-carrying habits in American society, a trend promoted in part by Sears and Roebuck.[164] Greater precision in clock mechanisms and stricter inspection systems for railroad timekeeping also contributed to railroad and wider social synchronicity — and punctuality.[165] As the biggest customers for American watches, the railroads encouraged the growth of the watch industry and spurred improvements in accuracy.

In 1851, William Cranach Bond, the first director of the Harvard College Observatory and owner of an instrument supply firm in Boston, became the first person to offer a public time service using signals telegraphed from the observatory; this service was used largely by New England railroad lines. According to Carlene Stephens:

> More than any other technical factor, the development of time-distribution technology systems based on telegraphy prepared the way for a uniform national standard time. Before telegraphed time signals, time transfer between observatory and railroad occurred with a simple comparison of mechanical timekeepers: a railroad employee checked his watch against a clock set to observatory time, and then carried his watch to a railroad terminal timepiece, from which other watches might be set. Telegraphed time signals permitted, for the first time ever, the virtually instantaneous synchronization of one place with another distant one.[166]

The railroads accordingly began using telegraphy to coordinate dispatching in the 1850s. The practice became widespread at the end of that decade and exerted its ultimate symbolic force in the relay of the hammer striking the Golden Spike that sealed the first American transcontinental railroad in 1869.[167]

The consequences of the adoption of standard time were dramatic. With the rationalization of time came the rationalization of markets coordinated by the railroads — which could now steam through the last remaining local obstacles that impeded the efficient pursuit of profit on a national scale. People and goods could now be regulated as a single unit, as the country could be regulated in relation to the city, and all territories could be bound together in the post-Civil War era. The United States began to shift from an agricultural to an industrial-based economy with the speed of transportation, which drove the engines of urbanization from the 1880s and oriented to commercial needs what was considered a peculiarly American obsession with speed.[168]

The effects on society were equally massive. Take, for example, the calculated erasure of local time. E. P. Thompson has drawn attention to the unprecedented disorientation in consciousness brought about by the imposition of factory time — regulated and disciplined by the clock — on a peasant population geared to seasonal, natural time.[169] The conversion to railroad standard time produced similarly disruptive effects. Replacing solar time with clock time implied a consciousness of punctuality — a temporal discipline not unlike that of the factory schedule.

Clearly, as Michael O'Malley points out, regulation of time by the railroads was not simply a mechanism to ensure efficiency; it was a way of expressing power. "Standard time posed a new authority for time, a new definition of its source. Newspapers frequently compared the railroad's innovation to Joshua's miracle at Jericho, and though they meant it in a spirit of fun the comparison made sense — in each case the authority for time bent to the will of social forces."[170] Scores of individual communities hostile to railroad time reacted strongly. Chris Clark cites an 1883 article in the *Indianapolis Sentinel*: " 'People will have to marry and die by railroad time . . . banks will open and close by railroad time. . . . In fact, the Railroad Convention has taken charge of the time business.' "[171] The slow adoption of standard time in rural areas parallels the transformation of the U.S. economy in its shift from a rural to an urban base. In almost all cases it was an issue of regional or local interests and customs. As O'Malley notes, "in fact the range of opposition to standard time was remarkably wide, and confined neither to rural people or small towns," but included commercial and political interests. Adoption of standard time was a state-by-state legislative process, which became truly standard only in the late 1910s.[172]

The single most important outcome of standard time was, in Stephen Kern's view, the abolition of local time, the imposition of public time, and the formation, in reaction, of multiple private times — symbolized most notably by

Proust's figuration of memory in *Remembrance of Things Past*.[173] As Kern points out, the new consciousness of time effected by the railroads can be described as "simultaneity" and "synchronicity." Clearly, the turn to national and then international standards of time involved a turn to "simultaneous" thinking: one's own time was now to be thought of in relation to concurrent times in faraway places. Kern cites the example of the simultaneous wireless communication of the *Titanic* disaster by David Sarnoff as a dramatic symbol of the major change in people's experience of the present. This experience, he claims, was conceived in two different ways in art, literature, and new technologies such as the telephone and the cinema: the present as a *sequence* of single local events vs. the present as a *simultaneity* of multiple distant events.[174] Certain technologies stimulated the simultaneist mode of thought, with cinema continuing and deepening the kind of temporal consciousness introduced by the railroad: simultaneity as an effect of the "annihilation of space and time."

Though characterized by its own unique articulation of temporality, the cinema owes much of its temporal sense to this train-infected consciousness. The most basic sense in which cinema fit into the new time structure was as a leisure pursuit made possible by rationalized time. In the 1890s, thanks to a greater rationalization of the production process, along with a greater shift from the country to the city, more time and amusements became available to the mass of Americans who worked for a living, especially in urban areas where the trolley or subway could easily deposit filmgoers at Kinetoscope parlors or nickelodeons near subway stops.[175] Distribution of film itself as one of these modern entertainments was almost wholly dependent on the railroad to ensure the smooth functioning of preset exhibition schedules, especially in cities. Thus, in an elementary sense, the rapid penetration of film throughout the United States — or, rather, rational distribution, with release schedules initially set by the Motion Picture Patents Company — was made possible by the railroad as a mode of transportation with access to communities everywhere.[176]

Exhibition practices of early film also displayed a temporality akin to the usually short trips of the subway or tram. Early film viewing took place first in Kinetoscope parlors in which the patron inserted a coin to see a continuous loop of a film subject such as *Fred Ott's Sneeze* (Edison, 1894) or the *Rice-Irwin Kiss* (Edison, 1894). When cinema became established as a projected entertainment, storefront exhibitors would run continuous shows all day and into the night.[177] The patron could come and go as she or he pleased, entering and exiting during the running of a string of films, on the assumption that no single film constituted a "program." In other words, there was as yet no concept of the individually *scheduled* program. One went to see the movies, not a particular film. Even when films were exhibited as part of a vaudeville program, they appeared as one "act" among many, not as a unique program. Both substantively and temporally, films were interchangeable with each other and with other forms of entertainment. Similarly, what editing of films there was in the early years of cinema was performed by exhibitors, who "arranged scenes" according to principles of variety and diversity, not continuity.[178]

This practice began to change in the nickelodeon era, when films such as *The Great Train Robbery* were advertised as single films on a scheduled program featured, crucially, in a space devoted primarily to cinema.[179] Thus, the earliest filmgoing habits were "inner-directed" experiences for the public, in which the time of viewing was controlled by the patron — nursemaids or housewives out on a walk or a shopping trip, schoolchildren playing hooky, workingmen and women on the way home from work, etc. The post-nickelodeon cinema as an institution developed into a more rationalized industry with a rationalized sense of its own schedule and an evolving standard of the length and duration of an individual film and program.[180] Film's liberation from vaudeville structures of paradigmatic time, and its transformation into syntagmatic, autonomous time, parallels the development of standard time by joining a high art format (the "performance") with an infinitely reproducible mass form.

Another sense in which film can be said to owe something to the railroad as a paradigm of temporality, however, is in its technique of evoking simultaneity.[181] In film, the simultaneist current was stimulated by actualities — the "you-are-thereness" of newsreels (again, the dominant filmmaking genre until 1904) that fostered a sense of things happening simultaneously with, or at least only a short time before, their projection.[182] The editing of disparate images, places, and times produced something of a leveling effect, a simultaneity by virtue of the condensed duration of projection of pictures taken far away. Though not literally simultaneous as with live television, the dramatic reduction in time between the occurrence of an event and its representation, something first accomplished by newspapers, encouraged an "eyewitness" effect in, for example, actuality films taken of the Spanish-American War or President McKinley's funeral — films rushed to spectators in a matter of days.[183] Musser notes that after William Dickson's camera shot Admiral George Dewey and his fleet returning from Gibraltar to the United States in September 1899, the "views" were shipped directly to New York to be processed before Dewey himself arrived in order to capitalize on his return.[184] Musser also quotes a *New York Clipper* review from November 1899 in which the reviewer's appreciation of projecting films shot the same day led him to assert that " 'the secret of Moving Pictures consists in the TIMELINESS. Without that feature, such an exhibition would inevitably fail. . . . ' "[185]

But early on, film form began to reflect a simultaneist inspiration in editing techniques that ranged from juxtaposition of two disjunct sites within the same frame (*Life of an American Fireman*, Edison/Porter, 1903), to "returns in time" from one narrative site to an earlier locale in the same narrative continuum (*The Great Train Robbery*, Edison/Porter, 1903).[186] Take *The Great Train Robbery*, a watershed film whose enormous popularity did much to set cinema on a firmly narrative path in 1903, the year of its initial release. The simultaneist structure of *The Great Train Robbery*, which follows one line of action and then doubles back on itself to pick up on the fate of a character knocked unconscious at the beginning of the film, was not edited as parallel montage, that is, through alternation, but it preserves the character of simultaneity nonetheless. *The Great Train Robbery* is significant in its advance of narrative continuity under the auspices of the station's railroad clock, which was criticized almost from the time the film was made for the apparent failure on the part of the filmmakers to change the hands of the clock from one scene to another. Instead of seeing this lack of change as necessarily an error, I would suggest that it perhaps should be seen as symbolizing simultaneity.[187] In other words, the doubling back of the text, returning in time to continue the line of action associated with the telegrapher, is marked as simultaneity by the fact that the clock has *not* advanced in time. Thus, the train's central role in grounding the narrative structure and dramatic potency of the story is further enhanced by its strongly coded connection to timekeeping.

The acknowledged master of simultaneity in American cinema was D. W. Griffith. In Griffith's films, including and especially his train films, the editing of separate but parallel actions according to the basic Dickensian technique of alternating plotlines incorporated tempo *and* speed.[188] Griffith used alternation and rapid cross-cutting to express simultaneity as well as symbolic and thematic parallels. Although, as Gunning notes, earlier Griffith films like *The Guerrilla* (1908) employed complicated editing patterns based on alternation, *The Lonedale Operator* (1911) is best known in film history for its complex use of cross-cutting.[189] As a film that involves a last-minute rescue, *The Lonedale Operator* was typical of Griffith's construction of narrative telos, as André

Gaudrault notes: "In most of Griffith's films, temporality assumes dramatic significance for its own sake. The 'last minute rescue' becomes a major innovation that implicates the very logic of film narrative since it emphasizes the *time* (last *minute* rescue). . . . "[190] The film uses parallel editing to tell the story of the girl telegrapher who is held up by thieves and of the engineer who loves her and rushes to her rescue in his locomotive. At one point, the film alternates among four different kinds of shots representing four different locales to produce an elaborate interweaving of disparate spaces, thus accelerating the temporality of the basic Dickensian technique.[191]

With Griffith, the *schedule* becomes a primary temporal narrative force with which to reckon, and the telegraph a primary instrument for negotiating it, along with the telephone and the clock.[192] The principle of suspense was inherited from the nineteenth-century novel, but the extent to which a plot unfolded according to the principle of a ticking clock — the amount of time allowed in a two-, three-, or four-plus-reel film, and finally a feature — was unique to the cinema.[193] Griffith institutionalized the spirit of the railway journey narrative, its speed, and its suspense, which included the prospect of disaster as well as that of intersecting with strangers.

Even before Griffith's innovations in editing, however, the motif of railroad time as inexorable and irreversible, as all-determining, affected the structure of early film in a number of ways. Railroad time and film time intersect literally in one genre of early films that say much about early cinema's grasp of its place in the "culture of time and space," to use Kern's apt phrase. In both preclassical and early classical film the tyranny of the clock as an expression of railroad time and power exerts a wide-ranging influence. The themes of missing the train and the anxiety produced around trying to catch it appear in French, American, and English films, along with a spectrum of "time-panic" films that do not actually involve a train. In *Monsieur et Madame in a Hurry to Catch a Train* (Gaumont, ca. 1901), *Five Minutes to Train Time* (AM&B, 1902), and *The Jonah Man: or, The Traveller Bewitched* (Hepworth, 1906), characters try to leave their homes in time to catch a train but are impeded by a series of obstacles.[194] The "bewitched traveller," for example, is unable to dress himself: as soon as he dons an article of clothing, it rebels and flies off his body. Monsieur et Madame are equally unable to remain fully dressed and become frustrated as a result. In these films, time is controlled by the railroad schedule, which, though not represented as such, is implicitly present; the entire temporal premise is built on anxiety and frustration produced as a function of an imaginary ticking clock.

The simple "beat-the-clock" linearity of the "catch-the-train" films becomes more complex in a narrative film like *Asleep at the Switch* (1910). In this Edison film a railway switchman is unable to carry out his job of switching the tracks at a designated time. The chaos that results from failing to meet the train schedule is made dramatically clear in the near-collision of two trains that would not have come so close had the switchman been alert to his duty. The anxiety produced as a consequence puts this film on a continuum with the earlier missed-train films and the later Griffith last-minute rescue train films and alerts us to a kind of cinematic subject whose roots in railroad "panoramic perception" and temporal authority bespeak a more complex psychic profile.

Shock and Subjectivity in Early Cinema

The early "catch-the-train" films refer to a kind of anxiety peculiar to modern industrial society. If anxiety over missing a train was the condition of the passenger before he or she boarded the carriage, however, it was no less the lot of the passenger after gaining a seat. The kind of perceptual overlap found in Hale's Tours, which depends to some extent on the simulation of pre- and post-journey temporal structures, but even more on the simulation of the journey itself, links the railroad and the cinema in deeper ways connected to the anxiety felt in relation to the train schedule. If one kind of anxiety is connected to a hyperconsciousness of time, of the tyranny of standard time, then another kind emerges from a different experience, a willful lack of consciousness of time: the forgetfulness produced while one is rocked to sleep or more generally hypnotized during a train journey.[195] As such, the passenger-spectator is vulnerable to unexpected events, or to "shock," as trauma was referred to before about 1880.

The experience of shock is a major feature of the perceptual overlap between the railroad and the cinema. In film, this kind of visual stimulation is represented by rapid shot changes, sudden cuts to close-ups (including the famous close-up of the robber in *The Great Train Robbery*), and even attacks on vision like those represented by the train charging headlong into the camera. With the railroad, the experience of shock was emblematized by the accident, both real and anticipated, which actually gave rise to a condition known as "railway spine," later called "traumatic neurosis." It is around this condition and its relation to shock that I would now like to explore a fundamental sense in which the railroad can be said to be a paradigm for cinematic perception or spectatorship.

As Schivelbusch notes, early railroad travelers lived a double relation to the train journey: the pleasure of speed, the thrill of the "projectile" being shot through space, matched against the terror of collision and its psychological effects — phobia, anxiety, and, in many cases, hysteria.[196] Certainly, as noted, with the marked increase in railroad accidents in the United States after 1853, the extent to which fear of collision had become bound up with the fabric of train travel could not be doubted.[197] The medical and legal professions were in any case obliged to take the connection seriously, since lawsuits mushroomed from the mid-nineteenth century on claiming damages for victims of "railway spine."[198] "Railway spine" was a condition analyzed as a deterioration of nervous tissue, a result of physical damage to the spinal cord — damage typically received in a railway accident. Pathological causes and effects were the only admissible evidence for claims against the railway companies until litigants began to demonstrate, with no corresponding physical source, symptoms such as anxiety, partial loss of vision, paralysis, and dyspepsia. Nerve disease studies taking place simultaneously in England, France, Germany, and the United States led the medical profession to expand its view of "railway spine" to include "railway brain," a more psychologically based disease. "From the early 1880s on," writes Schivelbusch, "the purely pathological view is superseded by a new, psychopathological one, according to which the shock caused by the accident does not affect the tissue of the spinal marrow, but affects the victim psychically. Now the victim's experience of shock is the main causative factor of the ailment. By the end of the 1880s, the concept of 'railway spine' has been replaced by that of traumatic neurosis."[199]

Very soon the notion took hold that fright alone from an accident could produce these states.[200] George Drinka notes in *The Birth of Neurosis* that even though not all cases were phobias (many involved hysteria, anxiety, or nervous exhaustion), victims of train neuroses all shared the experience of being frightened while simply in the proximity of a railroad. In short, "medical testimony and popular opinion concurred in establishing a firm connection between fright, nerves and the responsibility of the railways."[201]

If early railway travel caused its passengers considerable anxiety in anticipation of accidents, by the later nineteenth century improvements in railway travel had led to the reduction of anxiety and the internalization of panoramic perception as second nature, such that one no longer necessarily expected a violent interruption in the train journey.[202] The term "shock" then applies all the more to the phenomenon of the accident—which, though possibly less frequent (Schivelbusch overstates the case for the United States), had certainly not disappeared or faded as a "horizon of expectation." Schivelbusch, inspired by Benjamin, engages Freud's notion, developed in *Beyond the Pleasure Principle*, of the "stimulus shield" to describe the process of internalizing shock to form a protective shield against further shocks.[203] "Trauma" in Freud's book was the result of a particularly violent shock penetrating the protective shield of modern man's shock-habituated consciousness. Freud developed this psychic model in the context of World War I and the war neuroses that struck those who suffered the events of the war in a brutally violent mental, as well as physical, way. Schivelbusch sees "shock" as a technological and social phenomenon characteristic of modernity, of modern society since the dawn of full-scale industrialization (the railway era). Drinka is dramatic in his statement of the connection: "The progressive symbols of society, such as the railways, seemed to be responsible for the breakdown of the human nervous system. . . . Indeed the railway spine and brain stands [*sic*] forth as the classical Victorian neurosis, that is, a psychocultural illness in which the human psyche collided with the changing nineteenth-century environment and gave birth to an epidemic-like neurotic illness whose form and severity are rooted in the Victorian era."[204]

As part of that changing nineteenth-century environment, cinema certainly had its role to play in altering the ways in which people negotiated their world. In the paradigm of "panoramic perception," and the railroad perceptual model, film might seem to be already part of the "stimulus shield," just another shock of modern life that could easily be referred to past experience.[205] And certainly the emergence of projected moving images had its path prepared by the multitude of less-dynamic screen practices assisting the birth of the new medium.[206]

Moreover, the railroad accident even appears as a subject in early film—not an altogether unfamiliar "shock." Lubin shot a number of locomotive wrecks between 1903 and 1914, including *The Effects of a Trolley Car Collision* (1903) and *The Wreckers of the Limited Express* (1906). In *The Railroad Smash-up*, Edison brought together two locomotives and staged his own catastrophe (photo 10). The footage was released both autonomously as *Railroad Smash-up*

10. *Railroad Smashup*, Edison/Porter, 1904. Library of Congress.

and as the final scene in the 1904 *Rounding Up of the Yeggmen,* which follows a
bank robbery from its conception at a tramp campfire to its calamitous conclusion in the head-on crash of the locomotive that the robbers had stolen for
their getaway.

The immediate inspiration for this footage was not the train robberies so
widely reported in the 1890s and represented in stage plays, films, and popular
fiction (dime novels); rather, such footage was the product of numerous train
wrecks staged at county fairs throughout the United States from 1896 through
the 1920s. The first such head-on occurred in 1896 at Crush City, Texas, the
brainchild of W. G. Crush, general passenger agent for the Missouri-Kansas-
Texas Railroad. Some 30,000 people paid to see the crash, which caused the
deaths of two spectators, including a young girl whose skull was damaged by a
flying piece of chain. The negative press on this incident effectively killed
railroad company sponsorship of such events. But as late as 1929 a man
dubbed "Head-On" Joe Connolly made a fortune staging these disasters,
charging from 50 cents to $1.50 to thousands of spectators — as many as
150,000 for a single event.[207]

11. *B&O, Train Wreck*, c. 1900. National Museum of American History.

This "imagination of disaster," which clearly seems rooted in the fantasy of seeing technology go out of control (a sort of visual Luddism), had become associated with railroad travel early.[208] This horror was well-illustrated, commented on, and joked about throughout the nineteenth century. Toward the end of the century the representation of sympathy for the victims tended to fade, to be replaced by a focus on the mutilation of the machine itself, as postcards, photographs, popular illustrations, and films suggest (photo 11). Often, witnesses to accidents would have their photographs made and a postcard struck to send to friends or relatives. A 1909 card in the National Museum of American History, one of many in this genre, shows a man, woman, and child standing by a wrecked train car, as if posing for a studio family portrait. The card reads, "This is the car we were in when we went over. — Yours, Mr. and Mrs. J. B. Stout."[209] Such a document of survival and, in a sense, triumph over the machine is also clearly an orchestrated spectacle of aftermath.

Equating technological destruction with both pleasure and terror, the "imagination of disaster" says volumes about the kinds of violent spectacle demanded by a modern public, and the transformation of "shock" into eagerly digestible spectacle.[210] Yet the rhetoric of reception of the earliest films indicates that many were not yet immune to the "shock of the new," to use Robert Hughes's phrase. Perhaps the oldest cliché of film history is the reputed reaction of the first audiences to the Lumières' *L'Arrivée d'un train en gare de La Ciotat*. Spectators were said to have jumped from their seats in terror at the sight of the train coming toward the camera and running beyond its purview (in three-quarters' view), logically "into" the space of the spectator.[211] Descriptions of such a response in France and elsewhere survive in film history as rhetorical indices of film's initial novelty and the naïveté of the spectator confronted by a two-dimensional, dynamic representation.[212] Gunning sums this up: "Thus conceived, the myth of initial terror defines film's power as its unprecedented realism, its ability to convince spectators that the moving image was, in fact, palpable and dangerous, bearing towards them with physical impact."[213] He goes on to refer to this myth as a "primal scene" informing film theory's view of early film history. Gunning's point is not so much to puncture the myth of the terrorized spectator as to put it into historical perspective: "Restored to its proper historical context, the projection of the first moving images stands at the climax of a period of intense development in visual entertainments, a tradition in which realism was valued largely for its uncanny effects. . . . Far from credulity, it is the incredible nature of the illusion itself that renders the viewer speechless. What is displayed before the audience is less the impending speed of the train than the force of the cinematic apparatus. Or to put it better, the one demonstrates the other."[214]

Essentially, the idea that the train image inspires a threatened response — terror — and does so *as* a film image, returns us to the whole history of train travel as a paradigm for cinematic spectatorship based on shock. In one early film genre, "shock" was the very basis of its appeal. Concerned to establish the nonnarrative purpose and effects of early film camera movement, Gunning focuses on several examples of films in which movement is premised on "the thrill of motion" and the "transformation of space." He cites an early review in the *New York Mail and Express* of a Biograph film that mounts a camera on a locomotive (one of many such films) and moves through the Haverstraw Tunnel: " 'The way in which the unseen energy swallows up space and flings itself into the distance is as mysterious and impressive almost as an allegory. . . . One holds his breathe [*sic*] instinctively as he is swept along in the rush of the phantom cars. His attention is held almost with the vise of fate.' "[215]

In this and other examples, Gunning refers to the "enjoyable anxiety the audience felt before the illusion of motion." In films like *When the Devil Drives* (Urban, 1907), a train goes out of control and embarks on a crazed journey that plays off the fear associated with train travel. But to refer to Freud's distinction between fright (unexpected) and anxiety (anticipated), reprised in Hitchcock's distinction between surprise and suspense, the spectator presumably banked on being frightened as well as being anxious—the surprise of "unseen energy" being an indication of this reaction.[216] If shock was by this time a programmed unit of mass consumption and a principle of modern perception, it could clearly still frighten—or thrill—with the force of trauma.[217]

Walter Benjamin recognized this substratum of shock in his oft-quoted insight into Dada aesthetics, in which he compared the Dadaist work of art to ballistics, the effect of which—assault on the spectator—could be compared with film.[218] In the footnote to these remarks, Benjamin advanced a sort of stimulus shield theory of film (predating by three years the argument's more elaborate development in "On Some Motifs in Baudelaire"): "The film is the art form that is in keeping with the increased threat to his life which modern man has to face. Man's need to expose himself to shock effects is his adjustment to the dangers threatening him. The film corresponds to profound changes in the apperceptive apparatus—changes that are experienced on an individual scale by the man in the street in big-city traffic, on a historical scale by every present-day citizen."[219]

These changes were in large part brought about and imposed by the railroad. But Benjamin's remarks have a more specific thrust: big-city traffic and modern humans as urban creatures. Certainly a chief weapon in the bombardment of stimuli was the train, trolley, and subway. As Drinka points out, medical thought, especially as represented by George Miller Beard, the great American theorist of neurasthenia, blamed modern life—progress—for neurasthenia, the American "overwork" disease.[220] In an 1895 article Sir Clifford Allbutt, professor of medicine at Cambridge University, attributed nervous disability and hysteria to "the frightfulness, the melancholy, the unrest due to living at high pressure, the world of the railway, the pelting of telegrams, the strife of business. . . . " Living by the clock in a dense urban world electrified by a skein of traffic, the vulnerable urbanite succumbed to a host of nervous disorders.[221]

Early film registered the urban assault on the individual in, among other

12. *Uncle Josh at the Moving Picture Show*, frame enlargement, Edison/Porter, 1902. Library of Congress.

things, its fascination with the rube in the city. In *Rube and Fender* (Edison/Porter, 1903), for example, city-conscious spectators are asked to laugh at the unwary hick who ambles down a street only to be scooped up by the fender of a trolley approaching from behind. Early film's most famous rube is Uncle Josh, who in Edison/Porter's *Uncle Josh at the Moving Picture Show* parodies the Lumière spectator responding to the train.[222] Uncle Josh, a popular vaudeville and recording star at the turn of the century, plays himself — or rather his rube persona — in the 1902 film (photo 12). Seated in a loge just next to a film screen, he views three films, all by Edison, that elicit exaggerated responses. The first shows a dancer flinging her skirts, which titillates Josh's fancy and inspires him to leap from the balcony box to test the reality of the image. The second film is *The Black Diamond Express*, which shows a train rushing at the camera at an angle that cuts much closer than in the Lumière film. Uncle Josh appears terrified and, arms flailing, panics before the image. Is this the "primitive," terrified spectator? Or is it the modern, "train-trained" subject whose programmed response is a form of traumatic neurosis along the lines of railway brain? In the confusion of the two in Uncle Josh, we can identify a confusion or conflation of shocks that find a common center in the early film spectator, the hysterical, traumatized, and *thrilled* subject of both the railroad and film.

To understand early film spectators, and Uncle Josh, in terms of hysteria, we must first realize that hysteria was, according to popular wisdom, the quintessential condition of the Victorian woman. Read psychoanalytically (through Freud), such somatic states as paralysis, speech loss, convulsions, and somnambulism were, in the absence of a physical cause, taken as symptoms of repression — the repression of traumatic memories, specifically of a seduction scenario, and the consequent repudiation of sexuality.[223] Read socially, hysteria was an appropriate reaction against the oppressive roles that women were expected to play as wives and mothers.[224] In pre-Freudian medical thought, hysteria was nerve-related, and as women were assumed to have more highstrung, delicate nervous systems, they were thought to be particularly vulnerable. A basic premise of this view was that such diseases must have a pathological basis, even if traumatically induced (for example, a physical blow to the body that could be seen as a trauma-inducing paralysis), while a hereditary or genetic predisposition to weak nerves was typically assumed.[225] The "nerve literature" referred to above gradually modified its assumptions to admit a psychological dimension, but it held fast to the somatic and gendered roots.

One of the major correctives to this view was the phenomenon of male hysteria, which first came to medical attention in the context of the railway accident and the corresponding "traumatic neuroses" such as railway spine and railway brain. Many had remarked the appearance of neurosis in male subjects and its apparent relation to railroad accidents, as well as to "shocking" accidents of a more generic industrial nature.[226] But it was Charcot who seized on the phenomenon as a specific manifestation of hysteria. His primary examples in *Leçons sur l'hystérie virile* (1888–89) are derived from cases of railroad-related trauma, including railroad accident victims.[227]

Hermann Oppenheim objected to Charcot's assimilation of "railway brain" to the hysteria model. He preferred to call it "traumatic neurosis," insisting that railway trauma gave rise to a nerve condition, with "electricity coursing through the nerves as the causative agent."[228] His railway trauma cases often showed signs of hysteria, but just as often they exhibited simple anxiety or nervous exhaustion. But Charcot insisted with equal conviction that hysteria was the appropriate condition — both psychically and physically. He saw all the symptoms — anxiety included — as hysterical. "His essential proof was hypnosis," writes Michèle Ouerd, who notes further that, for Charcot, "since traumatic paralysis suggested all the analogies with the experimental paralysis he induced by hypnotic suggestion, the traumatic paralysis was therefore of a hysterical nature."[229] Clearly there was a problem of definition or, in semiotic terms, a crisis in signification: how many signifieds could be attached to a signifier, a symptom?

The rhetorical difficulties reemerge in Charcot's attempts to make a case for a properly male hysteria. He was struck by a number of things in his studies of male hysterics: (1) the similarity of the symptoms to those of female hysterics — here he took pains to stretch *the*, his own, standard model of female hysteria to encompass male traits less typical of women patients (e.g., symptoms that lasted or were sustained over a long period of time), meaning, as Ouerd points out, he had to obliterate sexual difference: if male hysteria was to be hysteria at all, it had to resemble or *be* female hysteria, already a redundancy in the medical imagination of the period; and (2) the astonishing appearance of hysterical symptoms in stereotypically virile working-class men — the assumption having been that one might expect to find hysteria among the "effeminate" men of the idle class, the "superior," hence more neurotically disposed beings of the delicately constituted upper classes, but among strong, vigorous proletarians, never.[230] The way around this latter paradox was a reference to heredity — a hysterical aunt or epileptic grandfather could always be produced to establish a genetic predisposition to neurosis — and an insistence on some real trauma, like the railroad accident. Still, Charcot was perplexed: "Male hysteria is very common among the lower classes of society; it even seems to be more typical there than female hysteria. We're speaking here of *la grande hystérie*, of massive hysteria as M. Marie calls it, for with mild hysteria, it's rather the reverse that one remarks."[231] This he connected with the appearance of male hysteria among vagabonds, tramps, society's peripatetic disenfranchised, what Ouerd refers to as "*les névropathes voyageurs,*" those who experience in their own bodies and lives the metaphor of a characteristic trait of hysteria — mobility.[232] Ouerd takes Charcot's insight into the class (or, as the case may be, nonclass) position of these patients further, noting that this position reveals a pattern. If mobility of mind is one of the chief characteristics of female hysteria (the rapid ease with which the hysteric passes from laughter to tears, for example), mobility of social place is the male hysterical equivalent. Ouerd draws a parallel with the fin-de-siècle view that the working class is, in the great social body of the Republic, the migratory uterus of traditional hysteria: "it moves, often convulsively as in the Commune — and it is thus necessary to suppress it, to channel it into its *faubourgs*, care for it if possible by all the means available in hygienic, prophylactic and mental medicine. . . ."[233]

In a kind of mirror image of otherness, one can see that cultural displacement as massive as nineteenth-century mechanization and urbanization — railway-assisted — traumatized its victims into a condition akin to female hysteria. In other words, it "emasculated" men, and not only those men of a certain class. Women, proletarian men, tramps, and other social marginals were made to bear the brunt of the shocks of modernity. Yet, as standard-bearers of the pathologies of modern culture, these signifiers of non-middle-class men were the frightening symbols of what middle-class men were in danger of becoming as potential victims of hysteria, the psychic disease of a modernism to which all were subject: the social and sexual Other.

The "emasculated" male, the male hysteric, might then be seen as the boomerang of white, male, technological culture against itself, a vision of the railroad neurotic as a man reduced to a female, or non-male state, like the proverbial woman tied to the tracks and assaulted or traumatized by the train. The paradox: investment or overinvestment (à la "overwork") in the male "culture of time and space" was emasculating for men of all classes. As Charcot had found, hysteria was not class-specific; even the most "virile" of men —

working-class types — were victims of industrially based shock, while hysterical upper-class men also had appeared in Charcot's experience. In a sense,
then, the working-class male hysterics pointed to what all men were potentially capable of becoming.

After making his own study of male hysteria in 1886, and more detailed
analyses of female hysterics with Breuer in 1895, Freud would be led to posit
trauma in psychic, not pathological, terms. Eventually he came to see the
"founding trauma" of hysteria as a fantasy of seduction, superseding his earlier
view that an actual seduction early in childhood was the repressed memory
that spoke, via displacement, across the body of the hysteric.[234] A seduction
fantasy — which in our time of "recovered memories" and widespread sexual
abuse is not to be interpreted as a conscious or welcome phenomenon — may
also be linked to "railway brain." To invoke Drinka's remarks on proximity to a
train as a basis for anxiety, if the mere threat of collision was enough to induce
"traumatic neurosis," or hysteria, in men and women, perhaps we might see
"railway brain" in relation to a technological seduction fantasy — a culturally
based fantasy of desiring displacement, movement, trauma, even destruction,
a fantasy whose apogee may have been World War I (which gave rise to Freud's
shock studies) or may be our present-day culture of desensitized violence.

Read in the context of "railway brain" and its implied trauma, Uncle Josh
is not just funny; he is hysterically funny. His hysteria, understood in popular
terms as the exaggerated fright, the bodily reaction to the train film (one
passes easily from hysteria to paranoia here), is not only a train phobia, but
a cinematic hysteria. Here, the commonplace understanding of hysteria as
frightened, wild gesticulation becomes for the film analyst an entry into an
understanding of hysteria as representation based in a traumatic experience
with psychoanalytic implications. As a proxy for the "naive" spectator, Uncle
Josh's reactions can be read in relation to shock — the shock not only of the
train image (the imagination of disaster, the railway brain cum railway eyes),
but of the filmic image: the panic of projection. But does this then make our
Uncle Josh an Auntie Josh?

In the guise of answering this question, I wish to offer an even more literal
example of the kind of spectator of early film that I am suggesting. *The Photographer's Mishap*, a 1901 Edison/Porter film, sets in motion the highly dynamic configuration of male hysteria, train, shock, and film that I identify as
a basis of more general spectatorship.[235] Reading this film in relation to a
slightly later example of the representation of male hysteria, Edison's 1910

Asleep at the Switch, I will suggest ways in which narrative cinema absorbs the hysterical premise for its own purposes, managing and controlling shock and its spectator.

In *The Photographer's Mishap*, a still photographer sets up a tripod on a railroad track to shoot an oncoming train. After covering his head with a photographer's dark cloth, he is hit by the train and his camera is destroyed. The photographer springs to his feet and moves to a parallel track, only to be menaced by another approaching train, with which he narrowly escapes collision. At the end, two men arrive to escort him off the tracks as the photographer breaks down, arms flailing in a hysterical fit of madness. The film consists of one shot and uses stop-motion photography to substitute a dummy for the actor when the train rushes over him.[236]

In one sense, this film is a literal illustration of male hysteria induced by railway trauma: a man suffers an unbelievable accident, the result of which is not so much physical as emotional or mental trauma and shock—the joke being that he suffers no bodily harm from being run down. His convulsions are a cliché of hysteria. In psychoanalytic terms the repetition of the main threat (the double running-over scenario) is not so much an exercise in retroactive defense and the production of protective anxiety (i.e., a preemptive, anticipatory strike), but rather the stimulus to an attack of fright, a prestimulus shield assault on the psyche. The hysterical symptoms point to a feminization—as emasculation—of the photographer as the victim of a metaphorical rape: run down by the train like the woman tied to the tracks, and knocked down from an erect to a prostrate position, the photographer suffers a technological seduction fantasy rooted in repetition every bit as terrifying—and thrilling—as the fantasies of Freud's hysterics. In a sense, within the masculinist coding of the locomotive, all obstacles run down by trains become women—or rather not-men. For what male hysteria shows us is not so much the coding of men as women, but the uncoding of men as men. Again, hysteria is a no-man's-land where gender falls apart, and both male and female hysterics resist given articulations of their sexes. Similarly, the photographer in our film exhibits many characteristics of the quintessential fetishist: run down once and more or less castrated, he goes against what he knows may happen (the reality of being hit by a train) and thus sets himself up for another assault. The fit at the end is a display of excess, of something that cannot be contained, as opposed to a limp, feminine subject. This photographer is in crisis.

That the butt of the visual joke is a photographer is suggestive. The other metaphor through which to read the "joke work" of this film is that of the still image versus the moving image, photography versus cinema. Like many an early film concerned to demonstrate within the film itself the superior powers of the moving image, *The Photographer's Mishap* offers graphic testimony to the ability of film to register movement, locomotion, and speed (the train). The still image folds under and into the dynamism of film — both the film in question, and the train as a displaced image of cinema — and is traumatized and repressed as a result. In a sense, we have here an allegory of early film as it emerges from photography.

The Photographer's Mishap also offers a view of spectatorship in its anticipation of *Uncle Josh at the Moving Picture Show*. The train hitting the photographer while he is behind his camera is an assault on vision — vision accustomed to static images and objects, a vision in the process of becoming outmoded. In this case the victim of railway brain is also a victim of cinema brain, of the aggression of the apparatus. Later, montage would absorb the aggressive function of a violent interruption of a journey, of a narrative — discontinuity as a shock principle, or rather that which terrorizes vision with the shock of the unexpected. If, as is commonly asserted, the repression of discontinuity is what classical, invisible editing is all about, then we could say that continuity editing is about the control of trauma as well.

Asleep at the Switch, for example, takes the trope of train trauma seriously by narrativizing it for a moral end; a lesson is to be learned about male hysteria in the proximity of the railroad and about the power of the moving image as a vehicle of trauma. In this film the hysterical representation of the man is linked to an excessive, "train film" kind of vision.

The film derives from the popular ballad of the same title, which enjoyed currency in the late nineteenth century.[237] In Charles Shackford's 1897 composition, a switchman tormented by wondering if his sick child will recover, falls dead at the switch (in the "big sleep"). His daughter Nell, who has come to tell him that the ill son has recovered, throws the switch barely in time. It turns out that the railroad company president and his family are aboard the train, and Nell is handsomely rewarded for her efforts.

Though structurally similar, the film departs from the song in certain key respects. In the film the switchman does not die but falls asleep, and it is his dutiful wife who stages the last-minute rescue, by resourcefully flagging the train with the dining room tablecloth. The railroad employee is given a test, which he fails and which his wife passes. She is made to bear the burden of his failure and to teach him a lesson in vigilance and fidelity — a function more generally accorded to women in Victorian culture, in which women were assigned the role of moral guardians, keeping watch over male laxity brought on by the stresses of the economic arena. In the film an opposition forms between two states: that of sleep and that of wakefulness. Ever awake, women are to keep men on the track, so to speak, and the system running.

What makes *Asleep at the Switch* interesting for the film analyst is its use of inset, superimposed fantasy images designed to underscore the price of "falling down" on the job. The switchman wakes up too late and, realizing his error, begins to hallucinate the probable outcome of his inaction. Inset in the upper left corner of the frame, we see two model trains crash head-on, to the switchman's manifest horror. Later, the window is filled with the rear-projected image of his would-be victims, who crowd the frame with arms outstretched. These psychic projections of guilt overpower the switchman, and he faints with remorse. Their primary function is to underline guilt, paranoia, and the moral and psychic consequences of being a negligent (if overworked and exhausted) employee and to make the woman's sacrifice that much greater — after all, she left her child at home to save the President's Special.

To read the switchman's reactions as hysterical requires no special effort: the somnambulistic character of his hallucination, the fitful bodily response (melodramatic gesture as hysteria), the anxiety — these are familiar symptoms. And the connection with work, with "overwork," to be exact, recalls the stress neurasthenia dear to American medical theory, as well as Charcot's emasculated railroad men. The film is saying something about the dangers of not only failing to perform one's job, but of gender reversal as a consequence of both too much work and railroad — or cinematic — trauma.[238] For the hallucination paralyzes and traumatizes the switchman, while his wife springs into action. It is as if he had suffered the shock of the imagined accident, or that of a traumatizing movie: a projected image like the matted-in crash. In terms of his relation to this "movie," to the imaginary scenario of collision, the male character responds physically and emotionally as if he had been assaulted by the trains, even as he imagines that he has caused the crash.

In theoretical terms, the assaulted spectator is the hysterical spectator. The fantasies of being run over and assaulted or penetrated produce a certain pleasure of pain — beyond the pleasure principle and in the realm of repetition compulsion — which is as much about will-to-submission (to loss-of-mastery) as it is about will-to-mastery or control (one might even say "suspension of disbelief" as submission). Where this will to submission becomes a social threat is the point at which the quest for thrill and shock exceeds ritualized containers of social legitimacy (the roller coaster), to refer to Ouerd's remarks on revolution and hysteria.[239] As Gunning points out, Siegfried Kracauer and others have seen the cinema, particularly silent cinema, as providing a potential launch pad for acting on restless dissatisfaction with modern experience.[240] And certainly the concerns of early reformers to clamp down on early cinema's lack of coherent or consistent morality provide a compelling index of the fear of social and moral threat its audiences may have posed.

The Photographer's Mishap and *Uncle Josh at the Moving Picture Show* unleash male hysteria and allow it to burst forth uncontained; *Asleep at the Switch* codes it, narrativizes it, and makes the feminization explicit. Such earlier films bear witness to a transitional moment in popular representation when codes were being broken down and re-formed around a dynamic, mechanical vision. Just as masculinity founders in the phenomenon of "male hysteria," which also puts into crisis definitions of femininity, so pre-cinematic vision breaks apart in relation to film. But early cinematic perception and its aggressivity, its discontinuous excess, to use Gunning's terms, would be put back on the track, so to speak, and gender given a more strongly narrative coding in early classical film.[241]

Does it then make sense to speak of a female subject, or of a male hysteric? Is early cinematic spectatorship an emasculation, a feminization, or neither? This question depends to some extent on how gender-coded are society's concepts of submission, vulnerability, and inability to contain and control — and they are so coded, of course. But before we posit some essentially "feminized" spectator — like a feminized railroad passenger or accident victim — we might instead consider the early film spectator as "undone," uncoded, a subject whose sexual orientation vis-à-vis spectatorship is broken down, put into crisis, and thus hystericized. Early train films are as often involved in the undoing of sexual difference, of a set of anchors for sexual identity that floats, comically, in an age of mechanical production. They embody the promise of modernity's destabilizing effects — the destruction of the old, the fixed, the Oedipal — and the confusion. We might then think of classical cinema, which is commonly described as the institutionalization of a male perspective, as the institutionalization of a female spectator, a properly female audience, and a regulated female point of view — certainly if we take into account the emphasis in feminist scholarship on the female spectator/consumer as practically a prototype for cinematic spectatorship.[242] In reference to the early German cinema, Heide Schlüpmann notes: "Melodrama froze the movement of female (self-) representation at the beginning of narrative cinema. . . . A hybrid form even before it insinuated itself into the cinema, melodrama abandoned the representation of woman's history in favor of the construction of a so-called 'female perspective.' "[243]

As chapter 2 will demonstrate, stabilizing the female image was only half the problem for dealing with the excess represented by the sexually heterogeneous audiences of early cinema and the "alternative public sphere" it represented, to use Hansen's well-founded phrase.[244] If, as *Asleep at the Switch* shows, feminized men, masculinized women, and excess of any sort were to be contained and narrativized, then the sex roles had to be sorted out according to the code of Respectable Woman, who began to assert a legitimating, reformist influence over film from about 1909.

TWO

Romances of the Rail in Silent Film

The world, my friend, will be turned on its head,
We'll no longer see anything that resembles the past;
The rich will be beggars, and the nobles ruined;
Our troubles will be blessings, men will be women,
And women will be . . . whatever they want."
—from "Dupont et Durand," Alfred de Musset[1]

Writing in 1838 about a new form of transportation, the train, the French poet
Alfred de Musset predicted a future in which the spread of railroads around
the world would entail the disintegration of codes and traditions, boundaries
in the largest and smallest senses. De Musset's ironic, faux utopian vision of a
new "world upside down" was not universally embraced by other Romantic
writers in the nineteenth century on either side of the Atlantic. As we saw in
chapter 1, wherever the railroad went, it left disturbance in its wake, mixing
progress with destruction and economic advance with social and cultural
confusion.

What I find interesting in de Musset's sketch of the emerging railroad-
defined landscape is the envisioned gender inversion that would be produced
by overturning established social codes and rules of understanding. In what

sense could the railroad possibly be thought to bring about a world in which "men will be women, and women will be whatever they want"? For Western countries in the nineteenth century this statement might refer to the sense in which the country and the city were considered to be violated, turned upside down by the iron horse, which reoriented the very ground of identity. Even more might it refer to the modern phenomenon of the public intermingling of the sexes, both inside the train and in the railroad station. In both cases the railroad was transforming spatial and social relations by the uneasy juxtaposition of masses — or, to be more precise, masses of bodies.

De Musset's linkage of the coming of the railroad and inverted relations between the sexes was far from premature. The railroad's intrusion into society mobilized and recoded sexual identity, providing a dynamic stage of romantic and sexual encounters. It is as if the very fact of accelerated motion and speed pulled the carpet from beneath the feet of traditional modes of social interaction in public space. Combined with the scale of such interaction — the increase in crowd size and density — the railroad's speed did much to further the sense in which all identities dissolve into a larger mass entity.

This chapter is about gender and the railroad — how the train and the cinema can be thought of in relation to sexuality. Specifically, it focuses on the relations of women, for the most part Caucasian, heterosexual women, to both trains and film, as well as to the men in and on the trains. The motivation for this focus is simple: the overwhelming majority of silent films that feature trains prominently are white, heterosexual "romances of the rail," and few of them manage to leave out women altogether. If in chapter 1, the discussion of legitimation centered on the overall social and cultural effects of the railroad and the cinema, in this chapter greater attention will be given to the moral issues involved, the sense in which both the railroad and the cinema were thought to be unhealthy for women. (Not surprisingly, white men and men and women of color were rarely included in discourse on the railroad, and almost never as historical agents.) In relation to the moral discourse on the railroad, I will also concentrate on the placement of women within and by each institution and look at how the cultural context of women's relation to technology informed their representation on screen along with the narrative and textual structures specific to the films. The transgression that de Musset hints at for the railroad became both a rich and contested source of narrative in silent cinema.

The Gender(s) of Trains

How can the railroad be conceived in terms of gender? One sense strikes us as obvious: the train as a metallic, mechanical phallus. Films like Alfred Hitchcock's *North by Northwest* (1959), in which a train entering a tunnel is meant to signify and parody sexual intercourse, epitomize this popular notion. Although Western culture's representation of the train as a specifically male object may have reached its fullest aesthetic expression in the early decades of the twentieth century in paintings by Giorgio de Chirico, Edward Hopper, Paul Delvaux, and others, and in the writings of Futurists such as F. T. Marinetti, the train has long carried this signification in popular imagery. For Klaus Theweleit, who has studied protofascist male sexual fantasies in terms of the oppositions high/low, dry/wet, hard/soft, and male/female, a turn-of-the-century postcard of a train riding on water is an emblematic image of these oppositions.[2] And in caricatures that illustrate antimodernist sentiment about the railroad in the late nineteenth and early twentieth centuries, the train appears ritually as an anthropomorphized white man threatening a female victim who allegorically signifies the city, the land, or the public.[3]

For the nineteenth-century American public the train carried sexual significance in relation to the land. The "machine in the garden" was seen as a virile projectile thrust upon "the garden," which was seen as both Mother Nature and as America's fertile, yet virgin frontier.[4] Henry Nash Smith's classic study *The Virgin Land* uses this gendered metaphor as its central trope in relation to time-honored Anglo-American themes of communion with nature and the threat that civilization represented to the natural world — enduring national myths about the land, the garden-nation, the Eden of the New World, the Great Mother Continent.[5]

Certainly the iron horse was a gendered creature. In *The Machine in the Garden*, Leo Marx reaches this conclusion after studying early responses, both literary and more popular, to the appearance of the railroad in America: "Most important is the sense of the machine as a sudden, shocking intruder upon a fantasy of idyllic satisfaction. It invariably is associated with crude, masculine aggressiveness in contrast with the tender, feminine, and submissive attitudes traditionally attached to the landscape."[6] Thoreau provides a vivid example in what he calls the Deep Cut — in Marx's words, a "wound inflicted upon the land by man's meddling, aggressive, rational intellect."[7] Thoreau attributes the Deep Cut to the " 'devilish Iron Horse, whose ear-rending neigh is heard throughout the town," and who " 'has muddied the Boiling Spring with his foot' " and " 'browsed off all the woods on Walden shore. . . .' "[8] The railroad-in-the-landscape as a sexual image can thus be seen in the context of the classic split between culture and nature.[9]

Perhaps the strongest association of the train with male sexuality in American culture, however, was and is as an extension of the male engineer who drives the train. Take, for example, a popular 1875 engraving representing the division between male and female in terms of the train and its "off-screen," off-the-tracks space (photo 13).[10] In the image, which shows a wife and child waving at the passing locomotive being driven by the husband/engineer, the wife and child appear off to one side. The engineer in his machine both expands and transcends the family circle, literally extending the engineer's self beyond that of father and husband. As John Stilgoe notes of the traits of the Western hero that overlap with those of the hero of train films in the 1920s, "he is frequently a loner, married to the railroad, and unable to be a loving husband."[11]

The association of the locomotive with male identity was established in childhood, or rather, boyhood. Both the cult of the model train and popular boys' fiction from around 1880 to World War I firmly linked masculinity with railroading. Toy railroads were boy territory; advertisements for model trains were addressed to male fantasies and aspirations. The 1929 catalog of the Lionel Company, the premier model train builder, asked the rhetorical question, " 'Is there a boy or man who doesn't thrill at the sight of a Lionel Passenger or Freight Train . . . ?' "[12] Lionel also built a self-promotional, Oedipal narrative into its pitch, noting that operating toy trains "strengthened father-son relationships, taught boys something of electricity, geometry, and mechanics, and prepared teenagers for responsible positions in the industrial world." Lionel touted itself as the seedbed for many toy-trained boys who grew up to become important railroad employees, thus marketing itself as a legitimate tool of male acculturation on a continuum with the giant railroad world. Clearly, Lionel saw itself as an anchor for heterosexual masculinity; a 1932 *Fortune* magazine article on the company's success asserts that " 'any man with pretensions to normality knows a lot about toy trains,' " noting that grown men are just as likely to be fascinated by toy trains as are boys.

In dime novels and serial railroad fiction from the late nineteenth and early twentieth centuries, most of which addressed adolescent boys, both men

13. *Lake Shore and Michigan Southern Railway*, poster, 1875.
National Museum of American History.

and boys identify themselves and their masculinity with the locomotive, as opposed to the world of girls and women that they leave and to which they return. Stories that appeared in such periodicals as the *Saturday Evening Post* and *McClure's* as well as more esoteric publications like *Railroad Man's Magazine* (which became *Railroad Stories* in 1932), bore titles like "The Luck of the Northern Mail: The Story of a Runaway Boy and a Runaway Train" (1900).[13] Boys who dreamed of railroad careers were encouraged by novels about "boy life on the rails" and even by "romances of the rail" that featured women who fell for railroad heroes in such novels as Frank Spearman's *The Daughter of a Magnate* (1903). Just as with the toy trains, this literature built into its premises an educational mission to train railroad *boys* and turn them into railroad *men*. As Stilgoe notes of the period from 1880 to 1920, "men chronicling their awakening into adulthood frequently emphasized the railroad as the place in which they discovered both personal and social change."[14] He credits the "national coming of age" during this same period with a monumental influence, noting that the man of the rails became initiated into a world governed by telegraphs, steam and electricity, and no longer by sunlight and horse-powered vehicles. In this sense, the nation's manhood and the individual's manhood converged in a single technology; the locomotive-obsessed boy was literally plugged into a national economy in some sense defined by the railroad.

It should not go without mention that many American boys who may have had fantasies of glamorous railroad careers were barred from fulfilling such dreams because of skin color. African American men were effectively shut out of positions on the railroad other than as porters and, more rarely, as shopmen, firemen, or trainmen well into the twentieth century. In no case were they allowed to be engineers or conductors, much less corporate personnel. Still, porters were held in high esteem in the African American community, and they did much to link black male identity with the railroads: "To say you were a Pullman porter was to say that you had a job that paid well compared to other kinds of work available to black men; it meant you were able to qualify for the position and thus had no police record and were both intelligent and trustworthy; it meant you were a black male who worked as a servant to the wealthy and powerful individuals who rode the Pullmans."[15] The emergence and growth of an educated black middle class in the second third of this century owes a great deal to the social stability established by the thousands of porters who worked for the Pullman company.[16]

Hence, "manhood" from the perspective of Lionel and the railroad industry would only ever refer to white men, while "manhood" from a wide-spread African American perspective could and did include trains in its definition. It is hardly surprising that in the shadow universe of African American-produced film — parallel to the white industry, just as the two definitions of masculinity ran side by side — one of the earliest efforts was entitled *The Rail-road Porter.* Produced in 1912 by Bill Foster, the first African American to have his own production company (established in 1910, predating Oscar Micheaux's company by eight years), *The Railroad Porter* was a short domestic comedy with an all-black cast.[17] The plot centers on a porter and his wife, who invites a young waiter from one of the " 'colored cafes' " over to eat while her husband is (she thinks) at work. When the husband returns early and catches the couple in the act of eating, a revolver is produced, a chase ensues, and all apparently ends happily without violence.

Interpretations of the film vary (it is no longer extant). Some have seen it as a positive representation of African Americans, others as reiterating through slapstick, Keystone-type comedy the same idioms in which blacks were represented — if at all — in white film.[18] Using such sources as film reviews in the *New York Age,* a weekly African American newspaper of the time, Mark A. Reid reads the film another way, seeing the clear middle-class setting, the references to a thriving urban, black middle-class culture (including cafés), and the representation of employed black men as a corrective to popular stereotypes of the "coon" character in American film and culture.[19] With this and other comedies, Foster sought and served an African American audience that desired images made from its perspective. And, as Mary Carbine has shown, such an audience thrived in Chicago's "Black Metropolis" (Foster's company was also based in Chicago) as well as in other Northern cities with a separate circuit of movie theaters and forms of specifically black vaudeville and musical performance to accompany film screenings.[20] As debates about the movies in the black press of the time show, "black audiences 'consumed' the movies in a context determined as much by the interests and tastes of the black community as by the economic and social agendas of the white majority."[21] Although more difficult to book in a distribution system that encouraged exhibitors to order more highly profitable Hollywood films, "race movies" thus found ready audiences across the country.[22] Even as *The Railroad Porter* affirms the sense in which the railroad world was a man's world, the film is for us an important alternative to the overwhelmingly white representation of railroads in the silent era.

The Genders in and on Trains

The sexual imagery of the train and its varied associations may have belonged primarily to men, but in providing a public stage for the display of sexuality, both legitimate and illegitimate, the railroad adopted a more ambiguous status in relation to gender. Whether in the station or on the train, class and sex mixed and converged in a space that could not always be socially defined or controlled. The sense of depersonalization and alienation alluded to in chapter 1, was brought about by industrial urban society's unfamiliar crowds and the forced intimacy of sharing space with a stranger.

In Paul Virilio's view, the de-territorializing effects of the railroad, that is, the dissolving of definable territories by their incorporation into the world economy, are also de-socializing. In the perfecting of systems of economic exchange, social exchange becomes abstract and dynamic, detaching the passenger from nature (the geographical and physical body) and from the social body as well.[23] Other people become simply *other*—transitory presences on the train, mere signifiers without reference, bodies bearing no familiar or regular relation to other passengers, bodies likely to disappear at any moment.

As such, the train is a quintessential heterotopia. Michel Foucault defines heterotopias as sites of temporary relaxation such as trains, cafés, cinemas, and beaches, sites that also "have the curious property of being in relation with all the other sites, but in such a way as to suspect, neutralize, or invert the set of relations that they happen to designate, mirror, or reflect."[24] The fact that they are outside all places, difficult or impossible to locate in reality, is what qualifies them as heterotopias. Foucault's classic example is the "honeymoon train," where the ancestral theme of the bride's deflowering takes place "nowhere," on a train or in a hotel, sites without clear geographical markers.[25]

The heterotopic anteroom to the chance meetings that flourished on the train was the railroad station. As the most visible and monumental cultural mask for the railroad, the station represented a microcosm of society in its channeling of bodies and its regulation of crowd flows.[26] Carl Condit notes that "the constantly expanding station not only shaped the urban fabric and the pattern of land use but became a special kind of urbanistic institution, a microcity mirroring the urban life around it."[27] The condensation of urban life, as well as the juxtaposition of all social types entering and leaving the city for the country, gave the station an eclectic, indefinable character with respect to class. W. P. Frith's famous painting of 1863, *The Railway Station*, like a number of English and American caricatures made throughout the nineteenth century, depicts the wild rush of the crowd to catch an imminently departing train as a kind of naive chaos that breeds crime.[28] In their social history of the railway station, Jeffrey Richards and John MacKenzie see the attempts to maintain rigid class divisions in the station as in some sense failed. "The station," they write "was an extraordinary agent of social mixing."[29] It was also an agent of sexual mixing. In European and American stations special attention was given to protecting women, as "stations were invariably seen as places of danger for women."[30] Jean Déthier describes the station as "a site for permissiveness," a "public space where intimacies abound."[31]

If the train station was a microcosm of the social sphere, the train car itself was simply a smaller, more condensed version of the station.[32] The station received and channeled the urban and rural flux that met on its platforms and in its hallways. The train in the case of departures was the endpoint of these flows, and in the case of arrivals a source of their outpouring. Once outside the station and en route to its destination, the train became a self-contained stage for romance, seduction, and crime, all encouraged by the "in-between" nature of the train journey and by such factors as the arrangement of compartments and seating.

In caricatures produced over some thirty years for such French illustrated humor magazines as *Le Charivari* and *Le Boulevard*, Honoré Daumier often addressed the hazards of train and bus travel for women. "*Intérieur d'un omnibus*" ("Inside an Omnibus") (1839) shows a terrified young lady wedged between a drunk and a butcher, with the implication that each is equally threatening and undesirable. "*En chemin de fer — voisin agréable*" ("On the Train — A Pleasant Neighbor") (1862) shows a woman overwhelmed by the cigarette smoke of the rude male passenger seated next to her. Another sketch from 1864 depicts a female passenger who refuses to enter a compartment in which a single male passenger is inside, demanding instead to board an all-female car.[33]

In the European train, which was divided into individual, unconnected compartments containing only a few seats, the resulting isolation encouraged murder, theft, and rape. Preventing crime was difficult, a fact that was sensationalized by the press.[34] Danger was particularly present to women. English paintings in the 1850s and 1860s by Abraham Solomon, Charles Rossiter, and others, take note of the flirtation that might occur in all classes of carriages, while caricatures were less subtle and romantic in suggesting the kind of attention women were likely to receive.[35] Schivelbusch quotes a series of *Punch* cartoons concerned with the mutual distrust among first-class passengers and an official report prepared for the House of Commons in 1865: "'There has been, indeed, a panic amongst railway passengers. Ladies, unable, of course, to discriminate at the moment between those whom they should avoid and those who should be their protectors, shun all alike; and gentlemen passengers, as well as railway officers of all classes, constantly refuse to travel singly with a stranger of the weaker sex, under the belief that it is only common prudence to avoid in this manner all risk of being accused, for purposes of extortion, of insult, or assault.' "[36] In one of the *Punch* cartoons, "Railway Morals," a woman tells the railway guard before boarding that she "must have a carriage where there are no young men likely to be rude to one."[37]

The legacy of this practical ambivalence — and its narrative potential — left an imprint on early film. *A Railway Tragedy* (Gaumont, 1904) takes as its theme the danger to women traveling alone on trains. Structured by a bracketing departure and arrival, the film concerns a woman waiting for a train who is eyed by a suspicious-looking male character. Inside an isolated compartment, the woman falls asleep under the unobtrusive gaze of the so far unnoticed man. While she sleeps, the man steals money from her purse and then removes his fake mustache. When the woman awakens and discovers her money has disappeared, she accuses the thief, who strangles her and throws her off the train. Outside the train, two men retrieve the woman's corpse from the tracks. At the next station the thief is accosted and taken away.[38]

Shot by Gaumont in England, this film is clearly a European "compartment drama."[39] The lesson seems to be that not only should women not travel alone on public transportation, but they also should not relax consciousness during their journey. The woman in the film is attacked as much for being a vulnerable creature, or, one might say, for providing an invitation to attack, as for her money. Yet even men were not safe from train compartment trickery. George Méliès's 1900 *Railroad Pickpocket* stars the filmmaker himself as a thief who takes advantage of an opportunity to make some money off of the dozing men in his compartment. In both cases, the filmmakers availed themselves of ready-made narratives and structured the action around the train's natural dramatic potential for bracketed (and unpoliceable) experience.

The problem of unsafe train travel for women was not exclusive to European railways. At one time American railroads were held up to Europeans as an example of openness and democracy, as well as safety, especially in their women-only cars, which lasted until the end of the century.[40] Even so, care had to be taken to ensure the safety of female travelers during the long and often remote journeys to which Americans of means became accustomed. Thus, when the railroads launched a massive self-promotional touristic campaign in the 1880s, one that continued through the 1930s, they emphasized the safety of travel for women as well as for children.[41]

"Personally conducted tours" began to appear in the 1890s. In an 1892 brochure advertising tours to Florida, the Pennsylvania Railroad explained the concept of "personally conducted": "The Chaperon, entirely an original conception of the Pennsylvania Railroad, has especial charge of ladies, particularly those unaccompanied by parents or escort, and also invalids. . . . In the Chaperon, the ladies find both a companion and guide. While furnishing all information that one could wish, and looking with watchful eyes after the comfort and pleasure of those in her charge, the Chaperon also stands to unescorted ladies in the exact relation that her title implies."[42] Most brochures from the 1890s and early twentieth century include illustrations or photographs of train car interiors that show women happily ensconced in seats while reading books or circulating freely in drawing room cars in the company of other women.[43] It is ironic that African American porters were often the effective "chaperons" to female passengers, but any threat they may have carried was effectively negated by the reassuring discourse of Pullman and other train travel literature, which reinforced the porter's character as a jolly, docile *servant*.[44]

The railroads were indeed interested in courting Caucasian women. But their interest in women went beyond seeing them as passengers, as ticket-buying riders of the rails. Women served a much larger function; they stood as symbols of cultural legitimacy and guarantors of respectability (photo 14). These associations were exploited in a number of cultural practices sponsored by the railroads — in particular, the railroad station. As indicated, the station represented the modern equivalent of the cathedral or temple. Culturally speaking, these were secular temples to progress.[45] The place of women in relation to this aesthetic is important. Take one of the great stations of Europe, the Gare de l'Est in Paris. Dominating the western façade is an allegorical statue of the city of Strasbourg, which commemorates the 1870 Franco-Prussian War. The city takes the form of a monumental woman seated in majesty on a throne and draped in Greco-Roman robes.[46] Recalling the virtues and victories of Antiquity, her dramatic immobility crowns a temple erected to mobility, dynamism, and progress. Like a muse who inspires poets, this femi-

14. *Brotherhood of Locomotive Engineers*, poster, 1877/1884.
National Museum of American History.

nine representation was chosen to sanctify a phenomenon constructed for and operated by men.

In this set of juxtapositions, woman is valued for what she represents against progress and for morality and tradition; she is an aesthetic veil thrown over the ugly, economistic face of capitalism. As Schivelbusch notes of the aesthetic function of stations generally, "The neoclassical character of the façades of the station buildings is quite certainly another expression of the typical nineteenth-century desire to disguise the industrial aspect of things by means of ornamentation."[47] Thus the "temples to progress" doubled as memorials to the past, and specifically, an imperial past.[48]

The aesthetic function of the railway station was paralleled in the movie palaces of the teens, which referred in their architecture both to the great nineteenth- and early twentieth-century stations and to the ancient Western cultures cited in their stylistic eclecticism. Hugo Munsterberg's 1916 treatise on film referred to the new movie palaces as "temples for the new goddess."[49] Certainly, the rise of the movie palace around 1912 and all through the teens can be linked with cinema's own bid for cultural legitimacy, specifically in relation to women. As Russell Merritt notes, women began to see themselves more and more during the nickelodeon era (1905–12), both on the screen and in the theater: "Statistically, women and children numbered only 30 per cent of the New York audience by 1908, even less than that during performances after 8:00 P.M., but they commanded the special attention of both the industry and its censors. In a trade hungry for respectability, the middle-class woman was respectability incarnate. Her very presence in the theater refuted the vituperative accusations lodged against the common show's corrupting vulgarity."[50] The great façades of the train stations provided, again, an aesthetic paradigm for such wonders as Mary Pickford's United Artists theater, an enormous neo-Gothic cathedral built in the early twenties in downtown Los Angeles. Women were integral to the aesthetic of the theater and entered its exotic space of fantasy to consume "transporting" images (in extremely rare cases like that of Pickford, they might own the space as well). The movie palace blends the architecture of the railroad station with the comfort and opulence of the luxury train car, while making use of high art *and* women to perform a legitimating function found in other practices of representation as well.

Popular fiction was one such practice. As noted in chapter 1, the American railroads were eager to counter their robber baron image and convince the public of their value to society. Several American railroad lines published

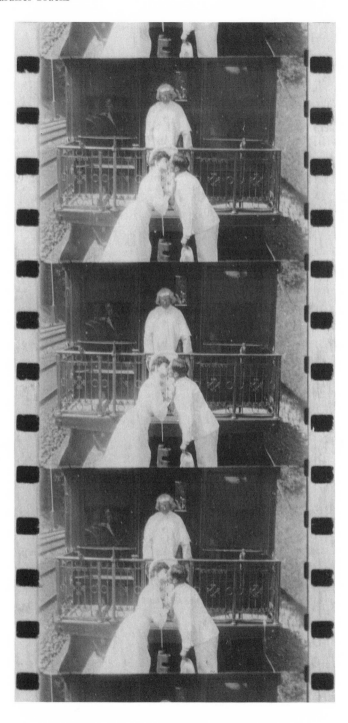

romantic fiction to be read on the journeys offered by individual lines. While most of the plots involved romances that sprang up in relation to generic train travel, descriptive passages on the services and sites offered by the particular line would often be inserted into the narratives. *The Vestibule* was published monthly by the Seaboard Airline railway and contained both contemporary and gothic romances.[51] The Lackawanna Railroad's 1907 "Mountain and Lake Resorts" brochure opens with "A Chase for an Heiress," a short story that stages the key romantic encounter on a voyage through the picturesque Poconos,[52] prime tourist territory for the Lackawanna. The story ends with a marriage — the perfect narrative and romantic resolution.

It is in this context that we must see the advertising impulse of Edison and Porter's 1903 film, *A Romance of the Rail*. Commissioned by the Delaware, Lackawanna and Western Railroad, the film traces the voyage of Phoebe Snow, the Lackawanna's established promotional figure used to advertise the cleanliness of the anthracite coal-carrying line and hence its attractiveness to passengers.[53] The "purity" of Phoebe's virgin-white dress remains intact from beginning to end, from the train station platform where she is "picked up" by a polite male Lackawanna chaperon, who will escort her on her journey and who is also attired in white, to the arrival of the train at another station. The film uses romance as a narrative frame within which to dramatize its claims to physical and moral purity. It goes without saying that Phoebe and her escort are Caucasian, the white cultural frame around everything that happens in the film (photo 15).

Phoebe and her beau eventually marry during the course of the journey, which transforms their observation car into a pulpit and underlines the "coupling" function of the train. They are shown admiring the scenery from the back of the car to demonstrate the cleanliness of the line, the attractiveness of the touristic excursion, and the containment of beauty and romance within the romantic couple — as opposed to an unchaperoned woman in danger of being seduced and hence soiled or dirtied, as in *A Railway Tragedy*.

The Heterotopia, Tricks, and the Joke Space

Had *A Romance of the Rail* been limited to the action described above, we might mistake it for a film made in 1907 or 1908, one that attempts to legitimate not

15. *A Romance of the Rail*, frame enlargement, Edison/Porter, 1903. Library of Congress.

only the aesthetic pretensions of the railroad, but those of the cinema. As discussed in chapter 1, the campaign to "clean up" the cinema in both the United States and Europe began in earnest at that time, with women and children as the battle's stake. One detail of the film, however, points to the "heterotopic" context of the film's production and to a whole genre of train films that were made before 1908 and contributed to an understanding of the cinema as an "illegitimate" space of moral heterogeneity rivaling that of the railroad station and train car.

At the end of the film, after Phoebe and her new husband have disembarked and demonstrated once again the cleanliness of the journey, a pair of tramps emerges from under the train car. The tramps are identically dressed in mock aristocratic attire, with top hats and tails; once they tip their hats in mock salute to the newlyweds, both of them also sport bald heads. The fact that the tramps are male only deepens the parody of the heterosexual couple they are clearly meant to mimic. Somehow, Edison and Porter could not play the "romance" advertisement completely seriously; literally beneath the romance-journey, buried within the narrative and functioning as an antinarrative coda, with its ending-beyond-the-ending, the ribald same-sex couple sabotages both the "straight" couple and the "straight" ending by repetition with a difference.

In fact, this aspect of *A Romance of the Rail* points to a typical genre of early train films, comedies in which, unlike *A Railway Tragedy*, the trope of threatened female sexuality is used as an excuse to mock the couple and the social codes on which it is based. The "honeymoon train" returns as a stage for parody in films like *Nervy Nat Kisses the Bride* (Edison, 1904). In this film, Nervy Nat, a tramp, takes advantage of a bride's irritation with her husband, who leaves the train car to go smoke a cigar. Offended, the bride turns her face to the window, and Nat slips into the groom's seat. When he attempts to kiss her, she consents, assuming it is her husband and that he has come to make up to her. Swiftly realizing the error in identity, she calls for help and Nat is thrown off the train, literally onto the tracks. The film ends with Nat brushing himself off and cursing the train as it passes out of sight.

Here the threat to the respectable middle-class couple does not come from a specific social class, but rather from a social outcast. Indeed, Nat's itinerant status as a tramp — with no home, no place either social or physical — makes him a signifier in Paul Virilio's sense, i.e., the passenger who is a mere transitory presence on the train.[54] Nat's trick is to turn the heterosexual couple into a question of point of view, of a shifting position in an impermanent space. Nat is a kind of Ur-passenger and Ur-cinematic image; what his representation suggests is that in both the train and the cinema, where appearances can be deceiving, identity is more a visual than a substantive phenomenon and one that is repeatable and replaceable.

A similar confusion based on mistaken identity defines the trompe l'oeil effect of *The Deadwood Sleeper* (AM&B, 1905), which, like *Nervy Nat*, uses substitution as a device to make fun of the honeymoon train and the sexual act it implies.[55] But where in *Nervy Nat* a middle-class bride and groom are prey to a prank, in *The Deadwood Sleeper* a rube couple is the butt of the joke. In this film a series of gags takes place in the corridor of a sleeping car framed on both sides by curtains concealing the beds. Since racism among white actors and filmmakers for a long time prevented African Americans, with rare exceptions, from performing in whites' films, a black-face porter escorts in a matronly white woman, then a rowdy group of white actors, a man and three women, who perch on their seats while drinking and laughing.[56] The matron throws a fit over the noise and drinking, which only encourages more of the same. By mistake, a man is shown to the matron's bed while she is in it, which prompts another tantrum on her part. Finally, a bumpkin newlywed couple claims a compartment and amuses the other passengers with their corny embraces. Before heading off to the bathroom, the rube husband has his wife stick her foot from the curtain so he will know which compartment is theirs. After he leaves, of course, all the other passengers thrust their feet into the corridor, which inspires confusion upon the groom's return; to find his bride, he must first fondle all the other passengers' feet.

In terms of sexual identity and its confusion, both *Nervy Nat Kisses the Bride* and *The Deadwood Sleeper* can be read in light of a passage in Jacques Lacan's "Agency of the Letter in the Unconscious" that bears an uncanny relevance to the theoretical point I wish to make: "A train arrives at a station. A little boy and a little girl, brother and sister, are seated in a compartment face to face next to the window through which the buildings along the station platform can be seen passing as the train pulls to a stop. 'Look,' says the brother, 'we're at Ladies!'; 'Idiot!' replies his sister, 'can't you see we're at Gentlemen.' "[57] The example illustrates Lacan's notion of the "sliding of the signified under the signifier," the sense in which meaning is to be found in the chain of signification, as opposed to any one of its components. "Ladies and Gentlemen will be henceforth for these children two countries toward which each of their souls will strive on divergent wings. . . . " What is significant is that the gap between signified and signifier is figured as a function of a view, a view that passes in turn through a frame, a window-screen; this is practically a prototype of point of view in the cinema, of the uncertainty of sexual identification on the train and in the cinema, and of identification as the construction of a variable perspective.

The repetition and sameness of train space, in which all spaces are interchangeable and only temporarily occupied by different people, is in these early films an excuse to upset expectations and the moral codes on which they are based. The space within the train, like that within the cinema, is perpetually recoded as it shifts constantly between boundaries and markers. Passengers come and go, and journeys are musical chairs of identity. The jokes on losing one's place or mistaking someone else's seat or sleeping compartment for one's own are premised on the endless possibilities of substitution, endless because they are dynamic, subject to timetables, clocks, and infinite turnover.

Substitution and haphazard juxtaposition as musical-chair devices appear in two Edison/Porter films that use the same streetcar set interior. In *The Unappreciated Joke* (1903) two Caucasian men are seated on a bench, when one turns to the other to point out something funny in the newspaper he is reading and proceeds to slap his friend's knee uncontrollably. Oblivious to the fact that his friend has gotten off at a stop and been replaced by a rather matronly white woman, he continues the knee-slapping — only now on her knee. Unamused, she knocks him off the bench. The film ends with the man making an "uh-oh" face at the camera. In *Streetcar Chivalry* (1903) the same matronly woman is forced to remain standing after all the men on the bench stand up to offer an attractive young woman a seat. When the streetcar hits a bump, the older woman is hurled onto the bodies of two of the men, creating a chaos that prompts them to get off indignantly at the next stop. Triumphant, she claims a seat.

Both of these one-shot, tableau-style films use the movement of the streetcar to allow a transgression to take place. But while the joke is in the end on the men, it cannot function without an understanding of the matronly woman as comic and unattractive. In *Streetcar Chivalry* the men honor respectability in one instance by giving up a seat to the pretty woman, and they disobey the code in another, which gives rise to an even greater aggression in the bodily contact of the large woman and the men.

This kind of transgression is even more extreme in *Queer Fellow Travelers* (Gaumont, 1904), an English film described in Gaumont's catalog:

> Scene, a Railway Carriage, in which a very dainty lady takes a seat. There follows into the same compartment a most eccentric family with heaps of luggage, including animals and pets, such as a parrot in a cage, tame guinea-pigs, etc. These they range upon the seats and racks without the least regard for the lady's comfort; in fact, the contents of one of the cages and some of the parcels are poured upon her. Eventually the small boy of the family, after climbing on the rack and falling on the lady, puts his head out of the window and, losing his hat, falls out after it. His mother, in an effort to save him, falls after him.[58]

The sense in which the very space of the train car interior produces an anarchic confusion around *place*, both social and behavioral, occurs here in relation to "a very dainty lady," a figure of *propriety*.

In these early train films, what I would like to call "train editing" points to a generalized temptation to transgress codes of propriety that involve respectability and, hence, the borders of sexual definition. Within the spectrum of early film's challenges to Victorian codes, the train often appears as a ready-made space of social instability not unlike that of early film viewing, where spectatorship, as Judith Mayne has noted, was far from an individual experience, especially among immigrant audiences.[59] To paraphrase Kracauer, it was a climate of distraction (or, as Gunning puts it, invoking Kracauer, "attractions imply the danger of distraction").[60] Looking at moving pictures meant that viewers had to negotiate noise, crowds, visual obstructions, mashers, the comings and goings of spectators—all of which were satirized in early films. Women in particular were addressed as potential victims of seducers; often theater exhibitors would project a slide before the films, warning women about mashers and advising them to alert the management in the event of an incident.

In a sense, early train films, like many early film theaters, could be said to define a joke or trick space of substitution. By joke space I mean not only a space in which joking takes place, though this is intended, but a space of displacement, of the substitution of a repressed meaning for an acceptable one, to use Freud's terms from *Jokes and Their Relation to the Unconscious*.[61] Trick space refers to the trick film, a genre of early film best represented by

Georges Méliès. In the trick film, Méliès used stop-action editing and other techniques to magically substitute one thing or figure for another. In the early train film this occurs profilmically, as a function of mise-en-scène; the resulting "interior montage" creates a shifting corporeal topography of often unexpected juxtapositions.[62]

As a kind of mise-en-scène equivalent of the trick film, the train film allows quick appearance and disappearance to occur within the diegetic space. Méliès's own *Tricky Painter's Fate* (ca. 1906) provides a good example. The film is a one-shot tableau set on a railroad platform. The tricky painter is the first to arrive to board a particular car. As a ruse to convince other passengers his car is full, he paints a series of portraits and places them in the windows to simulate real passengers. The deception is successful until a quick-witted passenger figures out what is happening. A mob of angry passengers then routs the painter from the car and smashes the paintings over his head — thus turning the joke on him. By replacing a previously blank frame, the windows, with an instant image, the painter effectively performs the function of a magician-editor — he "superimposes" images within the same frame where they previously did not exist. As a space where passengers flow in and out constantly and the question of whether a car is full or not is answered with a quick glance at the window, the train is here a very *cinematic* space of potential deception based on visual identification or appearance.[63]

The Tricky Painter's Fate makes obvious an important link between the train and the cinema found in many films: both machines of nineteenth-century visual culture are premised on a free-floating visuality, a kind of "now you see it, now you don't" perception. As such, the trick and train films propose an unstable identity where "men will be women, and women will be whatever they want."

In the films of Méliès, as Lucy Fisher has shown, trick editing is typically an expression of male creative power over the female body, turning women into skeletons, making them disappear and reappear, and more.[64] In at least one film by Méliès, however, the train is used to parody male authority through a kind of twist on the trick film concept. *Le Tunnel sous la Manche* (*The Tunnel Beneath the English Channel*, ca. 1906) mocks the common understanding of the train as a phallus and the euphemism of sexual intercourse expressed by a train entering a tunnel. The film incorporates fears surrounding train accidents and projects them as an unconscious homosexual fantasy in an over-determined space of terror, the train tunnel.

The project of constructing a tunnel between England and France had been entertained by both countries since the middle of the nineteenth century. From 1872 through 1883, several tunnels were attempted and then abandoned at the insistence of the English.[65] The tunnel notion still carried a certain weight as an ambivalent dream in the popular imagination when Méliès made his film. In Méliès's film two ambassadors, one English and one French, dine together and discuss the idea of building a tunnel between their countries. They retire to bed in adjoining rooms and dream the same thing: the tunnel is built, and one day two trains crash head-on in the middle. The "accident" rouses the diplomats from sleep simultaneously and effectively kills their common dream as they swear that henceforth they will never again sanction the construction of a tunnel.

The film is structured by doubling and symmetry. In typical "monstrative" fashion—that is, according to codes of exhibiting diverse objects and scenes within a single frame conceived as a tableau—the shot of the ambassadors retiring to bed shows the two rooms in the same frame, with a "wall" dividing the screen in half.[66] The wall is the only thing that separates their heads, which would touch back-to-back without this thin barrier. The two rooms, like the two men, are practically mirror images, and the mirroring is confirmed by the mutual dream, which seeks to do away with the wall, just as the tunnel seeks to dissolve boundaries between France and England. This is a dream engendered by two psyches, but one unconscious. In a simple sense, a hand-drawn shot of a transversal slice of the ocean and tunnel shows us a view of the unconscious, figured in the subterranean metaphor of submerged life that nourishes dreams with repressed desires.

The metaphor of sexual penetration of the trains in the tunnel suggests that the film is about, among other things, a fear of homosexual desire, whether unconscious or not. The work of displacement is clear on this point; the chain of substitution puts the ambassadors and the trains in the place of the countries as two substitutable representatives. The catastrophic union of the trains upsets the bodies of the diplomats in the shot following the accident; like the trains, the men experience a violent physical shock when they leap from their beds in terror. Their excessive denegation of the dream indicates that the dangerous force of the unconscious is precisely the crossing of the wall that separates the two men, which is in turn the crossing of a barrier separating sleeping from waking life. Méliès's film exploits the understanding of the train as a sexual object, as a phallic substitute, in order to caricature

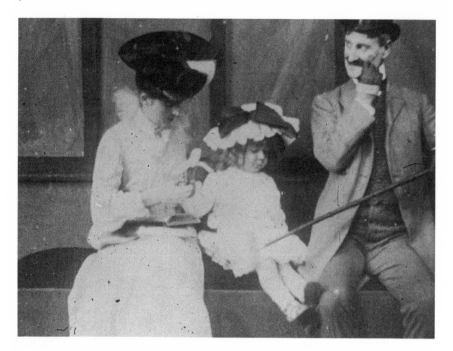

16. *Toodles and Her Strawberry Tart*, frame enlargement, American Mutoscope & Biograph Co., 1903. Library of Congress.

politics and the bases on which politicians make decisions. As such, his trau-matized diplomats exhibit many of the trademark traits of the male hysteric discussed in chapter 1.

American film contributed its share of films that toyed with male author-ity. In addition to *The Unappreciated Joke* and *Streetcar Chivalry*, AM&B's *Toodles and Her Strawberry Tart* (1903) grounds its humor in an apparent reversal of sexual power in the context of seduction on a moving streetcar (photo 16). Based on comic strip characters, Toodles and her pretty young mother are seated on a streetcar bench. The mother opens a bag, hands baby Toodles a tart, and then peels a banana. While Toodles eats the banana, the woman reads a book. A well-dressed gentleman sporting gloves, a cane, and a silk hat sits down next to Toodles and flirts with the mother. When Toodles begins to cry, the man, who had accidentally landed on Toodles's tart, rises and exhibits the tart stain on his coat (which covers his posterior) to the camera while the mother snickers, also for the camera.

It would not be stretching a point to call this an obscene joke. In Freud's analysis of obscene jokes, the purpose of which is smut,

> the smut is directed at a particular person, by whom one is sexually excited and who, upon hearing it, is expected to become aware of the speaker's excitement and as a result to become sexually excited in turn. Instead of this excitement, the other person may be led to feel shame or embarrassment, which is only a reaction against the excitement, and, in a roundabout way, is an admission of it. Smut is thus originally directed toward women and may be equated with attempts at seduction. If a man in a company of men enjoys telling or listening to smut, the original situation, which owing to social inhibitions cannot be realized, is at the same time imagined. A person who laughs at smut . . . is laughing as though he were the spectator of an act of sexual aggression.[67]

Insisting on the presence of a third person (a man) as necessary to the joke's humor, Freud uses this example to make the theoretical point that the purpose of jokes in general is to satisfy an instinct, lustful or hostile, in the face of an obstacle that stands in its way. The technique of techniques for achieving this purpose is displacement. In *Toodles* we have a situation analogous to smut, in which sexual desire is expressed humorously through displacement onto the little girl and figured metaphorically in the banana and what we imagine to be the blood-red tart. The strawberry filling connotes not only blood — menstrual or virginal — but other bodily secretions or excretions as well, namely semen and excrement. The stain is clearly about lack of containment and exhibition of the uncontainable: the flaunting of the inability to repress the taboo fluids of the body. The transgression is acknowledged in the embarrassed reactions of the man, and it is underscored by the sartorial signifiers of respectability (including a cross worn by the woman). All the signifiers of the sexual act center on the little girl and her banana; she is the rhetorical pivot of intercourse between the man and the woman, the site of both condensation and displacement on which converge two separate "trains" of desire. The third party considered necessary to the success of the joke is the spectator, whose laughter is summoned by that of the mother as she glances off-screen at the camera.

What complicates this reading, however, is the question of who is "telling" the joke. Though the seduction would seem to be authored by the man, it is actually the mother who initiates and produces the joke material, the banana and the tart, while the joke is clearly on the man. Again, Freud: "Smut is like the exposure of the sexually different person to whom it is directed. By the utterance of the obscene words, it compels the person who is assailed to imagine the part of the body or the procedure in question and shows her that the assailant is himself imagining it."[68] *Toodles* reverses the gender of the "assailant," making the man's flirtation merely a streetcar parapraxis, while the mother's act may be seen as the more transgressive one. The reversal effectively disempowers the gentleman, putting him in the aggressed position of the woman — which is the position of the proverbial woman tied to the tracks as well as that of the infant who cannot control its bodily functions.

This kind of reversal also marks Edison and Porter's *What Happened in the Tunnel* (1903), in which the tunnel plays a key role in articulating the transgression. As a space of the ultimate suspension of temporal and spatial markers, of time and space lost to pure speed and motion, the essence of the train journey itself, the tunnel multiplies this effect with darkness, the suspension of vision. In this film the tunnel is the mise-en-scène of a dislocation associated with threats to respectable white womanhood. Based on an old joke from the late nineteenth century, the film satirizes the popular image of the vulnerability of women on trains when a middle-class white man tries to kiss a white woman just as the train enters a tunnel.[69] The screen goes black, and in the next shot, when the train emerges from the tunnel, the man finds himself kissing the white woman's African American maid, who was seated next to her. The man is repulsed and ashamed, while the two women laugh hysterically at the switch they have effected.

Judith Mayne sees *What Happened in the Tunnel* as a film that resists the authority of the male gaze in allowing the women the last laugh, albeit through a racist prism.[70] The "resistance" indeed works at the expense of the African American woman, who is invested with the sexuality denied by the white woman. If, as Freud noted, substitution in jokes is always sexual, we might read the exchange of black woman for white as the substitution of sexuality for its opposite. In other words, the maid as an object debased by European-American culture is the sexual other of respectable white womanhood — and it is thus "proper" to aggress against her in another context. The humor derives from embarrassing the man and revealing the sexual aim of his aggression. Here fear of and desire for the other are conflated; it is not acceptable to desire respectable white women — just as in a Currier & Ives print illustrating another scene of "what happened in the tunnel," it is not acceptable to drink in public — but it is tacitly acceptable to desire un-respectable (black) women, as on plantations of the old South, only not in public. This is where the blackness of the tunnel and the blackness of the maid (and also of the black film frame that alternates with every other frame we do see) converge in a reversal of opposites whose relationship is normally repressed, i.e., kept invisible. It is only through a racist sleight-of-hand, then, that alternation in a basic sense subverts sexism within the context of a heterotopic inversion of "normal" rules of conduct. The women can laugh at the man because everyone can laugh at the black woman — an assumption entirely taken for granted by the film and the society in which it was produced.

All of these sexual and/or racial movements are underwritten by the implied principle of movement on the train car, the space in which the joke is played. In these films, desire, whether within or outside the romantic couple, is an effect of the machine and its movement. As spectacles of exhibitionism, which, as Tom Gunning has brilliantly argued, is a primary spectatorial mode addressed by early cinema's construction as "attraction," these movements take place in an in-between space, narratively speaking.[71] The heterotopia that sanctions illicit behavior also depends on a heterochronia — a slice of time bracketed off from a beginning or an end, a paradigmatic instance not necessarily reinserted into a syntagmatic narrative chain, a "willing suspension" of linear time.[72]

This kind of paradigmatic structure was not limited to American cinema. An Italian film from around 1914 known as *Foot Love* uses an unusual format to tell its tale of "unbound" sexual desire.[73] The roughly two-minute film is the story of a pair of male feet and their pursuit of a pair of female feet. The action involves various aspects of the pursuit, and it ends with the two pairs of feet leaping into bed. The shooting strategy of the film is a series of high-angle medium close-ups that focus on activity below the knees. These feet are cut off from a subjectivity that would otherwise be signified by the presence of a face — body fragments detached from the classical signifier of the psyche. The film satirizes romantic love in insisting on the seduction and physical desire literally at the bottom of the discourse on love.

In a central shot that occurs midway through the film, the female feet are followed by the male onto a train car, which is to all appearances a streetcar. Inside the car the female feet plant themselves beside the feet of a working-class woman whose skirt has been raised slightly to expose huge feet spread slightly apart. The male feet sit next to the object of their pursuit. Posed just on the near side of the working-class woman, the camera observes two types of activity linked to the movement of the train: a violent agitation on the part of the workingwoman's feet, and some tiny, hesitating movements on the part of the man's feet, directed at the shy feet of the pursued. Here the work of displacement follows a "train" logic: the movement of the train is the diegetic motivation that demands a movement of the feet such that they figure the desire of the coquettish feet (up to that point fairly restrained in their seduction). But there is not the same sort of motivation for the extreme movement of the workingwoman's feet; she is charged with figuring the excess desire of the others, just as the African American woman was burdened with representing the white woman's sexuality in *What Happened in the Tunnel.* Thus, it is not by chance that this is a second- or third-class car, where the seduction already connoted by the train in general is redoubled in a constellation of social class and sexuality. The displacement is at once sexual and social.

The seduction leads neither to marriage nor to "legitimate" sexuality. Rather, the fetishistic emphasis on feet suggests another movement of desire toward other points of investment, especially when they jump into bed at the end. The film proposes a subversive heterosexual desire, one that is channeled toward the union of two bodies, but not a romantic couple. The film also employs a narrative structure that hesitates between a linear, progressive reading, and a paradigmatic structure in which most shots can be rearranged, even substituted for each other, without significant loss of meaning.

Gender and Film Form in Early Classical Cinema

If the coupling function of the train and streetcar in early films was rarely tied to advancing either the romantic couple or continuous narrative, the opposite became the norm in American film after 1908–9. Indeed, it is at this time that representation of the couple and filmic representation by continuous narrative became joined at the hip through a moral and aesthetic aim. This is not to say, however, that such a configuration did not already exist in early film, or that, conversely, the heterotopia did not survive into the next phase of American film.

As a vehicle of narrative, the train had early been mobilized to represent romance, adventure, and crime. This coding clearly derived from a heavily determined narrative role with which the train already came to cinema. On the surface, this seems obvious. As noted, not only had the history of the railroad produced ready-made stories exploited in newspapers, journals, popular fiction, and theater, but the train in one sense would seem to be the very embodiment of narrative. In Tzvetzan Todorov's model, most narratives follow a basic a/b/a' sequence: they begin with a stable situation (a); the situation is disturbed by some force, which causes it to become unstable (b); and finally, through the action of another force, a restoration of equilibrium occurs with modifications incorporated, meaning the story ends with a newly stable situation (a').[74] The train ride can easily be conceived as a chain of units linked in a forward linear march, with events and the transformation of space and time framed by a departure and an arrival. This chain is realized in every train journey, even if the transformed event is simply that of motion and physical displacement from Point A to Point B.

In reference to the move in 1909 toward classical narrative form in cinema, Kristin Thompson notes of a 1913 Kalem railroad film, *A Race with Time*, that the "goal orientation" of the protagonists is established in relation to a deadline.[75] The desire to deliver a mail pouch by a certain time structures the plot and moves the main characters, a railroad president and his son, to achieve their goal. Going one step further, I would attribute an implicit "goal orientation" to almost any railroad film, and certainly to some preclassical examples, whether the journey ends on screen or not — *The Great Train Robbery* being perhaps the epitome and turning point of this inherent continuity. Still, the *"in-between"* experience — in which the goal is lost sight of — was emphasized in most early travel films.[76]

In early cinema the link between the railroad and narrative is complex and multiple. The earliest train films, drawing as they did on a photographic tradition of views of railroad journeys — views often published in a serial format — were both narrative and nonnarrative. Imbricated already in a touristic narrative, these successions of views and panoramas from the locomotive present narrative as spectacle in the very form of presentation. In these films, the journey is the spectacle; its movement between a beginning and an end is about moving through nature's display. The implied narrative of the travel genre merges with drama in hybrid films like *The Hold-up of the Rocky Mountain Express* to produce a narrative form that alternates between linearity and nonlinearity. Such hybrid films, discussed briefly in chapter 1, juxtapose interiors and exteriors, and the travel genre with the theatrical skit as aspects of points of view on a journey that again provides the overarching narrative frame.

"Narrative" in early cinema has been much debated. In revisionist literature since 1980 on early cinema, the realigning of what used to be called "primitive" cinema in comparison with classical cinema turns on a narrative argument. Early cinema, it is said, not only refuses the teleology of an inexorable drive toward linear narrative, but it actively wallows in its own nonnarrative modes of presentation and representation, of spectatorship and exhibition. As Tom Gunning, Charles Musser, Miriam Hansen, Noel Burch, and André Gaudreault have shown, Edwin S. Porter is wrongly made to play adolescent or infant to D. W. Griffith's mature classical form.[77] They point to Porter's ambivalence as a narrative filmmaker working within a more artisanal mode of production and producing a more ambivalent image and narrative, and to filmmakers like Méliès, who used narrative as an excuse for the display of tricks and magic acts and did not think of film primarily as a storytelling medium in the service of linear narrative.[78] They also underscore the extent to which Griffith was not the great inventor of every single narrative and filmic technique with which he has traditionally been credited, seeing many of the devices attributed to Griffith's films (e.g., the close-up) at work in earlier, and not necessarily narrative, films.[79]

Revisionist scholars recognize the early film audience as a mass of spectators drawn to a popular entertainment akin to many other "attractions," including, notably, the circus. Musser, Bowser, Robert Allen, Kristin Thompson, and others underscore vaudeville as a major context of the exhibition of early films, which were presented as acts in a program of diverse entertainments.[80] Gaudreault has dubbed the tendency of many early films to exhibit diverse objects and scenes within a single frame "monstrative," to emphasize the "demonstrative" or display character of such films, which were often conceived as tableaux. For Gaudreault, the codes of "monstration" are those primarily of *showing* as opposed to *telling*, which does not mean that stories are not "told" in such films; rather, they are told in the presentational mode.[81] Gunning refers to the whole of early cinema as a "cinema of attractions" in order to emphasize the display function of the films, which, like circus acts, were premised on multiple centers of attention as opposed to a synthesis of views organized narratively into an overarching point of view.[82]

For Gunning, early cinema's focus on display is more about exhibitionism than voyeurism — or rather, the voyeurism is not a hidden premise, as it is in narrative cinema.[83] Instead, it is acknowledged, often in direct address to the camera (e.g., actors' glances at the keyhole); the exhibition of the stained coat to the camera in *Toodles and Her Strawberry Tart* is an example. Miriam Hansen sees the voyeurism itself as ambiguous in many early "keyhole" films, in which characters within the film look through a keyhole, represented in matte framing, and invite the spectator to do the same. As quasi-pornographic, peep show equivalents, such films tend to assume a "patriarchal economy of vision," notes Hansen, but they also "occasionally acknowledge the threat — and thrill — of sexual disorientation and the confusion of gender roles."[84] This happens, for example, in films that make a woman the active voyeur peering through the keyhole, which for me implies a "joke" space. In these films and others in which the viewer's gaze is directly solicited by the film, the incorporation of the audience's point of view into the diegesis through an appeal to a gaze that is aware of the illusion, coupled with the multiple points of view often demanded of viewers, contributed to the "anarchic" viewing conditions of the collective film-watching experience.

Early classical cinema (after 1908) is narratively distinct from early cinema by virtue of the incorporation and organization of the spectator's attention, among other things. Hansen gives a succinct statement of this kind of spectatorship:

> From its inception in 1895–96, cinema was defined as the projection of films upon a fixed screen before a paying public. But the film spectator, as distinct from a member of an empirically variable audience, did not come into existence until more than a decade later. As a concept, a structural term, the spectator only emerged along with the set of codes and conventions that has been analyzed as the classical Hollywood cinema. Specifically, classical cinema offered its viewer an ideal vantage point from which to witness a scene, unseen by anyone belonging to the fictional world of the film, the diegesis. With the elaboration of a type of narration that seems to anticipate — or strategically frustrate — the viewer's desire with every shot, the spectator became part of the film as product, rather than a particular exhibition or show. As reception was thus increasingly standardized, the moviegoer was effectively invited to assume the position of this ideal spectator created by the film, leaving behind, like Keaton in *Sherlock Jr.*, an awareness of his or her physical self in the theater space, of an everyday existence troubled by social, sexual, and economic discrepancies.[85]

As David Bordwell, Kristin Thompson, and Janet Staiger point out, the narrative structure on which spectatorship was based in the classical era is premised on a linear structure of cause and effect, where everything that happens is motivated narratively (with the development of "goal orientation" being an important link in this chain). In addition, all effects can be explained within the sphere of the text.[86] Many early film narratives, like *Uncle Tom's Cabin*, did not build cause and effect into the exposition of the story, because it was assumed that spectators would be familiar with it and fill in the gaps themselves.[87] In other cases, lecturers accompanied film screenings to direct spectators' attention to important aspects of the story.[88] And in other cases still, spectators were left to their own devices to make sense of what was presented.[89] Both the lecturer and cinematic narrative techniques arose to assist audience understanding. Noting how a variety of methods were experimented with, Charles Musser emphasizes that the ultimate adoption of complex, cinematic narrative style in film "won out for many reasons," with "standardization, narrative efficiency and the maximization of profits . . . among the most crucial determinants."[90]

Once it "won out," classical cinema developed a system of techniques that it would perfect over the next decade (1908–17). "Continuity editing" developed as a method of connecting shots to subordinate everything to the progress of the narrative — i.e., to what *happens*.[91] Similarly, everything within the frame in classical film was composed to orient the spectator's attention to the most narratively significant action or object, whereas early films often filled the frame with a variety of competing characters, actions, and objects that tested the spectator's ability to discern the most significant action. Thompson rightly notes: "In short, classical narration tailored every detail to the spectator's attention; the primitive cinema's narration had done this only sporadically."[92]

As Hansen points out, the increasing narrative channeling of gazes and themes went hand in hand with more controlled, structured, and autonomous forms of exhibition — the nickelodeon, then the movie palace.[93] The desire to maximize profits through a standardized product, the multireel narrative film, was not unrelated to the desire to attract a broader and more respectable public. The shifts in film form and exhibition began to occur in relation to the effort to incorporate *more* middle-class white women — the growing public — into filmgoing.[94] The appeal to middle-class white women reflected the reformist current that had closed down New York's nickelodeons in 1908, and it thus established the greater moral control of cinema as an institution. With the reform of cinema at the behest of female reformers as well as religious male figures came an attempt to control an earlier type of spectator, one led to expect a transgressive pleasure in the representation of "immoral" subjects viewed in more or less disorderly spaces. The early perverse or "decoded" spectator discussed in chapter 1 — often a working-class woman — had to be channeled into line with middle-class values, as opposed to the subversiveness of the "joke space," both on the screen and in the theater. Such a spectator, whether biologically male or female, was perverse from a middle-class point of view by the very multiplicity of positions offered in films that thrived on the transgression of moral behavior. Sorting out gender in early classical film — clarifying sex roles apart from a context of subversion — was a project destined to please middle-class women, yet it also suited a fundamentally patriarchal point of view by limiting the expression of female desire.[95] Not coincidentally, this effort involved an unsuccessful attempt to repress comedy as a genre, the most common fictional form in 1907–8.[96]

The reformist transformation of cinema was therefore an appeal to the *middle-class*, white, female spectator, as Hansen notes.[97] Accordingly, film-makers turned to more "respectable" themes and to narrative as a system of resolving moral problems and economic concerns: how to tell a longer story efficiently, without relying on costly parafilmic devices.[98] They turned to the novel, the short story, and legitimate drama as existing literary and theatrical models that were familiar to many of them, while such models provided "respectable" stories that depended on internal coherence of plot and character. To preserve this coherence and a sense of focus, continuity editing developed as a complex system for "taming" and unifying the effects of cutting that can result in the radical juxtaposition of different times and places.[99]

It was D. W. Griffith who did much to systematize many techniques of early film, such as the close-up, within a continuity framework and to set the development of American cinema firmly on a narrative and more or less moral path, while self-consciously invoking the novel as a model.[100] As discussed in chapter 1, "parallel editing," the system of alternating between two spaces juxtaposed for the narrative effect of suspense (e.g., shots of a character being chased alternating with shots of the character who is chasing), was exploited by Griffith in such films as the 1909 *Lonely Villa*. His early train films in particular, made in 1911 and 1912, were important vehicles for working out the system of narration that would mark American filmmaking unalterably. In these films, Griffith responded to the changing times with female heroines who upheld Victorian codes, but within a greater scope of activity for women than was possible or conceivable in Victorian times. In both *The Lonedale Operator*

17. Dorothy Bernard in *The Girl and Her Trust*, D. W. Griffith, 1912.
Museum of Modern Art.

(1911) and *The Girl and Her Trust* (1912), the heroines are "girl" telegraphers
who are required to use ingenuity and daring to save the day—before having
to be rescued at the end by a male railroad employee (photo 17). These are
female characters who have left the "joke space" and its anarchy behind and
now act within a morally intelligible, narrative universe.

As textual equivalents of the move to morality in the exhibition sphere,
both these Griffith narratives link storytelling with gender-coding. The director who would make his racist reputation defending white womanhood in
Birth of a Nation (1915) earlier had created an image of white female purity
and/or goodness through a gender-defined mode of narration. Raymond Bellour's detailed work on alternation and narration in *The Lonedale Operator*
analyzes the ways in which the film can be seen as a seminal early classical film
by virtue of its system of alternation built on a fundamental opposition: the
couple.[101] Insofar as most silent train films are typically stories of a relationship
between a man and a woman, I see a ready-made railroad metaphor in *coupling*.
The train is a social force that puts bodies in relation to each other by chance

and joins them together, even if by accident. The train, as such, offers itself as a social ground of integration, a mobile support of attraction, an intermediary term in the engendering and channeling of desire. The railroad, as we have seen, is a medium of condensation, a site where a number of "trains of thought" or movement cross or meet. It is also a place where experience is bracketed, time is suspended for the duration of a journey, and anything can happen.

"Coupling" in Griffith's films is a textual strategy tied systematically to alternation. For Bellour, to alternate, that is, to cut back and forth between two different shots or sequences of shots, is to tell a story in classical American film. Alternation as developed by Griffith became a major feature of American film in the post-1908 era. In relation to gender, Griffith uses alternation in *The Lonedale Operator* to structure sexual difference. The film is the story of the wooing of a girl telegrapher (played by Blanche Sweet) by a train engineer and the crisis that brings them together as a couple. The operator is courted at the beginning by the shy engineer as he prepares to leave on his daily run. After he leaves, bandits come to rob the girl at the station. She tricks them into believing that the monkey wrench she has in her hand is a gun, holding them at bay until the boyfriend arrives, the hoodlums are arrested, and amusement at the trick — revealed in a close-up of the monkey wrench — is complimented with a kiss.

In *The Girl and Her Trust*, a variation on *The Lonedale Operator*, Grace, a tomboyish telegrapher (played by Dorothy Bernard), is pursued unsuccessfully by the young station agent. When she is held up for the railroad's gold, she at first tricks the thieves by hammering a bullet through a keyhole, producing a gunshot effect. This effect is emphasized, and made intelligible, in close-up. The thieves rob the chest anyway, and after she telegraphs for help, she rushes to the handcar escape vehicle and drapes her body over the treasure chest in a literal identification of her body, her womanhood (and, one may assume, her virginity) with the railroad's stolen property. Because she has telegraphed ahead (like the girl in *The Lonedale Operator*), the station agent is alerted, and he rushes aboard a locomotive to come to her aid. The film ends with Grace and the boyfriend sharing his sandwich while perched on the locomotive as it moves backward away from the camera — a humorous and symbolic statement of the train's role in forming the couple.

In Bellour's analysis, both films depend on a systematic alternation of terms that cluster around a basic opposition: male/female. Thus, inside/outside, close/far, thieves/good guys, motion/stillness, etc., are all restatements at the levels of both diegesis and text of the couple "he/she."[102] In both stories the narratives work to reunite the terms he/she separated at the beginning. In other words, the goal of the alternation is synthesis and resolution, i.e., the couple. From Bellour's essentially formalist position, this system is what distinguishes the classical Hollywood film *text* from both earlier American cinema and other national cinemas. Even more historically minded revisionist scholars of early film acknowledge the role of alternation — in the sense of parallel editing — in the system of film that succeeded early cinema's less systematically structured texts.[103]

For my purposes, what is important is that sexual difference, and the regulation of both point of view and the representation of women, became constitutive features of narrative cinema around 1908–9, and that alternation developed in Griffith as the chief vehicle and formal principle for articulating the narrative system.[104] Importantly, the train often functions as a key agent of synthesis: it literally brings the two terms of the couple together and provides an apt vehicle of dynamism to figure the "last-minute rescue," which Griffith would make so famous, and that depended on swift vehicles to make the acceleration work in relation to the ticking clock. The device of alternating between a speeding train and the "girl" in need of rescue established a pattern for future train films, as did the technique of alternating rapidly between one speeding vehicle and another.

In addition, Griffith transformed the train as a vehicle. No longer merely a space in which anything was likely to happen, the train in Griffith became an agent and an object made to serve human agents. In moving outside the vehicle itself, and emphasizing its proairetic dimension, its ability to move, and to move a story (literally by moving characters), as opposed to the train as space in between two stations, "in-between" space, Griffith made the train a more properly *narrative* figure. In a sense, one could argue that he tamed the train by recoding it for narrative purposes; his engineer-driven trains are a far cry from the out-of-control thrill trains of early films like *Le Voyage impossible* (Méliès, 1906) and *When the Devil Drives* (Urban, 1907). Picking up on early films like Edison's *The Train Wreckers* (1905) (remade by Lubin in 1906 as *The Wreckers of the Limited Express*) and *Asleep at the Switch* (1910) that made the train an endangered object in need of saving, Griffith gave the train a more central role in articulating narrative structure.[105]

It must be noted, however, that there was one genre in which the "joke space" and heterotopia of early film survived, parallel to Griffith, and at the heart of early classical filmmaking. As Gunning notes, "the cinema of attraction does not disappear with the dominance of narrative, but rather goes underground, both into certain avant-garde practices and as a component of narrative films, more evident in some genres (e.g., the musical), than in others."[106] Comedy was one such genre. In the 1910s, comedies wed the anarchy and nonsense of early film comedy with the storytelling techniques of continuity editing (parallel editing, match-on-action, alternation, the narratively motivated cut-in, etc.), while still clinging to earlier filmic form as a sort of challenge to the nascent classical system.[107] This genre included formal conventions as well as subject matter. As Bowser notes: "The idea that slapstick comedies were to be deplored as vulgar, tasteless, and not for refined audiences persisted as a legacy of the reform period, but the spirit of joy in pre-1909 slapstick cinema was too strong to be held down for long. Audiences loved it."[108]

Comedy was indeed enormously popular, and in the teens it was divided into the "vulgar, tasteless" shorts that starred Charlie Chaplin, Mack Sennett's Keystone Kops, Fatty Arbuckle, and others, and more feature-length, "high-class" comedies that were less slapstick and more realistic, as in the films of Douglas Fairbanks.[109] The class basis that had already formed in the gap between shorts (for the "'more transient trade'") and longer films (for "'a class of patrons formerly absent from picture theatres'") grafted onto these distinctions within the genre — distinctions that would disappear later in the lengthier comedies of Harold Lloyd, Buster Keaton, and Chaplin, which blended slapstick with melodrama.[110]

Pullman Bride (Sennett, 1916, with Gloria Swanson), one of many slapstick comedies employing a train in the teens, is a direct heir of early comedy. Its comic premise produces a series of inversions and perversions of gender, class, and age, mostly set within the confines of a moving honeymoon train. At the beginning of the film, a rich young girl (Swanson) is motivated by greed — and her mother — to accept the proposal of the rotund and unattractive Mr. Peabody, who to all appearances is extremely wealthy. A forlorn, rejected suitor discovers that Peabody is actually merely a cook in a restaurant, and he threatens to reveal his secret. A chase ensues, and Peabody manages to convince a policeman that the suitor has stolen his watch, when in reality Peabody has lifted the suitor's watch and brandished it as his own. The police banish the suitor from the town for his crime, but the train he takes out of town is also the honeymoon train taken by Peabody, his new bride, and her mother (who is clearly there to chaperon the newlyweds, to Peabody's chagrin).

Once the characters intersect, comedic collisions abound, fueled by a plethora of secondary characters who contribute to the confusion: a trans-vestite drunk, a tobacco-spitting gunslinger, an Annie Oakley-type cowgirl, a prim and proper bearded fat man, and various women (including the Sennett Bathing Belles) whose compartments are invaded by mistake.[111] In scenes reminiscent of *The Deadwood Sleeper*, the jostling movement of the train gives rise to a number of mistakes, including food exiting one window and returning through another to land on an unsuspecting passenger. The train's iconic role as a vehicle of the in-between, of heterotopic inversion and spatial deception, is rendered cinematically as a space of surprise through extremely rapid cut-ting that underscores the effects of surprise for both the characters and the passengers. The "happy ending," in which Peabody and his bride embrace, is clearly a parody, since the issue of Peabody's identity has been far from settled in the narrative, while the whole concept of marrying for money is ridiculed (at the beginning, a title tells us, "She knew he was a capitalist — he had told her so himself").

In this and other comedies of the teens, clichés of the train film were parodied and perverted, just as they had been in early films like *The Little Train Robbery* (1904), Porter's own takeoff on *The Great Train Robbery*. *Barney Old-field's Race for Life*, a 1913 Keystone picture with Mack Sennett, Mabel Nor-mand, and Barney Oldfield, the period's most famous race car driver and the "fastest man on wheels," makes fun of the "woman tied to the tracks" in pitting a race car against a villain-commandeered locomotive.[112] *Wild and Woolly* (1917), which starred Douglas Fairbanks as a wealthy Easterner with cowboy fantasies, was a spoof on the western in general and on city folks who still believed in 1917 that the Old West of legend existed intact. Included in the caricature is a fake train robbery, which the citizens of a town in Arizona stage for the benefit of the unsuspecting Fairbanks character (who gets to "foil" the robbery) in order to encourage his western fantasy — and attract his money to their town.

The Hazards of Helen

Although the familiar cinematic style of narrative film was developed at an early stage by Griffith, he was far from the only filmmaker making girl-train films between 1911 and the end of World War I (when the girl-based train films seem to disappear as a genre). According to Bowser, Kalem had estab-lished the "railroad thriller" with *The Railroad Raiders of '62* in 1911 (a civil war reenactment that gave Keaton the basis for *The General*).[113] *The Grit of the Girl*

Telegrapher and a host of other Kalem railroad films also were made during this period (e.g., *A Race with Time*, 1913; *The Railroad Inspector's Peril*, 1913; *The Lost Freight Car*, 1911; and *The Attempt on the Special*, Pathé, 1911).[114] "Boy telegrapher" films were made by Edison, who in addition made a few train films starring women. From all available evidence, however, far fewer boy-centered train film narratives appeared during this period.

These railroad films from 1911–13 look ahead to the serial format that would itself point toward features, which would come to dominate film production and exhibition after 1915.[115] Richard Koszarski states it concisely: "Serials were among the first attempts to develop very long and complex screen narratives, and they served as a useful bridge between the short film and the feature during the crucial 1913–1915 period."[116] Bowser notes the importance of the cross-promotional strategy of releasing a serial film simultaneously with the publication of its story in newspapers and magazines, particularly women's magazines.[117] These railroad films marked significant instances of the move to feature-length narrative and its development — both in Griffith's early girl and train films and in the serials, many of which involved a train. Just as travel films, especially those built around a train, were important steps in the transition from documentary actualities to dramatic shorts, so the one-reel Griffith melodramas staged at the station or on the train were important to working out longer narratives.

The "queen" of the railroad serial genre, post-Griffith, was *The Hazards of Helen* series that ran from November 14, 1914, to February 18, 1917 — the longest-running serial in film history.[118] As Ben Singer points out, the serial queen melodrama in general, which included *The Perils of Pauline* as well as many other woman-centered adventure serials, and *The Hazards of Helen* in particular, are remarkable for addressing female spectators through fantasies of female mastery and empowerment.[119] *Helen* is notable for the seriality of the narratives — their premise of "to be continued" already a variation within the nascent classical system of narrative closure (as was *Fantômas* in France) — for the railroad settings, and for the virile independence of the heroine, Helen Holmes. She truly represents the sense in which "women will be whatever they want" in relation to the railroad. Edison's "boy train films," by contrast, are neither serial nor woman-centered.[120] His films are as much an index, by virtue of neglect, of the changing status of women in American society in the teens and of cinema's various attempts to deal with the "female spectator," as are the Helen films — only the Helen films provide a more complex picture.

The Hazards of Helen was a weekly, one-reel serial produced by J. P. Mac-

18. Helen Holmes in "The Wrong Order," *The Hazards of Helen*,
J. P. MacGowan. Museum of Modern Art.

Gowan for Kalem. Some 119 episodes were produced. The first few episodes
featured two or three different actresses in the role of Helen, who was thereaf-
ter played by MacGowan's wife, Helen Holmes (photo 18).[121] So famous did
she become in this role that when MacGowan and Holmes left Kalem in the
late teens to begin producing railroad films for independent release and in
the 1920s reprised the telegrapher in a number of railroad films, her name in
the credits alone was sufficient to signify that the films were indeed heirs to the
old "Helen" episodes, since the titles did not feature the connection to the
legendary serial.

In the series, Helen is a telegrapher who in later episodes acts in the name
of her father, a "railroad man" named General Holmes. In a typical episode,
Helen saves a train from crashing or rescues a man from danger, usually a
railroad agent or engineer. This is consistent with the shift to the train as a
proairetic object or agent as opposed to an interior space for the unfolding of
action. The narratives involve rescuing money, goods, or people from crimi-

nals, who are then apprehended and punished. Helen herself is often rescued from danger, but only after having averted a prior disaster. In the episode "In Danger's Path" (June 1915), robbers lock Helen inside a refrigerated car. With characteristic ingenuity, she uses a knife conveniently hanging from her neck to whittle a stick, which she then rubs, Boy Scout-fashion, to produce a fire. The fire not only saves her from freezing, but attracts the attention of the engineers, who then rescue her and pursue the bandits. At the end, Helen summons her resources to save the station agent, Warren, who is locked in battle with the thieves and is threatened by a swinging track in the roundhouse switching yard. In another episode from 1915, Helen athletically stops a runaway train she happens to be riding by pulling a bolt from the locomotive.

Perhaps the best indication, however, of the extent to which Helen assumes active, indeed "masculine" roles is this excerpt from the plot summary update for "The Girl and the Game, Ch. 15: Driving the Last Spike" (1916):

> Story to Date: Helen Holmes prevents collision of train carrying her father and Storm; saves Storm from death on burning train; recovers accidental duplicate map of railroad cut-off, averting withdrawal of financial support; recovers payroll from thieves by desperate leap. Kidnapped by Seagrue; is rescued by Storm [and] Spike. Saves Storm, Rhinelander and Spike from death in runaway freight car; rescues Spike from lynching; captures ore thieves . . . ; accepts Storm's proposal of marriage. After daring ride, Helen uncouples freight and prevents terrible wreck.[122]

Helen is a direct successor to Griffith's "girls," as well as to those of other filmmakers. *The Grit of the Girl Telegrapher*, produced by Kalem (which was known for its westerns and railroad films), was originally made in 1912 with Anna Q. Nilsson. Allegedly because of stunt accidents that disrupted the *Hazards'* weekly release schedule, Kalem retitled the film and released it in 1916 as an episode of *The Hazards of Helen*.[123] The star of *The Grit* wields a gun to stop a thief and drives a locomotive while the engineer stokes the engine—all of which impresses her fiancé, who rewards her with a kiss at the end. The "virility" of these heroines seems to be a token of the genre, as both an attribute in itself and a means of attracting the attention of a man. In *A Railroader's Bravery*, for example, a young girl telegrapher performs amazing stunts to save the driver of a runaway train, including lassoing a rock from which she stretches a rope that she crosses hand-over-hand; she indeed "gets her man" as a result.[124]

More distantly, Helen is a descendant of Kate Shelley, the real-life hero-ine whose true story passed quickly into legend. Like the Griffith heroines who also followed in her tracks, Kate Shelley was a near-martyr whose popular image was based on heroic self-sacrifice and physical fortitude. According to the story, widely reported in 1889, Kate Shelley braved the gale-force winds of a massive rain storm to signal to an oncoming train that the trestle nearby was washed out. (Shelley's anticipation of the train came from knowing the sched-ule by heart.) Her successful crawl up a muddy slope and courageous signaling efforts were "rewarded" with a lifelong career as a telegrapher for the railroad, whose train she saved.[125] The theme of female bravery and sacrifice that trans-lates into early film narratives like *The Train Wreckers* and *Asleep at the Switch* thus refers to a popular literary image that provided early filmmakers with a potent narrative source.[126]

As with Kate Shelley and the Griffith heroines, a large part of the fascina-tion with *The Hazards of Helen* is that Helen does not normally operate the train—in other words, her function is to ensure the smooth running of the trains, but not to run them. Unable to be an engineer, Helen is given oppor-tunities to literally engineer: to stop a train, drive it, divert it, uncouple it, fuel it. Her heroism exists in the difference between not normally controlling the big machine and being able, having the resources, to do so. To make Helen the engineer would have been too feminist; but to allow her occasional opportuni-ties to display cleverness, competence, resourcefulness, and physical agility and strength is simultaneously to gesture toward a more "modern" woman and to underscore the unusualness of the gestures.[127] That a train film series could be based on a woman's adventures with the railroad is, in retrospect, extraordinary. This development speaks volumes about both the kind of spec-tator the American cinema was appealing to and the kind of viewer it was cultivating: an active female.[128]

In films like *The Railroad Inspector's Peril* (Kalem, 1913) and *The Dynamite Special* (Bison, 1917), the fact that these "girls" are largely working women was consistent with the greater emergence of women, and in particular middle-class white women, into the labor force in the early twentieth century.[129] Though women had been used as telegraphers since the 1850s, according to Andrew Carnegie they acquired a different status as part of a new cadre of workingwomen in similar positions starting in the 1890s.[130] Middle-class women moved into the urban bureaucratic force as cheap labor—secretaries, operators, sales girls—and as reformers, teachers, social workers, even doctors and lawyers.[131] As standard bearers of Progressivism and reform in the early 1900s, women professionalized maternal duty (e.g., Jane Hull, monitoring children's health and education) and helped legitimate at least one category of women's work. Thus, if American cinema could be said to be courting the middle class at this time, it was a new middle class that was being addressed, one in which many women now worked and hence had money to spend on entertainment. It was also a class in which women were beginning to recognize themselves as historical agents as well as consumers.[132]

The Hazards of Helen, already rooted in a consciousness of greater social and economic activity on the part of American women, was produced at a time when women's suffrage had "burst forth under fresh leadership in the second decade of the century."[133] The women's suffrage movement had begun to gain ground in the early years of the century with the growth in numbers of single women wage-earners and of increasing numbers of educated women entering the public sphere. The labor movement played a significant role in building momentum for the women's movement, with female strikers taking part in the picket lines by the tens of thousands from 1905 until 1915.[134] English feminism also greatly influenced the American suffrage movement during this period, which was overall a time of international solidarity for women's groups on both sides of the Atlantic. By the 1910s, as Nancy Cott notes, "woman suffrage was a platform on which diverse people and organizations could comfortably, if temporarily stand," adding that this "was the only decade in which woman suffrage commanded a mass movement, in which working-class women, black women, women on the radical left, the young, and the upper class joined in force; rich and poor, socialist and capitalist, occasionally even black and white could be seen taking the same platform."[135] The women's movement in both England and the United States was at this time very visible in the public eye, as a presence in both the streets and the media. Despite the vitriol unleashed on the movement by politicians and the press, the ferment of the teens yielded American feminists their greatest achievement in 1920, when women were granted the right to vote.[136]

But one need not look only to feminism to gauge the significance of Helen's active, youthful heroine. As Jackson Lears points out, advertisers targeted women early as an "inviting audience for offers of revitalization" in reaction to the popular perception of urban, modern unhealth in the early twentieth century.[137] In Lears's view, this stance was aimed at defusing women's demands for equality: "Feminist political claims were deflected into quests for psychic satisfaction through high-style consumption . . . to domesticate the drive toward female emancipation."[138] Christopher Wilson underscores the more "active" wifely role that supported this ethos as represented in late nineteenth-century and early twentieth-century women's magazines like *Journal*. According to *Journal*, the new housewife " 'did things' " and performed practical and managerial tasks as men's helpers rather than simply provide moral inspiration according to an older Victorian code.[139] Though Wilson wisely cautions against reading this encouragement of "practical" housewifery as feminist, his emphasis on the *active* woman dovetails with Lears's portrait of the modern, less passive woman — the consumer.[140]

Mary Pickford and Douglas Fairbanks played a monumental role in stimulating more emancipated and youth-oriented images of women during the 1914–18 period, the years of World War I.[141] The youth orientation is important: as a slightly pre-Pickford-era heroine, Helen embodies many traits of the changing representation of women, but she also performs energetically as a boy might. The fact of her dominating a "boy's" genre probably has much to do with an appeal to a growing audience of youth in general, as well as with her slightly tomboyish representation.[142] In combining male with female traits — activity with passivity — Helen is, like Griffith's "girls," a tomboy, albeit a feminine-*looking* one, whose sexuality is displaced onto her activity as a narrative agent. Thus, even if her action-centered narratives set in the West are not necessarily about consumption, Helen is very much about a "new woman" being formed in relation to a modern, urban-based, and increasingly advertising-directed mass culture and economy. In Singer's view, "the serial-queen genre gives shape to a pervasive social anxiety — one felt by both men and women — about the consequences of woman's emancipation and independence in the heterosocial public sphere. The serial-queen's oscillation between agency and vulnerability expresses the paradoxes and ambiguities of the woman's situation within the advent of urban modernity."[143]

From Seriality to Cliché: The American Railroad
Film in the 1920s

The films in which Helen Holmes appeared in the 1920s bear such titles as *Blood and Steel* (MacGowan, 1925), *The Open Switch* (MacGowan, 1925 or 1926), and *The Lost Express* (Anchor, 1926). While these titles (which are for individual features, not parts of a serial) might just as easily designate original

Hazards of Helen episodes, the plots evidence a shifting representation of both the railroad and the Helen character, a shift consonant with American film-making and larger cultural trends in the 1920s, as a number of formulaic "railroad films" produced at the time indicate. The shifts include a deemphasis on the train engineer and station personnel, while the railroad company or corporation — and its bureaucracy — rise in importance; the dominance of a male point of view at the expense of the female; a greater concern with the "properly" feminine traits of the heroine (where a heroine can even be spoken of); and an almost necessary juxtaposition of the train and the automobile.

The American train films of the twenties are studio products, generically stable feature films produced within a newly established system of mass production modeled on Fordism. These films form part of a genre of train films that was unique to the United States. It is in the wave of train films produced mostly by William Fox (who also produced Ford's *The Iron Horse*, to be considered in chapter 4) in the mid- to late 1920s that the generic changes from the teens to the twenties become clearest, while the Helen films form a telling complement to the Fox films.

Within the terms of the classical system formed in the teens, Hollywood railroad films in the 1920s structure gender around a set of oppositions in theme and form, both narrative and textual. So firmly do they adhere to narrative conventions of beginning/middle/end, extreme coherence of plot and structure, spatial and diegetic legibility, predictable couplings, good/evil characters, male point of view, happy ending, etc., that they form a series of tedious repetitions that nearly constitute a subgenre unto themselves. Stylistically, these films are entirely typical of the classical system, with visual style subordinated to story exposition. As Richard Koszarski notes, "For the most part, silent dramatic features failed to take advantage of their added length in any but the most peripheral ways. Continuing to operate in the melodramatic tradition that had worked so well during the nickelodeon era, they simply added larger quantities of information of plot, locale, and characterization. . . . The illusionistic power of the narrative was thus increased without altering the main ingredients of plot and characterization, which remained highly conventionalized."[144]

The Love Special (Paramount/Lasky, 1921) is typical of the genre. Based on "The Daughter of a Magnate" by Frank Spearman, a popular writer of railroad short stories, *The Love Special* weds action-adventure with romance in bringing together the railroad president's daughter, Laura Gage (Agnes

Ayres), and the brash, young, Fairbanksian construction engineer working for the Great Western Railroad, Jim Glover (Wallace Reid).[145] The film begins in the genre of a historical docudrama, with breathtaking landscapes as a paean to European-American progress: "No story in our history is more romantic than that of men who drove railroads through the Rocky Mountains — linking the civilization of the East with the West" (first intertitle). Before long, however, it is apparent that this is a contemporary tale, an updated version of the "giants of brain and brawn who builded those steel paths of progress across the Great Divide" (second intertitle). We first see Glover successfully directing a sand-bag operation to thwart a raging runaway river, a heroic operation soon "rewarded" with the job of guiding the railroad president, Rufus Gage (Theodore Roberts), and his daughter and sister through the mountains to various resorts. Glover at first repels Laura by mistaking her for his new stenographer and complaining about having to guide a bunch of "New York snobs." Although offended at first, Laura soon falls for him, and the two are supplied with many a contrived excuse to build a romance during the guided tour. Laura is simultaneously wooed by Allen Harrison (Lloyd Whitlock), director of the Great Western and an unattractive character who schemes to cheat a colorful old mountain man (and buddy of Glover's) out of his bit of property in order to "trade it" for Laura's hand. Glover's various acts of ingenuity and macho heroism, which include driving a train through a blizzard with Laura at his side, are enough to foil Harrison and ensure Gage's endorsement of Glover's betrothal to his daughter.

What should be noted right away about these films' plots is the disappearance of the tomboy female heroine and the shift to a corporate point of view. The locomotive engineer is replaced by the civic engineer or railroad manager as hero: Jim Glover in *The Love Special;* Gordon Steele (William Desmond), the construction engineer who earns the nickname "Slave Driver" for his brutal treatment of labor in *Blood and Steel;* David Burton (Malcolm McGregor), an engineering graduate who heads West upon finishing school in the East to work for the Overland Railroad in *The Overland Limited* (Gotham Productions, 1925); Tommy Tucker, the railroad official in *The First Year* (Fox, 1926; directed by Frank Borzage); and John Ralston (David Butler), the mail sorter for *The Arizona Express* (Fox, 1927). Even in *The Great K & A Train Robbery* (Fox, ca. 1921), which stars Tom Mix as an agent hired to protect the K&A from holdups, the point of view is resolutely corporate.

There are precedents in the teens for this perspective in films like *The Lost*

Freight Car (Kalem, 1911), in which a freight conductor wins the daughter of a railroad yardmaster when he saves the president's train and discovers a missing freight car. Train films before the twenties that reflect a corporate perspective, however, are more diluted in their expression as well as in their number. A 1912 film, *A Romance of the Rails* (Essanay), which bears little resemblance to Edison's earlier film, tells the story of Frank Denning (George Lessey), an assistant railroad superintendent, and Alice (Bessie Learn), the niece of squatter Silas Barton (William West), whom Frank must evict from railroad-owned property. Frank is given a childlike handcar to drive down the tracks to the place where Barton is squatting; on one of his eviction visits to the sour old man, Frank and Alice fall in love. Barton forbids their romance, but he eventually blesses the couple when Frank saves him from being run over by a train, and he rewards them on his deathbed with some money he had stashed beneath the bed. This legitimates the "downwardly mobile" intentions of the lower management executive. Even in films like *Alma's Champion* (Vitagraph, 1912), in which a railroad president's son disguised as a locomotive engineer (Willis Claire) wins the heart of the wealthy Alma (Lillian Walker), the heroism of the workingman engineer is preserved.[146]

In films of the twenties the transformation from one type of engineer to the other is often expressed as a family romance. In *The Overland Limited* the central character is bridge engineer David Barton, whose father, "Big Ed" Barton (Ralph Lewis), is the "crack engineer of the Overland," a man who "divided his affections between the throbbing steel steed and his little family" (intertitle). In that film and others the change is figured as a natural progression, with the son achieving success and heroism specific to modern times and outstripping the class position of the father — Oedipal narratives in the generalized sense. Though set in the West as a token reference to the original settings for train romances, the point of view is explicitly modern and urban Eastern, and it in fact uses its spatial expansiveness, its rhetorical connotations of the expansion of freedom and individuality, to legitimate the articulation of the male individual-as-hero within a corporate perspective.

The *social* movement symbolized by the train in film is rather specific to the 1920s, when automobiles had come increasingly to express the same thing. If the railroad holds any significance as such in a decade that would witness its slow decline as America's predominant form of mass transit, it is as a symbol of the American myths that it helped foster and in some sense create: mobility, flight from the past, progress, the "frontier spirit," technological mastery of the virgin land, and, paradoxically, individualism.[147] Thus, in many of these films, the bridge engineer is given the opportunity — or task — of driving the locomotive to pull someone, or some company, out of crisis (*Blood and Steel, The Love Special*). In other words, the new hero's legitimacy as a romantic individual — versus a mere corporate cog — derives from his similarity to the locomotive engineer hero, who is narratively and historically subordinate to the new hero.

Here the train comes to figure the classical American ethos of mobility in all domains — physical, social, and sexual. Appropriately, the new hero is linked to a new heroine: the romantic stake has shifted from girl telegraphers and station agents' wives or girlfriends to "daughters of magnates," and the magnates are typically good patriarchs. This basic Oedipal path is followed in *The Great K & A Train Robbery*, which features Madge Cullen (Dorothy Dwan), daughter of E. C. Cullen (William Walling), president of the railroad; in *The Arizona Express*, with Katherine Keith (Pauline Stark), the local bank president's daughter, pursued by the railroad mail sorter; in *The Overland Limited*, in which the civil engineer courts the daughter of an Eastern landowner who not-so-typically controls land in the West that the railroad is compelled to cross (the landowner is balanced, however, by the good president of the Overland, who is "self-made from the ranks of the workers"); in *The Love Special*, in which Jim Glover "earns" the hand of Laura Gage, the railroad president's daughter; and in *Blood and Steel*, in which Helen Holmes is featured as the daughter of the railroad's general manager.

Unlike the heroines of the teens, these women are meant to be classically female. Modern women do not operate trains; they adore the engineers and vent their spunk and restiveness organizing charity bazaars or vacationing in the resort-dotted wilderness. A certain tension around the feminization of the women characters develops, a tension most apparent in the transformation of the Helen Holmes figure. In *Blood and Steel*, Helen's role as daughter is established from the beginning. The beginning, however, is actually told from the point of view of the cruel taskmaster-engineer Devore Palmer (Mark V. Wright), with whom Helen falls in love. In short, the "Helen" story no longer belongs to Helen; the enunciation and narrative system belong to the male hero. Helen's appearance has changed as well; she sports a very feminine, dainty look, and in this film she no longer even works for the railroad. In *The Lost Express* her role as telegrapher is so understated, it is almost an afterthought. Her reduction to passivity is not total, since she does ride on horseback to warn the train of imminent disaster, but it is clearly meant to dilute any "masculine" traits associated with acts of heroism. In any case, the narrative logic requires that she be saved by her lover in an almost ridiculous parody of the former Helen Holmes, whose ingenuity in the films of the teens has all but disappeared in the 1920s.

The plots typically identify property and/or money with a woman: one is traded for the other, or the woman is ransomed, or the rescuing of one entails the rescuing of the other. This is a legacy of Griffith's "girl/trust" equations. In the later films, however, the stakes have been raised: these are *wealthy* girls being courted by largely middle-class or former working-class boys. As parables of consumerism, upwardly mobile aspirations to wealth, these 1920s films legitimate the struggle for success in two fundamental ways: (1) by romance, the couple, and a corresponding narrative structure of class transcendence; and (2) by establishing the hero as dedicated to middle-class values (in the line of Jim Glover's disdain for "New York snobs," or Tom Mix's cowboy mockery of civilization, "Sorry I couldn't stay for tea — or whatever your father drinks.").

Narrative Agency and The General

No longer in possession of narrative agency, the women in the railroad films of the 1920s have been made largely passive, the objects of enunciation. This return to a passive status involves a temporal relation to narrative agency that is also bound up with gender. In many of the train films that have been discussed here, the very proximity of a woman to a train often demands a certain kind of narrative logic designed to integrate or assimilate her to the narrative mission of the male character or characters, as evident in the films of Porter and Griffith, and again in the films of the 1920s. Male characters of these train films tend to be associated with the twin drives of narrative and cinematic force, both forces of a certain will to totalization, while female characters more often are swept up in the pull of photography, the still image, the nonnarrative delay, pause, or freeze. Certainly, in the "joke space" films, the presence of women can be absolutely antinarrative in halting or subverting male drive.

In film theory we find this active/passive division of narrative strategy argued most notably by Laura Mulvey. Mulvey identifies woman's nonlinear temporal status with the classical trait of passivity: "her presence tends to work against the development of a story line, to freeze the flow of action in moments of erotic contemplation. This alien presence then has to be integrated into cohesion with the narrative. . . . The split between spectacle and narrative supports the man's role as the active one of forwarding the story, making things happen."[148] In this view, classical Hollywood narrative is thought of as strictly active. Mulvey's view of narrative coincides with that of Stephen Heath in his analysis of Welles's 1958 *Touch of Evil*, where the woman's image comes to signify a sort of narrative vacation, a detour of linear temporal flow.[149] For Heath and Mulvey, woman represents the nonnarrative, pure and simple; she is the point at which "narrative wastes."[150] In another definition, we might see this nonnarrativity as related more to plot than narrative per se, since narrative systems tend to be made up of a variety of elements, both active and passive or, let us say, contemplative, with plot relating more closely to action. But the point is the same: in many of these films either the woman marches forward, so to speak, with the male protagonist or against him in some way that reorients the narrative.

For Peter Brooks, the theme of the train and engine in nineteenth-century fiction is a mise-en-abîme of the narrative motor of the novel, "an explicit statement of the inclusion within the novel of the principle of its movement."[151] Concerned with a textual erotics of force, and drawing on Freud's use of motor as metaphor for the drives, Brooks argues that in such works as Balzac's *Comédie humaine* and Zola's *La Bête humaine*, "life in the text of the modern is a nearly thermodynamic process; plot is, most aptly, a steam engine."[152] And that engine is invested with erotic and romantic power tied to male narrative agency.

In the Griffith-defined train film, even in the Helen variant, narrative and cinematic force are typically bound up with the train. This is especially true of the 1920s films. Insofar as the train is usually a substitute for the engineer, we can say that the engineer is himself a figure — indeed, an index — of narrative. One could say that in such cases narrative motive is locomotive. Consistent with both earlier and contemporaneous railroad films, in Buster Keaton's *The General* (1926) the steam engine literally sets the plot in motion. But *The General* presents us with an interesting variation on the logic outlined above. It seems to define its narrative twists with respect to the "other" logic of the development of classical cinema, that of narrative as a woman's system, a system straddling control and disorder. Yet it also throws into question the whole basis for distinguishing narrative according to gender, and it reveals how at the center of a prototypically classical Hollywood film, traces lurk of the early train film and its joke space, now integrated as a comic premise that exceeds the "classical" harness devised for it. In other words, *The General* is to the train film of the 1920s what *Pullman Bride* was to the 1910s, though the Keaton film is less overtly "anarchic." As such, Keaton's film provides us with a way of reading the classical film against itself, by opening it up to vestigial antinarrative traces it cannot successfully repress.

In terms of the temporal argument, *The General* generally tries to define the woman character in relation to the temporal logic of the photograph, as opposed to that of the film, i.e., mobilized photographs. The film at the same time, however, effaces the basis for this relation as a function of the central mechanism by which it is initially set up through both narrative and cinematic principles. To demonstrate, I would like first to trace the most obvious logic of this claim, that is, that male and female obey two different temporal schemes allied with (1) the photograph and (2) cinema.

The General is set in the South on the eve of the Civil War. Based on an actual incident that occurred in Georgia during the war, the film is the quasi-fictional story of a Southern engineer whose train is stolen by the Union army, and then retaken by him in a demonstration of Rebel commitment and romantic desirability. As the film begins, we see Johnnie Gray (Keaton) driving his locomotive to the station. This shot is followed by an intertitle that reads, "There were two loves in his life — His engine — and — ," which is followed by a cut to an oval portrait photograph of Annabelle Lee. Annabelle (played by Marion Mack), the beloved of Johnnie, is first presented to the spectator as a photo hung within the diegetic space of the locomotive. Her presentation is marked as different by virtue of the· fact that her image is given in place of language, as if words literally could not describe her. From the beginning, then, the film asks us to see her as a photograph, a still image, an object of visual contemplation.

Two key settings in the film support this reading. When Johnnie courts Annabelle at her father's house and gives her his double self/locomotive portrait photo, she props the photo up on the table as another image in the gallery of framed objects in the room. One might say that she inhabits a museum, a space where time has stopped, a repository of the photo and the memorial, a living room of the past. Certainly, her association with the photo is underlined in the middle of the film in the famous scene where Keaton gazes at her from under the table and through a hole in the tablecloth that comes to resemble a certain idealized matte framing, i.e., the iris. This tightly focused perspective frames her for the spectator as well, asking us to look at her as a framed picture. The effect is one of a restatement of the literal and figurative frames of the photographic space.

The first presentation of Annabelle is significant in its contribution to this logic. For one thing, the interruption in the story, which has barely begun, is a description in the structuralist sense, that is, the alternation of temporal advance and temporal pause that Gerard Genette analyzes as typical of the classical novel.[153] The descriptive passage is itself divided between a textual (written) and a figural (imaged) presentation. While both form part of a moment of textual and narrative freezing, when the film takes time out to fill in information on Johnnie's desire, one could say that Annabelle's representation is the more time-stopping of the two, since the spectator is less active when gazing at her framed image than when actually reading the words of the intertitle.

This should be contrasted with the initial presentation of Johnnie, who is shown driving his locomotive toward a destination, a precise location in space and time: Marietta, Spring of 1861. The intertitle tells us that the Western and Atlantic Flyer (the General) is *speeding* into Marietta; it imparts a distinct temporal character to Johnnie. Thus, to pursue the binary logic outlined above, Johnnie could be seen as the subject of dynamism, with the train as agent of force, both textual and narrative. The train certainly functions as the narrative motor, the vehicle and object of narrative development and plot. It is also the thing that propels history itself, while Annabelle figures as photo, as icon of the past, the body of the South, the civilization for which the war is being fought, and which is also stuck in the past. That is, she doubles as the sexual and historical stake of the narrative, while imparting a "respectable" aura to the locomotive she adorns as photograph.

Of course, there is the rectangular photo of Johnnie and his train, which would certainly seem to upset the logic. But before agreeing with this objection, I would like to defend that logic in terms of overall plot development. While it is true that Johnnie is initially presented as an annex of the train, of speed and dynamism, he is also by turns relatively passive and immobile, photolike, even to some extent feminine in his inability to integrate himself into the army or perform ordinary macho tasks (photo 19). But the narrative objective is in one sense precisely to mobilize him in a way that the army cannot, to dynamize him and push him toward his quest of obtaining the uniform and the girl, that is, to bring the hero from immobility to aggressive action, to narrative agenthood. Consider, for example, the interaction of

19. Buster Keaton in *The General*, 1926. Museum of Modern Art.

Johnnie with other modes of transport during the initial pursuit when he seems to take forever to regain control of the train: his handcar goes in reverse and eventually off the tracks, the bicycle simply folds up and dies, the cannon works only by accident. Mechanically speaking, Johnnie is a one-technology man.

As if to underscore the feminine coding of these bungled gestures, they are repeated or mirrored by Annabelle on the way back. In general, her activity on the train is antinarrative in the sense of threatening to halt or divert the central narrative action. Thus, as soon as she is put in a position where she must operate the train, it goes in reverse — and threatens thereby to reverse the narrative by disobeying the forward linearity of the plot controlled by Johnnie/Keaton. The reverse direction occurs, significantly, at a bend in the tracks, a curve in linearity.

Between the Johnnie of the first half of the film and the Johnnie of the second half intervenes the rescue of both the train and the woman. As Moews notes, the rescue constitutes the film's turning point.[154] With the plot reversal, the nature and direction of the pursuits return toward the film's beginning. In the exchange of narrative roles, power changes hands as well. Now Johnnie is in control of both his locomotive and his girl (emblematized by his literal possession of her when he conceals her in a boot sack soon after they are reunited in the middle of the film), and hence of the narrative — or so it seems.

The pivotal moment of the film is the pivotal moment of this analysis; my reading so far has been premised on a certain abstraction of the narrative logic and narrative agency. Yet the specific terms I have chosen to privilege can be used to buttress a very different analysis, with some further inquiry into the issue of "narrative control."

Another look at the structural design of these sequences should make us question the notions both of "narrative control" as the prerogative of a male subject and of the simple oppositional structure of the film. The fact that the rescue, for example, occurs at night, in the dark, is not merely a concession to some realistic claim on presumed durations of train chases from Georgia to Tennessee, but it is a key figure of the narrative rhetoric in its distribution of temporal, sexual, and narrative roles. It is Annabelle's presence that founds the reversal and becomes associated with the narrative rebirth. For one thing, the pause in the story is in a sense the pause of the photograph, a moment of temporal rest, an interlude in the film's flow. In addition, her narrative force is linked initially with the darkness that blankets the film in a key intertextual rhetorical connotation — the darkness of the train tunnel, a site of reversal and exchange of identities in films like *What Happened in the Tunnel*. (For the film analyst, it also connotes the black between film frames, the alternating obscurity of film's repressed other, glimpses of which pose a threat to continuity and can usually be caught only when the film has literally stopped or broken.) In *What Happened in the Tunnel* the blackness of the screen is overlaid on the darkness of the tunnel and the maid, all of which coincide to produce a diegetic as well as filmic alternation of light and dark. These train-aligned moments of darkness are moments of the reversal into the opposite or otherness, of the suspension of sense, linearity, continuity. Now the film must go backward in order to go forward; in a sense, it must bathe itself in femininity to be reborn as masculinity, as "the active role of forwarding the story" on Johnnie's part. Here it is important to note that unlike in *What Happened in the Tunnel*, "darkness" in *The General* stops short of evoking African Americans, who though forming a highly visible stake in the Civil War, are curiously all but invisible in the film, appearing only once, carrying trunks and bags for white passengers. (To a great extent, Keaton's concern in the film, blind as it is to the issue of slavery, is not really the Civil War or the South, but the train and the events giving it its legendary status.)

Insofar as the second half of the film is the mirror reflection of the first, and Annabelle is the spitting image of Johnnie with respect to management of the train and the narrative, she is indeed his double temporally displaced, i.e., reinvented.[155] In the film's second half, in fact, she is so much like him that when she tries to throw a twig instead of a log into the locomotive boiler, he feels compelled to strangle her playfully and then kiss her, as if to dilute the violence and/or acknowledge the likeness in what is a blatantly ambivalent kiss. In other words, Annabelle is Johnnie's past, the return of his other, incompetent self that he tries to repress during the return journey. She repeats his trajectory, and the similarity is frightening, so much so that he wishes to literally repress her. The sight of his own incompetence and its female embodiment is upsetting to his sense of identity and control; her repetition of his acts destroys his uniqueness.

But Annabelle's distressing mimesis is built on her reflection of not only his ineptitude, but his ingenuity. She performs some worthy deeds, such as rigging up the rope between two fir trees in order to act as a drag on, or at least slow down, the Yankee train. She is also allowed to control the train, successfully, at certain points when Johnnie stokes the engine. She fails, however, to gain Johnnie's recognition for her virtuous acts; he refuses to acknowledge the value of the tree-rigging exercise, even though it proves successful. In any event, whether Annabelle is stealing Johnnie's act for better or worse, it is not her difference that is at issue, but her similarity, her interchangeability, with him.

Johnnie also does not retain absolute control on the return journey; in a sense, he and Annabelle alternate roles here as well. Thus, for example, when they enter Rebel territory, Johnnie fails to understand why his comrades are shooting at him until Annabelle points to the Yankee uniform he had used as a disguise and forgotten to remove. In the game of musical chairs set up with the uniforms and narrative roles, the film leads identity along a chain of rhetorical substitutions implied in the attribution of agency to one character (or uniform) or another. This sets up a tension between the general and the specific, between the law as category and its application, between appearance and substance. Johnnie and company are inscribed in a double narrative that distances cause from effect, and intention from execution. This is the typical Keaton double narrative in which textual point of view is split in terms of the significance of actions. Keaton's protagonist is not aware of everything he does or that happens to him, while those around him often attribute his acts to another code; that is, they fail to "read" him correctly. For example, it is only when he views Annabelle from underneath the table that Johnnie realizes his pursuit of his General (the locomotive) turns out to have been a pursuit of his girlfriend as well. This split between signifier and signified, which accounts in large part for the humor of the parody, continues through to the attainment of the coveted Rebel uniform. Ideally, the uniform gives Johnnie access to the fulfillment of his desire with Annabelle, yet as soon as he attempts to kiss her, he is interrupted by the train of soldiers obliged to salute him for his newly acquired rank.

The basic problem of agency, however, comes back to Johnnie's relation with the machine, specifically with the train — one of his "two loves" — as enunciative device. The mechanization of Keaton as a performer — his machinelike movements and demeanor — is one of the clichés of discourse about him.[156] Johnnie's mechanical gestures and actions demonstrate from beginning to end the extent to which the machine pervades his body with its codes and aesthetic. The train drives him as much as he drives it. We can also describe Annabelle as a mechanical woman. Not only is she "cinematized" through the logic of narrative or her apprenticeship to the train on the journey back to Marietta, but the photograph tacked onto the wall of the locomotive at the beginning endows her with something of the pathos of the pressure gauge, her photo integrated into the series of round-framed measuring devices that enable the engineer to read the engine. Here woman is an element of combustion, a figurehead turned inward in a more properly functional (or narrative) arrangement instead of being decorative (or supplemental). This particular contextualization of her image makes her muselike status simultaneously narrative and nonnarrative, and to a great extent it undermines the distinction between the two. She is simultaneously form and function in her role as decor.

This logic leads us back to the photograph of Johnnie and the train. What is significant about his photo is not so much that he is frozen on film, as she is, but that the train appears with him as part of the portrait, that is, the train forms part of the photographic as well as the cinematic chain. This photo is the complement to the integration of Annabelle's photo into the train. The principle of contamination represented by the train, its cultural connotation as a public site of social-sexual heterogeneity and spatial-temporal confusion, is set in motion from the beginning.

Thus, when Johnnie's photo gets junked with old mail or already paid bills, junked no less by Annabelle's father, the photo seems lost to paternity's unappreciative whim. But it becomes reanimated, eventually finding its place in the cinematic continuum of images. Nothing illustrates this place better than the film's final scene, where the two photos — of Johnnie and train, and of Annabelle — are united to make cinema, but cinema that recognizes its debt to the photo: the final image of simultaneous mobility and immobility, the union of male and female as non-gender-specific, active/passive principles recoded by the machine.

In Moews's view, "if the machine is a machine and the humans are humans, in the affirmatively mechanical world of the film they have also been fantastically and approvingly presented as alike. Girl and train have been equated in their kidnapping and rescue and by the hero's equitably divided love. Hero and train have been equated as Johnnie, a Keaton kinetic hero in an age of admirable machines, acquired some of The General's mechanistic glory through being its expert engineer."[157] But the film goes further in its machine logic. The film's will-to-integration, its desire to equate man and woman, man and machine, culminates in the final image of Keaton and companion as a train-blessed desiring machine. Perched on and assimilated to The General, Johnnie and Annabelle glue their lips together as Johnnie mechanically salutes the passing train (*défilement*) of Rebel soldiers, as if the waving arms fueled the kiss, the desire, the flow between their two bodies (photo 20). This Matthew Brady salute to F. T. Marinetti is as close as classical cinema gets to Duchamp's bachelor machines.[158] Here resolution of desire is not so much synthetic as mechanical — it is desire as biomechanics.[159] The romantic couple is flimsy; just like the woman and man in *The Girl and Her Trust*, the couple here needs support, a prop for desire, a ground of identity that subsumes sexual difference in the train as agent and object of desire. As such, the train puts human desire at the service of technology.

In its ability to govern desire across and in ignorance of sexual difference, the General is more properly the Genre-al, or all the genres at once, the category of the Law itself. The name is charged with this significance. Keaton's pursuit of his General is also a pursuit of a *General*, of rank, authority, the

20. Buster Keaton and Marion Mack in *The General*, 1926. Museum of Modern Art.

father, identity in relation to the genre, the law. In this case, the "general" is the effacement of the proper name, as Derrida would say, the parricidal rubbing out of unique identity, of clearly differentiated instances of the law.[160] And it is the train that puts the genres into question, the law as the ground of identity; the law of noncontradiction, of either/or, is violated in the train's "both/and" principle, its inclusion of a double principle.[161] That principle is the Zeno's paradox of simultaneous mobility and immobility, which makes the train the perfect metaphor for cinema's relation to the photo and for relations between male and female. It condenses the paradox of sexual difference in spatiotemporal terms, and it forms the background for Keaton's final consideration of the simultaneous stasis/dynamism which is cinema, when at the end, the double figure of frozen bodies and waving arms gestures toward cinema's fundamental, pull-down mechanism.

In *The General*, then, man's simultaneous, unsuccessfully repressed identity is woman; the cinema's is the photo; and, we might say, action's identity is description, narrative's is nonnarrative. With the train as a fitting vehicle of paradox, the film ends in a dream of simultaneity: of past and present, male and female, photo and film, ending in what Thierry Kuntzel has called a "voyage immobile."[162]

The General brings the "romance of the rail" full circle in the silent period, from female joke space to nostalgic icon of the heterosexual couple. As such, it stands at the threshold between an early cinema heritage and an era of more complex usage of the train as a narrative, romantic space. Whether represented as girlish virginity (*The Lonedale Operator*) or tomboyishness (*The Hazards of Helen*), or channeled into the heterosexual couple defined by male authority (*Blood and Steel*), femininity left its mark on film texts with an ongoing instability shared by the train and the cinema. Though early classical American film after 1908 would attempt to control the female spectator and the joke space by codifying film texts narratively and morally, the heterotopia and subversiveness of early film — as filtered through the instability of train travel — survived *within* American classical films like *The General*, a comedy that is as highly coded as a classical text, albeit one marked by Keaton's unique approach to comedy.

THREE

The Railroad in the City

Cinema has always been an urban medium and art form. From the Grand Café in Paris, where the Lumière brothers staged the first public film screening, to the Wintergarten in Berlin, where Max Skladanowsky showed movies for the first time to a German audience in 1895, to Koster and Bial's music hall in New York, site of the first truly successful projected film screening in the United States in 1896, from Coney Island's penny arcade kinetoscope parlors and storefront film theaters, to the nickelodeon, perhaps the first true movie theater, cinema was marked as an entertainment that grew out of the *city*.[1]

American audiences for popular mass entertainments were already formed in metropolitan areas where recreation had become commodified in music and dance halls, vaudeville theaters, and amusement parks. The coming of cinema profited from the expansion of leisure time at the turn of the century—an expansion that resulted from a reduced working week, greater urban concentration, and greater disposable income for entertainment.[2] In the Unites States between 1840 and 1910, the urban populace grew from 10.8 percent of the population to 45.7 percent.[3] By 1920, for the first time, more than half the population lived in urban areas.[4]

The urban orientation of early cinema, often using the train to represent the fundamental city experience, is evident in the themes, conditions of exhibition, and intended audiences of early film. It is also evident in many of its sites of production, with the original AM&B studios located in Brooklyn, Edison's operation just across the Hudson River in New Jersey and eventually in Manhattan, the Lumières in Lyons, Urban in London, and Lubin in Philadelphia, to name a few.[5]

The city as an image is present at the beginning of cinema, forming a ready-made setting, a stage for a variety of early film subjects. The streets, buildings, sights, and crowds of New York, London, Paris, Tokyo, Beijing, and a host of other cities around the world formed an object of fascination in and of themselves.[6] Ceremonies for the opening of the New York subway in 1904 were filmed by Edwin S. Porter for Edison, while AM&B treated spectators to an unusual ride on a subway train, a journey illuminated by lights mounted on a flatbed car running parallel to the main tracks in *Interior, N.Y. Subway, 14th St. to 42nd St.* (1905).[7] *What Happened on 23rd Street* (Edison/Porter, 1901) and *Soubrette's Troubles on a Fifth Avenue Stage* (Edison, 1901) are New York-based comedies of street voyeurism, where a daring peek at what lies beneath women's dresses is afforded both the viewer and the passersby in the film. *Lifting the Lid* (AM&B, 1905), a parody of the vices of New York as seen through the eyes of tourists, takes a group of country bumpkins on a tour led by a guide with a megaphone, to expose in packaged form such big-city "curiosities" as the dance hall, Chinese restaurants, opium smoking, and dancing girls. And just as with the thrill train films, filmmakers made use of the urban railroad as a sort of fairground ride, taking audiences around New York on its elevated railroad (*Elevated Railroad*, AM&B, 1903), or Paris on its "Petite ceinture" (*La Petite Ceinture*, Méliès, ca. 1903), crossing the Brooklyn Bridge on the front of a locomotive (*New Brooklyn to New York Via Brooklyn Bridge*, Edison, 1899), or touring Boston on a streetcar (*Seeing Boston*, AM&B, 1906).[8]

The city also appears frequently as a setting for drama and comedy in early classical film. Griffith set a number of films in the metropolis, as did Charlie Chaplin and Mack Sennett. In France, many a Max Linder film took place in Paris, along with the *Fantômas* films of Louis Feuillade. But perhaps the greatest decade of city films in both the United States and Europe was the 1920s: Paris, Moscow, Berlin, and New York were the settings for numerous motion pictures that made the city part of their intrigue or their premise. *Berlin, Symphony of a Great City* (Walter Ruttmann, 1927); *Everyday* (Hans Richter, ca. 1928); *Entr'acte* (René Clair and Francis Picabia, 1924); *Paris qui dort* (René Clair, 1923); *Manhatta* (Charles Sheeler and Paul Strand, 1921); *People on Sunday* (Robert Siodmak, 1929); *The Street* (Karl Grune, 1923); and

The Crowd (King Vidor, 1928) and *Man with a Movie Camera* (Dziga Vertov, 1929), all were joined by countless other films that set their narratives in a city of some sort, even at times a generic "The City."[9]

It is only natural that the train would appear in many of the city films as a defining vehicle of the urban or interurban experience. The growth of the modern city was greatly motivated by the needs of the railroad, which dramatically accelerated the process by which the country was made to serve the city — as a source of cheap labor and raw materials and as a growing market for urban-made goods, especially in smaller cities whose growth was prompted by these same processes.[10] Railroads also expanded city limits, as middle-class suburbs mushroomed between 1880 and World War I. The great system of interurban transportation, defined mostly by the electric trolley, opened up a "metropolitan corridor" designed to relieve urban congestion and facilitate the passage between suburb and city.[11]

Just as the railroads fundamentally altered the interurban landscape, so they affected the urban landscape. The railroad station occupied a central place in defining the new form that urban culture and economy would take.[12] The station organized and marked the entry into and exit from the city and the city's relation to a whole economic system across the country. The station also contained a condensed version of the commercial chaos of city streets and marketplaces. Spreading out from the station were the trolleys and electric streetcars that came to dominate traffic in hundreds of cities around the country.[13] Railroad tracks charged across city streets, creating social and economic divisions defined by the needs of the railroad and erecting an aesthetics of steel, speed, and electricity.

Early film comedies often played off the division between city and country by privileging an urban point of view defined in relation to the train. In the 1912 Biograph film *The Tourists*, two Caucasian city couples disembark for a quick look and some shopping when their cross-country train stops momentarily at an American Indian village populated with a mixture of white actors made up as Indians and Native American extras (photo 21). The couples miss the train and, as the title tells us, "must wait for the next one." Even though one could hardly expect the "next one" to arrive for a few days, given the desert-like setting, another train does arrive about ten minutes later, which points to the urban, "subway consciousness" of the filmmakers. In between, the tourists are shown having precisely the sort of exotic experience promised by both the railroad and the cinema — a brief indulgence in "otherness" that enlists every conceivable cliché of American Indian culture in its parody of tourism.[14]

Trixie, one of the tourist women, is first shown buying armfuls of handmade baskets before the train leaves; it is her thirst for shopping that causes them to be left behind. To kill time, she sets off to tour the village. Her urban brashness is taken by the village "chief" for romantic interest, and he eagerly escorts her around, to the consternation of the jealous Indian women. The tourists are last seen running to escape the clutches of tomahawk-bearing Native women, who chase the white visitors onto the next train and out of sight. Though the city folks are caricatured, especially as shoppers, their point of view is privileged when compared to the extremely stereotyped Indians. Here the split between urban and rural is inflected with a racist division that underscores the alliance of the cinema and the railroad as touristic apparatuses of a hegemonic vision. For the spectator-tourist, stepping from the train is stepping into an altogether other world.

The urban viewpoint of early film was even more arrogant in train films set in the city. A whole genre of rube-in-the-city subjects that carried over from nineteenth-century vaudeville and popular music came to support an image of cinema as a medium based in the city.[15] *Uncle Josh at the Moving Picture Show* is a good example of cinema's anticountry bias: the rube who cannot grasp the cinematic phenomenon is to be laughed at, mocked. The same is true with respect to urban transportation: the train acts as a defining vehicle that separates the bumpkins from the cosmopolites. In *Rube and Fender* (Edison, 1903), for example, an unwary hick ambling down the street is literally swept off his feet and scooped up by the fender of a streetcar that otherwise would have run him down. In the inability to negotiate the city street, traffic, or large-scale machines, an old trope of country naïveté appears here around a lack in vision; the rube does not see or hear the tram coming. Uncle Josh's terrifying encounter with the *Black Diamond Express* is in a sense paradigmatic. Like Uncle Josh, the vulnerable rube is the object of mechanical aggression by a train, but, unlike Uncle Josh, he is unaware of it until too late. In both cases, a faulty or untrained perception is to blame, a cultural naïveté grounded in another, nonurban mode of perception.[16]

The real test of urban know-how was the subway. AM&B's *A Rube [Reuben] in the Subway* (1905; shot by Billy Bitzer) subjects a rube trio composed of a man and two women to the anarchy of the subway platform and creates a comedy around their inability to master the confusion. The film is a one-shot, fixed-camera view of a subway set that consists of a platform running down the middle of the frame, in perspective, with a track on either side.[17] A policeman tries unsuccessfully to uphold order on the platform (and symmetry within the frame), as crowds materialize and disperse, and the trains come and go. When the rubes step off a train and into the crowd in the middle of the frame, they instantly become the prey of a con artist. Realizing he has been robbed, and that the con man has disappeared while his female companions have left on the next train, the male rube panics and jumps onto the track to chase after the train. A subway official follows him out of frame, a puff of smoke appears, and the cop and subway official return escorting the burned and disheveled rube, who has clearly been run over, as another train pulls in and disgorges its contents onto the platform.

The subway confusion to which the rubes are victim occurs in this and other films within a "trick" space similar to that of the joke films discussed in chapter 2.[18] Joining *Streetcar Chivalry* and *The Unappreciated Joke* in this regard is *2 A.M. in the Subway*, which opens with a sleepy policeman half-dozing on a platform much like the one in *A Rube in the Subway* (photo 22). A train pulls in, opens its doors, and deposits a drunken trio of "city folk" on the platform — again, a man and two women. The man wears a tophat, tails, and a cape; he and his companions have clearly just returned from a night on the town. The cop is worried as the trio approaches the camera and the man bends down to tie one of the women's shoes in a sort of diegetic equivalent of the close-up cut-in in *The Gay Shoe Clerk*; the aim is to exhibit the woman's leg to the spectator. A train arrives on the opposite track, and the policeman shoves them aboard, while a passenger seen carrying a box on the platform and flirting with the women thrusts two dummy female legs from inside the train and through the window. The cop is shocked and hustles the two women off the train. The trick legs are then exposed as fakes, to the great amusement of the crowd.

Here the motifs of deception and substitution, and the extent to which they serve a confusion around sexuality, crop up in a joke space that is doubly defined by the appearance and disappearance of trains and the platform site of exchange in between them. The film is relatively complicated in its unfolding of "now you see it, now you don't." The confused policeman, like the naïve rube, is mocked for his failure to distinguish real legs from fake ones; it is as if the entire crowd of strangers were complicit in practicing the joke. Set up by

21. *The Tourists*, Biograph, 1912. Library of Congress.

the shoe-tying, the policeman is then fooled by the ersatz legs. The principle of the humor is underwritten by the speed-based "rules of perception" in the subway; one must be quick and alert to catch the real — and one's train.[19]

These films address an urban spectator whose "investment in the screen as mirror," to quote Miriam Hansen's reference to "local actuality" films set in cities, presupposes familiarity with an urban code.[20] Hansen notes that "if the spectator figure is embodied by a rube, the implied viewer is assumed to be more sophisticated and acculturated, familiar with the urban world of technology and mass entertainment."[21] The urban code in general is a code of prior knowledge, one of negotiating nonsense, scurrying through the crowd, knowing which trains to board, not falling for a trick. This code is hermeneutic — one that can be cracked only by those in the know — which is precisely what makes it a privileged point of view. Hugo Munsterberg refers obliquely to such a point of view in a passage from his 1916 study: "The applause into which the audiences, especially of rural communities, break out at a happy turn of the melodramatic pictures is another symptom of the strange fascination." This

22. 2 A.M. *in the Subway*, American Mutoscope
& Biograph Co., 1905. Library of Congress.

follows a passage on the vulnerability of neurasthenics to the "impression of
reality," thus linking susceptibility to film's illusion with presumably weaker or
more naive individuals.[22]

As a privileged point of view, urbanness in many early films connotes a
particular, middle-class position. In many films that make fun of tramps,
rubes, ethnic minorities, and other socially marginal types, "upward mobility
enters into film/viewer relations as already accomplished, inasmuch as spectatorial pleasure is frequently bound up with a position of social and epistemo-
logical superiority."[23] Certainly in 2 A.M. *in the Subway* the natty trio exhibit
the sartorial trappings of privilege. Yet, they also exhibit a transgressiveness
that defies class identity as fixed and "privileged" in an economic or social
sense only. Not only do the three make light of the law and actively contribute
to the disorder on the platform, but they converge in this endeavor with others
in the crowd who do not share the same social identity — for example, the leg
fetishist wearing distinctly lower-middle-class garb. Even if any of these characters could be said to appeal to "the rising class of white collar workers," who

may have identified "with a specifically American myth of success which blurred all class and ethnic distinctions,"[24] they also belong to "classlessness" in another, distinctly urban sense: that of the crowd.

Munsterberg describes a related phenomenon in the class character of movie audiences in 1916:

> Six years ago, a keen sociological observer characterized the patrons of the picture palaces as "the lower middle class and the massive public, youths and shopgirls between adolescence and maturity, small dealers, pedlars, laborers, charwomen, besides the small quota of children." This would hardly be a correct description today. This "lower middle class" has long been joined by the upper middle class. To be sure, our observer of that long forgotten past added meekly: "Then there emerges a superior person or two like yourself attracted by mere curiosity and kept in his seat by interest until the very end of the performance; this type sneers aloud to proclaim its superiority and preserve its self-respect, but it never leaves the theater until it must."[25]

In other words, films like *A Rube in the Subway* and *2 A.M. in the Subway* mixed and confused on-screen social types much as urban transportation and early film spectatorship did, and they provided a source of identification for city folk in general, while playfully undermining "proper" middle-class values. In these films the law is shown to be powerless in an urban crowd that moves according to the mechanical rhythm of the trains and responds like nerve endings to the stimulus of constant arrivals and departures. If "loose" behavior is to be expected in the subway (e.g., the exhibitionism of the drunken party), it cannot be located or fixed; it moves and depends on mobility and, to a large extent, anonymity. As in the early train films, its essence is that it is nonessential; it is an ephemeral representation, like the cinema itself, which draws the spectator into the search for meaning in a tangle of visual disorder.

These subway films project an ethos of "distraction." The great theorist of this concept was Siegfried Kracauer, whose 1926 essay on the "cult of distraction" is a central text.[26] The concept of distraction was, as Thomas Elsaesser notes, "originally a negative attribute (opposed to contemplative concentration)" that became recoded and endowed with a progressive meaning in the twenties in the writings of Kracauer and Walter Benjamin.[27] For Kracauer, the great Berlin movie theaters were "palaces of distraction" where the mass public saw itself reflected in the "pure externality" and fragmentation of surface glamor. Unlike the act of contemplating a traditional work of art, the attention of moviegoers was unfocused. Distracted spectators, according to Kracauer, could thus respond to film in a progressive manner because the whole act of cinema-going, including the film, exposed the inauthenticity, fragmentation, and disorder of the society that required them to engage in alienated labor and then asked them to appreciate the outmoded and static art forms of a repressive high culture. But, acknowledged Kracauer, the state of being distracted could, like its opposite, absorption, be reactionary in the case of films that organize the multiplicity of visual effects, the surface fragmentation, into a unified whole and make distraction an end in itself, which is precisely what Hollywood movies do.[28] Kracauer's revised perspective on distraction bespoke an ambivalence rooted in the accelerating breakdown of the Weimar Republic and the accompanying rise of Nazism.[29]

Hansen relates distraction to the urban mode of perception incorporated into the diversity of early film viewing:

> The rapid, seemingly random sequence of unrelated short films and live performances — which characterized the format of presentation even after cinema found its own exhibition outlet in the nickelodeons (from 1905) — was linked, furthermore, to perceptual changes ensuing from urbanization and industrialization. As early as 1911, a survey by the Russell Sage Foundation compared the variety format to "the succession of city occurrences," describing it as equally "stimulating but disintegrating." This trajectory is crucial to the concept of "distraction."[30]

A distracted attention in the case of the rubes is what renders them vulnerable to the deceptions of city life. Unable to focus on any one spectacle, yet equally unable to master the multiplicity of impressions, the rubes are fascinated, frustrated spectators who lack guides or cues to help them read what they see.[31] Yet the rituals of mass transportation and early film patronage cultivated their own form of urban distraction: a mechanical attention that permits one to move, zombielike, in and out of public vehicles and spaces while attending to other activities like reading or feeding a baby.[32] This is the attention of the mother and the shopgirl: the ability to attend to several things at once.[33] It is both states of distraction — being overwhelmed by and in some sense indifferent to sensations — that cinema recognizes in its mode of perception: a mechanical attention that is at the same time vulnerable to surprise and borne along by fascination with random, uncontrolled events, an attention that puts the perceiver in a hybrid state of mental relaxation and distraction. This hybrid distraction feeds on disorder, the transgressive disorder of the underground and the city, and reveals itself in the hermeneutic code of the urbanite as well as in the "cinema of attractions" that is to some extent founded on diversion. (As Hansen implies, "distraction" in one sense would then indeed approximate the model Gunning posits for early cinema.)[34]

The disorder of the crowd in *2 A.M. in the Subway* is based on a relaxation of inhibitions, with the display of sexuality and the anonymous passengers ganging up on the policeman, the "censor" of the underground—a highly charged topos for the figuration of unconscious desire. Down, underground, deep in the psyche, lurks an uncontainable sexuality, both male and female, that flouts the law and the respectability it upholds. The "danger" of this unbound sexuality lies partly in the display of a previously bound female eroticism that elicits predictable male responses (the shoe-tying display, the fake female legs). It is the crowd that releases sexuality, a crowd defined in relation to technologies of modernity emanating from the city: the train and cinema.

The "Unhealth" of Cities: The United States

The urban point of view that reigned in early film comedies did not go unchallenged. The representation of the city varied in individual films, as wider sociocultural attitudes toward the city, and toward urban transportation in particular, divided among embrace, alienation, and ambivalence. While anticity films were far from dominant in the first decade of the twentieth century, an attitude critical of the urban sphere became more and more common in the teens, starting at least with Griffith's sentimental idealization of the country and continuing in a variety of films through the teens and twenties. Antiurban sentiment in general was much older than the medium of film, as the time-honored literary genre of the pastoral demonstrates. But turn-of-the-century America raised the ante with an unprecedented acceleration: "If the booming factories brought affluence along with shocking working conditions, labor violence, and corruption, the booming cities dramatized the irony of the Industrial Revolution: the collision between progress and poverty—the wealth of Wall Street, State Street, Montgomery Street, and the wretched streets of Cockroach Row, Hell's Kitchen, and the Barbary Coast."[35]

Rapid urban growth in American cities in the late nineteenth century largely owed to a massive influx of immigrants, especially in the second big wave lasting from 1880 to 1910 when 18 million new arrivals swelled the immigrant portion of the urban population to a majority.[36] The pace of population growth in the cities far outstripped that of housing expansion, forcing huge numbers of poor people to live in tenements. The strain of the crowded city thus showed in its slums, where disease, poverty, crime, and social tension threatened to break the city apart.[37]

These contradictions became a subject for visual representation in late-nineteenth-century and early-twentieth-century photography and art. Jacob Riis's photographic documentation of "how the other half lives" (1890) profoundly affected both the role of photography as a medium of social documentation and the attitudes of reformers and politicians who were shocked by the images of slum life contained in Riis's work.[38] Years later, in 1912, Griffith's *Musketeers of Pig Alley* would project a fictional, cinematic equivalent of Riis's *How the Other Half Lives*, with a hard story of ghetto romance and crime set in real city streets. In a related story, James Kirkwood's *The Gangsters* (1914, Reliance Motion Picture Co., featuring Henry B. Walthall) ends with the gangster-protagonist retiring to the country to join the woman he loves, who had come to New York's Lower East Side fresh from the country, only to discover a world of corruption. Also made in 1914, *The Folks from Way Down East* (Photo Drama Motion Picture Co., 1914) is the story of the corruption of a country girl in New York and her eventual rescue by the rural divinity student who loves her.[39]

The antiurban bias that took hold in film was an outgrowth of the campaigns to make cinema respectable and moral, especially insofar as the city could be identified as an immoral place where women in particular were likely to be corrupted. As both the city and its entertainments grew, leisure itself came under study by groups who found it necessary as a check on the "unhealth" of Northeastern cities in the United States, with their teeming immigrant populations. In charting what he calls the "therapeutic ethos" that began to develop at the end of the last century, an ethos of which the city park was an early symptom, Jackson Lears identifies a "dread of unreality" among the educated bourgeoisie in the late nineteenth century: "The first and simplest source of a sense of unreality was the urban-industrial transformation of the nineteenth century. Changes in material life bred changes in moral perception. As Americans fled the surveillance of the village, they encountered the anonymity of the city . . . the corrosive impact of urban life on personal identity."[40]

Urban malaise would seem to have been compensated for by a new afflu-ence and material comfort produced by technological advance. This very af-fluence, however, was bound up with the sense of unreality; it was part and parcel of the growth of an interdependent national market economy: "As more and more people became enmeshed in the market's web of interdependence, liberal ideals of autonomous selfhood became ever more difficult to sustain. For entrepreneurs as well as wage workers, financial rise or ruin came to depend on policies formulated far away, on situations beyond the individual's control."[41] The evolution of the American city was similar, with the subor-dination of humans to the needs of the corporation.[42]

Writing in 1903, the German sociologist Georg Simmel defined the met-ropolitan citizen as an intellectual creature cut off from community and de-fined by a number of impersonal, interlocking circuits that stemmed from a money economy concerned only with exchange value.[43] The modern city threw together a heterogeneous collection of strangers, each of whom needed to compensate for the depersonalization and fragmentation by asserting indi-vidual expression — by distinguishing oneself in a crowd. But even in attribut-ing a sense of loss to the character of the metropolitan citizen, Simmel was loath to condemn the urbanite, seeing such individual expression as the sign of an unprecedented personal freedom that was impossible in small-town life with its narrowly prejudiced eye judging the individual's every move.[44] For Simmel, the greater nervousness that resulted from the wealth of constant stimuli produced by the city was only a natural adjustment on the part of a much more aware individual.

As noted in chapter 1, urban stimuli were, among other things, held re-sponsible for neurasthenia, the American "overwork" disease. George Miller Beard's studies of American neurasthenia linked a range of symptoms (dyspep-sia, insomnia, exhaustion, various phobias) with characteristically "American" behavior such as an accelerated pace of life, and with the dense and dynamic urban centers, the overambitiousness (hence, overwork), and the advanced state of modern, technological development in the United States.[45] Railroads were of course considered a major source of neurasthenic depression and of the modern, fragmented self, particularly for users of urban mass transit.[46] Neurasthenia even came to be identified with tram travel. An article in an 1896 issue of *L'Illustration* reports that "Tram conductors in America are, it seems, exposed to a special nervous malady that appears to be caused by the excessive mental tension demanded by traffic conditions in the busy streets of the na-tion's big cities.' "[47]

Inspired, significantly, by the likes of Edison, neurasthenia was identified by Beard with electricity and "sparks of force" that actually bespoke a higher development in its victims, the American "brain-workers."[48] But while stress and neurasthenia for Beard and Simmel represented signs of higher civilization, many who considered the price of progress too high to pay saw these same conditions as symptoms of decline. Prominent Americans such as Charles Eliot Norton scorned the "achievement ethos," partly in order to condemn neurasthenia. Norton — himself a certified neurasthenic — became part of the strong "antimodernist" current that arose in both Europe and the United States as a critique of the rapid pace of urbanization and modernization.[49] American antimodernism was supported by a heterogeneous collection of reformers, conservatives, doctors, health workers, aesthetes, and religious figures. Literary critics such as Silas Weir Mitchell, who mourned the displacement of Gothic romanticism by domestic realism in the literature of the 1880s, were joined by such psychologists as G. Stanley Hall, father of the Playground Movement in the early 1900s, who looked to medieval legend and folk tales as a source of revitalization of "the adolescent imagination."[50] Both antimodern militarism and primitivist vitalism represented a search for authenticity, and Protestants and Catholics alike joined the antimodern quest for meaning in the intense focus on premodern ritual.[51] Though often politically incompatible, antimodernists in general recoiled from the insubstantiality, fragmentation, and, for them, meaninglessness of modern urban life.[52]

A flurry of study, both scientific and paraprofessional, came to underpin the "therapeutic ethos" of consumer culture in the late nineteenth and early twentieth centuries and to ground the need for rest and recreation in greater sociological and psychological understanding. Leisure-as-therapy became an industry to which advertisers catered, developing to form the bedrock of a consumerist culture. "Unreality" was addressed first through entertainment: the captains of the leisure industry "commodified titillation at cabarets and in amusement parks; they catered to the anxious businessman as well as the bored shop girl; and they assimilated immigrants and WASPs in a new mass audience. Roller coasters, exotic dancers, and hootchy-kootchy girls all promised temporary escapes to a realm of intense experience, far from the stuffy unreality of bourgeois culture."[53] Clearly, cinema also formed part of this emergent culture of escapism.

Although, as Kathy Peiss points out, it would seem as if no one who had spent ten or twelve hours hunched over a sewing machine or standing at a sales counter could possibly summon the energy to go out dancing or to the amusement park, a surprising number of workingmen and workingwomen did.[54] Peiss's study of workingwomen's leisure in New York City between 1880 and 1920 shows how merely minimal improvements in the lot of working people during this time (shorter working hours, better wages) produced a space for leisure. The overwhelming majority of the female labor force during those years was composed of young single women who were either immigrants or daughters of immigrants.[55] They worked in the new department stores, factories, and offices as well as in more traditional occupations such as domestic service and sweatshops. Peiss notes: "These employment opportunities, the changing organization of work, and the declining hours of labor altered the relationships between work and leisure, shaping the way in which leisure time was structured and experienced. . . . Far from inculcating good business habits, discipline, and a desire for quiet evenings at home, the workplace reinforced the wage-earner's interest in having a good time."[56] "Having a good time" meant everything from walking in the street to frequenting the dance hall, from attending social clubs to patronizing vaudeville and the movies.

But while working people could not afford to flee to the suburbs and the country, the wealthy could, and did — to escape both the encroaching ghettoes and the pressures of city life brought on by "overwork." In the broadest sense, modern life in general, and urban life in particular, were understood by antimodernist men as a brutal force stripping society of its potency, its masculinity. As Lears notes of late nineteenth- and early twentieth-century male literary critics who decried the "feminization" of American culture, "they traced enervation to feminization because they equated masculinity with forcefulness."[57] The implication was that "a loss of will, both in themselves and in the culture generally," meant a loss of masculinity — for literary critics H. H. Boysen and Silas Weir Mitchell, "a decline of vital energy in art and life."[58]

As the shock waves of modern life rippled throughout society, a web of therapy practices arose to "heal" the wounds of progress. Within this web, the railroad defined a key role for itself. Consistent with its self-representation as a "civilizing factor," the railroad industry skirted the issue of its responsibility for some of the ill effects of modern society, instead concerning itself from the 1880s on with enabling middle-class vacationers and suburbanites to get away from the city.[59] Railroad companies were more than willing to serve the tired public; the train was indeed marketed as a primary instrument of escaping the pressures of urban life. The "Vacation Gospel" was published in 1890 by the Great Northern Railroad as a means of promoting its line for tourism.[60] Written as a "sermon" by one Rev. Dr. Bridgman of Hamline University in St. Paul, Minnesota, this treatise on the need for vacations recognized the toll that city life was taking on its busy subjects: "He who preaches the new *gospel of vacation* is a benefactor of his kind. He is a herald of health, happiness and hope. . . . Brain and body need to be released from books and business. One cannot afford to burn the candle of life at both ends and stick a red hot poker in the middle. . . . Leave Babylon by the fastest express for Arcadia."[61] In an undisguised address to male readers of "the gospel," the Rev. Dr. Bridgman advocated vacationing in the country to reinvigorate the male body and achieve "everything which goes to make up truest and most stalwart manhood."[62]

That same year the Pennsylvania Railroad stated in its brochure, *Winter Pleasure Tours*, which promoted travel to Florida, that after "six months' consecutive business life, to the average American there comes an imperative demand for rest, and man and woman alike must throw off the dual yoke of toil and social obligations and flee to some radically new scene and life. . . ."[63] This cautionary language was also used in a brochure published in the 1890s by the Brockville, Westport and North-Western Railway, which referred to "these days of rush and excitement and nervous strain" in answering the question, "Where Can I Get a Rest?"[64]

To escape modern life meant to escape the city and the clock — the kind of anxiety represented in the early train films concerned with train time and making or missing a train. But escape was not always possible. The early film *The Suburbanite* (AM&B, 1904) is a parody of a family's flight to the suburbs as refuge. Relocated to a New Jersey suburb, a family encounters a whole set of problems that do little to allay urban anxiety (photo 23). This anxiety is in any case inscribed in the suburban life itself: when the father misses his train to the city and stages a hysterical fit, we realize the extent to which the time of the railroad is bound up with the time of the city, infecting outlying communities with its tyrannical rule.[65] In other words, the suburb was not a dependable therapy or "cure" for the city.

Against its own self-promotion, the railroad was seen by many as part of the problem. Much antimodernist sentiment came to focus on whether an elevated railroad or a subway could alleviate the horrid traffic conditions of the nineteenth-century metropolis. Although in most large Western cities few people disagreed that something had to be done, the methods proposed by progressives, namely, allowing the city space to be penetrated by trains, generated passionate debate.[66] Alan Trachtenberg notes how the antimodernist

novelist William Dean Howells was troubled by the prospect of a technologized world that would "mechanize" morality: "Viewing New York City from an elevated car, Basil March in Howells' *A Hazard of New Fortunes* (1890) has a sudden perception of a 'lawless, godless' world, 'the absence of intelligent, comprehensive purpose in the huge disorder.' "[67]

Both the elevated and the underground railroad inspired such reactions. In Paris and New York, city dwellers feared that asphyxiation, disease, and death would result from an underground system, and they dreaded both the damage to the aesthetics of the city and the danger to pedestrians and property that an elevated railway would bring.[68] London, the first city with a subway system (1863), also encountered resistance when its underground was proposed in the 1850s. Paris refused the elevated in all but a few experiments (*La Petite ceinture*), while New York experimented with the elevated for more than twenty years before finally rejecting it as not only unsightly and unsafe, but impractical as a means of alleviating traffic problems. Both New York and Paris debuted their subways only in 1900.[69]

Well after the establishment of the subway and the elevated, antimodernist sentiment persisted, focusing on the destruction of the old city and its traditional values and aesthetics. A vivid trope often employed by antimodernists was the image of a violated Caucasian woman, which represented the threat posed by progress to both beauty and the past. In two late nineteenth-century French caricatures, the violated woman is shown as an allegorical figure of the city of Paris overrun with little trains.[70] An emblem of the reaction against the domination of the city by urban transportation, notably a proposed elevated railroad, the classicized woman in one of the cartoons is immobilized, indeed paralyzed, by the tiny trains, which are called "rats" in the cartoon. The "rats" crawl all over her monumental body, and threaten in particular her chastity; one train, for example, is posed like a dog trying to climb up her leg and under the waistline of her blouse.

The allegorical image of a woman threatened by the railroad also appeared in the New York press. A turn-of-the-century political cartoon shows a young woman strapped to the back of an "iron hobby horse" that is galloping down the tracks of an "El," or elevated railway.[71] In this parody of the Rape of Europa, the woman is bound with straps that read "6th Ave. Elevated Ry." A banner doubling as the horse's tail reads, "Individuals Have no Rights that

23. *The Suburbanite*, American Mutoscope & Biograph Co., 1904. Library of Congress.

Corporations are bound to Respect," while the buildings lining the tracks exhibit signs announcing, "To Be Sold for Taxes," "To Let," "For Sale on Account of the Noise," "Vacant," and "To Let—All the Inmates having been sent to the Insane Asylum." Clearly, the decline in the standard of living, not to mention property values, brought on by the intervention of the railroad straight through the heart of the city was received as something like a rape or violation, a physical aggression. In this allegory of corporate versus individual power—a theme to be taken up in greater detail later in this chapter—loss of power was represented as loss of masculine potency, or as feminization—the world upside down.

Weighing the City in The Crowd *and* Man with a Movie Camera

To be for or against the city or modernity as such was no black-and-white matter; one could despise modernity, and be either reactionary or progressive, while enthusiasm for the city could align the progress it represented with either capitalism or socialism. The feminine connotations of urban-based culture could also be received very differently, as two city films made in the late 1920s illustrate. These two films engage different notions of modernity and its relative value, while both use the train as a crucial means of articulating the modern male subject and urban experience. King Vidor's *The Crowd*, made in the United States (1928), is in spirit and subject linked to the early twentieth-century antimodernist ethos, but with a twist. In the film, the weight of urban alienation and depersonalized progress is so oppressive that it nearly kills its subjects. The fact that it does not result in death, but, in a dramatic turn of events, ends in a form of embrace, marks the film's approach to modernity as modern in a more capitalistic sense. Dziga Vertov's *Man with a Movie Camera*, on the other hand, made in the Soviet Union in 1928–29, is an avant-garde film set in the city that features railroad transport as a vehicle of modernity in order to celebrate progress in a more socialist, and certainly more experimental and creative, sense. By that decade, New York had come to symbolize all that was modern (and urban) in the United States, while in the nascent Soviet Union, Moscow, Leningrad, and other big cities acted as engines of opportunity driving the vast rural economy toward the future.

Analysis of these two films will shed light on a range of cinematic responses to an urban modernity in which trains played a crucial articulating role and permit us to appreciate the complexity of that role as it operates in specific film texts. Resuming the thread of this book as it points from early cinema to the twenties, these two films also bring together a number of themes and techniques identified in earlier films in both the United States and Europe. Both analyses will be framed by larger discussions of the cultural contexts that are important for understanding the particular significance of the train in each film, including the emphasis on consumption in *The Crowd* versus the focus on production in *Man with a Movie Camera*.

The City, the Train, and The Crowd

King Vidor's *The Crowd* (MGM, 1928) is a remarkable portrait of urban alienation in the United States of the 1920s — remarkable not only for its incorporation of some of the central social issues of its decade, but also for the extent to which these themes are embedded in the paradigm of modern, urban transportation, particularly the train. For my purposes, the film's primary relevance is thematic and narrative. *The Crowd* is largely a straightforward classical film, with some exceptional visual moments that distinguish its aesthetic as quasi-European (meaning German and French: the forced perspective of a few carefully composed shots, and the associationist montage that uses superimposition to express psychological states).

Vidor's film updates the rube-in-the-city film of early cinema and complicates its social premise to make the rube stand for the individual in modern society. Many of the great themes of the city identified so far — the loss of autonomy, the confusion of gender, new relations between work and leisure, the emergence of a new professional middle class, transportation, and deception with respect to identity — all come together in the film around one of the great sociological facts of modern society: the crowd, or the masses.

The Crowd is the story of a man who arrives in New York from a small town to "make his mark," only to lose his identity to the crowd and the city that throw up obstacles to the expression of his individuality.[72] John Sims (played by James Murray) is born in a generic American small town on July 4, 1900, an event heralded by his proud father's predictions of "great things" for his son. Twelve years later, as John boasts to his playmates of his own bright future, an ambulance pulls up to his house and a crowd gathers. John runs inside and to the top of the staircase, which is represented in Expressionist-style forced perspective, and hears the news of his father's unexpected death. Frozen on the landing with a crowd milling at the bottom of the stairs, the terrified John is told he will now have to be the "man of the house."

These early sequences set up the basic conflict of the film: the struggle of the individual to distinguish himself from the crowd, and even the nation, as his July 4 birthday reminds us doubly of the typicality of this American story and of the uniqueness to which John can aspire only with difficulty. The shot of John at the top of the stairs with the crowd at the bottom vividly illustrates the anxiety attached to this conflict; John's distinction from the crowd, both visually and narratively, has tragic overtones. The precariousness of John's position, which is underscored by the almost bird's-eye camera angle that makes it appear he is about to fall, strongly connotes the instability of point of view established by the narrative. But more importantly, perhaps, these sequences define the individual's struggle as a family romance, an Oedipal story to be allegorized on a larger social and national scale: John's later attempts to succeed are attempts to fulfill his father's wishes, to be the father, the man of the house, to wear "the mantle of patriarchal responsibility."[73] Thus will the "crowd" come to represent a crisis of paternal authority, a search for the position of the father.

Years after the father's death, after John has settled into New York City and tried without success to "make something of himself," his inability to submit fully to the force of modern life (the crowd) comes to a critical climax around his own perceived failure to be both a literal and figurative father (and husband) — in short, a patriarch.[74] The crisis of patriarchy is a crisis in confrontation of traditional with modern forms of authority. Paternal authority can hold sway only in the small town; in the metropolis, the crowd, which represents mass culture and consumerism, is the ultimate arbiter of values — one that demands unquestioning, even hypnotic, obedience.[75]

Crowds, Hypnosis, and the Subject

Vidor's representation of the crowd owes not a little to the crowd psychology of his day as well as to earlier attempts to characterize the masses and theorize about them. To grasp something of what Vidor's film implies for the hypnotic effects of the urban crowd on the male subject, I want to expand on the antimodernist attitude toward mass culture touched on earlier and the implications of that attitude for a greater psychological understanding of the crowd. This discussion will point to some of the most fascinating, yet least illuminated aspects of *The Crowd* as a train film.

The eponymous subject of Vidor's film is a quintessentially urban phenomenon, as seen in writings by Baudelaire and Poe, who were among the first to register the crowd as a distinctly modern entity.[76] Crowd psychology proper began with Gustave Le Bon's 1895 study, *The Crowd*, born at roughly the same time as the discipline of sociology, which also sought to explain mass behavior. Le Bon's work emphasized the subordination of the individual's conscious personality, and individual desires and values, to the "collective mind" of the crowd.[77] Accordingly, in a crowd, the collective or "herd" instincts dominate, particularly if the crowd has a leader.

For Le Bon, the individual in a crowd is like a hypnotized subject, in that "all feelings and thoughts are bent in the direction determined by the hypnotiser."[78] The individual behaves unconsciously, and irrationally, and is susceptible to suggestion, particularly when images are involved. Because of its inherent "suggestibility," as well as its character of impulsiveness, mobility, and irritability, Le Bon disdainfully considered the crowd to be like a woman.[79] Le Bon's perspective clearly resonates with the antimodernist fear of the feminizing effects of mass culture, whose shocks were thought to weaken the individual, whether, in sociological terms (the fragmented, no longer autonomous individual), or in medical terms (the nerve-racked, unstable urbanite).[80]

Le Bon's work was important to Freud's own theorization of the crowd, *Group Psychology and the Analysis of the Ego*, published in 1921.[81] But in analyzing crowd psychology, Freud wanted to go beyond the notion of "suggestion," which he felt explained nothing. Instead, he sought to explain "suggestion" in psychoanalytic terms. He saw the group relation to the leader and relations within the group as libidinal in nature and rooted in the primal love object relation that forms the basis for identification. Identification with the leader and with other members of the group involves the desire to be or to be like the other person, the Other. This identification within the group is emotional and, finally, erotic in nature.[82]

"From being in love to hypnosis," wrote Freud, "is only a short step."[83] The hypnotist enjoys the same idealized position, above reproach, as does the group leader/love object, and he becomes the *only* object for the subject. Since hypnosis is "a group formation with two members," it forms a paradigm of group psychology.[84] The comparison with the state of being in love evolves into something more complex, and more deeply rooted in the unconscious.

Freud ultimately derives the group, and hypnosis, from the primal horde in which the "dreaded primal father," the group ideal, satisfies the group's extreme passion for authority hypnotically, via an erotic, libidinal bond. This bond is where Freud locates "suggestion."[85]

Hypnosis, love, the crowd, and suggestibility are all concepts that have meaning in relation to cinema generally, and to *The Crowd* specifically. In film theory Raymond Bellour's work comparing cinema and hypnosis is well known.[86] Bellour suggests a fundamental similarity between the kind of subject or spectator articulated by the whole hypnotic apparatus and that of the cinema. He draws on Freud's metapsychology of the subject and Lawrence Kubie's metapsychology of hypnosis.[87] The hypnotic situation, according to both Freud and Kubie, requires an operation, a stimulus-apparatus to achieve it, a "suggestible" subject, proper conditions for encouraging suggestibility in the subject, and a "director" to stage the operation. Accordingly, the hypnosis proceeds via induction through the voice and/or a hypnotic object (a pendulum, a shiny object), each monotonous and rhythmic. The suggestible subject is put in a situation of immobility or a sort of somnambulism, while the hypnotist "director" who serves as a point of identification for the subject is an ideal Ego.[88]

The cinema is like a hypnotic apparatus insofar as it presupposes many of these components: a suggestible subject, an apparatus that entails physical immobility, vision as the means of seduction, and psychic regression, meaning that the borders of the ego relax with respect to identification with the camera, the fiction, and the apparatus itself, such that the cinema becomes for the subject a "hypnotist function."[89] (In narrative cinema, storytelling as a kind of narcotic inducement to fantasy redoubles the hypnotic effect in the spectator.)[90] The link with identification is crucial and rests on a body of theory produced in the 1970s around psychoanalysis and cinema. In brief, this theory found fault with a standard premise about identification—that as a process, identification occurred around stars and characters, as in "identifying with" a particular actor or character. Instead, Christian Metz compared the film spectator to an infant caught up in what Lacan called the Mirror Phase, a stage of psychic development—the Imaginary—in which the infant identifies with his/her image, as in a mirror.[91] This image does not depend on a literal mirror; the mother, for example, is the Ideal ego that the infant relates to as a subject. The point is that the scenario of a whole (hence imaginary) subjectivity takes place as an act of vision—Metz accents the "image" in Imaginary. In terms of

cinema, then, Metz posits an Imaginary and immobile spectator whose psychic regression to the Mirror Phase causes him/her to identify first and foremost with the look, and thus with the act of *looking*. This kind of primary
identification is then an identification with the camera—a proxy for the infant's gaze. Although the infant lacks motor mastery, it can imagine itself as
whole because it sees itself as whole. All secondary identification in cinema—
with characters and stars—thus presupposes a subject who is flattered as a
whole subject, one who literally sees all.[92]

Bellour considers the cinematic spectator to be fundamentally a hypnotized, suggestible subject.[93] His case rests on the analogy to the Imaginary, on
unconscious regression, and on the physical conditions of the exhibition of
film in which an immobile subject sits in the dark, focused on an image produced by a shiny point of light. Earlier and somewhat similarly, Hugo Munsterberg saw "suggestibility" as a fundamental trait of the film spectator,
whom he compared to a person under hypnosis. In discussing the role of
memory and imagination in the viewer's construction of meaning in film,
Munsterberg noted that the mental process of suggestion is similar to the
mind's reaction to a play or film, ascribing greater efficacy to the film: "The
spellbound audience in a theater or in a picture house is certainly in a state of
heightened suggestibility and is ready to receive suggestions. . . . The drama
as well as the photoplay suggests to the mind of the spectator that this is more
than mere play, that it is life which we witness. But if we go further . . . we
cannot overlook the fact that the theater is extremely limited in its means."[94]
Munsterberg also related suggestibility to neurasthenia, stating that "neurasthenic persons are especially inclined to experience touch or temperature or
smell or sound impressions from what they see on the screen. The associations
become as vivid as realities because the mind is so completely given up to the
moving pictures."[95]

The train presents some of the same conditions that give rise to suggestibility in the cinema: the rocking of the body as a kind of pendulum effect;
the monotony of the stimulus (the movement of the train); the presence of a
view and the dominance of the visual sense; and the hybrid state that makes
the subject simultaneously immobile and in motion, passive and active: seated,
the passenger is in perpetual motion and spatial displacement in relation to the
world outside, which makes it the perfect metaphor for the "transport" of the
subject in both cinema and hypnosis. This is the conjunction of *state* and *process*
that Kubie describes as characteristic of the hypnotized subject.[96] Put another

way, the physical conditions of train travel induce the sleepy state considered necessary to the ideal condition of suggestibility and the preparation of the body for its transport into dreams.[97]

The presence of the crowd in conditions of regression, of a state of near-sleep, and thus of heightened suggestibility in the train and the cinema, creates a situation that encourages fantasy and the lowering of inhibitions. One might say, following Freud, that the crowd encourages "an intensification of affect" — an aspect of what he called the "herd instinct" — such that the relaxing of the boundaries of the ego entails a pleasure that derives from identification with others as the Other.[98]

Though "hypnotized" is too literal a term to characterize the subjectivity of even the classical film's spectator, "suggestible" may be more to the point. Hypnosis provides us with a visually based analogy for exploring the means by which passengers, spectators, and consumers are constituted in relation to historically specific practices. In *The Crowd*, hypnosis functions globally and metaphorically as a kind of generalized discourse that addresses members of the crowd through mass media, entertainment, and transportation. The notion that the railroad could play a role in such behavior is something *The Crowd* sets in motion a decade before Hitchcock would make literal use of the idea in *The Lady Vanishes* (1938).

The Train and the Suggestible Subject

In a straightforward sense, the train appears in *The Crowd* as both an urban and interurban vehicle representing larger forces of mass society that control the individual. The train's primary significance is twofold: it is both an agent of social integration and a device of social and individual disintegration, of destruction of the self — particularly the male self; it also shows the way in which the film offers characters a path between the links that join the train and cinema through socially and filmically relevant discourses of the 1920s — namely, advertising and the new consumerism. What links these discourses both theoretically and narratively in the film is a subject (a passenger-consumer) and a rhetoric — techniques for persuading that subject to make use of the imaginary suggested by each discourse.

Trains in *The Crowd* appear first as part of a great chain of transportation in which public transport brings strangers together at random and creates coupling narratives as if by chance. This chain is constructed in four main sequences. As with many of the "romances of the rails" of early cinema, the train here plays a significant role in motivating the couple to come together.

John Sims sets out for New York at age twenty-one. His first encounter with the city is visual; he views its magnificent skyline from aboard a ferry that takes him from New Jersey to New York. The ferry boat is here an important site, as it is a fantasy space of vision, a cinematic arena in which John "sees" or imagines *opportunity* — even if a title has already told us that he is just "one of seven million that believe New York depends on them." A fellow traveler tells John that he will have to be "really good" if he wants to "beat the crowd." The words are a portent that endows the ferry boat with a subsequent significance; later, John promises his wife that they will move up in the world when his *ship* comes in. Just as the ferry will quickly be replaced by more dynamic and less contemplative forms of transportation, so will John have to give up his fantasy metaphor and confront the train and its urban proxies as his reality — and the symbolic measure of his success.

After this "boat entry" sequence, a montage of documentary city views that highlight transportation — buses, cars, the elevated railroad — takes us via an elaborate tracking shot into the office building where John works. John has become an accountant, one of many who work in a huge office at identical desks arranged in a grid pattern visible from the extreme high-angle camera that tracks in on him. His anonymity is underscored by both the scale of the shot, which highlights the sheer *number* of other corporate clones, and the number that occupies the place of a name tag on his desk: 137.

John's pal Bert (Bert Roach) invites him after work on a double date to Coney Island with Bert's girlfriend, Jane (Estelle Clark), and her friend Mary (Eleanor Boardman). Climbing to the second level of a double-decker bus, John follows Mary up the steps and suddenly notices her legs, a sensation marked for the spectator by the angle of the camera and its placement as his point of view. It is clear that even though he is only copying Bert's behavior (and point of view), John's desire stirs for the first time. The birth of his sexual desire in relation to this urban vehicle takes on a literal dimension when the two of them take their seats together and thereby position themselves as a couple. What is important about this coupling is that the top level of the bus is in the open air; John and Mary sit as tourists, as spectators watching the city and its crowds. Their coupling, then, is initiated in relation to a view, specifically of the city-as-spectacle (a sort of diorama where the spectators move and the view alters accordingly) and in relation to urban movement. As such, the city is linked with the carnival of the following sequence, and the practice of cinemagoing as an urban and romantic practice — which is a practice of the (primarily visual) "power of suggestion." The coupling of vision and transportation in this manner again reinforces the link between the train and the cinema, while the association of romance with a view, with spectacle, links this sequence with the boat entry sequence that expressed fantasy in visual terms.

At Coney Island the two couples are seen chiefly in motion. Vidor constructs a montage of carnival rides that shows the four turning and swaying in the wild movements of the roller coaster and other mechanical rides (photo 24). The last ride in the montage is the Tunnel of Love, where John and Mary kiss for the first time. The logic of the sequence is clear: love and desire require motion, displacement, instability, indeed vertigo, before becoming channeled (literally, in the case of the "love canal" of the ride) into the heterosexual couple. In the context of the film as a whole, love is represented as a social ritual that millions are programmed by and for; the tunnel of love is part of a machine of romance, of the social codification of desire in relation to the masses, the crowd.[99]

The narrative "motive" of the city bus and Coney Island images becomes manifest in the final segment of the sequence, when the two couples ride the subway (or elevated railway) home that evening on what amounts to the last "ride." Worn out and packed into the middle of an equally tired-looking crowd of passengers, Mary dozes on John's shoulder. This is the "perfect" moment for John to propose marriage, with inspiration taken from an advertisement he sees on the train that beseeches its implied male reader: "You Provide the Girl, We'll Provide the Home" (a reference to a real estate development in New Jersey). Asleep, rocked hypnotically by the train, Mary "consents" to the "suggestion" made by John, whom she has met only that day. It is not only the metro train, but also the other forms of transport which John and Mary have taken all day that place the "suggestible" woman in a state of powerlessness, of psychic and moral subjection to the man — himself "suggested" by the advertisement, which becomes important later when considering John's general suggestibility and ultimate feminization.

Here, the hypnosis takes place through the movement of the body and the state of quasi-sleep (instead of through a shiny object) and in relation to a crowd, a mob of other couples (instead of a single figure). Mary's acceptance of John's proposal is undercut by the fact that she is half-asleep, half-conscious when she says "yes"; dreaming, she agrees to the proposal in order to placate

John and remain asleep. Yet as soon as she says "yes," she is shocked awake by her own voice, and her doubting face reads, "Wait a minute — did I say that?" This moment is one of the few in the film where Mary's reactions are given a space, or where a female point of view flashes forth, since the film's story is primarily told from John's point of view.

The mise-en-scène chain culminates in the next sequence showing John and Mary on their honeymoon. The consummation of the couple takes place on the honeymoon train from New York to Niagara Falls, the newlywed cliché par excellence. Terrified by the thought of what awaits them, and also by their naïveté, John and Mary wait until the last second before going to bed (photo 25). Prodded by a sleepy African American porter who keeps hinting he would like to draw the curtains to their "compartment," John and Mary timidly wander off to their respective restrooms to prepare themselves for bed.[100] As stereotypical newlyweds, John and Mary are one repeatable unit among a hundred others retiring behind dozens of identical compartment curtains.[101]

The identity of spaces confuses John when he returns from the men's room and fails to locate the proper compartment. A humorous sequence ensues in which John mistakenly enters "wrong" compartments and mistakes their occupants for Mary — in one case, a huge family packed like sardines against their obese mother, and in another a bearded man. In a very simple sense, one sees illustrated or acted out the destabilizing effects of the fear of female sexuality: the dissemination of identity across regression to infancy (the family — the big mother) and latent homosexuality (the bearded man). This confusion of identity is, of course, made possible by the train as a "joke space" of potential fiction and deception (along the lines of *The Deadwood Sleeper* and *Pullman Bride*); all the stories that lurk "behind the curtain" to some extent by chance.

What distinguishes these train sequences from those in earlier films in which the train is shown as a heterotopia of potential role reversals and deception is their link with other forms of representation specific to the growing consumer culture of the 1920s. Given the extent to which motives are supplied the main characters by advertising and self-help books while on moving vehicles, we might more properly refer to the train as a space of *suggestibility*, as much as a space of trickery (and, to some extent, one presupposes the other). This makes John himself a "subject" of hypnotism or rather of the advertising suggestion that prompts him to propose to Mary. Robert Lang notes in passing that the behavior of characters and the turn of events in *The Crowd* can be

24. Bert Roach, Estelle Clark, James Murray, and Eleanor Boardman in the
"Tunnel of Love," *The Crowd*, King Vidor, 1928. Museum of Modern Art.

explained in terms of the influence of the mass media.[102] But advertising specifically defines that influence.

The popular association of advertising with "suggestion" and even hypnosis can be traced to the 1920s, when advertisers began to practice their own
"pop psychology" on the public by shifting the emphasis in sales techniques
from the product to the consumer.[103] Advertising had already arisen as an
urban institution in the last third of the nineteenth century to ease the shift
from a production-oriented society to one based on consumption.[104] Lears's
studies of the emergence of consumer culture show how advertising in the
early twentieth century began to promise "self-realization through consumption" — i.e., therapy.[105]

But the 1920s heralded a qualitative shift in the advertising industry itself.
Roland Marchand has drawn a detailed portrait of the two decades, the 1920s
and 1930s, in which the "personal tone" of advertising took hold, and advertisers began to think of themselves as "molders of the human mind and "consumption" or "psychological engineers."[106] Advertisers became concerned

25. Eleanor Boardman and James Murray on the honeymoon train in
The Crowd, King Vidor, 1928. Museum of Modern Art.

with the " 'mental processes of the consumer,' " targeting this consumer —
overwhelmingly female — as a tabloid reader, moviegoer, and radio listener.
"In a tone of scientific assurance," writes Marchand, "advertising leaders
of the 1920s and 1930s added that women possessed a 'well-authenticated
greater emotionality' and a 'natural inferiority complex.' "[107] Their presumed
emotional nature required that advertisements be pitched in emotional terms.
In the advertisers' view, as the primary targets of new advertising techniques,
women were in need of professional experts to guide — and persuade — them
on how to live life in the modern world that advertising was helping to
create.[108]

   According to Marchand, advertisers studied with "bemused contempt"
the lowest common denominator of both sexes, and they determined that it
could be influenced emotionally through techniques that addressed both a
limited mental development (advertisers' estimates of the average mental age
of the American citizen ranged from nine to sixteen) and the unmet needs of
a dislocated, mobile, predominantly urban population. They placed an un-

precedented emphasis on color and the *visual*, while developing "scare copy" (which played to the "inferiority complex" that all people were presumed to have), conversational copy (providing a "pseudo-*Gemeinschaft*"), and confessional ads (based on true-story magazine rhetoric). All were designed to gain the intimate confidence of a public cut off from traditional sources of advice and authority—the same urban crowd that was already the target of the "therapy" industry to which the railroads contributed.[109] In Marchand's words:

> Advertisers gradually recognized, consciously or subconsciously, that the complexities of an increasingly urbanized, specialized, interdependent mode of life were creating a residue of unmet needs. Perceiving new vacuums of guidance and personal relationships, they stepped forward to offer their products as answers to modern discontents. Thus, what made advertising "modern" was, ironically, the discovery by these "apostles of modernity" of techniques for empathizing with the public's imperfect acceptance of modernity, with its resistance to the perfect rationalization and bureaucratization of life."[110]

Among other things, advertisers saw their techniques as ways of helping their urban-based consumer cope with neurasthenia by pushing products that strengthened the nerves and made the consumer better able to keep up with the hectic pace of modern life. The basic premise was always that of "social therapy," expert advice on every conceivable subject. In short, advertisers, or their narrator-delegates in advertising copy and images, came to fill the shoes of trusted authorities such as priests or doctors (medical authority earlier had proved to be an effective technique in the shift to consumer-oriented advertising).[111]

These ersatz doctors were also seducers, or, in a social/psychological sense, hypnotists. The analogy with hypnotism is clear: the professional "molders of the human mind" were expert authority figures who, like the hypnotist and the leader of the group, attempted to persuade and "suggest" a primarily female subject by emotional, irrational, and, in psychoanalytic terms, unconscious means that played to the subject's desire.[112] "Suggestion" in advertising is *seduction;* and if it succeeds, it seduces both men and women.

John's main motives and desires, for example, are suggested by advertising texts planted throughout the film. Advertising is overall a thematic and narrative core of *The Crowd*, one that is interwoven with the transportation chain to produce a larger text of "suggestibility." For example, advertising plays a key role in three of the four transportation segments in *The Crowd*. First, on the bus with Mary, the two laugh derisively at a clown wearing a sandwich board advertisement for shoes; John sneers, "I bet his father thought he'd be President!" Second, on the elevated railroad, John's proposal to Mary is prompted by the ad he notices; its inspirational character is made clear by the glance-object editing as well as by its text. And third, on the honeymoon train, John and Mary stall for time by leafing through a *Liberty* magazine. As the fatigued porter looks on, we see a page with an ad for Goodyear Tires that exhorts, "It's time to retire," with an image of a little boy yawning and holding a candle. Only moments before, John had shown Mary an ad in the same magazine for a real estate development, promising her "the home" when his "ship comes in."

In all of these examples, the glance-object editing implies a causal relationship between the stimulus of the advertisement and the effect of John's behavior. If, as many have observed since Marx first wrote about the secret language of commodities, advertising made products "speak" their own language, John could be said to be responding to the "call of the ad."[113] The texts he reads are so many exhortations, so many messages that address him personally ("you"). His responses effectively inscribe him in a dialogue with an unseen enunciator, and in a chain of consumerism that includes millions of other addressees. John is certainly "other-directed" in availing himself of advice offered in ads, in guidebooks, and by peers (his pal Bert). Besides the ads themselves, there is "What a Young Husband Ought to Know," the guidebook John consults in the men's room on the honeymoon train. For this he is mocked by two gentlemen reading newspapers in the lounge area of the bathroom, which only points up how uneasy and yet clichéd the notion of "self-help" was in 1928, especially on matters sexual.[114]

The direct solicitation — or one might say interpellation — by advertising in *The Crowd* corresponds to the consumer-oriented advertising techniques Marchand sees as typical of the 1920s.[115] John and Mary in some ways personify the new consumer identified by Lary May in post-World War I American film. May charts the development of a truly modern, consumerist ethic that breaks with Victorianism in the work of Cecil B. DeMille, whose films link marital bliss with high-level consumption of goods and entertainment and, crucially, with romantic sexuality (which was located outside the family in premodern and more prurient times).[116] Sumiko Higashi characterizes the heroines of DeMille's sex comedies and melodramas: "A symbol of the con-

sumer culture, the 'new woman' was no longer a thrift-conscious and re-
sourceful housewife but a fashion plate who embodied market forces invading
the privatized domestic sphere."[117] In such films as *Old Wives for New* (1918)
and *Forbidden Fruit* (1921), DeMille worked out a consumerist ethic that legitimated sensuality as a "foreign" desire to be integrated into the married couple's lives and sustained with spending. The lesson that restive husbands and
wives were made to learn over and over was that "fun and sex can actually
strengthen marriage," and both can be purchased.[118]

The Crowd begins with the ideal of marriage as fun and romance and the
consumerist premise of the times.[119] Yet it also shows up the ideal for what it
is — often no more than a fantasy — while situating its characters, within a
solidly middle- (even lower-middle) class milieu. Still, though more realistic
and ironic than DeMille's movies, Vidor's film in the end tacitly supports the
consumerist culture that advertising — and cinema — legitimate.

What is significant is that the cues and clues the world gives to John
through advertising and other modes of communication are primarily visual.
As Louis Wirth noted of "urbanism as a way of life" in 1938, "a premium is
placed in the urban world on visual recognition" as a means of communication, since the alienation of individuals from each other in the city is so great,
communication must take place indirectly through media and delegation of
one's interests.[120] "Visual recognition" is the form of communication through
which advertising exerts its rhetorical power over consumers; it is also cinema's.[121] In John's case, the addressee is male; his desires count for the adver-
tiser in the text, and his perceived problem in identifying himself as masculine
is what advertising addresses. This ironically comes to mean that John must be
addressed — "seduced" — as a *female* consumer. As we will see, the very urban,
consumerist culture created by the railroad, cinema, and advertising — vehicles of the feminizing crowd — is what deprives John of the certainty of his
gender and makes him vulnerable to the image, that is, vulnerable to advertising and, ultimately, to cinema.

Transportation and Alienation

Beyond its function as social adhesive and platform for the messages of mass
culture, the train plays an equally important role in a second, more disintegrationist chain of transport that includes other kinds of vehicles. This chain of
transportation oppresses the individual and as such comes to figure the crowd

as an oppressive power. As an emblem of urban, mass fate, of a force so much bigger than the individual that its indifference overwhelms him or her, the train signifies a ground of unstable identity in a much more negative sense than that of the "joke" space. It does so in three principal sequences.

The first is a sequence directly following the honeymoon. While Mary is busy cooking in their tiny railroad flat, John strums a ukelele and gaily, if ironically, croons "Wife and I are happy/And everything is well/It is heavenly inside our flat/But outside it is El." The pun is on the elevated metro that we see in a shot from inside the flat looking out the window. The proximity to the elevated, and the equation of the "El" with "Hell," recalls the turn-of-the-century caricature showing the feminine figure of Europa strapped to the iron horse. The El is not merely "outside"; its intrusive presence in John and Mary's private space dramatizes the extent to which modern mass humans are deautonomized by forces beyond their control. Lang refers to the El as "the inhospitable outside world that cannot be wished away but which can be tolerated."[122] Indeed, because of the lack of *space*—and the lack of money to increase it—"inside" is not all that heavenly; John and Mary crowd each other and bicker constantly, especially when the unpleasant in-laws (Mary's mother and two brothers) come to visit. Although the train is here in the background, it bears an all-determining force that inspires nostalgia for the pre-railroad era (and for the nuclear family as a haven in a heartless world).

The next link in the chain of social oppressiveness is the truck that accidentally runs down John and Mary's three-year-old daughter and that can be considered a delegate for the train as a vehicle associated with the insensitivity and unintelligibility of the city—i.e., with Hell. Bored at his accounting job, John dreams up promotional jingles all day long, finally winning $500 in a contest. John rushes home with gifts for all. Ecstatic, he and Mary wave toys out the window to their son and daughter playing across the street. The parents then witness the death of the girl, who is hit suddenly while trying to cross the street, following the fatal lure of consumption—almost as a punishment for John's easy money. A crowd immediately gathers, but no one does anything to help until John implores someone to call a doctor. The absolute impersonality and indifference of the crowd, associated with this chance (therefore meaningless) death, is further magnified when John, grief-stricken, wanders the street begging people to be quiet, as his daughter is dying. He attempts to stop traffic, which prompts a policeman to escort him home with the chastisement, "You can't expect the world to stop because your baby's sick." Here the individual is powerless to control his life and feelings. This is the mirror opposite of the crowd that gathers in the home when John's father dies; in a small town, one can expect the world to stop for a moment when an unexpected death occurs. Urban transport — whether rail or motor — is identified with the cruelty of mass society and its indifference to individual expression, while it asserts the primacy of the machine over the human body as expressed very simply by traffic.

The moral of the story is in one sense that money not earned, not worked for, but won too easily demands some kind of punishment. The daughter's death sends John into a massive depression, an almost somnambulant delirium with hysterical symptoms in reaction to the trauma. At the office, John is paralyzed by thoughts of his daughter. The film represents this grief as a series of hallucinations, psychic projections in superimposition of the truck running over the little girl. As in *Asleep at the Switch*, John's somnambulant state is replete with its own masochistic repetition compulsion, the endless repetition of the incident as a rehearsal of impotence and guilt. John's listlessness and resentment of the world lead to his being fired, and they prevent him from holding a steady job. As such, the shock of the death induces in John symptoms akin to hysterical ones (including a semicatatonia).

John's depression comes to a climax at the railroad tracks, the third sequence in the chain. Mary has now been forced to work as a seamstress to make ends meet. Angry at John for his lack of motivation, she turns him out. Followed by his little son, John sets off for a bridge spanning the railroad tracks. The cliché of what Emile Durkheim referred to as "anomic suicide" is set in motion as John stares down at the tracks at an oncoming train — the symmetrical narrative reply to the daughter in the path of the truck.[123] Intercut with the rapidly approaching train, John climbs over the rail and peers down, but he is unable to leap. He continues walking and catches up with the son, who, completely unaware that his father was about to kill himself, announces gleefully that he would like to grow up to be just like his dad.

The son's desire becomes the stimulus to refound paternity, John's masculine identity as opposed to his emasculated one. Reborn, John takes the son by the hand and promptly goes off to find work as a clown-juggler wearing an advertising placard, the only job available to him, and the first he finds after a series of unsuccessful and uninspired efforts at door-to-door salesmanship. Lang sees the entire film as John's struggle to achieve "masculinity," i.e., to define himself as an individual and "beat the crowd."[124] This sequence makes it clear that masculinity is still an essential component of the family in the post-Father age, as well as being the stake of redemption.

In terms of the effects, both direct and indirect, of the railroad on the man, John Sims is the 1920s heir to the Uncle Josh hysteric and neurasthenic. Though hysteria may not be clinically accurate to describe John's distress, the convergence of symptoms and what I referred to earlier as the process of perceived feminization and/or emasculation support a sense of continuity with the urban nineteenth century. As with the hysterics of early cinema, John's breakdown effectively deprives him of his masculinity. His emasculation is played out as a role reversal; when he remains jobless, his wife works (albeit in a "woman's" job, sewing). His manhood is revived upon seeing his son, the token of his heterosexual potency. Submission to the train would have prostrated and violated him like the proverbial woman tied to the tracks. Not having control of one's destiny, the central experience of the crowded city, and the great signified of corporate-defined modernity, is tantamount to not having one's masculinity.[125] In terms of gender, John's status as a spectator-consumer — someone whose identity is shaped by the visual texts and urban experiences of modern culture — takes us back to Uncle Josh and to the suspicion that gender in cinema, advertising, and the railroad is inherently unstable. (It may well be that feminization — through submission to the crowd/the father/the culture industry — is the condition of all spectators, but I would argue that fluidity is more to the point.)

In the chain of transport associated with tragedy, with suicide, the train is a figure of the *social* — the social as an oppressive force and an urban "El." The juxtaposition of the individual (John) with the train underscores the sense in which the train is not only a vehicle of mass society, but a symbol of the crowd. To fight its power is fatal, as is unblinking submission; but to accept its premise and assimilate oneself to it is to succeed — hence, the redemptive ending. As such, the train figures an impersonal, mechanical authority that supersedes and replaces symbolically, traditional paternal authority. Indeed, the death of John's father early in the film is a parable of the death of the Father in modernity, a death mourned all the more (by the film) in relation to John's dreadful mother-in-law, whom he despises almost as much as she despises him.[126] If the choice is between a good but dead patriarch and an unpleasant but living matriarch (consistent with the "feminization of culture"), the film seems to be saying, then modernization has much for which to atone. The mother-in-law represents an emblem of the price to be paid in a world that has left traditional, paternal authority far behind.

The young John unable to cope with the responsibility brought on by the father's death parallels the twenty-one-year-old John unable to cope with the demands and responsibilities of work and family life in the city. A different set of demands produces different structures for negotiating them: professionals, peers, guidebooks, advertisements, the consumerist life-style — all of which arise to fill, therapeutically, the void left by the death of paternal authority. "As ancestral authority grew culturally or geographically remote," writes Lears, "advertisements replaced it with a merger of corporate and therapeutic authority — but often in pseudo-traditional guise."[127] The train in *The Crowd* encompasses these shifts by virtue of its omnipresence; it is everywhere in the film, just as it is everywhere in the modern city. With the status of fate or destiny (even Hell) on its side, the train effectively sums up the truism that the tide of progress cannot be turned; it commands assimilation to its ethic, its mode of perceiving, and the life-style with which it is inextricably linked as an economic motor. The hysterical, neurasthenic male subjects it molds are the underside of the success it promises — an underside that threatens to burst the fragile modern ego with all the force of uncodifiable resentment.

Vidor's story of a family man gone wrong, to be righted in relation to both his son and public spectacle, strongly recalls Griffith's *The Drunkard's Reformation* (1909). In that film, an alcoholic father is rehabilitated when he "sees the light" at a theatrical production of an antialcohol morality play that is also an allegory of the newly respectable and moral cinema. But *The Crowd* is far from the Victorian moralizing of Griffith's film. Vidor's family falls apart from stress, competition, and claustrophobia; mass society leads the man to drink. In Griffith's film, the family collapses from alcoholism, a character defect. Vidor's couple fights over mundane details: a broken bathroom door, burnt toast, a cramped apartment, money; Griffith's couple fights over moral do's and don't's. And as far as trains are concerned, they act in *The Crowd* as complex social spaces and obtrusive presences, while in Griffith films like *The Lonedale Operator*, they are heroic agents or victimized objects. If for both filmmakers the train is significantly bound up with the social body, Vidor suggests a much more negative reading consistent with the theme of urban alienation.

Yet John ultimately learns how to cope with modern urban life, with its crushing anonymity, by learning how to consume — i.e., to conform. Thus, early in the film he scoffs at the sandwich ad clown, but in the end he becomes one himself, after family and job have fallen apart. In other words, John integrates himself into the crowd by literally becoming the advertisement — the sandwich board that advertises a restaurant chain.

At the film's conclusion, the restabilized Sims family as integrated units in the huge audience/crowd cheerfully watches a vaudeville show. A man seated next to John opens his program and sees the "Sleight O' Hand" ad for which John had written the jingle and which is accompanied by an image of a clown; John proudly points out that he authored it, thus identifying with its values and with its generic nature. Here happiness is acceptance of being part of the crowd — to be the same as everyone else — and not to stand out from the crowd; happiness is being a consumer.[128] Although, as Miriam Hansen maintains, the ending cannot entirely overcome the ambivalence established by earlier sequences, the advertising here functions, again, as a medium of communication, redemptively enabling John to enter into dialogue with a stranger, a member of the crowd; its socially adhesive effects could not be more clearly illustrated.[129] The family's integrative functions pale in significance as its importance as part of a bigger unit (the crowd) grows. This is shown in the film's final shot: the camera tracks out from John and the stranger with the program to reveal, gradually, a larger and larger crowd, a mirror of the audience watching the film. This shot effectively doubles and responds to the extreme high-angle track-in on John's building and office at the beginning of the film; it offers itself as a cinematic resolution to the problem of "the crowd."

The perfect integration of "suggestions" from two media — theater and advertising — puts this final scene on a continuum with the train and cinema. With the theater and advertising acting as its proxies, the cinema finds its own bid for an audience reflected in the twin paradigms of mass transit and advertising; both are infected by suggestibility (or persuasion), by visual fields of transmission, and both define a mass audience. As two "seeing machines" that charge their consumers-passengers-spectators to see in perceptually and ideologically particular ways, both the train and the cinema can be situated in the same theoretical space vis-à-vis the modes of constituting their spectators. For John as a modern subject, regardless of gender, *is* constituted by the texts of modern urban culture; his identity *as* a man is one of appearance, constructed in relation to visual representation and a highly fluid, nontraditional platform for representation. In the end, the vaudeville/cinema spectacle is the culmination and summation of what the "space of suggestibility" implies about social integration and its accomplishment through images. Advertising is the bridge joining the railroad and the cinema in *The Crowd*, a bridge across which the spectator moves in a chain of displacement; she or he invests the same desire in each, and each poses its own problems of address and seduction, while each also premises that investment on visual consumption.

Dziga Vertov: Woman On the Track of the Avant-Garde

The Crowd uses the train to tell the neurasthenic's story — the lessons of the metropolis, the training in depersonalization, the assimilation to its force, the shift away from tradition, and the negotiation of masculinity in an age of multiple threats to its existence (active women, the pressures of overwork, speed, the clock, the crowd, the train). The train in Vidor's film functions as a potent mise-en-scène and symbol. Rather than wed the film to train vision as a function of film form, as in early train "thrill" films, *The Crowd* offers a paradigm for cinematic spectatorship in its *image*.

Dziga Vertov's *Man with a Movie Camera*, on the other hand, incorporates the train into the very fabric of its discourse as a metaphorical engine that drives the structures of perception and looking in the film. Unlike *The Crowd*, which basically falls within the classical paradigm, *Man with a Movie Camera* is an avant-garde film, one made with a deliberately unconventional style that often recalls the anarchy of early film.

Vertov does something quite different with the train from Vidor's approach. *Man with a Movie Camera* glories in the urban character of mass transit, reveling in the city and the railroad as part of a forward-looking vision. As a more or less classical Hollywood film in 1928, *The Crowd* tells one kind of city story, while *Man with a Movie Camera* is an experimental film telling a story based on a different set of cultural and historical circumstances at roughly the same time (1929). If *The Crowd* is heir to *Uncle Josh* and *The Photographer's Mishap*, *Man with a Movie Camera* is the descendant of the thrill film, the amusement park ride, and the Imagination of Disaster. And if *The Crowd* is concerned with male subjectivity, *Man with a Movie Camera* finds the female spectator a crucial — and problematic — part of its drive toward the future.

Man with a Movie Camera is one of the most celebrated avant-garde films in the history of cinema. Its representation of a particularly interesting moment in Soviet history, the late 1920s, combines revolutionary politics with a wildly inventive and experimental documentary style. Vertov's film is arguably the most experimental film to come out of the Russian avant-garde; it signals in hindsight one of the last great attempts to fashion a new form of filmic experience to correspond to the new Soviet society before the repressive hand of Stalin began to limit cultural production. The heroic status of *Man with a Movie Camera* has only grown since the twenties, influencing an entire generation of documentary and experimental narrative filmmakers in Europe in the 1960s. It is this heroism that has made the film difficult to criticize, since its innovative vision of Soviet society is so forward-looking and enthusiastic.

That *Man with a Movie Camera* is a "city film," as well as a "modernist film," is beyond dispute; this is indeed part of its aura. While the role of technology, of machines, is often honored in the critical literature on the film, what is much less noticed is that Vertov's film is about *trains*, or rather, that the train is one of the privileged machines in the film; even less noticed is that it is a film about *women*. What interests me about Vertov's film, however, is how it brings together several motifs of modernity and avant-garde experimentation — the city, the train, and machines in general — and weaves them together through the female body, using woman as a trope in the actual process of transforming her figurative power as an expression of social class and sexuality.

Man with a Movie Camera's point of view on women is double: it is divided between a critical and an affirmative perspective as well as between a feminine and a masculine voyeurism.[130] Underlying the organization of looking and point of view is the film's open acknowledgment of a fundamentally mechanical vision. In other words, all views are mediated by a mechanical apparatus, the camera, which is aligned with a technological paradigm that includes forms of transport — most notably the train — as well as machines of labor. At the same time, the placing of the female body within this technological paradigm produces a revolutionary heroine, a woman-machine equated with the modernist city as well. Vertovian woman is urban-mechanical, a fragmented yet harmonic blend of body, machine, and urban dynamism, at once distinguished from and of a pair with the bourgeois woman.

Woman, Machine, and Modernity

As an avant-garde Soviet film, *Man with a Movie Camera* is rooted in a type of filmmaking that was strongly influenced by avant-garde movements in the other arts. More than American cinema, Soviet film needs to be seen in the context of the artistic developments that affected filmmakers' aesthetic choices. This is especially true of an aesthetic based on the machine — an aesthetic that should be considered "urban."

For many early twentieth-century European avant-garde movements the machine occupied an important place in the theory and practice of aesthetic experimentation. "Machine aesthetics" varied from an interest in geometric forms and the breakup and dynamization of space begun with Paul Cézanne and continued with Cubism, to the bonding of organic to mechanical form in the creation of machine-bodies.[131] Various avant-gardes also seized on the link between the machine and the dislocation of modern life in appropriating the forces of transport and production for their own purposes. In Francis Picabia's *Entr'acte*, for example, the modernist spirit is fueled by the anarchy of mechanical speed in, among other things, a runaway roller coaster. Dadaists, Futurists, Cubo-Futurists, Simultaneists, Constructivists, Surrealists, Magic Realists; Fernand Léger, Kasimir Malevich, Marcel Duchamp, Max Ernst, Filippo Marinetti, Umberto Boccioni, Robert Delaunay, Naum Gabo, Oskar Schlemmer, Liubov Popova, and many others across Europe and the United States forcefully registered in their art the increasing mechanization of society and its subjects.

In early twentieth-century American art the paintings of Charles Sheeler, Charles Demuth, and Joseph Stella celebrated modernism in quasi-abstract paeans to technological progress. These three painters, known as Precisionists, depicted factories, railroad yards, steamships, and bridges with hard-edged, Cubist-inspired precision.[132] Stella's *Brooklyn Bridge* (1917–18) renders this technique dynamic, incorporating Futuristic "lines of force" to represent a quintessential emblem of New York City. Like Paul Strand, Alfred Stieglitz, and Edward Weston, photographers who in the teens and twenties aestheticized the industrial, railroad-defined zones of American metropolitan regions, these painters saw beauty in the large-scale technological and architectural fruits of corporate, urban modernism.[133]

The machine had certainly appeared earlier as a subject in modern art. Not surprisingly, the railroad apparatus (trains, tracks, signals, stations, roundhouses, etc.) was a recurrent image. As a speeding object incapable of being captured, frozen while in motion, the train was a specifically modern figure of the sublime that Romantic artists like J. M. W. Turner found so compelling, in paintings like *Rain, Steam and Speed — The Great Western Railway*. Edouard Manet, Camille Pissarro, Claude Monet, and other Impressionists and Post-Impressionists rendered the train and the train station as optical phenomena whose definition was precarious, though hardly sublime. As an omnipresent figure of modernity strongly associated with the urban centers of economic power it represented, the train provided modern artists with a suggestive surface for aesthetic experimentation, which increasingly incorporated the *mechanical* as a principle of style in twentieth-century avant-garde art.

The mechanical drive in avant-garde vision also singled out the female figure for a number of its experiments, and for widely divergent purposes. In both avant-garde discourse on the machine and mainstream concepts of "progress" and "modernity," woman has appeared as a figure of reflection, a topos of inscription of the conflicts and contradictions surrounding the modernization of late nineteenth- and early twentieth-century European culture and society.[134] In addition to the association of woman with mass culture, the hated Other of both traditional and modernist male culture, women and machines were often seen as belonging to two different paradigms: women to nature and the past, machines to technological progress. Similar to the narrative arguments summarized in chapter 1 with respect to *The General*, two kinds of history and two kinds of time became identified with one or the other gender: nonlinear, nondynamic, slow history and woman; linear, dynamic, future-oriented, accelerated history and man.[135] Just as in the antimodernist caricatures of the city and the railroad, women figure nature, civilization, and the past, while the train appears as a virile icon of progress, the machine that destroys everything in its path.

In ways not unrelated to the figuration of temporality and gender in *The General*, the juxtaposition of woman and machine in such views can be seen as a juxtaposition of two kinds of time. In the poetry of Baudelaire, woman was, among other things, a point of departure for another time and another world, a means of escaping time, the clock, in short, everything that would come to be regulated and standardized by the train and its schedules. In the prose poem "The Clock," Baudelaire speaks of this "vast, solemn hour, large like space, not divided into minutes or seconds, an immobile hour not marked on clocks," which he sees in the eyes of "la belle Féline," the "honor of her sex."[136] Female time is spatial, extending in all directions at once.[137]

A similar sense of time pervades the work of Giorgio de Chirico, where the past often appears as an inert, incoherent space weighted down with enigmatic frozen or dead figures, all impotent, frequently feminine. In such paintings as *Uncertainty of the Poet* and *Melancholy of Departure*, the twilight hour belongs to painting, to the atemporality of memory, the monument, the memorial, and, to the impotent, the feminine. The train appears in the background as progressive time materialized in the black line traversing the canvas. This horizontal axis is the axis of temporal linearity, of a troubling and anguishing emblem of the present and future.[138] The feminization and/or emasculation of everything the train displaces is expressed as the retreat of space, of particular spaces, before the trajectory of mechanical, male drive.

The bringing together of woman and machine meant something else entirely for Dadaist artists like Duchamp and Picabia. In such images as *The Passage from the Virgin to the Bride* and *The Large Glass* by Duchamp, and in *Amorous Display* and the *Udnie* series by Picabia, woman is reduced to a desiring machine designed to scandalize bourgeois morality. This wedding of woman and machine aimed to mock romantic love, to strip it down to a sexual function, a repetitive mechanism, by attacking a time-honored genre of academic painting, the nude. Picabia's love of racing cars notwithstanding, Dada's view of the machine was essentially ambivalent, if not sinister. Traumatized by World War I, the Dadaists viewed bourgeois control of technology as signifying destruction and enslavement.[139] At the same time, they were far from nurturing Romantic longings for primitive nature; Dada and Surrealism were firmly rooted in the city.

Fernand Léger, by contrast, celebrated the machine. His mechanized nude women in, for example, *Three Women* (1921), share none of Duchamp's irony.[140] Between Léger and Duchamp fall artists like Herbert Bayer, whose 1924 project for an exhibition pavilion at an industrial fair, which depicts a smiling woman's face filling the window of a Regina factory, draws on the desire to link woman and technology in the interest of advancing profit through a rhetoric of seduction, but not without a lurking sense of laughter.[141]

Probably no movement or single artist, however, celebrated the machine so affirmatively as did the Italian Futurists, though their legacy to the Russian avant-gardes is striking in this regard. The Futurist worship of the machine formed part of the exaltation of both speed and simultaneity of forms emblematized by F. T. Marinetti's "multiplied man" and celebrated in the paintings of Gino Severini, Giacomo Balla, Umberto Boccioni, and Carlo Carrà.[142] The train was included in this exaltation. Severini's *Suburban Train Arriving at Paris* is as forceful a statement of aggressive, urban dynamism as Futurism was able to make. The machine in general provided the paradigm of discipline and formal synthesis, of progress advancing beyond the moribund culture and society of prewar Europe and away from the past, from all that refused to be assimilated into the relentless charge toward the future.

This doctrine of burning bridges to history extended to the consideration of women. The well-known Futurist misogyny was summed up in one Marinetti essay, "Contempt for Women," where he advocated banishing women from the masculine world of speed, dynamism, and aggression.[143] Marinetti supported Suffragettes simply because he believed the incompetence of women in power would unwittingly hasten the demise of the parliamentary system, indeed of civilization, and hence further the cause of starting anew. Women, history, and the family, all were to be buried and steamrolled away by mechanical man. Temporally speaking, woman was history, time frozen, the past; hence, the significance of Marinetti's famous dictum, "A speeding automobile is more beautiful than the Victory of Samothrace." This forceful comparison between mechanical and female underscores the incompatibility of the sexes, the clash of worlds, and the Futurist race against organic culture, dead ancient time, and "woman" as a dying concept.

Yet, with Marinetti, woman represents a paradox bathed in ambivalence: she is as much a machine as she is bourgeois morality and romantic love. Consider, for example, Marinetti's references to the train. On the one hand, the train is an example of the cult of speed, of masculine power, an arm in the Futurists' antiwoman, anti-Romantic arsenal. They exploit the idea of mechanical as opposed to classical beauty in exalting "the love for the Machine that we have seen flaming in the cheeks of engineers, baked and soiled by charcoal. Have you never observed them when they lovingly wash the great body of their locomotive? This is the meticulous tenderness of a lover caressing his mistress."[144] In this configuration of sexual desire, the machine, the locomotive, displaces woman by becoming itself feminine, which places woman simultaneously at the margins and at the center of the masculine world — but as a machine.[145] In this respect it is not surprising that the Futurists recognized Émile Zola as a key precursor of Futurism.[146] One need think only of the detailed descriptions of the woman-train La Lison in *La Bête humaine*, who is a much more faithful mistress than flesh-and-blood woman.

It is this affective relation to the beloved machine that introduces a complexity into the gendering of the train. While the very image of the locomotive being driven by the engineer undoubtedly suggests a phallic reading — the train as an object under the control of a man — the locomotive was often endowed with feminine properties. This presents a paradox for gender definition, since the train can be invested with both male and female connotations and can be recoded endlessly in relation to a desiring subject, depending on who it is defined in relation to and for what purpose.

Thus, the attempt to banish woman from the Futurist scheme ends up reinstating her at its center. The harder Marinetti tries to purify his masculine vision, the dirtier it becomes with metaphors of female sexuality, as in the description of the locomotive as the engineer's "mistress." The metaphorical winds also blow in the other direction when Marinetti disparagingly refers to woman as an "engine of pleasure." These clumsy efforts to separate the sexes, and to further separate them with respect to the machine, illuminate what Jacques Derrida sees as the basic figurative character of language and its foundation in rhetoric.[147] In other words, language provides no hard-and-fast way to make the kind of distinctions to which Marinetti aspires. Discourses on both woman and machine are uncontrollably stained by each other: masculine machines come clothed in feminine figures, in woman-as-metaphor, while despised women are nothing better than machines.

Marinetti's inability to master his discourse is most obvious in his discourse of mastery, where he speaks of woman and machine in a rhetoric of domination, much as Expressionist discourse enmeshed woman and machine to signify, in Huyssen's terms, the threat of "otherness."[148] But Marinetti also tries to specify that the kind of woman he especially disdains is the contemporary bourgeois woman as typified by the wife, mother, and mistress—icons of the weak sex. Women might be tolerable had they been historically raised in the same ways as men. But as it was, women were hopelessly contemptible in their fragility, their embodiment of sentimentality and love, their function as guardians of the hearth. In Marinetti's eyes, women in his day were creatures it was too late to "masculinize."[149] Significantly, outside the Suffrage movement, no real attempt is made to address the modern workingwoman or female avant-garde artist, those in everyday life who stepped most heavily on the toes of the Futurists.

Yet, although Marinetti spat on the idea of woman as mistress, as "engine of pleasure," woman's serving the pleasure of man proved the least objectionable conception of female weakness. Her reinscription at the center of Futurist discourse distinguishes the sexual woman from the bourgeois woman of romantic love. Here it must be recalled that, as is true of almost any avant-garde discourse that singled out woman for social-sexual attack, bourgeois woman was a particularly visible social target, the most conspicuous sign of conspicuous consumption.

Marinetti's articulation of a double feminine in relation to the machine finds echoes in the work of Vertov, who drew inspiration from the Russian Futurist milieu dominated by the monumental figures of Vladimir Mayakovsky, David Birliuk, and Vassily Kamensky.[150] Russian Futurism was infected by the Italian Futurist adulation of the machine and the city, though not without some ambivalence — stemming in part, no doubt, from the Italians' connection to Fascism.[151] Still, it is striking though not surprising that the most fervent machine-loving discourse took root in nations that were industrial and technological latecomers.[152] It is as if the zeal alone for things modern would overcome the historical lag in "progress" compared to other European countries. In the nascent Soviet Union, Lenin's doctrine of productivism took the energy of industrial capitalism and wed it to the social aims of socialism.[153]

The mechanical, especially the urban-mechanical, was a central component of this modernist desire. In addition to the urban poetry of Mayakovsky and others, new technology as a theme and aesthetic infused a number of Russian Futurist and Constructivist visual experiments, like Mayakovsky's costume designs for the *The Seven Unclean Ones* (1919), El Lissitsky's *New Man* puppets (1920), Liubov Popova's *The Traveler* (1915), which represents a train, and Vladimir Tatlin's counterreliefs and *Monument to the Third International*. The conjunction of women and machines specifically ranges from Kasimir Malevich's *Woman with Water Pails*, to Ivan Kliun's *Cubist at her Dressing Table*, to Alexander Rodchenko's photograph of a female telephone courier, and his photo montages for Mayakovsky's writings.

The Russian Futurist sensibility, however, was far less misogynistic than that of the Italian Futurists, despite Alexei Kruchenykh's prescription of a future masculinization of the Russian language, which he felt should dispense with feminine endings.[154] Few Russian Futurists openly worked under the Marinetti banner, and Russian Futurism always counted a number of female artists and writers among its practitioners.[155] Vertov's own enthusiasm for both the machine and women is evident in his writings; "the theme of Woman is vast," he once stated in a project proposal.[156] Consider Vertov's "Lullaby," "the first song of a cycle devoted to the Free Woman to whom unemployment is unknown, threatened by neither violence nor hunger, neither torture nor the executioner's axe, the woman without fear for her children's fate, their present and future; to the woman for whom all doors to education, to creative and joyful labor are open."[157] Vertov is also affirmative in connecting woman and machine; even at his most aggressively enthusiastic, he criticizes bourgeois woman with more humor than virulence. It is to this enthusiasm as expressed in *Man with a Movie Camera*, which is still marked by traces of the Marinettian discourse, that I turn.

Vertov and the Cinematic Woman-Machine

Man with a Movie Camera establishes various relations between female sexuality and urban-based machines, especially the train, the camera, the factory, and communications machines. The association of the camera lens and shutter with the woman's eye is the most frequently cited example of the self-reflexive operations of Vertov's film. That this is first a woman's eye, however, is often overlooked. Here, the assimilation of the movements of the human eye to the mechanical designs of the camera formally engages female vision in a manner much less shocking than in, for example, *Un Chien andalou*. Both films ask us, however, to consider the female body as a surface of inscription for the filmic writing of a new vision and, in the case of Vertov, to look at the mechanical eye as forming part of a rhetoric that composes woman, cinema, the train, and the city in complex configurations.

Of all the machines mobilized by the film, with the exception of the camera and editing apparatus, the train is perhaps the most insistent. Urban railway transport lends itself both to visual disorientation and to a system of recurrences as a point of return. Of course, the role of the train in the Russian Revolution cannot be overemphasized as a potent historical symbol available to Vertov in the form of the agit-trains — trains specially outfitted with agit-propaganda and designed to disseminate information about the Revolution to the vast peasant populace.[158] Both Sergei Eisenstein and Vertov were connected with the agit-trains; Vertov began by editing the film that came back from the trains after traveling through the country. In a real sense, his "cinema of facts" was born on a train.

In *Man with a Movie Camera*, Marx's "locomotive of history" — revolution — is turned into cinematic agitprop. The train is used quite self-consciously as a metaphor for cinema. As in the opening sequence of the great city film, *Berlin, Symphony of a City* (Walter Ruttman, 1927), this machine that moves meaning is used first to inaugurate filmic force proper. In Vertov, this is the transformation of stasis (the city asleep, represented as so many "still" photos) into dynamism (the city awakened, the marriage of profilmic and edited movement). At this moment, a train rushes straight for the camera and the spectator, who then plunges with the waking woman into the rhythm of the film.

This is the same woman whose eye emblematizes the "kino-eye." ("Kino-eye" means basically "camera-eye," which is how Vertov referred to the superior, unclouded vision made possible by the camera.) She is "awakened" by the train through a kind of Kuleshov (or montage) effect: the train passes over the camera in the preceding shot, and the logic of editing links the force of the train to the drive to awaken, to open one's eyes, to see, to scopophilia.[159] The fact that the beginnings of profilmic movement coincide with setting a sexual imaginary in motion is even more clear in the alternation of shots that follow. The train continues, and the cameramen return to their car, which now runs in the opposite direction on the tracks, while the woman gets up and dresses, a performance highlighted by close-ups of her putting on stockings and bra. The least we can say is that we are dealing here with a seduction of vision through a classical voyeuristic scenario.

This scenario is, however, ironic. The voyeurism is ambivalent, since, as Yuri Tsivian points out, the scene turns out to be a parody of a film called *The Awakening of a Woman,* from a genre epitomizing bourgeois Russian filmmaking.[160] The title of the film appears in a poster, along with a painting by the academic painter Nikolai Perov. What is being mocked is the metaphor of the "awakening of the woman in a young creature." Through this abrupt awakening, Vertov opposes the bourgeois cinema of "dreams" to his cinema or "factory of facts," realized by means of the kino-eye.[161] Both the woman and the film awaken from the bad dream of the "artistic cinema," as Vertov called it.

In the awakening woman, we have the first kind of femininity to be invoked and then run down by a machine—a train—in *Man with a Movie Camera,* that of bourgeois femininity. The bourgeois woman is obsessed with beauty and the process of beautification, as later sequences at the beauty salon and the beach demonstrate. This femininity is in theory to be contrasted with that of women who are economically less privileged, whether in the form of workingwomen or of homeless women, like one we see asleep on a bench.[162] This image of a sleeping woman can be seen, as has been pointed out, as the reply to the first awakening sequence.[163] Here we have again that conjuncture of woman, train, and camera, a profilmic version of the earlier editing of the three together, only this time as a more documentary, "factual" image.

At the end of the film we again find the combination of desire, vision, and aggression linked to the relation between a woman, a train, and the filmic apparatus. *Man with a Movie Camera*'s best use of the train as a metaphor for cinema is in the film's last sequence, where the woman-editor looks at a strip of film composed of still frames of a train, which then become animated in a *défilement*, or filmic unfolding. The resemblance of the train body to a strip of film, and the coincidence of the film-in-motion with the train-in-motion, is complemented by the copresence of several images at once, many of which belong to the railroad — for example, the train signals. The woman's eyes then find themselves at the center of a rush of superimposed, quasi-abstract images, notably trains, signals, and the cameraman, all alternating with the audience watching the film-within-the-film. As an eye equal to the cameraman's, this eye is ambiguous; here the Pygmalion power to animate the still frame turns against itself and careens out of control in a visual frenzy. Though the spectator may have difficulty distinguishing the various images, given how rapidly they move, the woman's eyes remain stable, unmoving points of reference in the visual vortex. We might justifiably wonder if this is not the supervision of the editor, who alone can make sense of it all, or if it is not rather the catatonic vision of a spectator who can no longer identify the dizzying array of images flashing on the screen.

In between these opening and closing sequences, which establish the train as a *filmic* double, the film presents us with an array of women seen both as classically sexualized creatures and as parts of a less "feminine" machine of desire. As I suggested, two kinds of voyeurism are operating in the film, masculine and feminine. One seizes on the female body as sexual object, while the other seizes on the modern, urban, and mechanical world as a chain of bodies and objects rendered equal in the editor's gaze. We have, then, a division of voyeurism that corresponds to a division of labor in film production: the cameraman's eye and the woman editor's eye.

This point demands scrutiny in light of the femininity to which the film is most devoted, that of the woman-machine, which forms the prototype of the revolutionary heroine in the Vertovian universe. As in Marinetti, woman and progress join forces in the machine. In its continual repetition of both the mechanics of the labor process and the different types of machines employed by different kinds of labor, the film displays a striking obsession with the female figure. The man with the movie camera is fascinated by women at machines, women in machines, and woman as machine. In the representation of work in the film, the great majority of images present either female vocations or female workers at various kinds of occupations, many of them "modern," urban vocations: at the sewing machine and the telephone switchboard, in match, cigarette, and textile factories, as hairdressers, editors, street sweepers, secretaries.

By contrast, masculine vocations, which are segregated as such in the film, represent a minority of the images of labor and machines. With the male occupations, the accent is placed on the work itself and the power of the coal mines, hydroelectric energy, etc., while female labor represents at each moment repetition and the incorporation of the body, its gestures, into the mechanical rhythm of the work. In other words, images like that of a man "fitted" into the cogs of a huge machine are exceptional compared to images like that showing a woman's face superimposed on spinning cotton bobbins. In this comparison, the woman and the machine are identified cinematically, through superimposition, while the man in the machine represents a less experimental, more literal inscription of body in machine.

In the female paradigm we also have shots like that superimposing the face of a woman over the keys of a typewriter, which in one sense is a literalization of the relation between woman and writing. Views of women at the beauty salon performing various tasks (hairdressing, manicuring, etc.) also reinforce the association of the female body with repetition and routine, that is, with the *mechanics* of the machine. Finally, female bodies form part of an aesthetic machine when, for example, they perform exercises on the beach under the watchful direction of a male instructor who leads them as synchronized parts of a machine ensemble. This mise-en-scène is rivaled only by that of the cameraman, who roams the beaches exploring the female body in various poses and states of undress. In these shots, a male-defined mechanical vision is itself double, moving between voyeuristic leering and respectful reportage.

How are we to understand the status of woman in relation to the machine in these shots? Tsivian distinguishes between "aesthetic" vocations and "real" labor on the one hand, and between manual and mechanical labor on the other.[164] Stephen Crofts and Olivia Rose also emphasize the dual labor paradigms operating in the film: that of productive versus nonproductive labor, which correspond, respectively, to the beautification of the "new bourgeoisie" and participation in the proletarian labor process and to mechanical versus manual labor, which is set up in the editing to demonstrate the efficiency of machines versus the old artisanal methods, a sort of Vertovian version of *The Old and the New*.[165]

These distinctions put a truth (of labor) in opposition to an art, an aesthetic — indeed, to aesthetics. Vertov himself militantly opposed his "factory of facts" to what he called "artistic cinema": "But since this influencing is done through facts, not through acting, dance, verse, it means we devote very little attention to so-called art. Yes, comrades, as many of you know, we relegate 'art' to the periphery of our consciousness."[166] In Jacques Aumont's elegant phenomenology of *Man with a Movie Camera*, Vertov succeeds in situating vision between "symbolizing" and "seeing" — "seeing" in the sense of an almost pure vision.[167] For Aumont, Vertov is the master of *la vue*, the view, also the *seen*, an idea that resonates with Barthes's particular sense of photographic ontology. In any event, Vertov's documentarist impulse drove Mikhail Kaufman (his cameraman) to seek a "factual" vision, a new vision free of "symbolic" artistic trappings, free of overstatement, leaving the statement itself, in its cinematic articulation, as its own denuded affirmation of truth: "Kino-drama clouds the eye and the brain with a sweet fog. Kino-eye opens the eyes, clears the vision."[168]

In the scheme of a double vision, then, and of a double feminine, "bourgeois" femininity appears in the waking woman and her beach/salon counterparts as a figure of style itself — both as the seduction of style, and the style of seduction: "artistic" woman, art as woman. Factory woman, workingwoman, unemployed woman, these different embodiments of femininity are set up to transcend style, as the Revolution might be said to dialectically transcend the old order. The machine style itself as nonstyle, an expression of avant-garde will-to-stylelessness, was a reaction against the excesses of Academic style, as well as against the institutionalization of "style" represented by the museum.[169] Based on readings of texts by Le Corbusier, Maurice Vlaminck, and other nineteenth- and early twentieth-century avant-garde artists and critics, Donald Kuspit draws a distinction between "style" and "stylelessness" in reference to Picasso: "We see here a dichotomy between style and vision, the sense that style represents all that is really antithetical to art. Put another way, style represents only what art is superficially about — and the sense that the achievement of style can seriously interfere with what it is 'ultimately' about, indicates that desirability of the state of stylelessness as the state in which vision might be achieved."[170]

In *Man with a Movie Camera* the machine aesthetic or vision theoretically rescues woman from adornment, from useless decorativeness, and resituates her in the realm of practical activity, of (male) production. In the same way that bourgeois woman was once championed as a "useful" wife, mother, and helpmate of man against the excessively style-conscious and "functionless" aristocratic woman of the ancien régime, the revolutionary woman/workingwoman, as well as the female athletes in Vertov's film are privileged over the more conventionally "feminine" bourgeoise. This returns us to the paradigms of productive/nonproductive, authentic/aesthetic, and "fact" versus "art." Yet Vertov himself realized only too well the figurative power of his documentary montage of facts, the style constructed out of editing, "the organization of the visible world."[171] In Vertov's scheme, both art and labor are a woman; both figure and fact, lie and truth — just as in Marinetti. As Derrida says of Nietzsche's texts, "It is impossible to dissociate the questions of art, style and truth from the question of the woman. Nevertheless the question 'what is woman?' is itself suspended by the simple formulation of their common problematic. One can no longer seek her, no more than one could search for woman's femininity or female sexuality. And she is certainly not to be found in any of the familiar modes of concept or knowledge. Yet it is impossible to resist looking for her."[172] In other words, since woman's seduction, her dissimulation, is her truth — appearance as truth — she can represent only the truth of untruth, and of untruth as truth.

In *Man with a Movie Camera*, woman's status in relation to "truth" is not resolved merely by a distinction between bourgeois and proletarian femininity, or between dual labor paradigms. On the one hand, in terms of a mechanical metaphor, all the women in the film are put on a continuum that places work and leisure, truth and fiction, in relation to each other through the body and through machines of communication.[173] The typists and switchboard operators plug women into a giant board of interconnections and "disjunctive syntheses," points of disjunction giving rise to networks of new syntheses.[174] They are *operators* mediating style and nonstyle as two figures of style; they are women whose job it is to *represent* and connect others.[175]

On the other hand, Vertov's workingwoman herself asks to be considered as a style and source of figuration. The figurative power of woman, similar to the metaphorical force of the train, radiates brilliantly in the imagery and editing of the textile factory. Annette Michelson has drawn attention to the symbolic importance of the textile industry as represented in the alternation of the spinning cotton bobbins with the image of the cameraman shooting the mines and hydroelectric installations that power the factories. At the height of the accelerating alternation, which occurs at the structural center of the film, the cameraman is superimposed on the image of a worker at her textile machine, and the combined image turns and rotates according to the increasing rhythm of the hand-cranked camera (photo 26). For Michelson, this juxtaposition and superimposition of filmmaking and textile manufacture signify a unity that suspends the "natural" inequalities and contradictions once produced by a system of division of labor. "If film-work thereby shares in the paradigmatic status of the weaver's labor, it is because for Vertov, with that supercession, the eye has indeed 'become a human eye,' and 'its object a human social object created by man and destined for him.' "[176]

To Michelson's analysis, I add the observation that—returning to the eye/lens/shutter association—the eye belongs, again, to a woman. Between *textile* and *textual* (and here we should consider again the recurrent images of seamstresses stitching together fabrics as doubles for the editing process, itself the pivotal operation for J.-P. Oudart's suture),[177] there is a sense in which, as emblematized by the image of the face of the woman worker at the center of the spinning bobbins, the film and the filmmaking process literally spin out of the head and vision of a woman, specifically a female worker. Here, the spinning cotton reels, to be compared with reels of film and with train wheels, circulate as tokens of exchange, comparing the work of two women, the factory laborer and the woman editor. They give force to the role of woman in constructing not only a worker's revolution, but a revolution in perception and communication.

To pursue further what I am claiming is an identification of woman and film, we must return to the association of the train with filmmaking, and specifically the camera, which, as interchangeable figures of perceptual revolution, are wed in the representation of the city. Film is without doubt the urban art par excellence in its incorporation of the rhythm and fragmentation of urban speed and shock. *Man with a Movie Camera*'s well-known image of the gigantic cameraman superimposed on the city crowd (itself a montage of different crowds) brings to mind Walter Benjamin's famous notes on the figure of the crowd in Baudelaire and Poe: "Moving through . . . traffic involves the individual in a series of shocks and collision. At dangerous intersections, nervous impulses flow through him in rapid succession, like the energy from a battery. . . . Thus technology has subjected the human sensorium to a complex kind of training. . . . In a film, perception in the form of shocks was established as a formal principle. That which determines the rhythm of production on a conveyor belt is the basis of the rhythm of reception in the film."[178]

According to a similar rhythm, *Man with a Movie Camera* also places the train, labor, film, and the city in the same perceptual paradigm. In shots of multiple images of trams going in several directions at once, for example, Vertov exploits a montage within the frame, the "found" editing of intersecting tramways — Constructivist dynamism at its most energetic — to engender a specifically cinematic vision (photo 27). The city and its web of transport represented for Vertov "that whirlpool of colliding visible phenomena, where everything is real, where people, tramways, motorcycles, and trains meet and part, where each bus follows its route, where cars . . . do not obey the director's megaphone."[179] The tracing of cinematic processes in the urban landscape of public transportation ties the force of these shots to the force of editing, i.e., the principle of cut-and-splice, of a linkage that is simultaneously a separation or alienation. This is the force of the social space, of the public spaces that intermingle the sexes and social classes in the mass crowds, where identity is at once autonomous and anonymous, multiple and individual.[180]

Aumont sees the recurrent multiple-tram shots as so many figurations of the body of the city, of its nervous system, so to speak, especially in the numerous shots of train signals and traffic cops.[181] For my purposes, one crucial series of alternations effectively condenses the city, the body, the train, the film, and the idea of the constant cycle of social connection and disconnection: the sequence of the woman giving birth. Alternating with images of divorce, marriage, a funeral, the multiple trams, and the cameraman, the birth of the infant constitutes a "mother" figure of cut-and-splice, of organic-mechanical separation and integration: this is birth as dialectical montage. In a sense, the force of the trams and the force of the birth drama connect as parts of an enormous, urban libidinal machine, which, like Deleuze and Guattari's desiring machines, regulates work and play, life and death in an erotics of modern urban force and revolution.[182] It fuels the notion of social production and relations of production, labor, female labor, and woman-in-labor, as institutions of desire and zones of interpenetrating intensity.

The eye is force, says Jean-François Lyotard.[183] But so is woman, in this

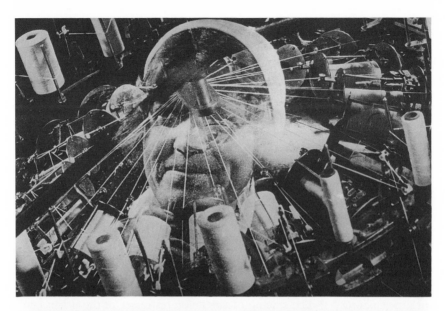

26. and 27. *Man with a Movie Camera*, Dziga Vertov, 1929. Museum of Modern Art.

28. *Man with a Movie Camera*, lithograph publicity poster, Stenberg Brothers, 1929.

sequence. Vertov and Elizaveta Svilova, his wife and editor, take a time-hon-ored figure of creation and of pictorial and textual birth and paste together a chain of modern images that identify the acts of creation and re-creation with the body of the woman, which is also the body of the film and the city, itself strongly defined by the urban railway network. A publicity poster from 1929 suggests that at least one marketing strategy took account of the extent to which the body of a woman is identified with the city and the film — no doubt simply as a strategy of seduction (photo 28). The image features the woman of the initial waking-up sequence bent over backward, with her arms spread out to form a "V," and her legs posed seductively as if pausing during a dance step; for today's viewer, it simultaneously evokes Olga Korbut and Ginger Rogers. The woman's body is traversed by Futuristic skyscraper lines of force to com-plement the diagonals of the arms. The circles of text, one of which contains the film title, echo the roundness of her head and the curve of her body. Here we have an image of total interpenetration of the female body and the city, as well as the camera, the lens of which is refigured in the circular forms of the titles. The pleasures of sexuality, the pleasures of the city, and the pleasures of the cinema cut each other at odd angles, to be situated with respect to each other according to the multiple shifts of a dynamic time and space.

Mechanical vision is, then, a female vision insofar as the editor's eye rivals that of the cameraman. Through a process of substitution that suggests Freud's joke work, and that in a sense is Vertov making a joke of his own voyeuristic stake in the film's images, the camera eye is the great leveler; to refer again to Michelson's argument, it mediates not only between different kinds of machines and labor, but between the sexes. To refer back to *The General*, we again have the mechanical mediation of male and female vision in a relationship of mirroring. Yet the look of the woman and the look at the woman slide into one another across the pivotal perspective of the camera-man, the one behind the kino-eye and its aggressive train double. This is, after all, entitled *Man with a Movie Camera*, not *Woman with a Pair of Scissors*; it is Vertov's film, not Svilova's. The vicious circle of this mechanical vision cannot help but lead the feminine, double or not, back to the masculine — and, as with Marinetti, vice versa. This is a circle that also leads to and from the trains that criss-cross the city, rendering it heroic, and not alienating, as in *The Crowd*.

FOUR

National Identity in the Train Film

One of the most symbolic moments in *October* (1928), Sergei Eisenstein's epic film account of the Russian Revolution, is when the Bolsheviks take over a night train of Cossacks bound for St. Petersburg. Suspense is built by the guerrilla stakeout of the railroad tracks, the switching of signals, the lying-in-wait for the train to pass. Finally, the revolutionaries stop and seize the train, achieving true triumph when, through rational argument and persuasive appeal to solidarity, they convince the Cossacks of why they should join the Revolution. From this moment forward, the train becomes an instrument of socialist, not capitalist, progress; it belongs to the Revolution. The sense in which the train is here an emblem of History is powerfully evoked in the narrative symbolism of the tracks. Taking control of the huge icon of modernity is taking control of history, of one's destiny, and engineering it along the railways of the collective future toward a new end — a new Russia.

Eisenstein's highly charged use of the train here borrows on the railroad's conventional associations with both progress and national identity. Other railroad motifs in the film support this usage, especially the sequence of Lenin's legendary reentry into Russia via the Finland Station. The train in *October* represents the nation allegorically in a more conventionally symbolic sense than in, say, *Man with a Movie Camera*. But it was far from the greatest 1920s Soviet train film identifying the railroad with the nation. That distinction belongs to two films made, like *October*, at the end of the decade: Victor Turin's *Turksib* (1929) and Ilya Trauberg's *China Express* (1929), also known as *The Blue Express* or *Goluboi Ekspress*.

Set in the far eastern reaches of the Soviet Union, *Turksib* is the story of the linking of regions by the railroad; the train is literally what unifies the USSR. A heroic agent drawing the remote southeast into the economic and social sphere of the rest of the country, the train brings water to the desert and goods to and from the region. The style of the film is Vertov-like in its use of rapid montages of images juxtaposed with simple textual messages: "Water!" or "Free the land for cotton!" or "Forward!" It also integrates the movement and speed of the train with that of the film. This is the Soviet version of the western.

China Express, the story of the coming-to-consciousness of a man whose sister is sold to a merchant, sets the tale on a train traveling from Nanking to Suchow. The train serves the function of agitprop, an agit-train of ideological enlightenment (just as *October*'s train does); over the course of the journey, the coolies and workers in the third-class car gradually rise up in revolt against the Chinese warlords and European dignitaries traveling in the first-class car and the middle-class merchants and professionals of the second-class car. Embodying the revolution, the train, "a microcosm of the political world hurtling through the night on rails towards a certain geographical point and an uncertain destiny," offers itself as an allegory of the Russian Revolution, with the Chinese standing in for the Soviet masses.[1]

Each of these films exploits and encourages a nationalist reading of the railroad and, simultaneously, of film. To the Soviet examples, we can add more from other countries, films that feature the railroad coded in nationally specific ways, whether overtly or obliquely: in the United States, *The General* (Keaton, 1926) and *The Iron Horse* (John Ford, 1924); in France, *La Roue* (*The Wheel*) (Abel Gance, 1921); in Germany, *Scherben* (*Shattered*) (Lupu Pick, 1921) and *Spione* (*Spies*) (Fritz Lang, 1928); in England, *Underground* (Anthony Asquith, 1927). The railroad/nation couple, which in some films expands to become the railroad/nation/cinema triad, is far more evident in films produced toward the end of the silent era than during the teens or earlier. This is not to say that national differences are not detectable in railroad films before the 1920s. Certainly, the sense in which both the railroad and the cinema could be conceived as vehicles of national identity predated the twenties. Both railroads and cinema were seen early in the history of each industry as means of homogenizing a far-flung and heterogeneous population through consumption at a national level—the goods and services made possible by the railroad-connected markets and the images, stories, and leisure practices disseminated in and by the cinema. But national cinematic differences were fewer, and mattered less, before World War I—before, that is, the rise of *national* cinemas as such.

Defining a "national cinema" is no easy matter, since the concept is based on a number of historically and culturally determined forces and rarely admits of an obvious or single definition. In this sense, it is like the concept of nation itself. It is a scholarly commonplace that "nation" has no natural or necessary meaning. Rather, it is a cultural construct, a collective set of representations woven through modes and styles of production and consumption in individual political and social groupings. No nation can ever be taken for granted as such. Indeed, the meaning of "nation" as we know it, the modern nation-state, emerged only in the eighteenth century and grew in the nineteenth in relation to political and economic boundaries drawn to fit the changing needs of the British-defined world economy.[2]

As an example, Theodore Zeldin notes that historically a sense of what it means to be French has seldom been simply assumed; rather, "the French nation had to be created:"

> One should not indeed unquestioningly assume that the French were a single people, clearly defined by their political boundaries. The process by which their unification was attempted continued throughout this period [1848–1945]: the resistance that patriotism met, the varieties of allegiance that resulted from the clash of innovation and tradition, exactly what was involved in being French and how the sense of belonging to the nation was spread among different groups, all this is usually glossed over, because the division of Europe into nation-states has been represented as natural and inevitable. But even the ideals that Frenchmen set themselves, the image of themselves that they formed, were not clear or distinct.[3]

Benedict Anderson refers to nations as "imagined communities," formed to draw attention to the *created* character of their collective representations and to the fact that "members of even the smallest nation will never know most of their fellow members, meet them, or even hear of them, yet in the minds of each lives the image of their total communion."[4] What holds these individuals

together is an arbitrary set of economic, political, and sociocultural relationships that, in nationalism, have the status of *natural* relationships.

As such, nationalism is a kind of myth, which, as Roland Barthes notes,
"transforms history into nature."[5] The mythology of the bourgeoisie, including the idea of the nation, is the elevation of the values of a historically constituted class into "the evident laws of a natural order."[6] Similarly, Anderson
writes, "It is the magic of nationalism to turn chance into destiny."[7] He links
the rise of the nation-state as an ideological force with the decline, thanks to
the Enlightenment, of religious modes of thought and authority in sociopoliti-
cal terms. Anderson attributes a key role to language, especially the rise of
vernacular languages, in hastening the transition to secular networks of authority and collective experience with respect to preexisting modes of representation (e.g., Greek mythology, feudal paternalism) in the articulation of
new institutional forms of power.[8] He also points to the powerful role played
by, first, the novel and, then, daily newspapers as agents of a *simultaneously*
experienced collective imaginary. To these one could easily add film in both
the United States and Europe, as well as in other countries, with visual imagery, especially mass media and, after 1895, film, coming to play important
roles in negotiating national identity.

If the "nation" is far from a natural formation, the same is true of a "national cinema." Philip Rosen points out that in most analyses of national cinemas, coherence is a determining criterion of what constitutes it as national:

> The discussion of a national cinema assumes not only that there is a
> principle or principles of coherence among a large number of films; it also
> involves an assumption that those principles have something to do with
> the production and/or reception of those films within the legal borders of
> (or benefitting capital controlled from within) a given nation-state. That
> is, the intertextual coherence is connected to a socio-political and/or
> socio-cultural coherence implicitly or explicitly assigned to the nation.[9]

This characterization far from solves the question of what constitutes a particular national cinema; it is entirely conceivable that a body of films might be
linked together as "national" cinema aside from any sense of coherence with a
national social given. And as Rosen points out, one must conceive of the nation
to begin with as something dynamic, something capable of change, and not as
a static, eternal object.[10] But the "coherence" principle does provide a useful
point of departure. There must be ways of grouping texts under the rubric

national, whether according to mode of production, aesthetic similarity, re-ception, themes, or site of production/exhibition. And clearly establishing a close link between a group of films and other cultural markers of nationality can assist the task of determining what is "national" about a particular national cinema. But none of these characteristics is any less arbitrary than the others. In a sense, one can construct national cinemas only ex post facto, since to label a film as "French" or "Soviet" means almost always to refer it to a preexisting body of films.

One can imagine a non-French director making a French film, for exam-ple, in much the same way that many contemporary British and French direc-tors (Adrian Lyne, Ridley and Tony Scott, Barbet Schroeder) and "classical" non-American directors (Alfred Hitchcock, Billy Wilder, Milos Forman) have made *American* films. And in today's world of international coproduction, a film by such an acclaimed director as Krzysztof Kiéslowski (*Red*) is ruled out of consideration for an Academy Award in the United States precisely because its national origin cannot be determined. To remove the criteria of the author's national origin and the site of production and exhibition from the equation, and to insist on both aesthetic qualities and a specific national, social, and historical context to which the film refers or out of which it comes, is to provide a slightly less arbitrary set of criteria, at least historically. Debate is inspired by the ways in which the films relate to that context, especially when the spectator is considered.

For example, with respect to German cinema after World War I, Sieg-fried Kracauer saw German films as reflecting domestic chaos and the psycho-logically impoverished German middle class clamoring for authority figures (and ultimately, Hitler) to order the anarchy.[11] Figures of the tyrant and the double, from *The Golem* to *M*, he felt reflected the German soul in a troubled time as a crisis of identity, which in retrospect has been interpreted as a crisis of masculine identity. Thomas Elsaesser argues, somewhat differently, that the fantastic film (and Neue Sachlichkeit films like G. W. Pabst's *Pandora's Box*) takes social reality and displaces it through a complex rhetorical relay that produces a distinctly German narrative structure — disunified, ambiguous, unresolved — and an equally disjunct visual style.[12] In his view, these films address a complex, historically specific *German* spectator, a split subject ac-knowledged as such, one that is sexually ambiguous, deeply ambivalent, and falling outside — indeed, opposing — the Hollywood Oedipal framework.

If so far I have avoided the question of national cinema in discussing the train and cinema, this is partly the result of a deliberately thematic approach that has focused on aspects of the train/film relationship shared across national boundaries. And, as noted, my focus is also skewed to American film examples because of the sheer quantity of them available. If we can point to any national differences in the early train films, however, the ambivalence toward the train would have to be seen as greater in European films than in American. As we know, the railroad entered into film in both Europe and the United States as an already marked cultural object around which much ambivalence existed. But based on the films screened for this book, and on plot summaries gleaned from catalogs and reviews, it can be asserted generally that the train tends to be represented in a more positive, heroic light in American films and as a more tragic vehicle in European film during the entire silent period. Even British comedies like *When the Devil Drives* (Urban, 1907), in which a railroad journey turns into a wild and hellish roller coaster ride under the nasty hand of the devil, invest the humor with an undertone of tragedy.[13]

Deeper ambivalence on the part of Europeans is understandable, even in England, possibly the greatest nation of railroad enthusiasts on earth. In Europe, as Schivelbusch notes, the railroad was overlaid on a preexisting, preindustrial transportation system, while in the United States the railroad imposed itself on vast expanses of previously untouched wilderness.[14] Social dislocation in Europe was necessarily more immediately visible and direct:

> While Europe experiences mechanization and industrialization as largely destructive, as they replace a highly developed artisan culture and an equally high developed travel culture, the case of America is the exact opposite. At the beginning of the nineteenth century, when steam power is first introduced, there is no developed American culture of artisanship or travel. . . . As it does not cause unemployment, every form of mechanization is experienced as creative. The mechanization of transportation is not seen, as in Europe, as the destruction of a traditional culture, but as a means to gaining a new civilization from a hitherto worthless (because inaccessible) wilderness. As the transport system does not merely take over preexisting traffic but opens up new territories for traffic, it appears productive to a degree unimaginable to Europeans.[15]

It is important to remember that while no European-American culture of artisanship had been developed, Native American cultures certainly became victims of European-Americans' industrialization. The point of view is crucial: only European-Americans could see the new rail transportation as productive.

But the distinction from a more homogeneous European culture is to be noted, including the more positive embrace of the train by white Americans.[16]

While such distinctions around the railroad hold true for some early films, these general national differences become more apparent in films of the 1920s in which the railroad plays an important part. *The Crowd* and *Man with a Movie Camera* are examples of two entirely different approaches to the train and the city, owing in part to different national contexts. Ironically, Vertov's film is much more consistently celebratory of the train than is Vidor's, but the Soviet cinema, despite its debt to Western European avant-gardes, is a case apart, because of the Revolution and the sheer vastness of Russian territory. It is, in the end, much closer to American cinema, while *The Crowd*'s negative image of the train is in a way more "European," even with a redemptive reading. In this chapter, however, I focus on films in which the notion of national identity has a more specific and direct relevance to the texts in question. In other words, the films I analyze invite discussion in terms of national identity, either because they use the railroad to embody the nation, or because the railroad plays a particularly determining role in a textual system specific to a national cinematic consciousness.

To return to an earlier point, it is difficult to argue for national, textual, or intertextual coherence in early film before the rise of national cinemas per se. Early film production, distribution, and exhibition were largely international. This was a universe in which films might be shot anywhere, by and with anyone, and shown on screens around the world without regard to nationality. Until around 1909, the borders of national production were as fluid as the subjects and genres of the films themselves. Eileen Bowser notes that of 1,200 one reelers released in the United States in 1907, only 400 were made in the United States, with the majority coming from France (most of them Pathé films).[17] Accordingly, "the values expressed in films the world over were scarcely distinguishable. In the beginning[,] the universality of the film medium was particularly evident: the same kinds of subjects and styles appeared the world over."[18]

Despite the fierce competition among producers in different countries, audiences were treated to a variety of attractions that only occasionally flaunted their national origin or required a culturally specific context to understand or enjoy. Indeed, many early filmmakers relentlessly plagiarized each other back and forth across the Atlantic as well as within the borders of a single country. Méliès, for example, sent his brother to open an office for his Star Films in New York in order to control the extent to which replicas and even outright dupes (duplicate copies) of his films were being claimed by others who obviously garnered the profits.[19]

Led first by the giant Pathé, the French were the dominant suppliers of film product to the world until about 1911, far outstripping even the United States.[20] Kristin Thompson has shown how pre-World War I film interests were national, mainly insofar as they affected markets and profit.[21] The Motion Picture Patents Company was formed in 1908 by Edison and others as a multinational means of controlling the world market for the production, distribution, and exhibition of films. Its members were Edison, who already controlled a substantial portion of the American market as the result of his own licensing and patent victories; Biograph; Vitagraph; Essanay; Kalem; Selig; Lubin; Pathé Frères; Méliès; and George Kleine, an importer of films in the United States.[22] Robert Sklar states that certain American producers were excluded from the trust because they were too small to make any difference, while "several of the leading British and Italian producers were to be kept out of the American market, apparently because they had angered Edison by siding with Biograph in the earlier patents dispute. Only two European companies (except for the two French producers who were members of the Trust), one British and one French, were allowed entry, and at the greatly reduced rate of three reels per week for both."[23]

Americans in this era regularly digested as many foreign films as American. If early American films are to be seen as arms of indoctrination of "Americanness" for immigrants, they have to be considered in relation to a host of other films coming from France, Britain, Germany, and Italy that shared the screen with American images. Miriam Hansen notes something similar for the case of pre-World War I Germany:

> How did the predominance of foreign films affect the inculcation of cinematic spectatorship? If one follows the argument Paul Monaco makes for the 1920s — that the most popular films as a rule were domestic productions — there still remains a considerable gap between the low degree of popularity of foreign films and their success at the box office. Unless one wants to explain the latter mono-causally as a result of economic control, one might investigate the possibility of a split between officially professed national preference and unofficially indulged cinematic pleasures.[24]

Thus, it is extremely difficult to speculate with accuracy on the "national" values absorbed by early film audiences in regard to specific film texts. And filmmaking as a practice in the United States was equally open to recently arrived immigrants and Anglo-Saxons like Edison who tried to block all attempts to rival his business, irrespective of national origin.

Film began to exhibit a "national consciousness" as early as 1908 in France, with *le film d'art*, and 1907 in Germany, with the hygiene movement and intellectual or literary *kinodebatte*.[25] In the United States, film was at first haphazardly an agent of acculturation for immigrants, and more consciously so after about 1907. In the teens the national, patriotic character of assimilation by means of the silver screen occurred clearly in relation to World War I, a crucial turning point in thinking of cinema as national.[26] Besides the ipso facto increase in nationalism on the part of countries involved in or affected by the war, during that time the American film industry gained dominance in production, distribution, and exhibition by profiting from Europe's production disarray.[27] These years were also when American film established its dominant structure and look. Since then, American cinema has been the crucial Other with which to contend, a dominant and domineering influence on the constitution of other national cinemas eager to define themselves differently from the American model.[28]

According to Kracauer, for example, the German film industry, which did not collapse during the war, renewed itself in part in response to foreign, especially American, representations of Germans projected on European screens.[29] One example is UFA. As first a state-run, and then both a state and private organization, UFA (or *Universum Film A.G.*, first organized as Deulig in 1916, and as BUFA in 1917) developed a self-consciously different system from that of Hollywood's organized studio regime and encouraged a different, German aesthetic, notably in the art film (e.g., films like *The Cabinet of Dr. Caligari* or *Nosferatu*).[30] Ironically, one of UFA's most successful directors was Urban Gad, and one of its most successful stars Asta Nielsen, both of whom were Danish.

Similarly, the French film industry came together in opposition to the overwhelming presence of American films in French movie theaters during and after the war, and it attempted to create a French identity in explicitly aesthetic movements like Impressionism (which occurred in film much later than the art movement of the same name).[31] Paul Monaco's study of French and German film from 1919 to 1929 shows in detail how widely held the view was during the 1920s that film should be a reflection of the "national mentality."[32] In both France and Germany various groups proposed ways to limit the imports of foreign films, including high import taxes and quota systems, practices that continue in some form today.[33] For many, including filmmakers, the notion of "national cinema" was strongly associated with actual national borders and was far from an arbitrary phenomenon.

To grasp what national difference meant in the 1920s with respect to the railroad film, I have chosen two films as case studies: *The Iron Horse* (John Ford, 1924, United States) and *La Roue* (Abel Gance, 1922–23, France). These films show how a unique triangulation of train, film, and couple went in two different directions owing to different national orientations on the part of the makers, critics, and audiences for the films. In *The Iron Horse* the train is explicitly charged, as in *Turksib*, with a nationalizing mission to unify the country; unlike *Turksib*, however, the story of nation-making in Ford's film is also the story of the romantic, heterosexual couple, a cornerstone of American identity in film as much as the railroad is or was. The train in *La Roue*, while not thematically identified with France, is invested with characteristically French cultural and social attitudes, and a "French" aesthetic that can be traced to a wealth of cultural representation embracing Zola, Jean Renoir, Léger, Blaise Cendrars, and many others. The couple is also important to *La Roue*'s identity as a French film and a train film, but in ways that distinguish it from *The Iron Horse*.

Compared to *The Iron Horse*'s textbook classical American system, *La Roue* is indeed "different" in narrative, visual, and thematic terms, and, importantly, in its representation and figuration of the railroad. A telling index of this difference can be found in the reception that similar films found both at home and abroad. *La Roue* and *The Iron Horse* were both extremely popular in their respective countries, but Gance's films in general, including *Napoleon*, fared badly in the United States.[34] Apparently, French films overall were not greatly appreciated by American audiences in the twenties — and not only the films of the "difficult" Impressionists — while American films received a mixed reception in France and Germany, according to Paul Monaco.[35] A comparison of these two films will tell us much about the fate of the train in the history of silent film and about the continuation of early cinematic modes of perception in avant-garde practice (*La Roue*) as opposed to the "channeled" perception of the train in classical Hollywood cinema (*The Iron Horse*).

Nation, Railroad, and the Couple in The Iron Horse

No evocation of the significance of the railroad in *The Iron Horse* surpasses that of Caroline Lejeune's review of the film in 1925:

The power of the engine has long been recognized on the screen. Film producers from France, Germany and America have made constant use of it. . . . But, with the exception of Abel Gance, who was feeling towards something of the kind in his film *La Roue*, no director has thought, until now, of freighting his engine with an entire theme and setting it at full pace along the track to adventure's end. No director, until now, has really done his railroad honour. No director has considered that an engine might be of more arresting interest than a man. Now at last a film has come from America which trusts the railroad, and sees magic in it, and power. . . . It is a spacious film. It is rather a splendid film. *The Iron Horse* is its name. John Ford is its director.[36]

Although we might take exception to the "firsts" that Lejeune claims on Ford's behalf, *The Iron Horse* is without question as accomplished a marriage of the themes of the railroad, the couple, and the nation as can be found in the silent period. The film brings together a number of figures and plot configurations from earlier train films and sets them on the track of Manifest Destiny, while it endows the train with a stabilized, and stabilizing, role. It does so, moreover, through a system of representation that is at once highly typical of the classical Hollywood style, and prototypical of Ford's later, and better-studied westerns. In other words, *The Iron Horse* is suffused throughout, as a text and as a narrative, with *American* national identity and with a great self-consciousness of its fabrication of American mythology.

The Iron Horse is outwardly the story of the building of the transcontinental railroad from 1862 until 1869. As such, it engages a potent historical and ideological myth that enthusiastically links the story of the railroad with the story of America — a story of Manifest Destiny, the mid-1840s doctrine that justified white American expansion and incorporation of Western lands and the decimation of Native peoples as an almost divine mission (photo 29). Henry Nash Smith quotes Walt Whitman as the poet of this doctrine, since the theme of westward American empire was sung in many of Whitman's works from the 1860s and 1870s, precisely the era of the extension of the railroad from coast to coast.[37] In "Years of the Unperform'd" (1865), Whitman extols the pioneer who "colonizes the Pacific, the archipelagoes," and who, with the aid of technology, "interlinks all geography, all lands." In the poet's view, "Never was average man, his soul, more energetic, more like a god."[38] And never, perhaps, was it more Eurocentric.

Early on, the railroad was seen as a key agent of nation-building. A rail-

29. Davy Brandon (George O'Brien) directs track-laying in
The Iron Horse, John Ford, 1924. Museum of Modern Art.

road promoter of 1847 employed the popular rhetoric of his day when he emphasized "the [railroad] system as the means — greater than any, we may say than *all* other — of perpetrating our glorious union. It will prove, literally . . . as bands of iron binding us together, a family of states — thus ensuring our greatness and permanence as a nation."[39] Such, at any rate, was the notion of which the railroads wished to convince the American public, and such was the myth that underpinned the nostalgic view of the Iron Horse.

The nineteenth-century metaphor of the iron horse, which endowed the machine with a friendly character, did much to encourage its acceptance in an age of mixed public sentiment about the monstrous intrusion of the railroad on the landscape, the "virgin land," to use Henry Nash Smith's famous epithet.[40] By the mid-nineteenth century the habit of identifying the country with the locomotive had also proved effective in legitimating the westward pretensions of the railroads, which promoted themselves as heralds of empire and keys to the wealth that lay beyond the Mississippi.[41]

The locomotive came to connote the essence of the "American character." This idea was encouraged by foreign observers like a Mrs. Houston, an English tourist of the 1850s who rode many American trains: " 'I really think there must be some natural affinity between Yankee 'keep-moving' nature and a locomotive engine . . . whatever the cause, it is certain that the 'humans' seem to treat the 'ingine,' as they call it, more like a familiar friend than as the dangerous and desperate thing it really is.' "[42] Mrs. Houston had hit upon a "national" characteristic: white Americans saw themselves as "locomotive." In the 1850s "promoters used the steam engine as a metaphor for what they thought Americans were and what they were becoming. They frequently discussed parallels between the locomotive and national character, pointing out that both possessed youth, power, speed, single-mindedness, and bright prospects."[43] An American observer declared in 1846 that " 'we are a preeminently locomotive people and our very amusements are locomotive — the greater the speed, the greater the sport.' "[44]

The progress and modernity of the railroad in and of itself came to stand for *American* progress, an important notion to uphold in the progress-driven, yet angst-ridden 1920s. In a sense, reaffirming American history as the myth of Progress — egalitarian, accessible to all — spoke to the therapeutic needs, as Lears might say, of a full-blown consumerist and managerial economy in need of historical myths to support the 1920s' version of the doctrine of Progress — and undoubtedly to combat growing civil rights claims by African Americans and women who could not see the "equality" guaranteed by those founding myths. According to Charles McGovern, advertisers in the 1920s learned from World War I the value and success of linking patriotism and "Americanism" with consumption, thus bending the myth of choice to mean freedom of choice in the marketplace.[45]

Without promoting consumption as such, Ford's 1924 film is virtually a manifesto of the myth of Progress as a specifically American myth. The use of the railroad as an emblem of this progress locates it in a specific historical context. Besides reenacting the completion of the transcontinental railroad in 1869, when the Golden Spike was hammered, Ford's film shows us a West in which the machine had a definite place, ready for (white) settlement and progress. At the point in American history when the film was made, the railroad was declining as the automobile gained in popularity and accessibility.[46] By the end of the twenties the reign of the iron horse would be over. Thus, with Keaton and Ford, it already could be figured nostalgically, but as an allegory for the contemporary United States, not for past history. Significantly, Ford's film, even as a story set in the past, reflects the shift away from the locomotive engineer to the management/civil engineer character and gestures toward the "daughter-of-a-magnate" plot more typical of 1920s' railroad films.

A Man's World

The Iron Horse tells the story of Davy Brandon (George O'Brien), the son of a surveyor who discovers a mountain pass before being brutally murdered by a band of Indians led by a two-fingered white man. Young Davy witnesses the murder and, growing up determined to build the railroad of which his father dreamed prophetically in the 1850s, plans to avenge his father's death. Separated early on from his childhood sweetheart, Miriam Marsh (Madge Bellamy), Davy meets her again by chance years later, just after Miriam's father (Will Walling) has begun contracting for the building of the railroad that Lincoln authorizes in 1862. She, however, has a fiancé, Jesson (Cyril Chadwick), who works for her father. Fired by greed and jealousy at Miriam's obvious attraction to Davy, Jesson is easily bribed by the evil land baron Deroux (Fred Kohler) to kill Davy on a scouting trip taken to search for the pass discovered by Davy's father. The pass would give the railroad a dramatic shortcut but deprive Deroux of profits if the railroad were to build instead through his land. Unknown to Jesson, Davy miraculously survives a "fall" down a cliff (actually set up by Jesson, though no one can prove it). He returns and finds the tracks being laid through Deroux's land, as Jesson has lied about the existence of the pass. Davy means to get even but, with romance between them blossoming anew, Miriam extracts a promise from him not to fight. Through a series of misunderstandings, Davy is forced into a fistfight provoked by Jesson. Miriam is taken aback but, out of shame at having broken his promise to her, Davy does not explain Jesson's unfair provocation and thus loses her a second time.

One day while laying ties at the end of track, Davy and the section hands are attacked by Indians. Davy leads a locomotive express charge that rallies the entire town, and, in a dramatic one-on-one fistfight with the Indian chief, discovers that the chief is Deroux, the two-fingered marauder and murderer of his father. Davy finishes the fight, exacting a proper revenge by killing Deroux. Still unable to explain himself properly to Miriam—because of his broken promise — Davy leaves to work on the rival Central Pacific Railroad. One year later, the two roads meet at Promontory Point, Utah, and Miriam and Davy reunite as the Golden Spike is driven.

Although *The Iron Horse* is primarily the story of both Davy and the railroad, the narrative point of view is dominated by other characters. Two key figures assist in the telling: Abraham Lincoln (Charles Edward Bull) and Miriam Marsh, Davy's sweetheart. Lincoln's basic function is symbolic: to set the story, the history in motion under the sign of divine law. Miriam's functions are more complex; she is both the narrative stake (a double for the virgin land) and a delegate for the Lincoln function of joining (coupling) two halves into a whole; her position as narrative motor is less important and less marked than Lincoln's.

Lincoln is constituted from the beginning as a central narrating agency. The second title of the film is a dedication "to the ever-living memory of Abraham Lincoln, the Builder — and of those countless engineers and toilers who fulfilled his dream of a greater Nation." This title is followed by a shot of a bust of Lincoln, and then two more titles about the Civil War, the division of the United States into both North/South and East/West, and Lincoln's heroic embodiment of the ideal of a unified nation — as represented by the "blood and iron" invested in molding it.

Lincoln, then, is the text's narrator-delegate, a kind of implied narrator located within the story itself. His benedictory presence at the beginning is virtually that of divine author: Abe the Builder, in the paradigm of God the Father. And, much like the proverbial "invisible" authorial hand, he is mostly everywhere and nowhere at once — it is his spirit, identified with Progress and History, that guides the plot forward. The sheer fact of his being identified as the "great rail-splitter president," and other recurrent instances associating him with rails, link him throughout the text with the railroad; it is his road, the *rail*-road.

Still, Lincoln is strongly present at the beginning of the story proper. The film begins in Springfield, Illinois, Lincoln's hometown. We are introduced first to Brandon, the backwoodsy surveyor, and Thomas Marsh, a small-time contractor, who is affable but skeptical of Brandon's vision. Their children, Davy and Miriam, play at "surveying" nearby; they are watched at a split-rail fence by the unmistakable figure of Lincoln, who ambles up to Brandon and Marsh as a friendly neighbor with a tremendous handshake. When Brandon and Davy set out a few days later to scout the West for a good railroad route, Lincoln chides Marsh for scoffing at Brandon: "Someday you'll be laying rails along that rainbow."

Lincoln makes one more diegetic appearance, in 1862, when, over the protests of skeptical congressmen who preferred to direct resources to the war, he signed the authorization for construction of the Central Pacific and Union Pacific Railroads that together linked East and West. Shown present at the historic occasion are Thomas Marsh and daughter Miriam, who asks Lincoln humbly if he remembers her. He does, of course. This continual threading of the everyday and the provincial through the great and the lofty—and vice versa—is a hallmark of Ford's approach to history. It is important that Lincoln's greatness be, at bottom, his ordinariness, his folksiness—this is Ford's concept of an American. And as surely as Lincoln's image circulates universally as the image on the smallest unit of American currency—the lowest coin in the realm, the lowest common denominator—so does his status as Ur-builder circulate in the film by humble tokens, the lowly but great human proxies, the "countless engineers" who built America.[47] The "countless" include Brandon and his son, but also Marsh and his daughter. Here we have a version of the daughter-of-a-magnate plot, but one popularized and legitimated through Lincoln.

In their seminal article on the "ideological project" of Ford's 1939 *Young Mr. Lincoln*, the Cahiers du Cinéma group referred to the significance of the Lincoln figure across a number of Ford films as "a sort of universal referent which can be activated in all situations," and as "a myth, a figure of reference, a symbol of America."[48] As a myth, the Lincoln of the 1939 film is a character whose morality—and moral mission—place him above politics, hence making him universal. This feature, as the authors point out, is basic to American capitalism—its elevation of its own politics to the level of divine right and natural destiny.[49] In *The Iron Horse* and *Young Mr. Lincoln*, "the enterprise consisting of the concealment of politics (of social relations in America, of Lincoln's career) under the idealist mask of Morality has the effect of regilding the cause of Capital with the gold of myth, by manifesting the 'spirituality' in which American Capitalism believes it finds its origins and sees its eternal justification."[50] As such, Lincoln's law is seen as absolute divine right and his discourse an idealist one.

Lincoln's universality inscribes all others in a chain of substitution, of interchangeability. For Lincoln's raison d'être in a Ford film is to sanction the

dissolving of difference, of hierarchy; he is the healer, the unifier, the *linker* —
Mr. "Link-un." As the copper penny of politics, Lincoln functions like the
bourgeois money of Roland Barthes's *S/Z*, which is all about lack of origin and
liberation from indexicality.[51] The sign of being American in Ford is analogous; from Lincoln on down, "metonymic confusion" operates ideologically
to make people equal — at least, white people. This fundamentally democratic
principle of narrative construction anchors the myth of progress and Manifest
Destiny in the film.

Constructing one nation is achieved in *The Iron Horse* by wiping out, or at
least suppressing, difference — geographical, social, religious, ethnic, racial,
political, economic, and sexual. The agent of this dissolution is the railroad;
hence, its aura of Manifest Destiny. The elder Brandon predicts he will help
realize the transcontinental railroad "with the help of God," as he and his
son are "impelled westward by the strong urge of progress" (title). Lincoln
watches the Brandons ride off and "sees the momentum of a great nation
pushing westward — he sees the inevitable" (intertitle). The inevitable is from
start to finish the America of one continent, "One nation, under God," in
which separation and difference theoretically do not count. *The Iron Horse* is a
tribute to all the utopian democratic discourse promulgated by the railroads
from the mid-nineteenth century on.

Geographical linkage is clear, East/West being the primary axis. North/
South, however, plays a significant role as a structuring opposition that begs to
be resolved. Shortly after Lincoln signs the bill, a title tells us, North and
South work side by side, their differences reconciled, laid aside in the interest
of the railroad and national unity. Thus does Lincoln's power to suture North/
South come to embrace other oppositions and splits within the country. The
geographical integration solves a problem of political integration.

Ethnicity and American Identity

Yet there is another civil war raging, a war within the ranks of the railroad
section hands — the Irish vs. the Italians, both vs. the Chinese, and everybody
vs. the Indians. The ethnic splits serve to illuminate the question of *American*
identity; who or what constitutes an "authentic" American is a question posed
repeatedly around the self-perception of the Irish in relation to "furriners":
Italians and Chinese. Seen through Ford's Eurocentric eyes, Native Americans are simply taken for granted, period, never to be included in the process

of questioning identity, never to be thought of as part of any civilization. Indeed, as "bad guys" go in the film, it is the Cheyenne Indians who are the ultimate Other; even the friendly Pawnee, who appear briefly to aid the whites during battle, do not offset the racist representation of the Cheyenne — who, it must be remembered, welcomed the evil Deroux into their tribe, allowing him to become their chief. Native Americans — the Americans here since pre-historic times — thus lurk at the margins of the text as "others" inhabiting nature, not culture, people that Ford's "melting pot" ideology could not conceive of embracing.

This essential blindness of the film reflects a larger, culture-wide blindness on the part of white American society in the 1920s. Ken Nolley notes that "as far as Native Americans are concerned . . . Ford's films function as if they were historical texts, constructing a sense of Native American life on the frontier, participating in the social and political debates of the era in which they were produced, and helping to construct much of what still stands for popular historical knowledge of Native American life."[52] Nolley attributes much of Ford's ignorance to a grounding in traditional Hollywood representations of Native Americans, noting how his construction of Indians as savages impeding American civilization meant that Indians were almost never shown as people.[53]

Certainly, the image of barbaric Indians attacking a beleaguered train (wagon or railroad) of white people has been ingrained in our imaginations through many forms of popular culture, including and especially the movies. They reflect a staggering European-American sense of divine right to conquer the West and remove or exterminate whole Indian populations. Of course, much of that history has been told at the expense of Indians — with *The Iron Horse* being a case in point — often by misrepresenting and sugar-coating the very conscious attempts on the part of whites to manipulate, deceive, and oppress Native Americans. Revisionist history of the last few decades has corrected some of the Romantic mythology that tended to emphasize the sufferings — and victories — of whites at the hands of Indian "savages," while ignoring the cruelty and injustice with which Indians have been, and continue to be, treated.[54] The fact that the U.S. government made and broke "permanent" treaties on innumerable occasions, beginning in the seventeenth century, has traditionally been romanticized as Manifest Destiny and rationalized through the land and gold rushes that lured "settlers" farther and farther West.[55] As part of the U.S. government's campaign to settle the West and unify white America, the railroads played a central role since the 1860s in helping push Native peoples off their lands and onto ever-shrinking reservations.[56] General Grant even wrote of the transcontinental railroad in 1866 that "the completion of these roads will also go far towards a permanent settlement of our Indian difficulties.' "[57]

The ideology of the melting pot represented by Ford in *The Iron Horse* thus skirts the issue of Native inclusion — American Indians were for long not considered "persons" under the Constitution — in part by erecting the thick-accented Irish as the Good Other, the already assimilated immigrants, those who served in the Civil War and defended the Union.[58] The newer Italian immigrants, shown in the film as more troublesome, are ethnically distinct as "dark" Europeans. Significantly, their otherness is always posed against the lovable Irish — Ford's much-extolled ethnic ancestors.[59] By the end of the film, however — by the time the two railroads meet at Promontory Point — the ethnic differences have been willfully and cheerfully suppressed in the name of technological and national unity. Tony, the recalcitrant Italian gang boss, announces proudly to Corporal Casey (played by J. Farrell MacDonald), "I become Irish now! I marry Nora Hogan!" thus reinforcing Irishness as an almost originary American identity. The Chinese are still outsiders, but even they are shown smiling when the railroads link up.

It should be noted that Chinese labor, which is represented in brief segments of the film, was central to the building of the transcontinental railroads, supplying the Central Pacific Railroad with a major source of cheap labor for laying track. *The Iron Horse* explains the role of the Chinese as one of absolute necessity, asserting that no "white labor" was available, and therefore the railroads "had to use Chinese" (titles). This was largely true, as most available white men either refused work on the railroad or quit soon after joining crews in order to try their hand at gold mining.[60] While the Union Pacific was adding newly freed slaves to its mostly white construction crews in the Plains, the Central Pacific's Charles Crocker had to work hard to convince his Irish construction boss to hire Chinese workers, so repugnant did he find the idea of working side by side with "coolies."[61] Using Chinese already in California (nearly 50,000 in 1865) and Nevada (mostly miners), and going through brokers in Hong Kong, Macao, and Canton, the Central Pacific was able to obtain by late 1865 some 7,000 Chinese men to work for monthly pay in gold (though for those imported directly from China, a form of indentured servitude required them to pay off to the broker an advance made to cover their travel). Some two thousand Caucasian men made up the rest of the crew. By 1867, about 80 percent of the CP railroad's work force was Chinese.[62]

According to railroad historian Oliver Jensen, the Chinese working for the Central Pacific were the targets of competitive and racist antagonism from the Union Pacific's largely Irish crews who, when the two lines began overlapping, would push boulders onto the Chinese track-layers and detonate explosive charges around them.[63] Even on the CP, though not particularly the targets of violence, the Chinese workers were organized into segregated gangs led usually by a white, often Irish boss. In general, whites kept the skilled jobs for themselves — trestling, masonry, and rail-laying — while the Chinese were put to work grading, cutting and filling, felling trees, and performing other types of common labor.[64] They were also subject to violent racism by white settlers in Nevada and other areas crossed by the Central Pacific.[65] Nevertheless, given the upheavals in China, most preferred to stick it out, occasionally even going on strike to try to raise their wages and reduce their hours to match those of white workers.[66]

In its own vision of progress, however, Ford's Eurocentric restaging of an American foundation myth — the melting pot — is founded on a concept of community that is, in his eyes, all-inclusive and tolerant of difference.[67] Community in *The Iron Horse* is represented by the teamwork of the section hands and the fraternity of comrades, and more emblematically by Hell on Wheels, the combination saloon/court of law that followed the railroad as it built westward. The Hell on Wheels entourage in the film is headed by Judge Haller, who can instantly transform his fun-loving, hard-drinking "bar of likker" into a "bar of justice" when fights that break out are not fought fairly.

Ford's ideal democracy is a balance of healthy competition (the two railroads) and teamwork/community, as opposed to unfair property ownership. In other words, it is about fairness within the European-American community, since the issue of rightful ownership of the frontier remains remote from the question of Indian rights to the land. But in its embrace of all manner and strata of social life, including prostitutes and other social outsiders, and its insistence on *fair judgment* in a court of law where all are meant to be equal, Hell on Wheels, together with the railroad world of workers and bosses, forms an ideal community of tolerance and social justice, much like the enclosed world of Ford's 1939 *Stagecoach*.[68] As such, it is both a mini-U.S. nation and a link in the chain of the nation, while Judge Haller is a democratic father-proxy in Lincoln's republican chain of rhetorical command.

Class conflict is also displaced onto community and ethnic rivalries, thus absolving the railroad of any but the highest motives (even if they are identified at one point as economic). "Class" is represented almost solely by Deroux, the malicious landowner. Ford's ideal democratic American universe has no place for such excess; it is instead a happy balance of workers and management, all dedicated to the country, the community, and the railroad. It is as if Lincoln's blessing alone were not enough to place the track-laying project above reproach and in the realm of unquestioned crusade. Ford rewrites the history of social relations between labor and management by first locating conflict among the workers, by segmenting out and identifying one unruly element within it (Italians), by ignoring a Chinese point of view, and by proletarianizing the hero, Davy. Davy's jack-of-all-trades persona legitimizes him as an all-American: he lays rails, drives a locomotive, and scouts passes for the railroad; he also hails from humble beginnings, like the rail-splitter Lincoln.

Without question, ethnicity played an agitational role in worker relations on the transcontinental railroad. But such belligerence, particularly between the Chinese and Irish, was matched by friction between labor and management, whether over poor working conditions, long hours, or low (or no) wages.[69] When the Italian workers in *The Iron Horse* refuse to work because the payroll train has not arrived and they have not been paid for two weeks, we are meant to scorn their lack of the spirit of American teamwork, because earlier we have seen the payroll train held up and sabotaged by Indians. Responsibility shifts from the railroad company to the real Other — Indians — pitching the plot snag at an emotional register that lumps all the bad guys together as forces impeding the expansion of the great railroad.

The Story of the Couple

The divisions of Otherness, and the sense in which the community can resolve them, extend beyond class and race to include the romantic heterosexual couple, perhaps the ultimate unit in the film that both "heals" divisions and itself needs healing. Caucasian men and women constitute a basic opposition that informs nation-building and are a constantly forming and dissolving unit of the community; Judge Haller dispenses justice and marriage and divorce rites with equal alacrity.

White women might be said to be the stake of the narrative. They are what the railroad is being built for — or rather the romantic heterosexual couple, cornerstone of the community and the nation, with woman as the muse and the prize. But there are different kinds of white women in *The Iron Horse* — good woman Miriam and bad woman Ruby, the prostitute, who is ultimately redeemed not from prostitution, which is "tolerated" by the community, but from having assisted Deroux in attempting to eliminate Davy. And beyond good and evil, there is, crucially, a third kind of woman, the absent mother. Good and bad woman are resolved in the spirit of the collective, the melting pot of different types — as women, they are dissolved into Ford's vision of Americanness.

But the missing mother is never fully resolved, or at least not diegetically, because she is never even addressed as such. We are first introduced to Davy and Miriam as children of Brandon and Marsh — the whole question of maternity is taken for granted. Brandon and Davy sell their belongings and trek westward with no mention of a mother or any other family. Marsh reappears as a Union Pacific railroad contractor with Miriam in tow, but, again, no mention is made of a wife or mother. Instead, we are given a series of fathers, from Abe Lincoln on down. Nationhood and democracy would seem to be about paternity and masculinity, were it not for Miriam's presence in the story — and her presence is heavily coded as a token for Lincoln. Ford's foundation myth of America as a whole nation is about creation ex nihilo — from the head and loins of Zeus/Lincoln, not Demeter — which *is* the American myth, period: liberation from the *Mother* Country, and appropriation and incorporation of femininity and the power of creation, even in railroad-building.

This is why femininity resides largely in the virginal Miriam — and in her monumental double, the American frontier, the virgin land. The conquering of the landscape, its penetration by the railroad, is the conquering of the woman, of Miriam, and the making of a nation. The train-inflicted cuts in the landscape, to use Thoreau's terminology, are marks of possession on a previously unmarked body, the body of the landscape, the earth, Nature — America. And while not "cut" by the railroad, the Brandons' discovery of the naturally "cut" passage is in a sense tantamount to the discovery of the female sex; its possession, its penetration by the railroad is a preeminently male act, as reinforced by the approving paternal gaze of Lincoln — a truly loving gaze, insofar as Ford makes brilliant use of the breathtaking landscape he exhibits as an object of desire.

As is so typical of classical American film, the first narrative sequence brings together and sets in motion the film's dominant sexual, ideological, and narrative currents.[70] It is a condensation of many important textual tracks that become separated, only to be reunited at various points in the narrative, and then ultimately recondensed at the end. The opening scene, set in Springfield, shows us Brandon, Marsh, Lincoln, and young Davy and Miriam. Although we are introduced by titles to the two fathers first, we know that the children are the most important. Their primary significance is marked in two ways.

The first shot after the introductory titles shows the two in long shot astride a split-rail fence, around which swarm herds of sheep. It is an idealized, pastoral image of idyllic innocence, an overdetermined symbol of "virginity" at large, the beginning of something, and of a couple, a holy dyad. A few shots later, after Brandon and Marsh seniors are introduced, we see Davy and Miriam playing in the snow with a surveying apparatus. Watched by Lincoln at a nearby split-rail fence, their union is blessed by the gaze of the father, thus setting it up as the union of the country.

The two children play at surveying — the practice of marking out visually the path of the railroad. As they play it, surveying is also surveillance — a chain of watching that goes from Lincoln to Davy to Miriam, the one surveyed. Miriam's role in the game is to hold the string tied to the apparatus manned by Davy and to walk backward at his command.

This scene evokes Freud's famous fort/da scenario, in which the infant comes to symbolize the presence and absence of its mother by rolling a spool back and forth.[71] More to the point, it engages a mise-en-scène of the cinematic apparatus, which in classical cinema typically positions women as objects of the male gaze. As such, Miriam is made structurally equivalent to the landscape, which is theoretically also the surveyed object. As if to underscore this identification, little Miriam steps back, on Davy's orders, and unwittingly falls down a snowy hill. Davy rushes to her rescue and helps her brush off the snow, literal marks of her association with the land. Control through the apparatus of both the cinema and the railroad is here doubly control of woman and Nature. It is thus the couple that is born of this surveying (read: scrutinizing) operation that is watched (read: projected) by Lincoln, his cinematic vision of the future of America, his vision of America as a woman, and a couple — all mediated by an act of looking, namely, film spectatorship.

These same terms return in the next scene, when, a few days after the first scene, Davy and his father prepare to leave for the Cheyenne Hills. Marsh, Lincoln, and Miriam are there to see them off. As Lincoln chats with the men, his back turned to the camera, Davy and Miriam steal a kiss for the camera.

Lincoln turns around and smiles down on the budding couple. Then, in truly classical style, the departure of Davy is represented in shot/reverse shot, cutting between his sad expression and Miriam's tearful face as she bids goodbye.

This technique, which weds the two by means of their glances, even as it separates them in editing, finds an echo in the narrative: pleasure deferred, the couple will not be truly integrated, literally placed in the same shot as a legitimate couple able to kiss again, until the story's end, when the railroad and the nation have brought them back together. These hallmark traits of classical American film — repetition, rhyme, the destabilization and restabilization of the couple, the articulation of desire visually and primarily through editing — are in turn supported by Ford's theme of the project of integration, linkage, coupling in several senses, especially that of the railroad, doubling as making equal.[72]

The final scene of the film is absolutely clear and literal in its restatement of the parallels set up earlier: couple, community, railroad, nation, the world. This scene is preceded by key narrative moments that build toward it, moments when Davy and Miriam have come together on or before the train or tracks in an expression of train-induced coupling in the great tradition of almost every American train film made up till then, and parodied by *The General*. The two reunite and rediscover each other, for the first time since childhood, on a moving train, and later they are seen standing before the locomotive. And in the great romantic moment of embrace, the embrace that sums up by default many other erotic urges, Davy and Miriam avow their love in her caboose compartment.

The coupling metaphor of the railroad gains momentum as we approach the end of the film — and the Golden Spike. Just after the two railroads have laid their last rails, Davy stands alone on the tracks, at night, to contemplate "the consummation of his father's dream." While reflecting on this relationship between paternity, train track, and the land, with the majestic mountains visible in the background, Davy caresses the rails lovingly, and a title informs us: "With his own hands, Davy has driven the golden spike [not the actual Golden Spike]: the buckle in the girdle of a continent — America."

This symbolic buckling of the railroad, which anticipates that of the couple, is repeated the next day, in the next scene, which is also the last scene of the film (photo 30). A title opens this sequence: "The wedding of the rails, May 10, 1869," followed by a note on the use of the original locomotives that met in Promontory Point: the Jupiter (CPRR) and the UPR 116.[73] We then see

30. George O'Brien (*middle-ground left*) and Madge Bellamy (*middle-ground right*), at the Golden Spike ceremony in *The Iron Horse*, John Ford, 1924. Museum of Modern Art.

the locomotives preparing to meet as a crowd gathers. Davy stands with the CPRR locomotive on one side, in one shot; Miriam stands in the other, the reverse field. This is their first reunion since Davy left to work on the CPRR a year earlier. She bids him join her on the UPR side — "You belong on this side, Davy." Davy shakes his head and announces that they both belong on both sides, and that when the Golden Spike is driven, they'll belong to each other. It is difficult to imagine a clearer statement of the sense in which personal, social, and national destiny are joined in the railroad.

Davy watches as Governor Leland Stanford drives the spike, a sexually coded act literally consummating a physical union, while Miriam watches Davy. When the telegraph wire placed on the spike is struck, the crowd cheers, Davy rushes to Miriam, and the two kiss and hurry off-screen through the crowd. In long shot, very much like the final shot of *The Crowd*, we see Davy and Miriam run through the crowd, dissolving into the community, as the locomotives inch forward, champagne bottles are smashed, and a photograph is taken, mimicking the famous photographing of the original event. Similar to the last shot of *The General* two years later, the photo crystallizes what has been set up in the shot/reverse-shot editing: the joining of two perfectly symmetrical fields (the locomotives and the crowds around each are arranged identically), and the halting of movement (narrative, filmic and profilmic) — the welding of difference into one frozen image of unity. The railroad completed, the nation "buckled," the couple restabilized, and the community united, the film can now literally end.

The Assumption of Woman by the Buddy Plot

The romantic couple, built on male-female difference and the subsuming of female identity (difference) into male identity, paralleled by the erasure of racial difference in the triumph of white America, may be the bracketing terms of the film, but the significance is rivaled and in a sense undermined throughout by that of an altogether other type of couple: the same-sex, male couple. This type of couple is far from secondary, while there is simultaneously a sense in which the object of sustained looking in the film, by both the spectators and the characters, is often unproblematically male. Ford in general is good at representing friendship in his films, and *The Iron Horse* is no exception, especially in its homoerotic articulation of male friendship. Although the narrative is overall an Oedipal one — the deaths of both a good father (Brandon) and a bad one (Deroux) as necessary for Davy to gain access to the virgin land and the woman — it sets up a shadow "buddy" narrative that occupies far more textual time than the moments accorded the heterosexual couple. The doubling male narrative is a more subtle equivalent of the tramp couple that appears at the end of *A Romance of the Rail* (1903) as a hidden narrative parody effected through same-sex coupling.

Male bonding rituals permeate the film, from the section-hand sing-alongs, to the various antics of the "Three Musketeers" — Sergeant Slattery (played by Francis Powers), Corporal Casey, and Private Schultz (played by James Welch) (photo 31). These three secondary characters are the heart and soul of the film's "buddy system," and they provide much comic relief in the often tense narrative. One comparatively lengthy scene involves Casey and Schultz escorting the extremely reluctant Slattery to the dentist to have his tooth pulled. There is much ado about the dreaded extraction, and by the time

31. Corporal Casey (J. Farrell McDonald), Sgt. Slattery (Francis Powers), Private Schultz (James Welch), and Dinny (Jack O'Brien) in *The Iron Horse*, John Ford, 1924. Museum of Modern Art.

the dentist and Slattery's sidekicks manage to hold him down for a moment, the scene is approaching sadomasochistic dimensions. The dentist reaches for the tooth, and simultaneously Casey pricks Slattery's upper thigh with a long hat pin; the result is a double scene of victimization played off a metaphorical castration and sodomy. "Go on — be a man and a soldier!" chides Casey. This whole scene is very much a comic questioning of what is a man, of masculinity.

The Three Musketeers have intense bonds with other men as well. Their symbolic father is General Dodge, chief engineer for the UPR and the trio's commander in the Civil War. All four reunite by chance in Marsh's office in North Platte, a reunion marked by rituals of backslapping and war story remembrance. More significantly, the three are Davy's buddies, too. When Davy decides he cannot tell Miriam why he fought Jesson when she had asked him not to, Casey merrily volunteers to join Davy on the CPRR, thus offering himself as a substitute for her, and reminding Davy in cartoonlike Irish brogue: "Shure an' you'll have to take me along — you'll be worth nawthin without me." Later, when the CPRR and the UPR gangs gain sight of each other as their respective tracks draw closer together, the great scene of integration, of joining, is symbolized by Davy — "For whom no rivalry exists" — and is played as one of male bonding and brotherhood: the reunion of old pals.

The reunion is enthusiastic; the two sides cheer at each other in shot/reverse shot and rush to embrace. There follows a series of two-shots of buddy couples embracing that begins with Davy and Dinny (a young pal we have seen before on the UPR, played by Jack O'Brien) locked in a poignant embrace and passionately (the only fitting word) gazing into each other's eyes. Davy's gaze conveys to Dinny his sympathy and grief over the death of Dinny's brother at the hands of Indians, an event not properly mourned by either. But compared with the reunion of Davy and Miriam, which is marked by an extremely brief peck on the lips before the two run off to get married, the pathos is remarkable. This mise-en-scène of male coupling has the effect of mirror doubling, the perfect statement of equality as symmetry, the end of rivalry and difference. It actually completes the ideological system of Ford's film.[74] And not coincidentally, it is built on a mutual disdain for Native Americans.

Even Davy's "buckling" moment, when he stands alone in contemplation on the tracks the night before the Golden Spike ceremony, belongs not to Miriam, but to someone else: Davy's father, the explicitly evoked object of Davy's contemplation. Brandon, Sr., and son are in a very simple sense the Urcouple of the *The Iron Horse*, the doubling template for all other couples. Their relationship is privileged by virtue of both their physical closeness and the amount of screen time they are accorded. Their mutual affection is underscored in the scene in which the father is killed and scalped, when Davy breaks down hysterically, melodramatically, and weeps over his father's body. The traumatic scene the son has witnessed from the bushes, evokes Freud's famous primal scene — the child's witnessing of a sexual act between it parents. Compared to all other scenes in the film, this one is excessive by virtue of its sustained focus on affect. In a sense, Davy's uncontainable expression of mourning marks him as feminine.

The father-son relationship as a couple is also marked by virtue of a structure of looking. Their departure from Springfield is watched by Abe Lincoln, and by Miriam, in the same point-of-view pattern that characterizes Lincoln's benediction of the Davy/Miriam couple; the text holds on a shot of Lincoln gazing at the two off-screen. This is followed by the title, "He feels the momentum of a great nation pushing Westward — he sees the inevitable."

Davy, played by the ruggedly built George O'Brien is, finally, an object of contemplation as a beautiful man. His erotic image is invested with the look that elsewhere fuses with the landscape, while, paradoxically, Miriam is presented not at all as visual spectacle, but tending to be shown *looking* at others. Even Ruby the prostitute, with whom Miriam bonds in a couple of scenes, has a more active and less contemplative function. Although narratively Miriam occupies a fairly classical female role, the greater visual role accorded Davy bears testimony to the weaker points in Ford's otherwise tight system of difference.

For example, during the fight with Deroux, Davy's shirt comes off gradually, until his muscular body is exposed from the waist up. When the fight ends, after Davy has choked Deroux (also half-naked) to death, Davy poses by the opening in the stack of ties that acts as a kind of doorway-threshold onto the frontier (a stock compositional device in Ford's films). Davy pauses, and we are meant to look, to take in his physique, pitched as it is between the "savage" prairie and the civilization embodied by the railroad (the threshold of significance). As Janet Bergstrom has shown with the films of F. W. Murnau, the male body and the landscape can act as substitutes for the gaze displaced from the female body.[75] The contemplative gaze in Murnau's films invests the male form and the landscape with the same charge and eroticism normally applied to the female body. To a degree, this analysis applies to Ford's film, though his male types are less androgynous, and more classically masculine than Murnau's (hence, "American").

The paternalist buddy text ends where it began, with Lincoln's bust, the real framing image of the film. Lincoln's head floats, decapitated, as an abstract, ethereal symbol that visually as well as narratively indexes the penny image of universal circulation and equivalence. The words "His truth is marching on" appear with the bust in the final image of the film. By this point, however, "his" truth may as well be "her" truth, for the discourse of unity and healing — Lincoln's discourse — has begun to sound less paternalistic and more maternalistic. In one crucial scene, Miriam is specifically entrusted with this function — the Lincoln function, the mother function. The Italian workers refuse to continue laying track because the payroll and supply train has been sabotaged by Indians and no one has been paid in two weeks. Only Miriam's plea to Tony, the gang boss, restores them to their jobs. Using a discourse of both unity and seduction ("Tony — please — you'll go back for another week — won't you?"), Miriam achieves a Lincolnesque miracle and heals the rift. "Anything to oblige a lady!" is one worker's answer, while Tony's stereotype of an Italian response is, "For the beautiful Signorina, Tony he build the beeg railroad heemself alone."

Earlier in the film we have seen other instances that equate Miriam with Lincoln. In the first sequence, a point-of-view structure unites Miriam and Lincoln and makes her Lincoln's double in the scene where Davy and his father ride away to travel west. The use of off-screen space, with both Miriam and Lincoln looking off-screen, puts her in the structural position of Lincoln — or Lincoln in hers. In short, the doubling of the two characters is a textual device, a function of point of view as much as of narrative. It is then that we realize paternity has come full circle to embrace maternity. The absent mother has been absorbed into the paradigm of patriarchy — Lincoln is the displaced mother; he has dissolved sexual difference in his benevolent vision, a vision that is represented and realized by the railroad. Railroad-building is, then, like filmmaking, the male version of creation, or procreation, a work of labor that for the filmmaker and the railroad worker elides and transcends the "female function" in society.

The railroad in *The Iron Horse* thus embodies Ford's restricted, white, male-centered doctrine of egalitarianism and democratic utopia at many levels. Ford's is a grand vision, nearly a textbook illustration of the Manifest Destiny myth, and at the same time it illustrates the myth's circular contradiction. In the end, a seemingly rigid white male hierarchy that puts women, Irishmen, Italians, and Chinese on a sliding scale, with Native Americans at the bottom, truly does dissolve into one big nothing with the subsumption of everyone's identity into a white man's vision. *The Iron Horse* erects a sentimental version of history that gives American national identity a perversely narcissistic and racist character in its effort to deal with difference and to glorify a morally righteous point of view embodied by the railroad.

La Roue: *"Frenchness" and the Impossible Couple*

As a film that puts femininity in its place by literally replacing it, *The Iron Horse* makes a clear statement about gender in relation to the nation and the railroad, especially insofar as it figures national identity and masculinity in the railroad: women are only the rhetorical stakes of a nation-building that idealizes the absence of difference in the name of white male agency. The suppression of difference that haunts the text, especially racial difference, produces minimal textual/aesthetic effects, however, compared to another film that struggles with the difference between male and female as figured through the railroad: Abel Gance's *La Roue*, shot in 1920–21 and released around the same time as Ford's film.

Gance's 1923 epic train film (it was originally nearly nine hours long) is not about French national identity as such. In other words, "national identity" is not thematized by the film as it is in *The Iron Horse*. *La Roue* is marked, however, from beginning to end as a "French" film in both form and content. The railroad and the train play a crucial role in articulating the film's "Frenchness," insofar as the train is the great agent and metaphor of all meaning in the film. All the characters' identities, male and female, are bound up with the railroad world, while the story, which derives from a great tradition of French literature, expresses a vision of French working-class life and of the presence of the railroad in French culture that comes out of a complex history of each.

Crucially, the very rhythm of the film's construction is defined by the train, making *La Roue* at one and the same time unique in its style and a paradigm of a certain kind of French film aesthetic in the 1920s. The train is a highly unstable object in the film, evoking both the wild, thrill train films of early cinema, and the "joke" space of confusion of identity, although little action takes place within the space of the train itself. The train is a proairetic object, as such recalling Griffith; but its status as a vehicle of integration, of coupling, is equally, simultaneously disintegrationist. Gance's often delirious representation recalls Griffith's excessive editing style in *Intolerance* (1916) — an acknowledged inspiration — and may even be considered yet more excessive.[76] It is with a view to *La Roue*'s aesthetic, as defined by the filmmaking milieu of which Gance formed a key part, that analysis of *La Roue* as a "French" film must begin. Since the parameters defined by that milieu were so often articulated in opposition to American film, this analysis will begin comparatively and then extend to consideration of theme and narrative.

Aesthetics and National Identity

As noted, many European national cinemas and avant-garde movements like Impressionism arose partly in response to the classical Hollywood film that was ubiquitous in European theaters during and after World War I. Through what came to be called by the mid-twenties "Impressionism," French filmmaking resolved to define itself, much as German cinema did, as art *and* as national cinema. The extent and popularity of cine clubs and journals devoted to film criticism in the early twenties were a vibrant testament to the strength of this conviction.[77] Aesthetics — meaning the *cinematic* — served as the organizing pole of screenings, lectures, and salons. In filmmaker Marcel L'Herbier's view, " 'none of us — Dulac, Epstein, Delluc or myself — had the same aesthetic outlook. But we had a common interest, which was the investigation of that famous cinematic specificity.' "[78] All the Impressionists and their fellow travelers, like Gance, were obsessed with making *art*, which, for them, meant making films that were different from both American films *and* mainstream French films of the period. The great slogan of the Impressionists was, "the French cinema must be cinema; the French cinema must be French."[79] Such nationalism was not restricted to that film movement alone; nearly all the leading French filmmakers of the twenties declared their commitment to national "emotions," traditions, and culture. Jean Renoir stated unambiguously in 1919: "I know that I am French, and that I should work in a way that is *absolutely national*."[80] Although clearly identified with an extreme patriotism, the French right wing had no monopoly on nationalism following World War I; nationalistic sentiment — often articulated as populism — spanned the political and cultural spectrum, with only the Communists — and in art, the Dadaists and Surrealists — maintaining a more international or less nationalistic stance.[81]

Aesthetic concerns were across the board expressly nationalistic, even when inspired by non-French cinema. For Louis Delluc, Cecil B. DeMille's *The Cheat* (1915) — and Colette's review of it — were a kind of epiphany of how artistic the cinema could be, and he began to advocate "a truly French cinema art" at the same time that he focused on American films at the expense of French serials and literary features.[82] In contradistinction to Henri Diamant-Berger, who advocated a French film practice based on the mainstream American model, Delluc, who also loved American cinema, advocated an alternate French cinema, in part by singling out "certain French films and filmmakers who were developing a form of film discourse in parallel with, but differing from, the Americans," including Gance's *J'Accuse*, L'Herbier's *Rose France*, and Germaine Dulac's *La Fête espagnole*.[83]

Paul Monaco has shown how instrumental the press was in calling for films that reflected national themes and a national "tone," and how such consciousness permeated every level of the industry, including exhibition, with theater owners competing to carry the most "French" films.[84] Box-office successes throughout the twenties were routinely attributed to the films' grasp of the "national mentality," while failures were chalked up to a "national inability to comprehend the spirit of the cinema and cinematography."[85] Such views were propounded mostly by elitist critics opposed a priori to cinema as an inferior art form. In any case, the popular context for "French" films was highly conducive to the creation of a national cinema. As Monaco asserts: "The rhetoric of 'national' cinema that was common in both France and Germany during the 1920s reflected the economic realities of the movie business in both countries. The competitive nature of that business in both France and Germany meant that everyone involved in commercial feature film production 'had to slave to make something which was popular.' To be popular meant to appeal to the mass, national audience. To do this meant to develop standardized, national types of films. . . . "[86] As has been suggested, "national" criteria informed even the artistic cinema, the noncommercially oriented avant-garde.

Film scholars of French avant-garde cinema — Impressionism, "pure cinema," Dada, and Surrealism — also emphasize the extent to which a *French* film was not an *American* film. In a now classic article, Noel Burch and Jorge Dana established a taxonomy of films defined in relation to the "dominant" codes of Hollywood film, whether in a relation of imitation, experimentation, or opposition.[87] Acknowledging this model, Richard Abel sets up a somewhat different categorization of the French *narrative* avant-garde (to be distinguished from optical cinema, a style privileging formal relations of images, and Dada filmmaking), seeing it as a filmmaking practice that breaks with, adds to, and reconstitutes the conventions of classical narrative cinema.[88] David Bordwell's baseline definition of Impressionist film is the expression of subjective experience through representational techniques that bespeak a consciousness of their art.[89] This definition is included in Abel's scheme, in which such filmmaking (1) deemphasized story in order to highlight filmic discourse (L'Herbier's *photogénie*); (2) privileged the image, and avoided titles, as a means of telling the story and focusing on the subjectivity of the characters; (3) developed a syntax that employed continuity, but relied more on associational and rhythmic editing to achieve a more symbolic, and less narrative sense of structure; (4) exploited the rhetorical power of the image in metaphor and symbol; and (5) experimented with narrative structure that did not necessarily oppose the linearity of Hollywood film, but played with the conventions to produce hybrid structures that often approximated the structure of dreams in exploiting incoherence or discontinuity as a principle.[90] Almost all of these traits can be found in the German cinema of the twenties as well, and though their particular articulation in French cinema is tied to further defining factors — language, locations, literary traditions, themes, etc. — to some extent we must recognize the framing role of discourse around the French cinema as a key element in its own definition.[91] In other words, the territorial articulation of "French" films had everything to do with linguistic and rhetorical acts of marking and distinction of the time — identity by fiat — enunciated by self-appointed arbiters of cultural identity.

By insisting on the cinematic, rather than subordinating image to story, as in Hollywood film, French filmmakers felt they could distinguish their practice as artistic and French. In reference to such consciousness, Gance claimed long after the twenties that, at the time, he realized he "could never work happily with Americans because of their formula methods of shooting."[92] In *La Roue*, narrative structure and style relate to the wider context of the avant-garde in France during the first two decades of the twentieth century. *La Roue*'s ambling, elliptical plot, which critics disliked for being too long and excessive, full of slow passages and confusing symbols, and its obsession with its characters' obsessions, distinguish it from the sort of highly motivated narrative of *The Iron Horse*, in which no detail exists outside the film's tight economy of construction, with its clear synthesis of parallel plotlines resolved in a neat conclusion.[93] The same pertains to visual style. Gance's excessively image-based editing style, which yields some striking and beautiful montage sequences, could be said to be both Impressionistic and montagist or optical. As Richard Abel notes, "*La Roue* is predicated on not one but several competing conceptions of film then emerging in France."[94] Abel is referring primarily to a realist, almost documentarist film aesthetic (indebted, we might add, to Zola and the nineteenth-century naturalist novel) and also to that of a "pure" or optical cinema. Accordingly, *La Roue*'s incorporation of Impressionist rhetoric in, for example, the use of superimposition and symbolic close-ups, along with a unique rhythmic, associational montage (an acknowledged inspiration for Soviet filmmakers, along with Griffith's earlier work), mark it as an aesthetic text and a "French" film.[95] And both qualities, its "art" and its "Frenchness," were remarked by critics in relation to Gance's use of the train.

Gance's conception of "art" in *La Roue* embraced the use of a series of literary quotations that, to the embarrassment of many of his contemporaries, threw a desperate mantle of cultural legitimacy over the story set in *les bas fonds* of the railway milieu. The range of quotes is wide, from Sophocles to Shelley, but the majority are French: Baudelaire, Hugo, Cendrars, Pascal, Chamfort, Zola, Claudel, Pierre Hamp. Critics attacked the quotes precisely for imparting a literary quality to the film, insisting that Gance should be content to focus on cinema, on its own aesthetic, and not on other, traditional arts like literature.[96] They pointed to the "poetry of machines" expressed in Gance's representation of the train, a machine already considered a beautiful, aesthetic object by French avant-garde filmmakers (and avant-garde artists across Europe, like Blaise Cendrars, cited below; cf., somewhat later, *Berlin, Symphony of a Great City* and *Man with a Movie Camera*). Even though Impressionism owed much to Romanticism, Gance, Delluc, L'Herbier et al. were modernists in their fascination with machines (a fascination nonetheless minor compared to that of truly modernist filmmakers like Fernand Léger) and in their interest in everyday life and popular culture. They shared a sense of what Blaise Cendrars, the French avant-garde poet who wrote the screenplay of *La Roue*, expressed about "the poetry of the rails" in his 1913 poem on the Trans-Siberian Express: "I have deciphered all the confused texts of the wheels and I have gathered together the scattered elements of a violent beauty."[97]

In a 1923 text written about *La Roue*, avant-garde filmmaker René Clair praised the film's lyricism and its romantic conjunction of the sublime and the grotesque, asserting that "the real subject of the film is not its curious plot, but a train, rails, signals, jets of steam, a mountain, snow and clouds" — in other words, its "impressive visual themes."[98] Dulac, whose 1924 review of the montage sequences of *La Roue* was subtitled "The Song of the Rails" (after Gance), described its aesthetic: "A theme but not a drama. . . . The railway, a crisscrossed road of straight steel tracks, the railway, all that is distanced from life, a poem, whose rhymes are lines that move first singly then in a series: I don't think cinema has ever come so close to the peak of its potential as in this short poem by Abel Gance, our master. A play of light, of forms, of perspectives."[99] Dulac was fascinated above all by "wheels, rhythm, speed," a "complex visual orchestration" that is, simply, "Cinema!"[100]

Jean Epstein also referred to Gance as a poet, declaring that with this film "the first cinematographic symbol is born," namely, the wheel.[101] He saw in Gance's film a rare lyricism and drama in the locomotive rods "darker than the whole of Greek tragedy."[102] Emile Vuillermoz also considered Gance a great poet, praising his handling of the train: "Certainly, the most beautiful, moving, and original parts of his film are the experimental study of a mechanical fairyland, from drive-rod traction to hissing steam, and the description of the supernatural magic of snowy landscapes. He has learned how to analyze the hallucinatory beauty of speed, the drunken frenzy of the wheels' intelligent labor, the steel rods and gear wheels, the great stirring voice of organisms made of sheet iron, copper, and steel."[103] "Pure cinema" advocates like Léger insisted even more strongly on the abstract qualities of the film. Léger, who designed a poster for *La Roue*, wrote about the film's "plastic qualities" in reference to the machine, which, he claimed, had become the leading character and actor in the film.[104] He stated that " 'with *La Roue*, Abel Gance has elevated the art of film to the level of the plastic arts.' "[105] Even Pierre Hamp, author of the novel on which *La Roue* was based, lectured on "The *Photogénie* of the machine world" in a cine club series in 1925–26 (*La Roue* was screened over and over as a model of filmmaking to budding cinephiles in cine clubs in the early twenties).[106]

Ceci n'est pas un film américain

The aesthetic distinction of *La Roue* as a French film can be traced through analysis of certain key themes and motifs that also distinguish it from American film. By first juxtaposing *La Roue* with *The Iron Horse*, and then considering particularly French themes in the Gance film, this analysis will integrate the various aspects of "Frenchness" that come together in relation to the railroad and questions it raises about gender — questions that both differentiate *La Roue* from, and link it with, the great train films of other countries.

In many ways *La Roue* resembles *The Iron Horse* remarkably. Although the railroad in *La Roue* does not play a thematic role as a national emblem, as it does in *The Iron Horse*, many motifs at first glance link the two films above and beyond the central role of the railroad in each. Each film is concerned with the heterosexual couple and its constitution, which is a problem in both; each film takes care to evoke a realistic representation of the world of the railroad and especially of railroad work; in each film, conflict exists between labor and management; and in both films, the marked absence of mothers is virtually taken for granted. Finally, both films' narratives are driven by male characters possessed by nearly fatal visions, desires, and forces far beyond their control.

It is the extremely divergent treatment each film accords to these motifs, however, that drives them apart as texts representative of different national cinemas or different national characteristics. The representation of the trains illustrates this split. In *The Iron Horse*, the train is a positive figure, conceived in an absolutely optimistic spirit of constructive progress; in *La Roue*, the train is an ambivalent figure at best, and more often a tragic vehicle linked with the double inescapability of oppressive social conditions and a destructive Fate. Conversely, the train is hardly exploited as an aesthetic and dynamic object in *The Iron Horse*, while *La Roue* focuses a great deal on these aspects of the machine and exploits the train's metaphorical properties in relation to film. The realism of the railroad world in Ford's film is meant to evoke a popular spirit of teamwork, the communal sweat that, all things being equal, is the essence of America, doubly signified by the railroad "ties" that bind. The railroad milieu in Gance's film is claustrophobic, sooty, and alcoholic, a depressing trap for oppressed workers. Management is "righter" than labor in *The Iron Horse*, and ultimately the two sides make peace; like Vidor's *The Crowd*, the Ford film defines a very American concern, characteristic of the 1920s, to integrate the individual with the community — the corporation — in all senses. Management in *La Roue* is evil scum, while the engineer and the fireman are heroic (and even as a hero, the engineer Sisif is tainted by alcoholism and blind, transgressive lust). Divisiveness marks the life of the individual in all milieux, a fragmentation of the subject that in part reflects a national context of crisis and social fragmentation in postwar French political and social life. Maternity is absorbed metaphorically into paternity in the American film; in the French film, it is literally killed and buried in a train wreck at the beginning of the film, and thenceforth repressed. The legitimate couple is the goal and final outcome of *The Iron Horse*; in *La Roue*, it is desired, but impossible. And while the desire that drives Davy Brandon is both pure and nationalistic—Manifest Destiny and Oedipal father replacement—the desire that drives Sisif, the protagonist of *La Roue*, is impure, mad, and fatal as well as fateful.

Set in and around the railroad yards of Nice, *La Roue* begins with a Victor Hugo quotation: "Creation is a Great Wheel which does not move without crushing someone."[107] The quotation is taken seriously. Soon after it appears, we see a train wreck, from which Sisif emerges; he is holding a little girl whose parents have died in the crash. Identified by a tag that reads, "Norma—London," the child is taken home by the widowed Sisif, who raises her as his daughter and as a sister to his son, Elie. Elie and Norma grow up believing they are siblings, while developing an intense and, to them, inexplicable desire for each other. This desire is expressed in Elie's medieval fantasies, in which he courts Norma with a mandolin (the grown-up Elie is a maker of violins). Sisif also falls in love with Norma as a young lady, and, now a jealous alcoholic, he dares his railroad comrades to so much as look at her (photo 32).

Meanwhile, Norma is courted by the sleazy Jacques de Hersan, a wealthy railroad civil engineer and Sisif's boss. Crazed by his own obsession with Norma, Sisif confesses his secret one day to Hersan and then tries unsuccessfully to commit suicide under his locomotive. Hersan blackmails Sisif into giving him Norma in marriage, threatening to tell all if he refuses. Norma is led to believe Sisif's madness is a result of the poverty in which they live, and she agrees, reluctantly, to marry Hersan in order to take herself off Sisif's hands. Both Elie and Sisif are horrified by Norma's decision, but Sisif drives the train that transports Norma from Nice to Paris for her wedding. En route, Sisif attempts to wreck the train and unite himself with Norma in death—thereby keeping her for himself, and from Hersan. Machefer, Sisif's fireman, prevents the second suicide at the last moment, and Sisif loses Norma to marriage.

In the second part of the film, "The Death of Norma Compound," Elie learns the truth about Norma, and both he and Sisif confess their love for her. Elie castigates Sisif for standing between the "brother" and "sister." Sisif is partially blinded by a blast of steam from a valve released through Machefer's negligence on the "Norma Compound," the locomotive Sisif has rechristened

32. Sisif (Séverin-Mars) in *La Roue*, Abel Gance, 1923. Museum of Modern Art.

in her name ("compound" refers to the type of locomotive). He attempts once more to destroy both himself and his locomotive by ramming it into an embankment. Sisif again survives, but the locomotive is hauled off the tracks for good. Looked upon by his superiors as somewhat deranged, Sisif is demoted to running a funicular railway on Mont Blanc, where his worsening eyesight encourages a dependence on his dog, Toby. Elie joins him and works on discovering the secret of the violin of Cremona. One day Elie attends a concert that features one of his violins at a neighboring resort, and he spies Norma, who happens to be vacationing there with Hersan. Elie and Norma reunite, and he forbids her to make her presence known to Sisif. Elie sends her a secret, never-to-be-read love letter tucked into a panel of a violin; Hersan finds the letter, and the next day he and Elie fight on a mountain slope. Elie falls off a cliff and clings desperately to a ledge, calling Norma's name. She rushes to the cliff, reaching the edge just as Elie falls to his death.

Sisif blames Norma for Elie's death and banishes her from the mountain. A year later, the waiflike Norma reappears and secretly reenters Sisif's life; she moves into the cottage, silently maneuvering around Sisif, until he eventually senses and then accepts her presence. Sisif is now totally blind, but finally at peace with Norma and himself. In early spring, Norma joins the locals in their annual circle dance on the mountainside. As they dance ever higher in the Alps, Sisif sits tranquilly by the window and dies. The film ends with an image of clouds encircling the mountain peaks, which are then crowned by a super-imposed image of a rolling locomotive.

Several themes stand out that, while not essentially French, might be said to have French significance, for French audiences at least, in reference to a tradition of French Naturalism: the impotence of individuals to change their destiny, whether individual or social; the inability of the individual to ascertain absolutely his or her identity; the equation of sex with death (and the imbrica-tion of the machine in this equation); and the impossibility of the couple, itself a subtheme of the impossibility of happiness. All of these themes exist in *La Roue* in the shadow of the basic premise of fatalism, of which the railroad, and the train in particular, are central instruments.

Fate, The Railroad

Though Gance allegedly based *La Roue* on *Le Rail*, a "proletarian novel" by Pierre Hamp,[108] the film (and, one can assume, the novel) is clearly in-debted to Zola's Rougon-Macquart series, more specifically to *La Bête hu-maine*. The setting of the railroad world, along with the alcoholic engineer and locomotive-cum-woman, by themselves are enough to evoke the Zola novel. Considering as well the motif of illicit desire and the obsessive focus on death, it is as if Hamp had written the next installment in the series. The sense of ineluctable fate that hangs over events and characters and seems to compel them to do things — or to stay where they are — informs both Gance's film and Zola's novel. Both are also marked by the worldview of Zola's contemporary, the positivist philosopher Hippolyte Taine, whose famous epithet, "Le race, le moment, le milieu," emphasized that history's actors are determined by large forces outside the individual's control. (Zola's treatment of class still falls short of the reactionary disdain for democracy and the common people that Taine's doctrine came to signify.)

As one such "large force," the train shares in the irreversible march of events that pushes Sisif to commit acts of violence (much like Jacques Lantier in *La Bête humaine*). One might even say that the train is a handmaiden of Fate.

It is associated with death and destruction, with tragedy, at every turn in the story, from the beginning train wreck sequence, through Sisif's three suicide attempts, to the "crash" of a toy locomotive that drops out of Sisif's lap as he passes away at the end. The film's final image suggests what the story has implied all along, that all "Pursue their pattern as before/But reconciled among the stars."[109] The locomotive's symbolic location here gives it a divine status, as if it truly descended from a greater power. At the same time, it figures the ascent of Sisif's soul to heaven.

The title of the film is the strongest clue to a reading of the train and the railroad as figures of Fate. "The wheel," as Abel notes, is the primary metaphor of the film: "the tragic wheel of fate."[110] Abel charts its recurrence and transmutation across the film, from the image of the locomotive wheels repeated in the catastrophe sequences, to the recurrent use of 360-degree pans, figural traces of the unbreakable cycle of suffering and joy. Pointing to the Victor Hugo quote that opens the film, Abel refers to Ixion, the mythological figure punished for desiring Hera by being bound to a chariot wheel.

> The chariot wheel that Ixion was tied to (for desiring Hera) becomes the locomotive wheel that Sisif is bound to, first out of love and then as a form of punishment. It is this crushing punishment that the film hammers out, over and over, in repeated sequences of suffering, separation, and loss. In fact, the wheel even seems to become a figure for the film itself. As a series of structural variations on the initial tragedy, the narrative acts exactly like a wheel revolving.[111]

We should note that the figure of Ixion is embedded diegetically in the film. After Elie's death, Sisif goes through his son's belongings, throwing out a small engraving that, revealed in close-up, shows an image of a martyr tied to the wheel. And the name "Sisif" itself connotes unchangeable — and tormented — suffering fate: the Sisyphus of Greek mythology, who was condemned perpetually to push a boulder up a mountain, only to have the boulder roll back down on every attempt. Collectively, the Greek intertext of *La Roue* is one of punishment, suffering, and tragedy. If this intertext is also easily coded as French, with respect to nineteenth-century French literature and French film of the twenties and thirties (Poetic Realism), since suffering is a "French" obsession, it is also the fact that the suffering is built around romantic love that further distinguishes it as French.

The train also figures Fate in a more mundane sense; it is associated with

Sisif, but controlled by Hersan, the devious superior. In other words, the railroad belongs to the destiny of class, or power as expressed in the privileging of one class over another. In French Impressionistic films by directors like Dimitri Kirsanoff and Jean Epstein, the fatalism of class is a strong theme. In *La Roue*, the class struggle between worker and boss, between working class and bourgeoisie (or even aristocracy) is the basic social split overlaid with a geographical division, that between Paris and Nice (which also signifies the provinces).[112] The distance between Nice and Paris is the distance between the classes. Hersan, who lives in Paris, disempowers Sisif by dispossession, which is expressed in details like his taking credit for Sisif's inventions, the toy locomotive prototypes scattered symbolically throughout the film. Sisif's curse is also that his poverty and inability to transcend his social position leave him vulnerable to Hersan's ability to buy Norma and take her away from him.

This tragic view of class, reinforced by the suffocating atmosphere of railroad life, is the antithesis of Ford's melting-pot worldview. The railroad in Gance's film divides more than it links; it tends to reinforce differences in class and is not at all about democracy. The railroad had signified from the beginning a kind of outside force unwelcomed by the French public (the first French lines were even built by English railway workers).[113] Unlike in the United States, where the railroad literally expanded the nation by four-fifths, the railroad in France was imposed on long-existing networks of transportation. Although ideologically bound up with the increasing unification of the country — a country divided sharply by regional differences and the split between the provinces and Paris — the railroad suggested none of the optimistic limitlessness of American trains.[114] The expansion of markets in Europe via the railroad also meant a threat to French autonomy, and, within France, to regional identity. In the gargantuan United States, trains roamed the continent for thousands of miles before national borders even became an issue.

Significantly, the history of the French railroad shows that railway ownership by nobles actually increased in the later nineteenth century, and even more so after 1902.[115] Though by 1923, the year of *La Roue*'s release, the French railway system was in the process of converting to outright state ownership, the contemporaneous struggle of the railway unions against both the state and the Grandes Compagnies (the six companies that controlled the French railway system) was marked by precisely the sort of unbridgeable class differences the railway was meant to erase.[116]

Fate and the Couple

The theme of incestuous desire, the tragic theme of Oedipus, is articulated in *La Roue* around a time-honored French theatrical and literary convention, the impossibility of the couple. In making this impossibility tragic, with a higher, purer, and ultimately spiritual resolution, Gance is a direct heir to nineteenth-century Romanticism — in particular, the poetry of Alfred de Musset, Alfred Vigny, Alphonse Lamartine, and Hugo. Given the narrative relay of Zola (even Flaubert) in the articulation of this theme, one is tempted to reread *les Rougon-Macquart* in the light of an inverted Romanticism, one in which submission to higher forces is turned earthward.

The theme of the impossibility of the couple in *La Roue* is premised on a frustrated and unrealizable desire: incest. The tragedy is that incest is socially, not biologically, a problem, and that knowledge of the true relations is divulged, if ever, *only* at the wrong times. Sisif desires his adopted daughter, while Elie desires his adopted sister, and Norma her adopted brother. In fact, all these desires are legitimate; it is the social codes of familial liaisons that tarnish them with taboo. Paradoxically, the most perverse desire of all is Jacques de Hersan's, since his desire for Norma represents pure lust and the droit du seigneur of upper-class privilege. This is the perversion of an unjust social system in which conflicting codes of transgression are caught. Elie's love for Norma is absolutely pure, as represented by his medieval fantasies (shared by Norma) and the euphemism of music, his very noncorporeal and beautiful courtship/seduction when he serenades her on his violins. Sisif's desire falls between that of Elie and that of Hersan; his raging lust, which he creates (the construction of his desire around its taboo is clearly one thing that fuels the lust), is tempered by his paternal, reverential love for her (though even this love poses a paradox, since he confesses to Hersan that never telling Norma of her true origins safeguards his own love for her). Sisif's is truly the most impossible of loves, since, on top of everything else, Norma does not return his desire; she loves him as a child would a father. This point is where the symbolism of the name "Sisif" rings truest and parallels the wheel imagery; Sisif is condemned to eternal return, the unending repetition of what is essentially a circular situation, pushing the boulder or driving the wheel.

Abel touches on the Oedipal structure governing the characters' forbidden desires, the incest taboo that determines that structure: "For what drives

La Roue's narrative is Sisif's 'incestuous' passion for Norma and his desperate attempts to repress that passion."[117] It begins with Sisif placing the little Norma he has just rescued literally in the same bed with his son. Sisif's cheerfulness belies the profundity of this scene, for he is witnessing, indeed creating, a kind of "primal scene" in reverse. Instead of the child happening upon the unaware parents making love, we have the parent deliberately coupling the children. Elie's status as the mediator of Sisif's desire is made explicit when, fifteen years after Norma's arrival (a period of time signified in the print I viewed by an ellipsis and a title), Sisif explodes with jealousy upon seeing Elie and Norma playing together, and he forbids his son to spend any more time with her. This reverse primal scene is also a perverse inflection of the Oedipal myth and psychoanalytic scenario: it is as if Elie and Norma were the parental couple, and Sisif the son-rival desirous of killing the father in order to possess the mother.

The film is one long, extended attempt on Sisif's part to "desperately repress his passion." For example, Sisif catches himself voyeuristically peeking at Norma while she swings outdoors. We see Sisif at the window, then the object of his glance in a point of view shot of Norma's legs. Sisif looks away, then peeks again, and finally draws the curtain, sobbing into it "as if it were her skirt."[118] Sisif knows his desire is perverted, but he does not recognize that his attempts to repress that desire and preserve the fiction of the family are equally perverse: "The more he asserts the 'law of the father' and tries to maintain Norma's false identity . . . the more he suffers. . . . As a consequence, in order to preserve the relation of father to 'daughter' and, by extension, the Oedipal bonds within the family, the repression he imposes on himself perversely almost destroys them."[119] It literally destroys Elie and even Sisif — his loss of eyesight is the Oedipal price of his desire, but it is a punishment meted out by the locomotive, Norma Compound.

Fate, Woman, and the Train

Sisif ruins his eyes in a blast of steam escaping from a valve on the locomotive. Though narratively this accident is caused by Machefer, who fell asleep on the job, psychologically and symbolically the film finds fault with two conflicting agents: Norma, clearly, but also Sisif, insofar as he also identifies with the locomotive. In terms of the first, both La Lison, the locomotive of *La Bête humaine*, and Norma-Compound are women-machines that signify the undoing of their respective masters. Post-Zola machines are doubly invested with the ambivalence of modernity: oppressive monsters that, in the right hands, have the power to liberate humanity from toil.[120] It is the identification of the locomotive with a woman that makes it destructive and fatal, beyond the control of the engineer. As in *The General* and in the writings of Marinetti, the locomotive signifies both the engineer and the woman. Norma's association with the locomotive identifies her with the larger force of fate that puts her at the center of the tragedy affecting Sisif and everyone else, including herself, her martyrdom (thus, the martyr on the wheel could also be Saint Catherine). The train has a life of its own as a displaced figure of Norma. It refuses to die or be killed, and it refuses to kill Sisif. Whenever Sisif attempts to wreck it, or to kill himself and/or Norma, something prevents him from achieving his ends. It is as if the locomotive were possessed by Norma's will-to-life at such moments, a transference of power through nomenclature of the tag that reads "Norma-London" and that Sisif hangs in the engine cab (reminiscent of Annabelle's photo in *The General*).

Sisif's own identification with the locomotive makes his punishment a self-mutilation, a mea culpa autoflagellation. It is simultaneously a sadistic sexual act authored by Norma, targeting the eyes as transgressive organs, and an act of masochistic sexual release; both are, in a sense, forms of pleasure. "Pleasure, orgasm," writes Baudrillard of J. G. Ballard's *Crash*, "perverse or not, has always been mediated by a technical apparatus, by a mechanics, of real objects, but more often of *fantasmes* — it always implies an intermediary manipulation of scenes or gadgets."[121] And in the case of *La Roue* the "intermediary manipulation" takes place through the train, the vehicle that absorbs and releases the sexual tensions of the story and that takes on the displaced figuration of a potentially fatal female sexuality.

Sisif's "dirty" desire for Norma is indeed mechanical in that it is at first mediated by the train — he finds her, "La Rose du Rail," as he dubs her, in the train wreck. The train is the vehicle that unites and, in a sense, couples Sisif and Norma in the accident that brings them together and sets in motion a chain of events and images that further confuse and split identity as mediated by the train. The sequence of the accident is preceded by an abstract, visual prologue that establishes a paradigm of identification. The film opens with first Gance's face, then Sisif's face superimposed, Impressionistically, over images of locomotives. The symbolism is double. On the paradigmatic level, we have images of men and their machines, with the train clearly representing the machinery of film as well. On the syntagmatic level, we have a succession from film director/narrator to his diegetic proxy, the film character. The locomotives racing through Gance's sad face mirror in a sense the film running through his brain.[122] Sisif's face appears on the front of a locomotive advancing toward the camera; underlighting gives it a demonic character, and asks us to identify right away the engineer and his train as a portent of doom. Finally, there is an image of a woman's face in snow; this is Norma, the stake of the portent, the reason for the tragedy.[123]

These opening images are succeeded in the first sequence, "La Rose du Rail," by the abstract images of train tracks shot from a moving train in such a way that the tracks appear to blend together and move apart calligraphically, an effect aided by the use of vertical matte framing. A montage of locomotive wheels and pistons in motion follows to complete the initiation of this abstract opening built on rhythm and circular motion.[124] The sustained focus on the beauty and rhythm of the machinery is interrupted suddenly and unexpectedly by a cut to a long shot of a train wreck. "The next minute or two," writes Abel, "literally explodes with images (apparently tinted red in the original print)—cars tilted in the air, people caught in the wreckage or struggling along the tracks over an embankment, billowing smoke, lights flashing across the control shack, figures in silhouette before a flaming car, a woman hanging lifeless from a window, another collapsing beside a squalling baby, a hand grasping out of twisted metal, locomotive wheels lying about, a close-up of a rose lying against a rock, and a begrimed, staring Sisif holding a little girl (Norma). All of these shots are intercut so rapidly and jarringly that it is difficult to take them in."[125]

This montage is soon followed by another. Sisif, holding Norma, notices that the signal has not been changed, while another train is fast approaching. A series of shots alternates at a rapidly accelerating pace: Sisif trying to lift a train wheel and axle, the oncoming train and its engineer, the people of the wrecked train. A quick series of shots concludes the montage with the successful signaling of the approaching train, and the scene ends on a shot of the rock and the rose, with baby Norma beside it.

The sequence is a kind of creation myth. The story begins with a bang, and out of the explosion, literally born ex nihilo from the ashes (and the train, as well as the film), the parentless Norma is delivered to Sisif. This mise-en-scène of disaster represents simultaneously a black cloud (death, trauma), the silver lining (Norma), and the hint of more tragedy to come (the near-crash of the second train). The single image that sums up the web of contradictions is the rose on the rock: the austere juxtaposition of soft and hard, living and dead, which is represented later by Norma's sheer presence in the midst of the filthy railroad world. Norma is a kind of "fleur du mal," an unintentional flower of evil blooming in a man-made, metallic, grimy environment.

This symbolic juxtaposition, and the sense of the train as the ambiguous mediator of all identities in the film, is recovered in the sequence in which Sisif rams the locomotive into a bank of flowers in an attempt to kill himself and his engine. He has at this point rechristened the locomotive "Norma Compound," an identification of woman with train underscored previously by the superimposition of her face over the steam on the locomotive as Sisif was preparing to wreck the train with Norma aboard on the way from Nice to Paris. Here, Sisif's unsuccessful attempt to kill himself and Norma further imbricates the train in the chain of coupling. Since a wreck is what brings them together at the beginning, it is in a way only fitting (and symmetrical) that a crash weld them together at the end: the perverse ideal of bodies and souls merging in a tangle of hot metal. Sisif vows just before trying to wreck the train, "The Rose of the Rail and the Man of the Wheel were meant to die together!" As such, the proposed act of coupling recalls that of Jacques Lantier in *La Bête humaine*. Lantier is pushed by an inherited criminal tendency to murder the woman who tempts him; the killing is the ultimate act of possession, as the text tells us: "Finally, finally! he had satisfied himself, he had killed her. . . . He derived from it a surprising sense of pride, a sense of expanded male sovereignty. He had killed the woman, he possessed her, as he had desired for so long to possess her, completely, to the point of annihilating her. Dead, she would no longer belong to anyone."[126] Both Sisif and Jacques derive an intense and very male-coded pleasure from a violent control over the threatening female body.

The association of sex with death is an old French theme in both high art and popular culture. Besides the nineteenth-century literary obsession in Zola, Gustave Flaubert, Baudelaire, to name only a few, there is the linguistic slippage between "l'amour" and "la mort"—only a nuance of pronunciation separates them verbally. The French language has enshrined this slippage in the idiom "la petite mort," the little death—a euphemism for orgasm. This idiom haunts the ending of *La Roue*, which represents the symmetrical train

33. Sisif in *La Roue*, Abel Gance, 1923. Museum of Modern Art.

crash, the wreck Sisif could not achieve three times before, only this time it happens in miniature. When Sisif dies, the toy locomotive he is caressing falls and crashes to the floor, signifying a double death that takes the form of a "petite mort" (photo 33). We see Sisif stroking the engine, both a phallic metaphor and a proxy for Norma, as his eyes roll back in his head; here the representation of blindness, emphasizing the whites of the eyes in uncontrollable movements, is transformed into the representation of *jouissance*, or orgasm. The dog Toby barks, and Sisif says, "Tell me, Toby—is the wheel still turning?" As a cloud representing Sisif's soul passes over them, we see the dancers, followed by the train steaming through the clouds around the mountain peaks.[127] The last shots of Sisif show him white-eyed and head back, with his pipe smoke rising above him in the form of rings—an organic, indexical sign of his connection with the wheel, Norma's wheel. It requires no complex analysis to read the pipe smoke as the trace of ejaculation that the broken train has initially figured. In short, Sisif's death is strongly coded as a sexual act, and one that is displaced onto the train.

Ideal Love and the Transitivity of Gender in Film and the Train

The ideal of desire posited by the film is ethereal, noncorporeal: Norma is to be kept innocent, as far as possible, both of her true origins and of her sexuality. Elie's fantasy sequences define his desire, and Norma's, within a medieval world of lutists and ladies, the allegorical world of *Le Roman de la Rose* — the medieval French literary classic blatantly recalled in these sequences and in the oft-repeated phrase used to describe Norma, "La Rose du Rail."[128] It is clear that this innocent, mutual love between Elie and Norma is the "right" love, the proper couple. As such, the film privileges the beautiful, effete son who could not be more different from his macho, animalistic father. Like other aesthete-heroes in French Impressionist film of the twenties (in those by L'Herbier and Jean Epstein, for example), Elie reincarnates a Romantic hero, one attuned to things spiritual, cerebral, beautiful, feminine — and one who is doomed by fate.

The sense in which Elie is indeed a "feminine" figure must be read against an ambiguous Norma. Her identity as a female is both a source of trouble for the other characters and an undefined, unclear representation in and of itself. Consider the way in which Norma as a grown-up girl is first introduced to the spectator: in drag. In this sequence we first see Elie, now a young violin maker, working on his craft in an "atelier," a room inside Sisif's small house wedged between the railroad tracks. A tomboyish Norma comes gleefully bounding through the door wearing engineer's overalls, sporting a false mustache, and straddling a goat decked out to resemble a train: its tail drags a string of violins meant to represent train cars. Compared to Elie, Norma is the one who "wears the pants" and is the "son" to Sisif, the child who follows in the father's footsteps by imitation, even to the point of denying or at least disguising her sex. Impersonating Sisif, however, she also "rides" him, if we see the goat/train as a double for Sisif's locomotive; as such, she presents an image of sexual domination, which extends to Elie as well, since his violins represent him in the intimate mise-en-scène of sexual play.

Norma's playful transvestism bears all the marks of children's sexuality, innocent of rigid gender determination. It is Sisif's desire, defined specifically — and cinematically — by his gaze, that marks her as a woman, i.e., as a sexual being (note the scene where he peeks at her while she swings). This is the problem of Norma's identity, symbolically expressed in the confusion of her transvestism, and it is a problem that both the film and Sisif attempt to repress, through both ideal love and absolute denial — which, taken at its most extreme, implies the death by train wreck that is desired, though not achieved, by Sisif. Thus, the "male" connotation of Norma's tomboy identification with Sisif in a sense *gives* her a sexual identity, while Elie's "femininity" desexualizes him, hence the chaste fantasies. Sisif's masculinity is by definition, then, the sexual that is expressed as such. What precipitates a crisis in this definition is both a woman (his terror at desiring her) and a machine (the train to which he is libidinally attached).

It is clear that, on the one hand, Sisif and his locomotive are identified with each other, and, on the other, that the locomotive is a substitute for Norma as well. This transitivity of the locomotive recalls that of *The General*, in which the machine is at the center of the de- and resexualization of the characters and of their interchangeability. In *La Roue* the machine is more bound up with confusion and ambiguity of identity, though interchangeability is often the governing trope. As such, Norma is much like the train; her identification with it through narrative motifs and visual imagery, such as superimposition, gives her a kind of transitive, ambiguous status. Recall that Norma is found without mother or father, since both of them have died in the train wreck; she is literally reborn from the ashes, from the train itself. In this regard, Norma's name is significant. Sisif learns it from a tag she bears, "Norma — London."

Norma is, in other words, a foreign "other" whose entrance into the world of these highly French characters in a sense contaminates it. For one critic of *La Roue*, writing in 1923, the "foreign" connotations of the actress playing Norma were strong — and distasteful; he contended that Gance had sold out to the demands of mass taste, which included "an American clientele." The critic, Emile Vuillermoz, wrote: "According to the same rules of prudent international distribution, he [Gance] conferred the role of a young working-class woman, French by education, to an English actress [Ivy Close] who, although charming, distorted the character by performing in a resolutely American manner."[129] The "American manner" refers no doubt to her acting style in such scenes as Norma's riding the goat, in which the evocation of an energetic, American, even Griffith-style actress is striking and certainly not especially French (*or* stereotypically female). Similarly, the name "Norma" connotes "normal" (a French-English cognate).[130] And since the codes of what is "normal" (and taboo) are continually put into question, both her name and ambiguous gender haunt the narrative from the film's beginning.

Confusion, ambiguity, interchangeability — beyond the train, all are figured rhetorically by the filmic process, which is charged with the same transitive functions as the train in identifying and confusing characters, especially Elie and Norma. Narratively, Elie is identified with Norma not only by his femininity, but by his vocation. Having apparently spurned the occupation of his father for more ethereal pursuits, Elie, a maker of musical instruments, and by implication, of music, is also a thing of beauty blossoming in the grime. His medieval "Roman de la Rose" fantasies are, textually, embedded or nested moments of "flowering" in the midst of the tragic plot. They serve "Normafunctions" and link the two as ideal objects. But it is cinematically in which Elie and Norma become linked most closely. Elie's death sequence, when Norma is running to him as he calls her name and clutches the rock on the cliff before falling, is edited to identify the two lovers in what is tantamount to superimposition.

An accelerating montage alternates Elie's face, Norma's face, Norma's eyes, images of Norma in medieval dress, and flashbacks to Norma from earlier in the film. Abel offers an interpretation of the acceleration that culminates in a one-to-three frame alternation:

> The sheer speed and density of this accelerating montage clearly functions as a representation of Elie's last moments of consciousness, as he remembers images of Norma from various periods of her life. Yet the very rapidity of the cutting (making the two characters synonymous), the pause in her eyes, and the shifting association of the several masking devices seem to include her changing emotional state as well. Through this interchange of shots, Elie's love and pain seem to coalesce magically in Norma. Their subjective states become so intermeshed that they literally seem wedded in an expanded instant just before the moment of his death.[131]

Thus are the two "aesthetic" characters of the film resolved, aesthetically, in an editing pattern that refers back to the opening train wreck sequence that expresses the same urgency.

A similar aesthetic resolution, by editing, in the end redeems Sisif's love through participation by displacement in the kind of love defined by Elie and Norma. Chastity and virginity are the lingua franca of this ideal sacred love, which infuses the mountain and cloud imagery of the final sequence. Already in the virgin-white Alps, high up in the realm of spirit, Sisif dies and his soul ascends to heaven in the figure of the locomotive, which is shown in superimposition as an ethereal image floating above the clouds. It is as if Gance wanted to redeem the earthly — heavy, dirty, mechanical, sexual — by literally freeing it of all corporeality and concreteness and by making the locomotive abstract. As such, the locomotive becomes identified cinematically with the clouds, which moments before have represented Sisif's soul passing over the ring of dancers, including Norma. The film offers this metaphor as a token of spiritual as much as sexual reunion, the only couple that ideally can respond to the innocent child couple of baby Elie and Norma at the beginning of the film. The locomotive brings full circle the train as the mediator of desire, the agent of impossible coupling, and the double of the cinema: both are machines that separate and link Sisif and Norma, that "edit" them as characters whose ultimate identities are resolved through the juxtaposition of noncorporeal images.

Thus, the ending of *La Roue* is a beautiful, yet tragic, resolution to the problems of the male subject as represented by Sisif, problems engendered by confusion over, contamination by, and fear of female sexuality. Having posed Norma's identity, and by implication "woman's," as a problem for the characters and the text, Gance's film indulges in a protracted repetition of suicide, depression, unattainability, and unhappiness. In a sense, by repressing maternity so strongly, as does *The Iron Horse*, but without recourse to a symbolic mother, as with the Lincoln figure, *La Roue* invites the return of the mother as the vengeful return of the repressed. His split subject, Sisif, is incapable of absorbing maternity into paternity, just as he is incapable of working through the Oedipal scenario. Oedipus is Oedipus in *La Roue;* even homoeroticism is not a safety valve for frustrated sexual tension.

The machine is such a valve, however. As the universal medium of exchange that mirrors the film's exchange function (interchangeability of identities through editing), the train recodes desire in its own image, uniting "the rose of the *rail*" and "the man of the *wheel*" in a machine logic that can absorb any sexuality, any gender. We have seen this logic at work in a number of train films, from early cinema's train and streetcar comedies to *Man with a Movie Camera*. But while this logic operates narratively and diegetically in *The General* and narratively and metaphorically in *The Iron Horse*, in *La Roue* it is an aesthetic logic, a logic of modernity that looks ahead to Vertov's film through a uniquely French lens.

Conclusion

Isn't it interesting how the three great movie farces are all set on trains? . . . "Palm Beach Story." "Some Like It Hot." "Twentieth Century." It's because the action has to be contained. People have to enter and exit but have no way out. — Scott Rudin[1]

The journey this book has taken ends at the threshold of a great era in train movie history, that of sound cinema. While silent film produced some remarkable train engineers — Keaton, Ford, Gance, Griffith, Sennett, Edison, Vertov, Vidor, and countless early filmmakers — sound film has added scores more to the roster: Jean Renoir, Alfred Hitchcock, Fritz Lang, Max Ophüls, Josef von Sternberg, Cecil B. DeMille, René Clément, John Stahl, Jean Mitry, Richard Fleischer, Satyajit Ray, John Frankenheimer, Costa-Gavras, Sergio Leone, André Delvaux, Jiri Menzel, Robert Aldrich, Sidney Lumet, Wim Wenders, Arthur Hiller, Luis Buñuel, and Andrei Konchalovsky — directors, respectively, of the films *La Bête humaine* (1938), *Strangers on a Train* (1951), *Human Desire* (1954), *Letter from an Unknown Woman* (1948), *Shanghai Express* (1932), *Union Pacific* (1939), *The Battle of the Rail* (1945), *Leave Her to Heaven* (1945), *Pacific 231* (1949), *The Narrow Margin* (1952), *Pather Panchali* (1955), *The Train* (1965), *Compartiment de tueurs* (1965), *Once Upon a Time in the West* (1968), *One Night, One Train* (1968), *Closely Watched Trains* (1966), *Emperor of the North* (1973), *Murder on the Orient Express* (1974), *Alice in the Cities* (1974),

Silver Streak (1976), *That Obscure Object of Desire* (1977), and *Runaway Train* (1985).

Closer in time to our time, and perhaps more easily remembered because of this, railroad films from the last several decades tend to eclipse the multitude of such films made before 1930. The shared fascination with the train, however, is built on continuity from one era to the next, from Edison to Frankenheimer. Take, for example, Scott Rudin's narrative intuition regarding three American train films from the sound era — *Palm Beach Story* (Preston Sturges, 1942), *Some Like It Hot* (Billy Wilder, 1959), and *Twentieth Century* (Howard Hawks, 1934). Producer of some of the most popular Hollywood films of the 1990s (*The Firm, Sister Act, The Addams Family*), Rudin has put his finger on a major reason for the enduring appeal of railway journey narratives for cinema: "the action has to be contained." We have seen this logic at work in many silent railway films in which trains functioned as containers, stages for action — from *What Happened in the Tunnel, The Great Train Robbery*, and *The Deadwood Sleeper* to *Pullman Bride, The Hazards of Helen*, and *The Crowd*. The sense in which the railway journey provides a contained space and time, a special "nowhere" outside the sphere of normal rules and codes of conduct, has been seized upon by directors from the beginning of film history.

Silent cinema's treatment of the train as kinetic sculpture also established a visual language of wheels, steam, and speed in both classical and experimental films that set the stage for future treatments of the image. Jean Mitry's essay film *Pacific 231*, a short ode to the train with music by Arthur Honegger, is an ode to Gance and Vertov as well, as is British filmmakers Basil Wright and Harry Wett's 1935 documentary *Nightmail*. Although the train in sound cinema settles into a role more as vehicle or stage and less as aesthetic object per se, there is still a clear fascination with the way the locomotive defines the screen that is a legacy to the nineteenth-century photograph and stereograph and was exploited ever since *L'Arrivée d'un train*. The visual language for representing the train embraced not only the concatenation of wheels, steam, and tracks, but the compositions, the rapid perspectival filling of space, the rush of movement from a dot on the horizon to an all-consuming foreground presence.

There are thematic continuities as well. The work of everyone from the Lumière Brothers, to Edison, Griffith, and Ford — themselves drawing on earlier modes of representation of the train — informs almost all Westerns of the sound era, from *The Virginian* (Victor Fleming, 1929) and *Dodge City* (Michael Curtiz, 1939), to *Duel in the Sun* (King Vidor, 1946), *High Noon* (Fred Zinneman, 1952), and *Butch Cassidy and the Sundance Kid* (George Roy Hill, 1969). The same holds for the standard linkage of the train with hobos or tramps that we associate with the thirties, from *Sullivan's Travels* (Preston Sturges, 1941) to *Emperor of the North* (Robert Aldrich, 1973) and *Fried Green Tomatoes* (Jon Avnet, 1991), all descendants of Nervy Nat and his early cinema brethren. And *A Romance of the Rail* set the thematic and narrative course for perhaps the greatest obsession of railroad films made in the sound era, including the western: stories of men, women, and locomotives.

Without question, the great themes of this book—panoramic perception, tourism, voyeurism, seduction, romance of the rails, thrill and shock, an orientation to simultaneity—continue well into the sound period. What all train films share is the voyeur, the tourist, an incorporation and showcasing of the passenger/spectator in the fiction through an imaginary journey into another reality—escape as escapism. In both silent and sound film a major way in which this escapism has played out is in a concerted attention to looking and deciphering, beginning with films like Méliès's *The Tricky Painter's Fate* and continuing with films by directors such as Fritz Lang, whose silent and sound films used trains to make a cinematic statement of desire connected to the act of looking. In many of Lang's films—*Spies* (1928), *Fury* (1936), *Man Hunt* (1941), *Ministry of Fear* (1944), *Scarlet Street* (1945), *Human Desire* (1954)— the train is typically an optical apparatus, a metonymy of vision itself; it is also a vehicle of libidinal movement.

Lang's great thriller *Spies* (*Spione*) gave silent cinema one of its best examples of train-embedded, cinematic dream screens where characters' desires are translated into plot. Toward the end of the film a female double agent on her last mission for evil spymaster Haghi (a Mabuse-like figure who sees/controls all) boards a train. Through the window of her compartment we see, framed in the window of another train, on a parallel track, the man she loves, a spy whose journey will end in disaster thanks to Haghi. She does not know he is in danger, but she cannot reveal herself to him in any case, as she must carry out her mission in order to be free to join him. Her desire is literally framed by a screen—as ours is framed by her point of view—and the image vanishes with the departing train almost as soon as she notices it. She also notices the number of the train as its passes—a number she had seen earlier, but cannot remember where — which will later make sense to her in the middle of the night when she bolts upright in her compartment bed and realizes her lover's train is destined to crash into another train in a tunnel.

What is cinematically interesting about this scene is that the female spy awakens on her train at the moment her lover's train crashes, even though they are nowhere near each other. The film represents this connection filmically, through editing, in such a way that it appears she awakens because of the crash. In a reciprocal, symmetrical movement, her lover awakens just before the crash because his train car, detached from the rest of the train and left to be smashed in the tunnel, comes to a halt, causing a medallion she had given him to fall onto his chest. In a sense, she saves him: although he will suffer the crash, he will not die, in part because he awoke early enough to see what was coming. The lovers thus communicate through a dream logic that is also a train/cinema logic charged with danger and longing. As such, the psychic space of the film collapses into the train journey — for the characters, a journey taken in bed — in which both shock and sexuality can be anticipated but not predicted. Lang has put a literal and figurative frame, a railway frame, around desire.

Some twenty-five years later, Lang would reprise the device of the train window as cinematic screen in *Human Desire* (1954), a remake of Jean Renoir's 1938 *Le Bête humaine*. The very beginning of the film sets up a marriage of train and film — and passenger and spectator — in the alternation of shots of two train engineers looking from the front of a locomotive in motion, and shots of the track, scenery, a tunnel, bridge, and passing trains on parallel tracks. In this opening sequence, no dialogue and little sound occurs, other than music over the credits and generic train noise as the train rolls along. What Lang establishes here is an almost pure desire to look, to be a passenger/spectator, to be carried along toward a story, but through the seduction of vision, the act of looking. What will eventually come to fill the screen in a metaphorical sense will be precisely a woman, seduction in another sense that picks up on the desire of the characters and the spectator to look, to see — a desire framed and in a sense created by the embedded screen of the double locomotive window. As the sequence progresses, the rapid forward movement of the train keeps our vision glued to the screen, while the stark marriage of the two machines keeps the spectator in a balance between looking and imagining, which is what tourism/voyeurism are all about; we are on a train/in a movie, after all, and this always promises that something will happen. This sequence is the logical heir to Hale's Tours and the thrill films with the camera mounted on the fronts of locomotives drawing the spectator inexorably into the film. It is the original seduction of the train film.

To be sure, there are important differences in representation from one era to the next. Sound, of course, is the major axis of difference, even though we know that silent cinema was never actually screened in silence, without music or sound effects. In addition, it could be fairly said that silent film only began to explore and develop feature-length narratives involving train journeys, while sound cinema lavished attention upon the vehicle as precisely a vehicle, a hotel-on-wheels of drama and comedy. And while it is difficult to generalize about the fate of the train in various national cinemas in the sound period without benefit of a systematic study, it seems clear that in American sound cinema the train disappears overwhelmingly into the past — the western — or the exotic, with some notable exceptions, Hitchcock's and Lang's thrillers being chief among them. In the United States the further away we get from the last decade of the train's preeminence as mass transit — the twenties — the more the iron horse becomes an object of nostalgia.

In European cinema, by contrast, the train appears more consistently as a contemporary vehicle in a world where trains remain a major force of social life for millions of citizens — in, for example, Delvaux's *Un Soir, un train* (*One Night, One Train*, 1968), Buñuel's *That Obscure Object of Desire* (1977), Alain Robbe-Grillet's *Trans-Europ Express* (1966), and Wenders's *The American Friend* (1977) and *Alice in the Cities* (1974). A film that combines the sense of contemporary, everyday life such as that which the train represents for Europeans and the exoticism it represents for Americans is *Before Sunrise* (1995). Made by American director Richard Linklater and featuring Ethan Hawke, whose American student-tourist character meets and falls in love with a young French woman played by Julie Delpy, the film begins with an extended "meet-cute" (Hollywood's term for the contrived first meetings of characters who usually end up falling in love) set in a key fantasy space of America's imaginary of Europe: the train. This could not have been set in the United States and have the same aura of normalcy associated with train travel. The European railway is a cliché of American touristic consciousness and a potent figure of fantasy — precisely for the reasons it has always been: chance meetings, adventure, and voyeurism, windows onto other countries, landscapes, and lives.[2]

One director whose work embodied this cliché while transposing it to an American context was Alfred Hitchcock. Like Lang, he established a body of films in which the train played a major role, beginning in Europe and continuing in the United States. In *The 39 Steps* (1935), *The Secret Agent* (1936), *The Lady Vanishes* (1938), *Shadow of a Doubt* (1943), *Spellbound* (1945), *Strangers on a Train* (1951), and *North By Northwest* (1959), Hitchcock made great use of the train in narratives that expand upon earlier film treatments of the subject. One Hitchcock film in particular for me measures the distance between silent and sound cinema's treatment of the train. That film is *The Lady Vanishes*, made toward the end of the 1930s while Hitchcock was still in England. The distance measured is small enough to show continuity with earlier train films, and yet large enough to illustrate the differences. Two scenes that occur close together in the film will exemplify what I mean.

A spy thriller that involves English tourists returning home from an unnamed, generic East European country, the film takes place for the most part aboard a train en route back to England. The plot twist promised in the title occurs near the beginning of the journey. Seated in a compartment filled with various East European types who appear "suspicious" as well as the kindly old English lady Miss Froy (Dame May Whitty), our main character Iris (Margaret Lockwood) falls asleep after having earlier been hit on the head by a suitcase. Her last image as she goes out is of Miss Froy smiling comfortingly. When Iris comes to, she asks for Miss Froy, only to have the entire compartment deny that she ever existed. The lady has vanished. Miss Froy, who will become a fugitive from Nazi-like Balkan spies, has become a fugitive image.

Earlier, we have seen Iris meeting Miss Froy for the first time in the dining car. Just at the moment when Miss Froy is to tell Iris her name, the train enters a tunnel and the resulting noise makes it impossible for both Iris and the spectator to hear what she is saying. Miss Froy decides to write her name for Iris in the dust (or is it grease?) on the train window, which later becomes a half-erased clue in Iris's search for evidence of Miss Froy's existence. Very much like the lady herself, the name ends up nearly disappearing, becoming an ambiguous trace of what we, like Iris, know to be the truth.

The first scene shows us the legacy of the joke space, with its paranoia based on visual deception, and its equation of hysteria with the train — only this time, it is female hysteria, Iris madly battling the chorus of disbelievers who want her to think she is crazy for having hallucinated Miss Froy. The scene is a direct heir to *Nervy Nat Kisses the Bride* and *The Tricky Painter's Fate:* the sense of "now you see it, now you don't" exploited in those early films. It also recalls *Uncle Josh* and *The Photographer's Mishap*, two early films in which seeing and believing are put into doubt in relation to the train and an image. And it reinforces the sense in which the train journey is both a dream and a nightmare in which anything could happen, and the sudden passage from one state to the other — much as in hysteria — is reflected in cinema's own handling of the dream/fantasy voyage.

We should recall that the more prosaically hysterical "joke" space of early train films was very much premised on surprise and the chance juxtaposition typical of train travel, which became integrated into the space and in some cases the very textual fabric of the film. In such films this instability gave rise to scenarios of confusion and inversion of identity, and often to perversity as well (*Toodles and Her Strawberry Tart*, *What Happened in the Tunnel*, *The Deadwood Sleeper*). In films like *Nervy Nat Kisses the Bride* and *What Happened in the Tunnel* (and its British precursor, *A Kiss in the Tunnel*), the identity of spaces within the train created a "joke space" of substitution, of interior montage, a shifting corporeal topography underwritten by movement.

The second scene from *The Lady Vanishes* shows us the role that sound can play in the double representational system that is train/cinema. The effect of live accompaniment and Hale's Tours-type sound effects notwithstanding, *The Lady Vanishes* is a profound demonstration of the rich possibilities of integrating train sounds into a picture; it gives the sounds a powerful role in increasing narrative complexity. Train noise obscuring dialogue is a reference to silent cinema, where reading lips becomes a game of deciphering and interpretation. Hitchcock cleverly evokes the abandoned intertitles of silent film in the very diegetic space of the fiction, using the noise of the train as an excuse for having Dame May Whitty inscribe her character's name literally on the dream screen, the window. There is thus a narrative role for noise, a way in which the film is not offering dialogue as a replacement for intertitles, but sound as a partner with images in creating and unraveling enigma and mystery. The cinematic train has entered a new realm of signifying potential.

A more immediate predecessor to *The Lady Vanishes* in this regard is Josef von Sternberg's 1932 *Shanghai Express*, which features the very images of wheels and steam made famous by *La Roue* and *Man with a Movie Camera*, and adds the shrill sound of the whistle. Like no other film, *Shanghai Express* embodies what it means to marry sound with an image of a railroad. From the opening whistle over the first shot, the train literally screams "Sound!" We quickly realize how difficult it is to imagine a train film without the characteristic sound of a whistle blowing or the clickety-clack of the wheels on the tracks.

The train in *Shanghai Express* also falls squarely within the "joke space" paradigm in staging a number of "meet-cutes" among various characters. Its "coupling" role (like that of *The Lady Vanishes*, which also brings a couple together) harks back directly to the early films just mentioned as well as to *The Crowd*. In such films what I have called "train editing" points to a generalized temptation to transgress codes of propriety that involve respectability, not unlike the "temptations" produced in the viewing spaces of early film. *Shanghai Express* makes great use of train editing to bring its couple together and advance the romantic and sexual aim of the journey. The film even includes a very proper female character as a foil — a prudish, small-minded, and annoying older woman traveler, the embedded morality police whose petty judgment of Dietrich's and Anna May Wong's sexuality we are meant to disdain.

In *Shanghai Express* the train is associated strongly with Dietrich's sexuality, as in many ways the train functions as an elaborate display case — more shop window than stage — for her character Shanghai Lily. One scene in particular makes a direct association between the train and the sexual act. Midway through the film, Lily joins her former lover, Captain Harvey (Clive Brook), on the observation deck. In the course of correcting a past misunderstanding that had caused him to have contempt for her, she ends up seducing him. As the two kiss, we cut to an image of steam gushing out of the locomotive smoke stack, accompanied by a whistle and clanging bells. When we return to the couple, who are completing their kiss, the first thing Harvey says to Lily is "I wish you could tell me there had been no other men."

Beyond the obvious displacement of desire figured in the cut to the steam and locomotive wheels, the line uttered by Harvey firmly establishes the sexual character of the exchange by referring to Lily's other lovers or, more precisely, to the fact that she had sex with them. At that point, Dietrich confesses to one thing she wishes she could change about the past — her hair. Donning the Captain's hat, she claims she would not now have bobbed her hair or, in the sense in which long hair has always signified femininity in comparison to short hair, become a man.

In using Dietrich to throw both Captain Harvey and the spectator off-balance, *Shanghai Express* recalls *The Crowd*, where the train is the crucial zone in which identity is made and unmade. Putting masculine identity into crisis, both *The Crowd* and *Shanghai Express* use the train as an important object and space to underwrite the male character's breakdown. In the twenties, as American train films demoted women as heroines and subordinated them to male characters, while simultaneously increasing the focus on women as objects of the male look, women came into their own as consumers, as sexual beings, and as consumable objects with "deficiencies" created and addressed by advertising. Men as well were entreated to think of themselves as deficient subjects — partly in relation to the increased visibility of women in the public sphere, particularly since femininity in the early twentieth century was literally not in its place, but moving out of traditional, fixed spaces and places, in a sense calling masculinity into question.

Before the imposition of the Hays Code in 1934, women were given an even more overtly open sexuality on screen. But whether it was explicit or implied, brazen or "proper," the train as a figure of female sexuality, and as a vehicle for perversion — a leitmotif that translates into homophobia in the case of *Strangers on a Train* — continued to mark film texts with a vertiginous instability. If we never again attain the level of female engagement with the machine that *The Hazards of Helen* offered (or even *The General*), we also rarely get the engineer and his toy without some kind of female marking of the machine and its space. Trains become coded even more as sex chambers, places where female and male desire are negotiated, in some cases literally — for example, in *Twentieth Century* and *Some Like It Hot*.

Throughout film history, dealing with female spectatorship has meant devising various strategies in different cultural contexts for incorporating, controlling and expressing the changing place and demands of women as Western societies moved out of the nineteenth century and into the twentieth. Female spectatorship in the train films of the silent period, like female sexuality, is far from a single, unitary, and unproblematic thing — much, in fact, like male spectatorship.

The machine is the guiding paradigm, since it is the machine — both the train and the cinema — that can decode and recode subjectivity and gender by virtue of its discontinuous shock effects on the subject and by further virtue of its status as a *vehicle* of identification that can be invested and coded with any desire, any subjectivity, which, in the age of emergent consumerism, defined all spectators a priori as consumers. The courting of the middle-class female spectator is a case in point: beneath the rhetoric, the legitimation of both the railroad and the cinema was about wooing consumers, purchasers of tickets. It is, after all, cinema's business to cash in on the instability of identity, to offer its mode of coherence, and to provide narrative and textual pleasure as a response to crisis, as in *The Crowd*.

Simply, cinema has attempted to control the return of the female and male spectator time and again to pay for the experience of reliving its crisis and its fictive resolution, its happy ending. But if such exchanges are more or less regulated, controlled at the till as well as in the text, they are never completely absent as a dynamic ground for the variability of spectatorship. Efforts to resolve identity in films of the teens and twenties, in both classical and avant-garde train pictures, are in a sense about this fluidity of codes precipitated by early cinema. Because train films tend to foreground the similarities, the doubling between the railroad and the cinema, they illuminate especially well the leveling effects of the apparatus, the absorption of spectatorship into the joke space of the imaginary, and the incorporation of the railroad paradigm into film's narrative and aesthetic systems. The almost originary power of the double, the mirror shows us what drives the narrative so central to the train-cinema relation and so powerful to the film spectator-passenger: the mise-en-abîme of the journey, the overwhelming expectation of plot, surprise, action, of something promising or threatening to happen.

The attempt in this book to understand cinema's fascination with the railroad began with a hunch: the suspicion that before there was cinema proper, it already existed in the railroad. As we have seen, the establishment of the railroad as a precursor to and a paradigm for early cinema, both American and European, was determined in a number of areas: technology, tourism, public spectacle, photography, the institutionalization of standard time, and the railroad's cultural reception in society. Early cinema revealed its fascination with and debt to the railroad in exhibition practices (Hale's Tours), in subject matter (*Arrivals*, *A Railway Tragedy*), in its mode of representation (thrill/travel films), in stories (*The Hold-Up of the Rocky Mountain Express*, *Le Tunnel sous la Manche*), and in discourses on the reception of cinema in society.

It is in the spectator/passenger that the train and the cinema converge most closely, as each creates its tourist, its visual consumer, its panoramic perceiver, its subject out of a fundamental instability: discontinuity, shock, and, ultimately, suggestibility. The visually based, fantasy-oriented subjects of the railroad and the cinema are also those of the city and its raison d'etre, consumerism. These are subjects whose ability to make judgments is influenced by images, and whose psyche is based on the destabilization of traditional modes of perception, consumption, sexuality, social interaction, and the framing of vision by a window/screen.

If early cinema set up a relation between the train and itself based in part on panoramic perception and a kind of virtual reality experience — one in which visual perception was wedded to the physical sensation of reality — later cinema only deepened the effect of "now you see it, now you don't," of putting into doubt all appearances. Deception, suggestibility, and the uncertainty of representation, these form the modus operandi, the currency, of modern life in which so much becomes subject to confusion and the influence of image-based culture. Extrapolating from Georg Simmel's insight into the advantages of city life over the village, it is clear that modern, urban-based culture makes deception easier. And the phenomenon of railway travel made deception easier, still, in part though high-speed, physical displacement, a disorientation that in cinema translates into a visual questioning of what is true and what is false.

What is ironic today is the train's nostalgic value as a symbol of the historical, the traditional, the "good old days" of white Main Street America when everybody knew their place. Cinema itself has acquired some of these quaint associations as a technology of the last century surviving in the age of the World Wide Web. We forget that it is precisely the train, and later the cinema, that threw social place into crisis and created rupture with the past on an unprecedented scale. To a very great extent, the world we live in still bears the imprint of the railroad — witness the Internet, a vehicle of chance meetings where identity is nothing if not secret, anonymous, a bracketed charade incapable of being verified. The railroad gave us our first mass vehicle of deception — based on a fundamental perceptual shift in which speed and the visual framed every encounter with the Other. The cinema gave us our second such vehicle. And with both, we got machines that would guide us as tourists and consumers through a world made by and for each.

Notes

Introduction

1   C. A. Lejeune, Review of *The Iron Horse*, Nov. 14, 1925, in *The C. A. Lejeune Film Reader*, ed. Anthony Lejeune (Manchester, U.K.: Carcanet, 1991), 75.

2   Dominique Noguez, "Fantaisie férroviaire," *Traverses* 13: Le Modèle férroviaire (Dec. 1978): 95–102.

3   The Golden Age of railway travel in the United States was 1890–1910. See Oliver Jensen, *Railroads in America* (New York: American Heritage, 1975) 192.

4   Jensen 12.

5   Jensen 13–14, 16–17.

6   See Jensen 20; and Guy Chaumel, *Histoire des cheminots et de leurs syndicats* (Paris: Librairie Marcel Rivière, 1948) 4–5; Henri Vincenot, *La Vie quotidienne dans les chemins de fer au XIXe siècle* (Paris: Hachette, 1975), 20–21, 34–35; Alfred Cobban, *A History of Modern France*, vol. 2: *1799–1871* (1961; Harmondsworth: Penguin, 1977), 124; and Paul Hastings, *Railroads: An International History* (New York: Praeger, 1972), 50–51.

7   Hastings 44–45.

8   Jack Simmons, *The Railways of Britain* (London: Routledge and Kegan Paul, 1972), 7, 15–22; Jensen 20, 25; and John Stover, *The Life and Decline of the American Railroad* (New York: Oxford UP, 1970) 17.

9   See Jensen 87–91; and Lloyd J. Mercer, *Railroads and Land Grant Policy: A Study in Government Intervention* (New York: Academic, 1982), 6–7, on how much government had given away to railroads by the late 1930s: 179,187,040 acres, or 280,000 square miles, or an area 5 percent greater than California and Nevada combined.

10 Theodore Zeldin, *Politics and Anger*, vol. 1 of *France 1848–1945* (Oxford: Oxford UP, 1979), 189–191.

11   Chaumel 12–13; Simmons 36; Michael Freeman and Derek Aldcroft, *The Atlas of British Railway History* (London: Croom Helm, 1985), 103; and Jensen 299. Only passenger traffic, however, was nationalized in the United States with the development of Amtrak in the late 1960s and early 1970s.

12   Jensen 144.

13   Simmons 17; Hastings 50, 60; and Stover 93. Stover 100 notes that the American system increased by an astonishing 25 percent from 1900 until 1910 alone.

14   See Jensen 22; Simmons 10.

15   Simmons 26–27.

16   Jensen 222.

17   See William H. Harris, *Keeping the Faith: A. Philip Randolph, Milton P. Webster, and the Brotherhood of Sleeping Car Porters, 1925–1937* (Urbana: U of Illinois P, 1991), 2–3, on George Pullman's use of former slaves as porters for cheap labor that would flatter whites' perceptions of their own status.

18   Ronald E. Robinson, "Introduction: Railways and Imperialism," in Clarence B. Davis and Kenneth E. Wilburn, eds., *Railway Imperialism* (New York: Greenwood, 1991), 2.

19   See Robinson, "Introduction: Railways and Imperialism," 1–6, and several excellent essays on informal empire and the railway in different countries around the world in *Railway Imperialism*, only some of which are cited below.

20   William J. Fleming, "Profits and Visions: British Capital and Railway Construction in Argentina, 1854–1886," *Railway Imperialism*, 71–84. See also Robinson, "Introduction: Railway Imperialism," 4–5, and Robinson, "Conclusion: Railways and Informal Empire," *Railway Imperialism*, 194–195.

21   William E. French, "In the Path of Progress: Railroads and Moral Reform in Porfirian Mexico," *Railway Imperialism*, 85–102.

22   See David F. Holm, "Thailand's Railways and Informal Imperialism," *Railway Imperialism*, 124–132; Robinson, "Introduction: Railway Imperialism," 5, n. 2; R. Edward Glatfelter, "Russia, the Soviet Union and the Chinese Eastern Railway," *Railway Imperialism*, 137–154; and Clarence B. Davis, "Railway Imperialism in China, 1895–1939," *Railway Imperialism*, 155–173.

23   Stover 133–141; Hastings 130–132.

24   See Wolfgang Schivelbusch, *The Railway Journey: Trains and Travel in the 19th Century*, trans. Anselm Hollo (New York: Urizen Books, 1979).

25   See, for example, Robert Sklar, *Movie-Made America: A Cultural History of American Movies* (New York: Vintage Books, 1975), 18ff.; Russell Merritt, "Nickelodeon Theaters: Building an Audience for the Movies," *Wide Angle* 1, no. 1 (1979): 4–9; and Lewis Jacobs, *The Rise of the American Cinema* (1939; New York: Teachers College P, 1978), 63–66.

26   In Jonathan Crary's terms, "Very generally, what happens to the observer in the nineteenth century is a process of modernization; he or she is made adequate to a constellation of new events, forces, and institutions that together are loosely and perhaps tautologically definable as 'modernity.'" Jonathan Crary, *Techniques of the Observer* (Cambridge, Mass.: MIT P, 1991), 9.

27   Schivelbusch 57–72.

28   Schivelbusch 152–160.

29   The notion of "suggestibility" comes from theories of hypnosis. See chap. 3, below.

30   See Tom Gunning, "The Cinema of Attraction," *Wide Angle* 8, nos. 3–4 (1986): 63–70; Tom

Gunning, "An Aesthetic of Astonishment: Early Film and the (In)credulous Spectator," *Art & Text* 34 (Spring 1989): 31–45; and Charles Musser, "The Travel Genre in 1903–04: Moving Toward Fictional Narrative," *Iris* 2 (1984): 47–59.

31   Although the different individuals might be referred to as an "audience," we would do well to heed Donald Crafton's caution regarding claims that can be made for concrete, historical audience members (or as he calls them "attendees"), who may be so diverse that it is impossible to abstract them as a single audience — and yet "[a]lthough cinema-going was an activity, analyzable in a sociological sense, it was at the same time a textual activity, with the attendees participating in the construction of many meanings." Donald Crafton, "Audienceship in Early Cinema," *Iris* (Summer 1990), 9–10.

32   Mary Carbine, " 'The Finest Outside the Loop': Motion Picture Exhibition in Chicago's Black Metropolis, 1905–1928," *Camera Obscura* 23 (May 1990): 9–41.

33   See Miriam Hansen, *Babel and Babylon: Spectatorship in American Silent Film* (Cambridge, Mass.: Harvard UP, 1991), 117–125.

34   Christian Metz, *The Imaginary Signifier: Psychoanalysis and Cinema*, trans. Celia Britton et al. (Bloomington: Indiana UP, 1982). Jean Baudry, "Ideological Effects of the Basic Cinematographic Apparatus," *Apparatus*, ed. Theresa Hak Kyung Cha (New York: Tanam, 1980), 25–40. See Janet Bergstrom, "Alternation, Segmentation, Hypnosis: Interview with Raymond Bellour," *Camera Obscura* 3–4 (1979): 71–104.

35   Walter Benjamin, "On Some Motifs in Baudelaire" and "The Work of Art in the Age of Mechanical Reproduction," *Illuminations*, ed. and intro. Hannah Arendt, trans. Harry Zohn (New York: Schocken, 1969), 155–200, 217–252. For a rereading based on a different translation of Benjamin's "Work of Art" essay, see Miriam Hansen, "Of Mice and Ducks: Benjamin and Adorno on Disney," *South Atlantic Quarterly* 92 (Winter 1993): 29–32.

36   Schivelbusch 135–160.

37   Benjamin, "On Some Motifs in Baudelaire," 175–176.

38   Roland Barthes, *Mythologies* (New York: Hill and Wang, 1982); and Roland Barthes, *S/Z*, trans. Richard Miller (New York: Hill and Wang, 1974).

39   Barthes, *S/Z*, 20.

40   Michel Foucault, *The Archaeology of Knowledge*, trans. A. M. Sheridan (New York: Harper Torchbooks, 1972), 48–49, 74–76, 184–186.

41   Foucault, *The Archaeology of Knowledge*, 38.

42   Michel Foucault, *Discipline and Punish*, trans. Alan Sheridan (New York: Vintage Books, 1979).

43   See, in particular, Gunning, "The Cinema of Attraction;" Tom Gunning, "An Unseen Energy Swallows Space: The Space in Early Film and Its Relation to American Avant-Garde Film," *Film Before Griffith*, ed. John Fell (Berkeley: U of California P, 1983) 355–366; Miriam Hansen, *Babel and Babylon*; Miriam Hansen, "Early Silent Cinema: Whose Public Sphere?" *New German Critique* 29 (Spring/Summer 1983): 147–184; and Anne Friedberg, *Window Shopping: Cinema and the Postmodern* (Berkeley: U California P, 1993).

44   Giuliana Bruno, *Streetwalking on a Ruined Map: Cultural Theory and the City Films of Elvira Notari* (Princeton, N.J.: Princeton University Press, 1993).

45   Sigmund Freud, *The Interpretation of Dreams*, trans. James Strachey (New York: Norton, 1963), 312–315; Sigmund Freud, *Jokes and Their Relation to the Unconscious*, ed. and trans. James Strachey (New York: Norton, 1963); Jacques Lacan, "The Agency of the Letter in the Unconscious or Reason Since Freud," *Ecrits: A Selection*, trans. Alan Sheridan (New York:

Norton, 1977), 146–178; Sarah Kofman, *Le Respect des femmes* (Paris: Editions Galilée, 1984); Jean-François Lyotard, *Discours, figure* (Paris: Klincksieck, 1971); Richard Feldstein and Judith Roof, eds., *Feminism and Psychoanalysis* (Ithaca, N.Y.: Cornell UP, 1989).

46   Tzvetan Todorov, *The Poetics of Prose* (Ithaca, N.Y.: Cornell UP, 1977); Barthes, *S/Z;* Barthes, *Mythologies;* Stephen Heath, "Narrative Space," *Questions of Cinema* (Bloomington: Indiana UP, 1981), 19–75; Stephen Heath, "Film and System: Terms of Analysis," parts 1 and 2, *Screen* 16 (Spring/Summer 1975): 7–77, 91–113; Laura Mulvey, "Visual Pleasure and Narrative Cinema," *Screen* 16 (Autumn 1975): 6–13.

47   Jackson Lears, *No Place of Grace: Antimodernism and the Transformation of American Culture, 1880–1920* (New York: Pantheon, 1981); Kathy Peiss, *Cheap Amusements: Working Women and Leisure in Turn-of-the-Century New York* (Philadelphia: Temple UP, 1986); and Lary May, *Screening Out the Past: The Birth of Mass Culture and the Motion Picture Industry* (Chicago: U of Chicago P, 1983).

48   Gunning, "The Cinema of Attraction;" Gunning, "An Unseen Energy Swallows Space;" Hansen, *Babel and Babylon;* Hansen, "Early Silent Cinema: Whose Public Sphere?" 147–184; Judith Mayne, "Immigrants and Spectators," *Wide Angle* 5, no. 2 (1982): 32–41; Robert C. Allen, "Motion Picture Exhibition in Manhattan, 1906–1912: Beyond the Nickelodeon," *Film Before Griffith*, ed. John Fell (Berkeley: U of California P, 1983), 162–175; André Gaudreault, "Les Détours du récit filmique: sur la naissance du montage parallèle," *Les Cahiers de la Cinémathèque 29: Le Cinéma des premiers temps (1900–1906)* (Winter 1979): 88–107; and Charles Musser, *Before the Nickelodeon: Edward S. Porter and the Edison Manufacturing Company* (Berkeley: U of California P, 1991), in particular 260–265.

49   Leo Marx, *The Machine in the Garden: Technology and the Pastoral Ideal in America* (1964; London: Oxford UP, 1981); Jeffrey Richards and John H. MacKenzie, *The Railway Station: A Social History* (Oxford: Oxford UP, 1986); and James A. Ward, *Railroads and the Character of America, 1820–1887* (Knoxville: U of Tennessee P, 1986).

50   See, in particular, Raymond Bellour, "Alterner/Raconter," *Le Cinéma américain*, ed. Raymond Bellour, vol. 1 (Paris: Flammarion, 1980), 68–88; Thierry Kuntzel, "The Film-Work 2," *Camera Obscura* 5 (1980): 7–69; and Janet Bergstrom, "Enunciation and Sexual Difference (Part 1)," *Camera Obscura* 3–4 (1979): 33–65.

51   Robert Allen, "The Archeology of Film History," *Wide Angle* 5, no. 2 (1982): 4–13.

52   Noguez 85–86; Mary Ann Doane, "'when the direction of the force acting on the body is changed.': The Moving Image," *Wide Angle* 7, nos. 1–2 (1985): 42–58.

53   Musser, "The Travel Genre," 55–56.

54   Raymond Fielding, "Hale's Tours: Ultrarealism in the Pre-1910 Motion Picture," *Film Before Griffith*, ed. John Fell (Berkeley: U of California P, 1983), 116–130.

55   Frank Kessler and Gabriele Jutz, "Panoradigmes," unpublished seminar paper, Université de Paris III, 1982–83.

56   John Huntley, *Railways in the Cinema* (London: Ian Allan, 1969).

57   Tom Gunning, *D. W. Griffith and the Origins of American Narrative Film: The Early Years at Biograph* (Urbana: U of Illinois P, 1991); Hansen, *Babel and Babylon;* Musser, *Before the Nickelodeon;* Charles Musser, *The Emergence of Cinema: The American Screen to 1907*, vol. 1 of *The History of the American Cinema*, Charles Harpole, gen. ed. (New York: Scribner's, 1990); Eileen Bowser, *The Transformation of Cinema, 1907–1915*, vol. 2 of *History of the American Cinema;* and Richard Koszarski, *An Evening's Entertainment: The Age of the Silent Feature Picture, 1915–1928*, vol. 3 of *History of the American Cinema.*

58   Ben Singer, "Female Power in the Serial-Queen Melodrama: The Etiology of an Anomaly,"

Camera Obscura 22 (Jan. 1990): 90–129; Lauren Rabinovitz, "Temptations of Pleasure: Nickelodeons, Amusement Parks, and the Sights of Female Sexuality," *Camera Obscura* 23 (May 1990): 70–89; Sumiko Higashi, *Cecil B. DeMille and American Culture: The Silent Era* (Berkeley: U of California P, 1994); Michael O'Malley, *Keeping Watch: A History of American Time* (New York: Penguin, 1990).

One. Inventors and Hysterics

1 See Tom Gunning, "Non-Continuity, Continuity, Discontinuity: A Theory of Genres in Early Film," *Iris* 2, no. 1 (1984): 111; Musser "The Travel Genre" 47–59; and Tom Gunning, " 'The Whole World Within Reach': Travel Images Without Borders," unpublished paper presented to the Second International Domitor Conference, "Images Across Borders/Images sans frontières," Lausanne, Switzerland, June 1992.

2 This is judging by titles alone; one can only assume that dozens more involve or image the railroad, but without indicating this in the titles. For example, it is likely that many of the tramp films take place around the railroad. See Musser "The Travel Genre" 47; and *Production Catalog of the American Mutoscope and Biograph Company (AM&B), 1896–1902*, Museum of Modern Art Records (N.p., n.d.). Among the titles included in the MOMA Records: *Train Coming Out of Station, Philadelphia* (1896 or 1897); *Getting Off Trolley — Atlantic City* (1896); *Third Avenue Elevated Railroad* (1903); *Train Passing Hooksett Falls* (1899); *Down Kicking Horse Grade* (1899); *The Farmer and the Trolley Car* (1900); *Fast Mail, UPRR* (1900); *Arrival of Tongkin Train, Tsin Tsin, China* (1901); *New Brooklyn Bridge Panorama* (1902); *Girls Getting on Trolley* (1903).

3 See the numerous titles described in Huntley 7–48. See also Musser, *The Emergence of Cinema*, 118, on early views of New York City shot by Edison, including elevateds, streetcars, and a head-on collision of two trains in 1896. The Film Archive of the Library of Congress contains a number of train films produced before 1914. The following is a sampling of the many films screened for this book: *Arrival of Tokyo Train* (Edison, 1898); *Arrival of Train, Cheyenne* (AM&B, 1903); *A Railway Tragedy* (Gaumont, 1904); *Railroad View — Experimental* (AM&B, 1903); *Panoramic View, Horseshoe Curve, Penna. R.R., no. 2* (Edison, 1899); *A Trip Down Mt. Tamalpais* (Miles Brothers, 1906); *In The Valley of the Esopus* (AM&B, 1906); *Canyon of the Rio Grande* (Edison, 1898); *Down Western Slope* (AM&B, 1903); *Philadelphia Express, Jersey Central* (Edison, 1897); *Black Diamond Express* (Edison, 1902); *City Hall to Harlem in 15 Seconds via the Subway Route* (Edison, 1904); *Empire State Express* (AM&B, 1902); *Lonesome Junction* (AM&B, 1906); *I Due Machinisti* (Cines, 1913); *The Grit of the Girl Telegrapher* (Kalem, 1912); *The Girl and Her Trust* (D. W. Griffith, 1912).

4 See the following sections on railroad series, listed by page numbers, in *Complete Catalogue — Edison Films* (Orange, N.J.: Edison Manufacturing, 1901): 9–12, Northern Pacific Railway Series; 39–40, Mexican International Railroad Series; 41, Denver and Rio Grande Railroad Series; 42, Atchison, Topeka and Santa Fe Railroad Series; 43–44, Southern Pacific Company Series; and 93–94 "Trains." See also British Film Institute, *Early Filmmakers' Catalogues* (London: World Microfilm, 1983); in particular, W. Butchers & Sons, 1905–06, *A Trip to Southend or Blackpool*; W. Butchers & Sons, 1906, *Honeymoon, Panorama from a Descending Car of the Reichenbach Railway, Meiringen, Switzerland, Glasgow Trams*, and *Panorama in North Wales*; W. Butchers & Sons, 1907, *The Train Wreckers: Travel Series*; Gaumont & Co. — The "Elge" Lists, Dec. 1903: *Railway Panoramas*, and Clarendon Films, July 1904: *Off for the Holidays, Attempted Murder in a Railway Train*; Hepworth & Co.

Catalogues, 1903–1912, 1903: *Express Trains, Arrival of Train-Load of Visitors at Henley Station, View from an Engine Front*; and Special List of Films—Selig Films, 1903: 29–35 (Railway Scenes), 49–73 (Colorado Series). See also Fielding 119, n. 9, which describes the numerous films produced in both England and the United States in which moving trains, trolleys, or subway cars provide the filmmaker with a shooting platform; and Peter Morris, "Images of Canada," *Film Before Griffith*, ed. John Fell (Berkeley: U of California P, 1983), 67–74, which describes the all-determining role of the Canadian Pacific Railroad as a commissioner in stimulating a film industry in Canada from 1896; the numbers of train films made in the early years of Canada's industry rivaled the American output.

5   See Robert Conot, *A Streak of Luck* (New York: Seaview, 1979), 203ff.; William K. Laurie Dickson and Antonia Dickson, *The Life and Inventions of Thomas Alva Edison* (New York: Thomas Y. Crowell, 1894), 177–181. What makes Edison's experiments doubly interesting for our purposes is that he conducted them for Henry Villard, the great Northern Pacific Railway baron. Conot 203–204.

6   See Gordon Hendricks, *The Edison Motion Picture Myth* (Berkeley: U of California P, 1961), 143–157. Musser notes that George R. Blanchard, president of the American Mutoscope Company (later the American Mutoscope and Biograph Company, and then Biograph), was one of the most prominent railroad executives in the United States (*The Emergence of Cinema* 148).

7   See Musser, *The Emergence of Cinema*, 167; and Alan Williams, "The Lumière Organization and 'Documentary Realism,'" in John Fell, ed., *Film Before Griffith* 156. There is also George Spoor of Essanay, who, according to Musser, managed a theater in Waukegan, Illinois, but made his living from a newsstand at Chicago's Northwestern Railroad Station. Spoor apparently was also one of the backers of the development of a 35mm projector in 1896, the magnascope, built by Edward Amet (*The Emergence of Cinema* 162).

8   See Hendricks 1ff.; Jeanne Thomas Allen, "The Decay of the Motion Picture Patents Company," in Tino Balio, ed., *The American Film Industry* (Madison: U of Wisconsin P, 1976), 119–134; and Lewis Jacobs, *The Rise of the American Film* (1939; New York: Teachers College P, 1978), 81–84. See also Musser, *The Emergence of Cinema*, 109–111, on how Edison's name became attached to Thomas Armat's Vitascope, with Armat's consent.

9   See Kenneth MacGowan, *Behind the Screen: The History and Techniques of the Motion Picture* (New York: Delta Books, 1965), 47–48.

10 Kenneth W. Maddox, "The Railroad in the Eastern Landscape: 1850–1900," *The Railroad in the American Landscape: 1850–1950*, exhibition catalog (Wellesley, Mass.: Wellesley College Museum, April 15–June 8, 1981), 26. See also "Artists Excursion Over the B&O Railroad," *Book of the Royal Blue* 3, no. 11 (1900): 1–10.

11 Maddox 26.

12 Maddox 33.

13 *Book of the Royal Blue* 1 (Oct. 1897): 2–4.

14 The Transportation Department Photo Archive at the National Museum of American History contains several production stills of camera operators filming just such views.

15 See Musser, "The Travel Genre," 54; and Gunning, "'The Whole World Within Reach,'" 9–10, on film catalogs and railway companies.

16 *Complete Catalogue—Edison Films* 9. See n. 4 above.

17 G. W. Bitzer, *Billy Bitzer—His Story* (New York: Farrar, 1973), 24–27. See Musser, *The Emergence of Cinema*, on Bitzer and train films (150); and on James White, whom Edison hired in October 1896 to head up production, which included shooting a rash of train films

in cooperation with the Lackawanna Railroad (including the Black Diamond Express) (164).

18 The term "legitimation crisis," which refers to moments when mass loyalty to the legitimizing system can no longer be taken for granted, is taken from Jürgen Habermas. See Habermas, *Legitimation Crisis*, trans. Thomas McCarthy (Boston: Beacon, 1975), 46–48.

19 See the articles collected in *Traverses* 13: Le Modèle férroviaire (Dec. 1978), published by the Centre Pompidou, Paris; in particular, Paul Virilio, "L'Empire et l'emprise," 3–23; Pierre Sansot, "Réseaux: Structures ou rêveries férroviaires," 36–48; Marc Ferro, "Images de l'histoire," 52–53; Anne Querrien, "Le petit train," 95–102; and Révérend Père François de Dainville, "Cartographie industrielle de l'Europe au 19e siècle," 120–127.

20 Jean-Luc Evard, "Ferry Dick," *Traverses* 13: Le Modèle Férroviaire (Dec. 1978): 60.

21 Marx, *Machine*, 192–194.

22 Quoted in Marx, *Machine*, 195.

23 Quoted in Marx, *Machine*, 202.

24 See Marx, *Machine*, 192–193, 209–214.

25 Leo Marx, "The Railroad-in-the-Landscape: An Iconological Reading of a Theme in American Art," ed. Jack Salzman, *Prospects* 10 (1985): 109.

26 Both Barbara Novak and Marx stress a negative, or at least ambivalent, reading of the painting as a critique of capitalism — its sheer revelation of a whole technological complex, a system that includes a roundhouse, tracks, a station, in short, a capitalist enterprise, as well as a plethora of tree stumps indicating destruction of the wilderness. Marx, "The Railroad-in-the-Landscape," 110. Barbara Novak, *Nature and Culture: American Landscape Painting, 1825–1875* (New York: Oxford UP, 1980), 172–174.

27 Schivelbusch 73.

28 See Chaumel 5; Schivelbusch 42.

29 Quoted in Marx, *Machine*, 234. See Ward chaps. 6, 7, and 10.

30 See "Passage to India" (1868), quoted in Marx, *Machine*, 223–224; and Walt Whitman, "Chants Democratic," no. 4, *Leaves of Grass*, intro. Stuart P. Sherman (New York: Scribner's, 1922), 495.

31 See Marx, *Machine*, 187–192, 203–208.

32 Querrien 96; Richard F. Kuisel, *Capitalism and the State in Modern France* (Cambridge: Cambridge UP, 1983), 8–11.

33 See the section on "Time and the Railroad" in this chapter, below. The railroads also strongly contributed to the development of the science of economic cartography in the nineteenth century. See de Dainville 120; Lewis Mumford, *Technics and Civilization* (1934; New York: Harcourt, 1963), 198–199.

34 See Schivelbusch, chap. 6 ("The American Railroad") for a succinct analysis of cultural differences between American and European attitudes toward the railroad: "While Europe experiences mechanization and industrialization as largely destructive, as they replace a highly developed artisan culture and equally highly developed travel culture, the case of America is the exact opposite. . . . The mechanization of transport is not seen, as in Europe, as the destruction of a traditional culture, but as a means to gaining a new civilization from a hitherto worthless (because inaccessible) wilderness" (94).

35 Schivelbusch 43ff., 58–62; Marx, *Machine*, 194–195, 211–212, 249ff.; Marc Baroli, ed., *Lignes et lettres* (Paris: Hachette Réalités/SNCF, 1978), an anthology of the representation of the railroad in nineteenth- and early twentieth-century European (mostly French) literature and painting. See, in particular, Alfred de Vigny's "La Maison du berger" (1842) in

Baroli, 84–85; John Stilgoe, *Metropolitan Corridor: Railroads and the American Scene* (New Haven, Conn.: Yale UP, 1983), 140–159.

36   Quoted in Baroli 81–82.

37   Schivelbusch 44.

38   See Schivelbusch 47–50, for his Benjamin-influenced reading of the loss of regional and local autonomy as a loss of aura by virtue of the collapsing of distance. The notion of "aura" was developed by Benjamin, who defined "aura" as "the unique phenomenon of a distance, however close it may be." (Benjamin, "The Work of Art in the Age of Mechanical Reproduction," 222)

39   See Angie Debo, *A History of the Indians of the United States* (Norman: University of Oklahoma P, 1983), 183, 202–205, 213–218, and 296–297, on various lines' major roles in advancing through duplicitous means the Eurocentric agenda in the West.

40   Dee Brown, *Bury My Heart at Wounded Knee: An Indian History of the American West* (New York: Bantam, 1972), 134–135, 147, 152–157, on the role of the Union Pacific in the Plains Indians wars of the 1860s; 391 on the Northern Pacific; Philip Weeks and James B. Gidney, *Subjugation and Dishonor: A Brief History of the Travail of the Native Americans* (Huntington, N.Y.: Robert F. Krieger, 1981), 100–102, on the Northern Pacific in 1872–73.

41   Brown, *Bury My Heart at Wounded Knee*, 134, 242.

42   According to Debo, Cody killed over 4,000 in eighteen months for the Kansas Pacific, which began selling tickets for such excursions in 1868 (Debo 213–214).

43   Brown, *Bury My Heart at Wounded Knee*, 135, 147, 153, 155–157, 177–186; Weeks and Gidney 102–104.

44   See Marx and Schivelbusch, n. 34, above, and O'Malley 60–62 on ambivalent and negative reactions to the railroad's noisy, nasty intrusion on the land, particularly that of Hawthorne, who in 1843 published his rant against the railroad in the form of the short story "The Celestial Railroad."

45   See Marx, *Machine*, 250–252, 260, which quotes liberally from *Walden*. The references can be found in Henry David Thoreau, *Walden and Other Writings*, ed. and intro. Joseph Wood Krutch (New York: Bantam, 1982), 174, 177, 190–196.

46   Marx, *Machine*, 263.

47   Evard 63. The train "desocialized" as much as it socialized. See Virilio, "L'Empire et l'emprise," 4.

48   Schivelbusch 80.

49   See Schivelbusch 81–82; and Daumier's *Third Class Carriage*, reprinted in Honoré Daumier, *Les Transports en commun*, preface Max Gallo (Paris: Editions Vilo, 1976).

50   See Robert C. Reed, *Train Wrecks* (New York: Bonanza Books, 1968); Schivelbusch chaps. 8 and 9; and Julie Pêcheux, *L'Age d'or du rail européen (1850–1900)* (Paris: Berger-Levrault, 1975), 174–185.

51   See Daumier, plates 5, 8, 45, and 46; *L'Illustration*, 1895–1897 (all issues, vol. CVI–CIX; see, in particular, the column "Documents et informations"); Anthony J. Lambert, *Nineteenth-Century Railway History Through the Illustrated London News* (London: Newton Abbot, 1984); Box 62, Warshaw Collection, National Museum of American History, Washington, D.C., contains several examples of *Punch* illustrations from the 1840s and 1850s that caricature the danger of railway accidents.

52   Reed 17.

53   Reed 25ff.; Schivelbusch chaps. 8 and 9; Jensen 178. Even the railroad industry was sensitive to its dangers. Reporting on "Railway Accidents in the Third Quarter of 1904," which lists

411 killed and 3,737 injured between July and September, an article in *Railway Age* noted: "Notwithstanding that a very gratifying decrease is shown in the number of employees killed, the quarter under review may, as a whole, be termed the most disastrous on record in fatal accidents to passengers." "Railway Accidents in the Third Quarter of 1904," *Railway Age* 27 (Jan. 1905): 105.

54 Archibald Williams, *The Romance of Modern Locomotion* (London: Seeley, Service, 1912), 121.

55 Chaumel 4–5, 118–130; Schivelbusch 176–179; Benson Bobrick, *Labyrinths of Iron: A History of the World's Subways* (New York: Newsweek, 1982), 142–148, 158–160.

56 See Matthew Josephson, *The Robber Barons: The Great American Capitalists, 1861–1901* (1934; New York: Harcourt, 1962); Stover 78–87; Jensen 136–144.

57 See Edward Winslow Martin, *History of the Grange Movement, or The Farmer's War Against Monopolies* (1873; New York: Burt Franklin, 1967), 253, 313. See also Stover 89–92.

58 Martin 407–416; Stover 90–91.

59 Stover 92; Jensen 156–160.

60 See Gerald G. Eggert, *Railroad Labor Disputes: The Beginnings of Federal Strike Policy* (Ann Arbor: U of Michigan P, 1967), 152–191.

61 See Eggert 1–6, and 24–27.

62 Bernard J. Brommel, *Eugene V. Debs: Spokesman for Labor and Socialism* (Chicago: Charles H. Kerr, 1978), 35–40; James Alan McPherson and Miller Williams, eds., *Railroad: Trains and Train People in American Culture* (New York: Random House, 1976), 104–112; Stover 88–89.

63 African American participation in railroad labor struggles, as with labor more generally, was long rejected by white unions, but it reached an apogee of autonomous success in the all-black Brotherhood of Sleeping Car Porters, formed in 1925 in response to both Pullman *and* racist white union attitudes, and it was led by the famous intellectual A. Philip Randolph. See *Keeping the Faith*, 4 on Debs, and 12–27 and 35–41 on formation of the BSCP; Herbert R. Northrup, *Organized Labor and the Negro* (New York: Harper, 1944), 48–101.

64 Brommel 35–40; McPherson and Williams 104–112.

65 Alan Trachtenberg, *The Incorporation of America: Culture and Society in the Gilded Age* (New York: Hill and Wang, 1982), emphasizes the profound ambivalence of popular and high cultural attitudes toward the railroad in the late nineteenth and early twentieth centuries as part of a larger context of ambivalence toward industrial culture in general. In the Gilded Age, he notes, "Along with regional and local autonomy, age-old notions of space and time felt the impact of mechanization as a violent wrenching of the familiar. . . . And the chief agent of such cultural changes, was, of course, the most conspicuous machine of the age: the steam-driven locomotive, with its train of cars." (57) As such, the railroad formed part of the representation of the monumental event of mechanization in "ambivalent cultural images of machines and inventors, and in displacements running like shock waves through the social order." (69)

66 The Warshaw Collection in the National Museum of American History contains a number of pamphlets stating the views of both sides in the matter of regulation. See, in particular, L. D. McKisick, "Addressed to the Lawyers in Congress—In the Matter of Funding the Debt which the Central Pacific Railroad Company owes to the United States," *San Francisco Examiner*, Jan. 28 1896: n.pag. (Box 76); Samuel Rea, *How the States Can Co-operate in the Efficient National Regulation of Railroads* (N.p.: Pennsylvania Railroad, 1917) n.pag. (Box 91); *Railroad Facts* 4 (Chicago: Western Railways' Committee on Public Relations, 1926)

(Box 91); J. M. Mason, *The Right to Regulate Railway Charges* (New York: National Anti-Monopoly League, 1881–1882) (Box 76).

67 *Sayings and Writings About the Railway — By Those Who Have Managed Them and Those Who Have Studied Their Problems* (New York: Railway Gazette, 1913), 15.

68 *Sayings and Writings About the Railway* 24.

69 *Railway Age Gazette* (Feb. 13, 1914): 2.

70 Stilgoe 3–15. The term "culture industry" comes from Max Horkheimer and Theodor Adorno and refers to the rationalization of art, leisure and life itself through self-described industries of mass culture that reduce everything to the unrelenting sameness and conformity of consumerism, while maintaining the illusion of individual freedom. See Horkheimer and Adorno, "The Culture Industry: Enlightenment as Mass Deception," *Dialectic of Enlightenment*, trans. John Cumming (New York: Seabury, 1972), 120–167.

71 Robert C. Allen, "The Archeology of Film History," 6.

72 See May 36; Merritt 5–9, on nickelodeons as "democracy's theater;" and Miriam Hansen, "Universal Language and Democratic Culture: Myths of Origin in Early American Cinema," in *Myth and Enlightenment in American Literature* (in honor of Hans-Joachim Lang), ed. Dieter Meindl and Friederich W. Horlacher in collaboration with Martin Christadler (Erlangen: Erlanger Forschungen, 1985), 321–342, on the lineage and development of the notion of democracy and American cinema, especially in relation to Griffith.

73 Hugo Munsterberg, *The Film: A Psychological Study* (1916; New York: Dover, 1970), 64, 73ff.

74 Munsterberg 12.

75 Musser, *The Emergence of Cinema*, 183; see also Bowser, *The Transformation of Cinema, 1907–1915*, 1–4.

76 Musser, *The Emergence of Cinema*, 183–184.

77 According to Eileen Bowser, there were about 2,500 nickelodeons at the beginning of 1907, and 4,000 to 5,000 by the end of that year. Bowser, *The Transformation of Cinema, 1907–1915*, 4.

78 Merritt 6.

79 Merritt 6. See Mary Carbine's valuable article on black spectatorship and film exhibition in Chicago in the first quarter of the century (" 'The Finest Outside the Loop': Motion Picture Exhibition in Chicago's Black Metropolis, 1905–1928," 9–41).

80 On film exhibition in the vaudeville context, see Robert C. Allen, *Vaudeville and Film, 1895–1915: A Study in Media Interaction* (New York: Arno, 1980); and Robert C. Allen, "Vitascope/Cinématographe: Initial Patterns of American Film Industrial Practice," *Film Before Griffith*, ed. John Fell (Berkeley: U of California P, 1983), 144–152. See also Douglas Gomery, *Movie History: A Survey* (Belmont, Calif.: Wadsworth, 1991): "Until the explosive growth of the nickelodeon in 1906, American vaudeville theatres provided the movie industry regular access to potential patrons." (14)

81 Michael Chanan, *The Dream That Kicks: The Prehistory and Early Years of Cinema in Britain* (London: Routledge and Kegan Paul, 1980), 133.

82 Donald Crafton in his study of the French cartoonist and early film animator Emile Cohl emphasizes the fact that the middle classes constituted the original film audiences in France: "From its origins, in France cinema was defined as an urban, middle-class phenomenon, competing for the same market that constituted the readership of *Le Rire, La Caricature*, and other great French humor magazines." *Emile Cohl, Caricature and Film* (Princeton, N.J.: Princeton UP, 1990), 241; see also 231, 239–245 on the bourgeois public of early French film; and Crafton in "Audienceship in Early Cinema," 1–12, 6–7, on the social and eco-

nomic diversity of "the audience" for early cinema, which was, it seems, never rigid but perpetually middle-class in its essential identity. See Richard Abel, *The Ciné Goes to Town: French Cinema, 1896–1914* (Berkeley: U of California P, 1994), 33, on ways in which different French cinema venues and programming formats catered to different classes of audience, with the development of permanent cinemas and stabilized programming contributing to the development of a regular white-collar and bourgeois audience between roughly 1907 and 1911. On fairgrounds as exhibition sites, see Jacques Deslandes and Jacques Richard, *Histoire Comparée du Cinéma*, vol. II: *Du cinématographe au cinéma, 1896–1906* (Paris: Casterman, 1968), 21–28; 83–250. See also Jean Mitry, *Histoire du cinéma: Art et industrie*, vol. I: *1895–1914* (Paris: Editions Universitaires, 1967), 106ff.; and Georges Sadoul, *French Cinema* (London: Falcon, 1953), 7.

83   See Bowser, *The Transformation of Cinema, 1907–1915*, 19; Sklar 18–19, 30–32, 89–90; Mayne, "Immigrants and Spectators," 32–41; May 31, 36, 48, 110–114; and Garth Jowett, *Film: The Democratic Art* (Boston: Little, Brown, 1976), 38ff.

84   Mayne, "Immigrants and Spectators," 38.

85   Sklar 30–32; Jacobs 62–66; and May 43–59. See also Bowser, *The Transformation of Cinema, 1907–1915*, 37–40.

86   Sklar 30–32; Jacobs 62–66; May 43–59.

87   Besides Jane Addams (Hull House), motion picture reformers included Joseph E. Lee (Playground Association) and Fredric Howe (National Board of Review). The board's membership included representatives of major universities, the Federal Council of Churches, the YMCA, the New York City school board, and the Society for the Prevention of Crime, along with Samuel Gompers and Andrew Carnegie, among others (May 54). It is important to note, however, that church reformers who wanted the nickelodeons curbed (through Sunday closings, for example) and more progressive reformers who wished to regulate it toward a more socially acceptable kind of experience represented two different currents within the motion picture reform movement. See William Uricchio and Roberta Pearson's illuminating *Reforming Culture: The Case of the Vitagraph Quality Films* (Princeton, N.J.: Princeton UP, 1993), pp. 26–40.

88   Sklar 18.

89   Sklar 18ff.; Jacobs 63–66.

90   See Bowser, *The Transformation of Cinema, 1907–1915*, 48; May 43ff.

91   See Gunning, *D. W. Griffith and the Origins of American Narrative Film*, 155; Bowser, *The Transformation of Cinema, 1907–1915*, 41–43 and 48–52. See also Sklar 31–32; May 54–60.

92   See Sklar 32; Jacobs 65–66; Mitry 254ff; Sadoul 69ff.

93   Mitry 254ff; Deslandes and Richard, p. 242. See Uricchio and Pearson on how cultural masterpieces in other media provided a source of "uplifting" images and subjects for filmmakers, especially the Vitagraph Company, which staked its reputation on its "Quality Films" based on high art stage plays, literature, and other socially sanctioned works (Shakespeare, Dante, the Bible, etc.) (Uricchio and Pearson 48ff). See also Bowser, *The Transformation of Cinema, 1907–1915*, 42.

94   See Abel, *The Ciné Goes to Town*, 40–41.

95   Hansen, "Early Silent Cinema: Whose Public Sphere?" 167–177. See also Sabine Hake, *The Cinema's Third Machine: Writing on Film in Germany, 1907–1933* (Lincoln: U. of Nebraska P, 1993), esp. chap. 2 "The Cinema Reform Movement," 27–42; and an earlier article in which she laid out some of her key theses, "Girls and Crisis: The Other Side of Diversion," *New German Critique* 40 (Winter 1987): 147–164.

96   Hansen, "Early Silent Cinema: Whose Public Sphere?" 168.

97   Hansen, "Early Silent Cinema: Whose Public Sphere?" 169; and Hake, *The Cinema's Third Machine*, 28–36.

98   See Jean Déthier, ed., *Le Temps des gares*, exhibition catalog (Paris: Centre Pompidou, Dec. 13, 1978–April 9, 1979).

99   Hansen's characterization of the early cinema as "a collective forum for the production of fantasy" applies to the railroad as well (*Babel and Babylon*, 111).

100   See Gerald Mast, *A Short History of the Movies* (Indianapolis: Bobbs-Merrill, 1976) 297; Chanan 174; Linda Kowall, "Siegmund Lubin, The Forgotten Filmmaker," *Pennsylvania Heritage* (Winter 1986): 18–27. Musser, *The Emergence of Cinema*, 32: "Photography provided the first key element of standardization in screen practice."

101   Many of these observations were initially inspired by Patrick Loughney at the Library of Congress.

102   On travel images generally, see Tom Gunning, "The Whole World Within Reach': Travel Images Without Borders." Gunning discusses a range of travel images that fulfilled this "surrogate" function. For train images specifically, see William Darrah, *The World of Stereographs* (Gettysburg, Pa.: W. C. Darrah, 1977) 185–188; and William C. Darrah, *Cartes de Visites in 19th-Century Photography* (Gettysburg, Pa.: William C. Darrah, 1981), 88ff., 156–157. I am grateful to Patrick Loughney for introducing me to Darrah's work.

103   Darrah, *The World of Stereographs*, 185–188; and Darrah, *Cartes de Visites in 19th Century Photography*, 156–157. See also the wealth of stereographic and postcard views of railroads contained in the Warshaw Collection of the National Museum of American History, and in the Library of Congress, Photographic Division.

104   Robert Taft, *Photography and the American Scene* (1938; New York: Dover, 1964) 374–389; and Patricia R. Zimmerman, "Filming Adventures in Beauty: Pictorialism, Amateur Cinematography, and the Filmic Pleasures of the Nuclear Family from 1897 to 1923," *Afterimage* 4 (Dec. 1986): 8.

105   Taft 374.

106   This view is based on the study of approximately a hundred photos in the Division of Transportation Photo Archive, National Museum of American History, and the considered opinion of John White, curator, Division of Transportation, National Museum of American History. A number of these photos, which were taken for various companies, caption the image with the speed at which the train is traveling.

107   See Susan Danly Walther, "The Railroad in the Western Landscape: 1865–1900," *The Railroad in the American Landscape: 1850–1950*, Exhibition Catalogue (Wellesley, Mass.: Wellesley College Museum, April 15–June 8, 1981) 44. See also Gunning, " 'The Whole World Within Reach,' " for a compelling analysis of the direct relation between travel films and the ideology of colonialism (8–9, 11–12).

108   "Immediately after the invention of the new camera and its name, Eastman began a national advertising campaign, describing his new instrument and its ease of operation in the popular and well-known magazines. He thus reached the general public and a new class of patrons was actually created." (Taft 389)

109   Zimmerman 8.

110   The Warshaw Collection in the National Museum of American History is rich in documents of the promotional efforts of the American railroads in relation to tourism from the 1870s through the early years of the twentieth century. Pamphlets, journals, flyers, books,

and visual advertisements of all sorts were used to advance a more mass-oriented, albeit middle-class surge in tourism in the late nineteenth century.

111   Susan Sontag, *On Photography* (New York: Farrar, 1977), 9. On the railroad and tourism more generally, see John A. Jakle, *The Tourist: Travel in Twentieth-Century North America* (Lincoln: U of Nebraska P, 1985), 84–100.

112   Sontag 64.

113   See Jensen 96–99. Jackson and Russell were two of many photographers and artists who could count both railroad companies (as corporations) and wealthy railroad magnates (as individuals) among their patrons. (Walther 37)

114   See Gunning, "The Whole World Within Reach," 8.

115   See Sontag 51–84. As Gunning notes, "The image becomes our way of structuring a journey and even provides a substitute for it. Travel becomes a means of appropriating the world through images." (" 'The Whole World Within Reach,' " 4)

116   See Musser, *The Emergence of Cinema*, 30–42 and 221–222; and Musser, "The Travel Genre," 52–53. The epigraph to Burton Holmes's *The World Is Mine* (Culver City, Calif.: Murray and Gee, 1953) reads "To travel is to possess the world." See also Burton Holmes, *The Burton Holmes Travelogues*, vol. 1 (New York: MacClure, 1908); and Burton Holmes, *The Burton Holmes Lectures — Illustrated in Color, Accompanied by a Series of Original Motion Pictures Projected by the Chronomatographe* (Chicago: E. Burton Holmes, 1897–98). Trains and travel figured into a related music hall entertainment that also segued into early film exhibition, the sing-along. The early filmmaker Sigmund Lubin, for example, actually helped popularize early movie houses (his 1899 movie theater is perhaps the oldest) with his glass lantern slides produced for "rousing movie house sing-alongs" that came before or after the films; the only extant Lubin slides were made for the popular tune, "In the Baggage Coach Ahead," a song about a train ride. (See Kowall 18–27.) See also Charles Musser in collaboration with Carol Nelson, *High-Class Moving Pictures: Lyman H. Howe and the Forgotten Era of Traveling Exhibition, 1880–1920* (Princeton, N.J.: Princeton UP, 1991), on Lyman Howe, the turn-of-the-century traveling showman who built his own projector to show films to "high-class" audiences (see, in particular, 47–68 on Howe's "Animotiscope").

117   Holmes, *The Burton Holmes Travelogues*, "Biographical Note," n.pag. See also Musser, *The Emergence of Cinema*, 221.

118   Musser, "The Travel Genre," 47–50. Gunning notes that travel films and railway films overlapped so closely in early film that they are practically indistinguishable genres ("The Whole World within Reach," 9; and earlier in this chapter).

119   Musser, "The Travel Genre," 56.

120   Musser, "The Travel Genre," 57.

121   Musser takes Noel Burch's notion of ambivalence in Porter's films and extends it to the analysis of a number of films that incorporate several genres at once (which explains, in his view, the popularity of *The Great Train Robbery*) ("The Travel Genre," 57). See also Charlie Keil, "Steel Engines and Cardboard Rockets: The Status of Fiction and Nonfiction in Early Cinema," *Persistence of Vision* 9 (1991): 37–45.

122   On women and shopping in relation to tourism, Friedberg notes: "The subjective effects on the tourist are not unlike those of the cinema" (*Window Shopping* 59ff.).

123   See Richard Koszarski, *An Evening's Entertainment*, 1–9, on details of the trip and the event.

124   See Charles Musser, "Toward a History of Screen Practice," *Quarterly Review of Film Studies* 9 (Winter 1984): 59–69; and MacGowan 25–75.

125   Friedberg 94.

126   Helmut and Alison Gernsheim, *L. J. M. Daguerre: The History of the Diorama and the Daguerreotype* (New York: Dover, 1968), 6–7. See also Evelyn J. Fruitema and Paul A. Zoetmulder, eds., *The Panorama Phenomenon* (The Hague: Foundation for the Preservation of the Centenarian Mesdag Panorama, 1981), 17–40.

127   Gernsheim 6.

128   Kessler and Jutz 9.

129   Gernsheim 16. The diorama Daguerre created in 1821 was inspired by the Diaphnorama of Franz Niklaus Konig.

130   Quoted in Gernsheim 17.

131   Kessler and Jutz 14.

132   Kessler and Jutz 14; see also Schivelbusch 64.

133   A. T. Ry and S. F. Ry, *The Grand Canyon of Arizona* (Chicago: Rogers and Smith, 1915) (Box 81, Warshaw Collection, National Museum of American History, Washington, D.C.). See "The Great American Panorama" (ca. 1875), advertised by the Central Pacific Railroad (Division of Transportation Photo Archive, Photo 77-14566).

134   Schivelbusch 41.

135   Schivelbusch 58–65.

136   Schivelbusch 66.

137   Crary 14. He adds: "The loss of touch as a conceptual component of vision meant the unloosening of the eye from the network of referentiality incarnated in tactility and its subjective relation to perceived space" (19). Crary sees the stereoscope as a "major cultural site" where this new kind of vision occurs: "No other form of representation in the nineteenth century had so conflated the real with the optical" (124).

138   Schivelbusch 48.

139   Schivelbusch 63.

140   Doane, 44. See also Noguez 85–94; and Musser, "The Travel Genre," 47–60.

141   Friedberg 20

142   Friedberg 29. Also rejecting Foucault's panoptic model as the only way to view nineteenth-century spectatorship, Crary notes: "The production of the observer in the nineteenth century coincided with new procedures of discipline and regulation. [I]t is a question of a body aligned with and operating an assemblage of *turning and regularly moving wheeled parts.* The imperatives that generated a rational organization of time and movement in production simultaneously pervaded diverse spheres of social activity. A need for knowledge of the capacities of the eye and its regimentation dominated many of them" (112, author's emphasis). See also Crary 112–113 on the diorama, where he draws conclusions similar to Friedberg's.

143   Gunning, " 'The Whole World Within Reach,' " 14. Explaining the popularity of moving camera shots in early travel cinema, Gunning further notes: "First, they allowed a broader view of the landscape. Second, the actual movement seems to carry the viewer into the image, realizing what Charles Musser has called the 'spectator as passenger convention' " (" 'The Whole World Within Reach,' " 15).

144   The most comprehensive source on Hale's Tours is Fielding 116–130. 1904 was for long the standard date given for the first exhibition of Hale's Tours. Musser, however, has found promotional material and advertisements that would indicate the first exhibition was in 1905 at K.C.'s Electric Park (*The Emergence of Cinema*, 428). In any event, Fielding notes that the Electric Park appearance was Hale's Tours' first commercial installation.

145 Friedberg 84 describes the virtual Transsiberian Express exhibit at the 1900 Paris World Exposition, which simulated the journey using the old convention of rolling painted scenery.

146 Gunning links the term "traveling shot" to this kind of camera movement that created the effect of actually penetrating space, noting that panoramic travel films also gave the spectator a privileged point of view, one even tourists riding in a real train could not enjoy, as Gunning points out (" 'The Whole World Within Reach,' " 15, 18). According to Musser, the popular lecturer Lyman Howe projected the Black Diamond Express simultaneously with a phonographic recording of an approaching train, which led one newspaper to report how " 'startlingly realistic' " the scene was (*The Emergence of Cinema*, 178). See also Musser, *High-Class Moving Pictures*, pp. 65–66; and Bruno 44, who notes that apparently as early as 1908 an Italian film magazine was calling for "cinema cars" to exhibit motion pictures during train travel.

147 Deslandes and Richard 196

148 Deslandes and Richard 244–246.

149 Terry Ramsaye, *A Million and One Nights* (1926; New York: Simon and Schuster, 19), 351–352. Jonathan Crary cites an early nineteenth-century English mathematician, Peter Mark Roget (author of the first thesaurus), an important precursor of theorists of "persistence of vision" who in 1825 theorized the illusion of movement based on his observations of effects produced by observing moving train wheels through the vertical bars of a fence: "Roget pointed out the illusions that occurred under this circumstance — the spokes of the wheels seemed to be either motionless or to be turning backward. . . . Roget's observations suggested to him how the location of an observer in relation to an intervening screen could exploit the durational properties of retinal afterimages to create various effects of motion" (106).

150 Ramsaye 352.

151 Munsterberg 10–17, 35–36, 39–48, 74–80.

152 Munsterberg 10. Caroline Lejeune, who in a 1925 review of John Ford's *The Iron Horse* went on at length singing the praises of cinema's love affair with the railroad, also saw a direct connection between the two machines — and precisely as modern machines: "The kinema — why should it be forgotten? — is a mechanical thing. It was born of science out of industry, and its whole life runs on wheels. This, the modern medium of expression, fulfils itself most completely in the presentation of modern forms in the shaping of things industrial, the service of the machine. Wheels, piston-rods, screws of steamers, turning lathes, the glow of blastfurnaces, the polished bellies of guns, are all materials of splendour to the motion-picture camera. They and the kinema are of the same stuff and time. In expressing accurately these mechanical things, conveying into flat image their build and texture and power, the kinema is most itself, most forceful, and, because mechanical, most nearly an art" (75). And, as noted, Lejeune saw the railway engine as the most potent machine of all in which the "kinema" realized itself, the ultimate symbol of cinematic potential.

153 *The Moving Picture World*, 22 June 1907, 249–250. See a cartoon drawn in 1901 by Henri Avelot entitled "Le train qui regarde passer la vache" ("The Train Watching a Cow Go By"), which shows an exaggerated quivering cow as represented from the unstable, jiggling perspective of a speeding train window (reproduced in Crafton, *Emile Cohl: Caricature and Film*, 248).

154 Crary 91.

155 Vachel Lindsay, *The Art of the Moving Picture* (New York: Macmillan, 1922/orig. 1915), 165.

156 See Eviatar Zerubavel, "The Standardization of Time: A Sociohistorical Perspective,"

American Journal of Sociology 88, no. 1 (1982): 1–23; Barbara Liggett, "A History of the Adoption of Standard Time in the United States, 1869–1883," unpublished thesis, U of Texas, 1960; Christopher Clark, "Time Consciousness and Social Change in Nineteenth Century America," unpublished paper, Department of History, University of York, 1975. See also O'Malley 1–54 on the confusion in the early to mid-nineteenth century over local time in relation to the introduction of clocks prior to the railroad's establishment of standard time.

157 Zerubavel 8.

158 O'Malley 82; Zerubavel 9.

159 Timetables represented as best they could the differences in time, often with elaborate visual diagrams. See, among others, *Appleton's* and *Baby Pathfinders's* in Boxes 80, 83, 85, The Warshaw Collection, National Museum of American History, Washington, D.C.

160 Frederick Werner Allen, "The Adoption of Standard Time in 1883: An Attempt to Bring Order into a Changing World," unpublished paper, American Studies Department, Yale U, 1969, 10.

161 See O'Malley 276–295 on the various debates surrounding the passage of and ongoing challenges to DST; and Carlene Stephens, " 'The Most Reliable Time': William Bond, the New England Railroads, and the Formation of Time Awareness in 19th-century America," *Technology and Culture* 30 (Jan. 1989): 7–11, on the negotiations of various interests vis-à-vis standard time in the decades leading up to the Time Convention.

162 O'Malley 111; Frederick Werner Allen 29.

163 O'Malley 123; Frederick Werner Allen 38. Finally, in 1884, the world was divided into its twenty-four time zones by representation of twenty-five countries at the Prime Meridian Conference in Washington, D.C., where all agreed on Greenwich as zero meridian. See Stephen Kern, *The Culture of Time and Space* (Cambridge, Mass.: Harvard UP, 1983), 12; and O'Malley 109.

164 Clark 32–33; and O'Malley 183 on Sears.

165 Stephens 16–21.

166 Stephens 11.

167 The striking of the Golden Spike, the official emblem of the joining of the Central and Union Pacific Railroads into one Transcontinental Railroad, was conveyed simultaneously via telegraph. As the hammer hit, the wire tapped out "D-O-N-E" to telegraph offices all over the United States, including President Grant's office in Washington, D.C. Simultaneous celebrations occurred across the country: a parade was launched in Chicago, firebells rang in San Francisco, and a magnetic ball dropped from a pole atop the Capitol dome (Stover 53; Jensen 99). O'Malley notes how, without public knowledge, Leland Stanford, who was given the honor of swinging the sledgehammer, missed the spike and hit wood instead; another official ended up executing the telegraphed blow (73–74).

168 See Stephens 22–24; Mumford 162–163.

169 E. P. Thompson, "Time, Work-Discipline, and Industrial Capitalism," *Past and Present* 38 (Dec. 1967): 56–97.

170 O'Malley 124.

171 Clark 52. See O'Malley 126–144 on individual states' and towns' reactions to standard time.

172 O'Malley 133–144. Quotation on 133.

173 Kern 68.

174 Kern 66–68. See also David Harvey, who insists on the sense in which control over time derives from or demands railroad conquest of space: "But there were all kinds of equally

significant indirect ways in which the conquest of space after 1840 shifted the whole sense and valuation of time for all social classes. The rise of the journey to work as a phenomenon of urban living was itself connected to the increasing partition of time into 'working' and 'living' in separate spaces. And there were all manner of secondary effects of such a journey to work upon customary meal times, household labor (and its sexual division), family interactions, leisure activities and the like. The rise of mass-circulation newspapers, the advent of telegraph and telephone, of radio and television, all contributed to a new sense of simultaneity over space and total conformity in coordinated and universally uniform time." *Consciousness and the Urban Experience: Studies in the History and Theory of Capitalist Urbanization* (Baltimore: Johns Hopkins UP, 1985), 9.

175 See Robert C. Allen, "Motion Picture Exhibition in Manhattan," 162–175; Peiss 5–56; and May 12–40. Guiliana Bruno offers a lengthy discussion of the spatial condensation of cinema/railroad in Naples in the early silent period, noting how common it was for movie houses to spring up in and around railway stations (Bruno 44ff.).

176 I am grateful to Tom Gunning for driving home this crucial point. For more on the MPPC and distribution, see Gunning, *D. W. Griffith and the Origins of American Narrative Film*, 63–65, 144–146; Bowser, *The Transformation of Cinema, 1907–1915*, 21–36; and Lee Beaupré, "How to Distribute a Film," in Paul Kerr, ed., *The Hollywood Film Industry* (London: Routledge, 1986), 189.

177 Jacobs 3–5; Sklar 13–17; and MacGowan 64–75, 92.

178 Musser, *The Emergence of Cinema*, 179.

179 Musser notes how the nickelodeons, electric theaters, theatoriums, etc., created a new kind of spectator: the moviegoer — one who did not see a movie as part of something else (*The Emergence of Cinema*, 430).

180 Merritt 8–9; Jacobs 52ff. See Bowser, *The Transformation of Cinema, 1907–1915*, on the slow acceptance of feature films, standardized lengths, and streamlined, longer programs — i.e., control by producer vs. exhibitor and distributor (191ff.). She notes: "The public continued to cling to the habit of entering at whatever point in the program they wished, which did not matter much when, in the short film program, each new reel was a new beginning" (192).

181 While O'Malley devotes an entire chapter to this concern (200–255), offering analyses and arguments very similar to what follows in this chapter, I must point out that my research and analysis were conducted independently of his and submitted in dissertation form before his book appeared, just as his was conducted and published independently of mine. [I also want to point out that while O'Malley and I were both research fellows at the Smithsonian in 1986–87, his work on standard time did not include, as far as I was aware — based on his dissertation prospectus — consideration of the cinema.]

182 See Munsterberg 10; and Charles Musser, "The American Vitagraph, 1897–1901: Survival and Success in a Competitive Industry," *Film Before Griffith*, ed. John Fell (Berkeley: U of California P, 1983), 43: "Audiences generally acquired prior knowledge of events shown on the screen through a variety of cultural forms, providing an explicit framework for appreciation. At the time of the Great Naval Parade in the North River, newspapers were filled with drawings of the participating ships. Detailed descriptions were given of their firepower, their commanding officers, and accomplishments during the war. Unlike today's audience for television news, vaudeville spectators generally read the papers and could appreciate the films within this context. The cinema itself was increasingly looked upon as a visual newspaper." Perhaps the most famous example of film taking itself seriously as an instantaneous

medium of reportage is Méliès' faked coronation of Edward VII (1902), which was exhibited only hours after the real coronation in England. See Vincent Pinel, "Petit guide chronologique du cinéma français (1895–1909)," *L'Avant-scène du cinéma* 334 (Nov. 1984): 11.

183 See Munsterberg's train example, above; film history is full of examples of filmmakers collapsing the process of shooting, processing, and exhibiting films as rapidly as possible to bring spectators a "visual newspaper," as Musser calls it (*The Emergence of Cinema*, 225).

184 Musser, *The Emergence of Cinema*, 264.

185 Musser, *The Emergence of Cinema*, 275.

186 André Gaudreault, "Les détours du récit filmique (Sur la naissance du montage parallèle)," *Les Cahiers de la Cinémathèque* 29 (Winter 1979): 88–107.

187 Gaudreault, "Les détours du récit filmique," 99.

188 See Gunning, *D. W. Griffith and the Origins of American Narrative Film*, 95–97, 103–106, 205–207; and Sergei Eisenstein, "Dickens, Griffith and the Film Today," *Film Form*, ed. and trans. Jay Leyda (New York: Harcourt, 1949), 195–255.

189 Gunning, *D. W. Griffith and the Origins of American Narrative Film*, 133. See Bellour, "Alterner/Raconter," 68–88; and William Johnson, "Early Griffith: A Wider View," *Film Quarterly* (Spring 1976): 2–31.

190 André Gaudreault, "Temporality and Narrativity in Early Cinema, 1895–1908," *Film Before Griffith*, 324.

191 See Gunning, *D. W. Griffith and the Origins of American Narrative Film*, for a good definition of parallel editing: "Parallel editing can be defined by three characteristics. First, it alternates two separable series of shots (and in 1908 was referred to as 'alternating scenes'), setting up what is most often described as an *a-b-a-b* pattern. In addition, parallel editing indicates specific temporal and spatial relations. The actions shown alternately are signified as occurring simultaneously in different places, most frequently fairly distant locals. The temporal specificity that parallel editing entails brought enormous changes to the tense of film's narrative discourse" (95). On the "contrast edit" in Griffith, Gunning notes: "The contrast edit does more than simply present events; it intervenes to comment on them and expresses that comment by an ideological reference" (134). See Bowser, *The Transformation of Cinema, 1907–1915*, on the nuances of "crosscutting" and "parallel editing" (58–59).

192 On early cinematic methods for representing telephone calls, including alternation, see Bowser, *The Transformation of Cinema*, 64–71. See also Tom Gunning, "Heard over the phone: The Lonely Villa and the de Lorde tradition of the terrors of technology," *Screen* 32 (Summer 1991): 184–196, on the role of the telephone in the development of suspenseful parallel editing in early narrative films.

193 "Although deadlines, and even deadly clock mechanisms, appear in stage melodramas, film supplies a manipulation of time which the stage could not easily match. . . . The climax of *The Fatal Hour* evokes the cutting edge of the instant; time is measured in moments, and the smallest interval spells the difference between life and death" (Gunning, *D. W. Griffith and the Origins of American Narrative Film*, 105).

194 See *Catching an Early Train* (Edison/Porter, 1901), which, through the technique of printing the film backwards, shows a man dressing rapidly by holding out his hand and having items of clothing come to him. Such films fall into a broader genre of films about the repetition of frustrated desire.

195 See Schivelbusch 60–62. The notion of hypnosis as a mode of consciousness specific to both the train journey and the cinematic experience will be taken up in Chapter Three. See also Patrice Petro's "After Shock/Between Boredom and History," *Discourse* 16:2 (Winter 1993–

1994), 77–99 on the flip side of shock, the in-between of boredom which "seems to be about both too much and too little, sensory overload and sensory deprivation, anxieties of excess as well as anxieties of loss" — which applies only too well to the anxiety of train travel in the nineteenth century (81).

196 Schivelbusch 131.

197 Reed 17.

198 Schivelbusch 135ff.; and George Drinka, *The Birth of Neurosis: Myth, Malady and the Victorians* (New York: Simon and Schuster, 1984) 118ff.

199 Schivelbusch 136.

200 Drinka 109.

201 Drinka 121.

202 Schivelbusch 153.

203 Schivelbusch 153.

204 Drinka 122. See also Crary 89 and 93 on the contributions of Johannes von Müller to the early nineteenth-century's reorientation of medical science to nerve theory and nervous energy.

205 See Susan Buck-Morss's provocative "Aesthetics and Anaesthetics: Walter Benjamin's Artwork Essay Reconsidered," *October* 62 (1992): 16–18 on the sense-deadening effect of overstimulation of the modern world, the anaesthetics applied to too much shock, in relation to Benjamin's "Artwork" essay. See also Miriam Hansen, "Of Mice and Ducks: Benjamin and Adorno on Disney," *South Atlantic Quarterly* 92 (Winter 1993): 27–61 for an intriguing and insightful analysis of Benjamin's reading of Mickey Mouse in relation to the experience of technological destruction and the potentially revolutionary aspects of collective laughter.

206 See Musser, "Towards a History of Screen Practice," 59–69.

207 Reed 59–60; Jensen 186; B. A. Botkin and Alvin Harlow, eds., *A Treasury of Railroad Folklore* (New York: Crown, 1953), 354–356; and "Accidents de chemin de fer en spectacle," *L'Illustration*, May 30, 1896, 454.

208 The term "imagination of disaster" is Susan Sontag's. *Against Interpretation* (New York: Farrar, 1966), 115.

209 The Warshaw Collection and the Photo Archive of the Transportation Division, both of the National Museum of American History in Washington, D.C., contain numerous postcards, photographs, stereographs, and illustrated magazine reprints of railroad accidents from the mid-nineteenth century on. See also Reed 25ff.; Schivelbusch 131–160; Anthony J. Lambert, *Nineteenth Century Railway History through the Illustrated London News* (London and North Pomfret, Vt.: Newton Abbot, 1984), 88ff.; and Darrah, *The World of Stereographs*, 185ff.

210 See Gunning, "An Aesthetic of Astonishment," on how the experience of assault was in many cases part and parcel of the entertainment value of early films (36–37).

211 A report on "Le Cinématographe" in the popular Paris illustrated magazine *L'Illustration* provides a typical example: "Let us repeat what has been remarked over and over about the naturalness and life-likeness of the scenes Lumière presents to us. . . . The Locomotive appears small at first, then immense, as if it were going to crush the audience. One has the impression of depth and relief, even though it is a single image that unfolds before our eyes" (*L'Illustration*, May 30, 1896, 446–447).

212 See, for example, Jacobs 6; Benjamin Hampton, *A History of the Movies* (London: Noel Douglas, 1932), 13–14.

213 Gunning, "An Aesthetic of Astonishment," 32.

214 Gunning, "An Aesthetic of Astonishment," 33–34. Gunning adds: "The audience's sense of shock comes less from a naive belief that they are threatened by an actual locomotive than from an unbelievable visual transformation occurring before their eyes, parallel to the greatest wonders of the magic theatre" (35).

215 Gunning, "An Unseen Energy Swallows Space," 363.

216 Gunning, "An Unseen Energy Swallows Space," 363. With respect to the allegedly terrifying train arrival films, he says: "The on-rushing train did not simply produce the negative experience of fear but the particularly modern entertainment form of the *thrill*, embodied elsewhere in the recently appearing attractions of the amusement park (such as the roller coaster)." ("An Aesthetic of Astonishment," 37). See Sigmund Freud, *Beyond the Pleasure Principle*, trans. James Strachey (1920; New York: Norton, 1961), 6–7.

217 See Gunning: "Shock becomes not only a mode of modern experience, but a strategy of a modern aesthetics of astonishment. . . . These screams of terror and delight were well prepared for by both showmen and audience" (Gunning, "An Aesthetic of Astonishment," 42–43). To some extent, the avant-garde "flicker film" of the 1960s is a perennial tribute to film's power to stimulate, provoke, and shock at a highly visceral level. I am thinking not so much of Peter Kubelka's *Arnulf Rainer* (1960) as Tony Conrad's *The Flicker* (1966), an abstract, rapid-fire alternation of pure blacks and whites that, following a screening that unintentionally brought on an epilectic fit in a spectator, was exhibited with a warning.

218 Benjamin, "The Work of Art in the Age of Mechanical Reproduction," 238.

219 Benjamin, "The Work of Art in the Age of Mechanical Reproduction," 250.

220 Drinka 120ff. See Buck-Morss 19.

221 Drinka 121. See also Schivelbusch 157; Kern 125, on the turn-of-the-century disease known as "Newyorkitis"; and an article in an 1896 issue of *L'Illustration* on American tram conductors, who, it seems, "are exposed to a special nervous malady that appears to be caused by the excessive mental tension demanded by traffic conditions in the busy streets of the nation's big cities" (*L'Illustration*, May 30, 1896: 454). See chap. 3, below, for more on this subject.

222 Musser, *The Emergence of Cinema*, 322, notes that this is itself a variation on Robert Paul's *The Countryman's First Sight of the Animated Pictures* (1901).

223 Sigmund Freud, *The Pelican Freud Library*, vol. 8: *Case Histories I: "Dora" and "Little Hans"* (Harmondsworth: Penguin, 1977).

224 See Toril Moi, "Representation of Patriarchy: Sexuality and Epistemology in Freud's Dora," *In Dora's Case*, ed. Charles Bernheimer and Claire Kahane (New York: Columbia UP, 1985), 181–199.

225 See Charcot, *Leçons sur l'hystérie virile*, intro. by Michèle Ouerd (Paris: Le Sycamore, 1984) 39–54.

226 Charcot 36–39; Drinka 109–113.

227 Charcot 36–54.

228 Drinka 118.

229 Michèle Ouerd, introduction to Charcot, *Leçons sur l'hystérie virile* (Paris: Le Sycamore, 1984), 20.

230 Ouerd 37–39.

231 Charcot 280.

232 Charcot 214; and Ouerd 26.

233 Ouerd 27. See also Neil Hertz's excellent "Medusa's Head: Male Hysteria Under Political Pressure," *Representations* 4 (Fall 1983): 27–54.

234 Sigmund Freud and Josef Breuer, *The Pelican Freud Library* vol. 3, *Studies on Hysteria* (Harmondsworth: Penguin, 1974); and Freud, *Case Histories I.*

235 Musser, *The Emergence of Cinema*, 329–220 refers to a film called *Photographer's Mishaps* (1901), produced first by Lubin and remade by Edison later that year.

236 *Moving Picture World* relates an interesting story about the shooting of *The Photographer's Mishap* that has to do with the stop-motion technique. It seems that, although he was instructed to run over the dummy, the train engineer refused to believe it was not a real man and screeched to a halt too soon — still hitting the dummy, which in turn upset some of the equally incredulous passengers (May 18, 1907, 166).

237 See Norm Cohen, *Long Steel Rail: The Railroad in American Folksong* (Urbana: U of Illinois P, 1981), 345. Eileen Bowser describes a similar film plot: "THE PHANTOM SIGNAL (Edison, 1913), in two reels, was an attack on corporate heads of an unnamed railroad in New England, who are at fault for train wrecks resulting from the long hours and exhausting work of men at signal stations. A double-exposure animated skeleton forecasts each of several tragedies, while another shows two trains approaching on a V switch." (Bowser, *The Transformation of Cinema*, 248)

238 Musser describes a similar narrative where a woman is the main character. In *Mother's Dream* (Lubin, 1907), a woman tucks her children into bed, then falls asleep and dreams she dies, leaving her children orphans, which causes her to awaken in a panic that soon turns to joy. She and the switchman are virtually interchangeable in their roles and reactions (*The Emergence of Cinema*, 482).

239 Ouerd 27; see also Hertz 27–54.

240 By laying bare the lack at the core of modern life with a climate of distraction, the cinema of attractions' "jolt experienced becomes a shock of recognition. Far from fulfilling a dream of total replication of reality — the apophantis of the myth of total cinema — the experience of the first projections exposes the hollow center of the cinematic illusion" (Gunning, "An Aesthetic of Astonishment," 42). For a more extended consideration of Kracauer's views on cinema, see chap. 3 of this book.

241 See Gunning, "Non-continuity, Continuity, Discontinuity: A Theory of Genres in Early Film," 101–112; Gunning, "The Cinema of Attraction," *Wide Angle* 8, nos., 3–4 (1986): 63–70; and Hansen, *Babel and Babylon*, 121–123.

242 See Mary Ann Doane, *The Desire to Desire* (Bloomington: Indiana UP, 1987), 2: "It is as though the historical threat of a potential feminization of the spectatorial position required an elaborate work of generic containment." See also Friedberg 32–38, 57–58; Bruno 50ff. Hansen also offers some provocative insights into the relation of female spectatorship to early cinema and its complication of the institutionalization of male spectatorship: "We thus return to the paradox sketched out above, between the industry's thriving on — and catering to — female audiences and the masculinization of the spectator position concomitant with the institutionalization of classical cinema. For one thing, the implementation of the classical system was not instantaneously effective and perhaps never as total as film theorists have made it seem. . . . Industrial efforts to address the large number of women viewers took a variety of directions, some responding to the changed status of women in both private and public life (as in the serials), some reviving the discourse of domesticity and moral guardianship (as in films debating the U.S. entry into World War I). While both directions of female address lingered after the war in the work of individual directors and stars, the contradic-

tions and resistances they presented were soon absorbed by the large-scale appeal to the female spectator as consumer. . . ." (Miriam Hansen, "Adventures of Goldilocks: Spectatorship, Consumerism and Public Life," *Camera Obscura* 22 (Jan. 1990): 65.

243   Heide Schlüpmann, "Melodrama and Social Drama in the Early German Cinema," *Camera Obscura* 22 (Jan. 1990): 75. This is to be contrasted with the emerging "social drama," which in its less sentimental appeal to female spectators "constructs the rudiments of formulating a first-person narration on the part of the female protagonist" (79).

244   See Hansen, *Babel and Babylon*, 90–125 for a compelling argument regarding early cinema's realm of alternative potential for female spectators in particular.

Two. Romances of the Rail in Silent Film

1   Alfred de Musset, "Dupont et Durand," *Lignes et Lettres*, ed. Marc Baroli (Paris: Hachettes/ SNCF, 1978), 79.

2   Klaus Theweleit, *Männerphantasien*, vol. 1: *Frauen, Flüten, Körper, Geschichte* (Frankfurt am Main: Verlag Roter Stern, 1977). The image appears on the dust jacket.

3   See chap. 3 of this book.

4   Marx, *The Machine in the Garden*, 249–262.

5   Henry Nash Smith, *The Virgin Land: The American West as Symbol and Myth* (1950; Cambridge, Mass.: Harvard UP, 1978), 123–210, 187.

6   Marx, *The Machine in the Garden*, 29.

7   Marx, *The Machine in the Garden*, 260.

8   Henry David Thoreau, *Walden* (1854), cited in Marx, *The Machine in the Garden*, 260.

9   The idea of woman-as-nature and man-as-civilization revolves around the identification of the female body with the earth and her relative exclusion from the male world of culture, progress, and technology. A good summary of these issues can be found in Sherry B. Ortner, "Is Female to Male as Nature Is to Culture?" *Woman, Culture and Society*, ed. Michelle Z. Rosaldo and Louise Lamphere (Stanford, Calif.: Stanford UP, 1974), 67–87.

10   J. A. Burch, "The Fast Mail," 1875. Reproduced in Jensen 164.

11   Stilgoe 261.

12   Stilgoe 12 for this quotation and the following Lionel quotations in this paragraph. See also Stilgoe 11–15.

13   Stilgoe 4.

14   Stilgoe 8.

15   Jack Santino, *Miles of Smiles, Years of Struggle: Stories of Black Pullman Porters* (Urbana: U of Illinois P, 1989), 10.

16   Santino 14–15; Harris 15. Despite the positive images porters carried for African American men, the wages all black railroadmen were paid for the jobs they were allowed to hold were far below what whites received for comparable work. This was in part because the "Big Four" railroad unions—the Brotherhood of Locomotive Engineers, the Brotherhood of Locomotive Firemen, the Brotherhood of Railway Trainmen, and the Order of Railway Conductors—all outlawed black membership in their constitutions. It took the creation of the Brotherhood of Sleeping Car Porters, formed in 1925 by A. Philip Randolph, to even begin to alter perceptions and practices of racism in the railroad industry, which eventually happened when the union at long last won federal and Pullman recognition as the sole bargaining agent for Pullman porters in 1935, signing its first collective bargaining agreement two years later. See Harris 4–5, 16, 26–65, 202–216; Santino 10, 36; Northrup 48–

101; and Paula F. Pfeffer, *A. Philip Randolph: Pioneer of the Civil Rights Movement* (Baton Rouge: Louisiana State UP, 1990), 21–25.

17   For this and what follows, see Mark A. Reid, *Redefining Black Film* (Berkeley: U of California P, 1993), 7–9. I first learned about Foster from Charlene Regester of the University of North Carolina in an illuminating paper she delivered at the Domitor '94 "Cinema Turns 100" Conference on June 18, 1994, at NYU: "African Americans in Early Cinema History: A Period of Protest and Self-Assertion, 1900–1914."

18   Reid 7–8; Thomas Cripps, *Slow Fade to Black: The Negro in American Film, 1900–1942* (New York: Oxford UP, 1993), 80.

19   Reid 8.

20   Carbine 9–41. Indeed, Reid 7 sees Foster's productions as coming out of the black theater with its innovative black comedians and musicians.

21   Carbine 12.

22   See Carbine 20; Gregory A. Waller, "Another Audience: Black Moviegoing, 1907–16," *Cinema Journal* 31 (Winter 1992): 3–25, on African American early film audiences in Lexington, Kentucky, and black-owned and/or operated exhibition venues.

23   Virilio, "L'Empire de l'emprise," 3–27. See also Schivelbusch 77–82.

24   Michel Foucault, "Of Other Spaces," *Diacritics* 16 (Spring 1986): 23–24.

25   Foucault, "Of Other Spaces," 24–25.

26   See Stilgoe 36–41 on crowd flows in stations and the concept of "steady-flow machines."

27   Carl Condit, *The Railroad and the City: A Technological and Urbanistic History of Cincinnati* (Columbus: Ohio State UP, 1977), x.

28   See C. Hamilton Ellis, *Railway Art* (Boston: New York Graphic Society, 1977), 78–88.

29   Richards and MacKenzie 137.

30   Richards and MacKenzie 158.

31   Déthier 83.

32   "The train became a mobile equivalent [of the railroad station], a special kind of microcity moving over the ground." Condit x.

33   Honoré Daumier, *Les Transports en commun*, preface Max Gallo (Paris: Editions Vilo, 1976) plates 32–34, 38–39, 45.

34   Schivelbusch 84–92.

35   See Ellis 74, 82, 83.

36   Schivelbusch 87–88.

37   Schivelbusch 87.

38   See the English film *Attempted Murder in a Railway Train* (Clarendon/Gaumont, 1904), which involves a similar succession of scenes, including "The attempt to throw the girl from the train" ("Gaumont 'Elge' Lists 1904," British Film Institute, *Early Filmmakers' Catalogues* (London: World Microfilms, 1983). Though this could possibly be the same film, the description mentions scenes not included in *A Railway Tragedy*; for example, cardsharps performing tricks and a passage through a tunnel.

39   The term is Schivelbusch's (82–84).

40   See Schivelbusch 88–92, 104–105; Jensen 22, 50.

41   A large number of documents of this campaign can be found in Warshaw Collection, National Museum of American History, Washington, D.C. (Hereinafter Warshaw Collection.)

42   *Tours of Florida* (Washington, D.C.: Pennsylvania Railroad, 1892), 5. (Box 85, Warshaw Collection.)

43   See brochures in Boxes 84, 85, and 88, Warshaw Collection.

44   Santino 84.

45   Déthier 8–11.

46   An allegorical statue of a woman representing a battle or war was a typical adornment for railroad stations in Europe and the United States. See Déthier 39, 96.

47   Schivelbusch 166. Déthier analyzes the aesthetic roles of the train station, whether Greek Revival or neo-Gothic, in terms of the railroad's desire to smooth over the brutal path cut by the machine through traditional culture and society, as well as space (Déthier 9).

48   Trachtenberg 118–121.

49   Munsterberg 95.

50   Merritt 73. As Tom Gunning has informed me, Merritt probably underestimates the number of women and children in audiences at the time, as some sources indicate higher figures for both categories. See, for example, Gaylyn Studlar, *The Mad Masquerade* (New York: Columbia UP, 1996).

51   *The Vestibule* (Norfolk, Va.: Sam. W. Bowman, 1894); and *The Vestibule* (Norfolk, Va.: Sam. W. Bowman, 1895). Both brochures are in Box 81, Warshaw Collection.

52   Box 88, Warshaw Collection. See also *My Canadian Sweetheart or Aunt Tabby's Summer Boarders* (N.p.: Connecticut Valley and Passumpsic Railroads, 1885) (Box 84, Warshaw Collection).

53   See the Phoebe Snow print advertisements contained in a 1906 Lackawanna brochure, which uses photographs of a woman in white to illustrate its "scenic" premise, promising that "A daylight trip over the Lackawanna is a flying picture book whose pages will hold your interest every minute of the way between New York and Buffalo. . . . " *Lackawanna Railroad* (New York: American Bank Note, 1906) n.pag. Box 82, Warshaw Collection. Stilgoe 5 refers to a piece put out by the Lackawanna in 1905 entitled *A Paper Proposal*, "a story in which two strangers fall in love on a fast express."

54   On the figure of the tramp in early films, see Charles Musser, "Work, Ideology and Chaplin's Tramp," in *Resisting Images: Essays on Cinema and History*, ed. Robert Sklar and Charles Musser (Philadelphia: Temple UP, 1990), 40–41, 44–46.

55   See similar "honeymoon train" films by the English filmmaker Cecil Hepworth from 1903–4 as described in the Hepworth catalogs reproduced in *Early Filmmakers' Catalogues*.

56   See Cripps 12–18.

57   In terms of sexual identity and its confusion, both *Nervy Nat Kisses the Bride* and *The Deadwood Sleeper* can be interpreted in light of a passage in Jacques Lacan's "Agency of the Letter in the Unconscious" that bears relevance to the theoretical point I wish to make: "A train arrives at a station. A little boy and a little girl, brother and sister, are seated in a compartment face to face next to the window through which the buildings along the station platform can be seen passing as the train pulls to a stop. 'Look,' says the brother, 'we're at Ladies!'; 'Idiot!' replies his sister, 'can't you see we're at Gentlemen.'" Lacan, "The Agency of the Letter in the Unconscious or Reason Since Freud," 152. The example illustrates Lacan's notion of the "sliding of the signified under the signifier," the sense in which meaning is to be found in the chain of signification, as opposed to any one of its components. What is significant is that the gap in meaning is a function of a view, a view that passes in turn through a frame, a window screen. This is practically a prototype of point of view in the cinema, of the uncertainty of sexual identity, and of identification in general.

58   *Early Filmmakers' Catalogues*. See *A Trip to Southend or Blackpool*, listed in "W. Butchers & Sons 1905–6 Catalogue," which describes the trials suffered by a dandy who has the misfor-

tune to enter a railway carriage full of "costers with their wives, sweethearts and kiddies." ("W. Butchers & Sons 1905–6 Catalogue," *Early Filmmakers' Catalogues*).

59 Mayne, "Immigrants and Spectators," 35–36. See also Hansen, *Babel and Babylon*, 93–114, and Noel Burch, "How We Got Into Pictures" (text to accompany Burch's film *Correction Please*), *Afterimage* 8 (Spring 1981): 33.

60 Gunning, "An Aesthetic of Astonishment," 39.

61 Freud, *Jokes and Their Relation to the Unconscious*, 101.

62 See Tom Gunning, " 'Primitive' Cinema—A Frame-up? or The Trick's On Us," *Cinema Journal* 28 (Winter 1989): 3–12, in which Gunning takes apart the conventional wisdom about how the trick film was constructed and illuminates the role of the substitution splice in the trick films of Méliès and others.

63 See Doane for an incisive analysis of the association of trains in psychoanalytic thought and cinema with trompe l'oeil and visual deception ("The Moving Image" 42–48).

64 Lucy Fisher, "The Lady Vanishes: Women, Magic and the Movies," *Film Before Griffith*, ed. John Fell (Berkeley: U of California P, 1983), 339–354.

65 Pêcheux 42–44.

66 Gaudreault has developed the concept of "monstration" in relation to early cinema in numerous articles, including: " 'Théâtralité' et 'narrativité' dans l'oeuvre de Georges Méliès," *Méliès et la naissance du spectacle cinématographique*, ed. Madeleine Malthête-Méliès (Paris: Klincksieck, 1984), 199–220; and "Film, récit, narration: le cinéma des frères Lumière," *Iris* 2, no. 1 (1984): 61–70. See n. 81, below.

67 Freud, *Jokes and Their Relation to the Unconscious*, 97.

68 Freud, *Jokes and Their Relation to the Unconscious*, 98.

69 "A Kiss in the Dark," 1881, Currier & Ives. Reproduced in Jensen 227.

70 Judith Mayne, "Uncovering the Female Body," *Before Hollywood: Turn-of-the-Century Film from American Archives*, ed. Jay Leyda and Charles Musser (New York: American Federation of Arts, 1986), 66. Mayne further elaborates on the film's significance for "primitive" narration and the stereotyping of people of color as "primitives" in her *Woman at the Keyhole: Feminism and Women's Cinema* (Bloomington: Indiana U P, 1990), 173–174, 182.

71 Gunning, "The Cinema of Attraction," 63–70. Gunning's theory is discussed later in this chapter.

72 Foucault, "Of Other Spaces," 26.

73 Tom Gunning thinks that the film is probably *Amore Pedestri*, an Italian comedy from 1914 by Marcel Fabre. The title *Foot Love* appears on the copy I viewed in the archive of the Cinémathèque universitaire in Paris.

74 Todorov 111. See Gaudreault on narrative.

75 Kristin Thompson, "The Formulation of the Classical Style, 1909–1928," in *The Classical Hollywood Cinema: Film Style and Mode of Production to 1960*, eds. David Bordwell, Kristin Thompson, and Janet Staiger (New York: Columbia UP, 1985), 180.

76 Articulating somewhat ironically the democratizing influence of films for the less privileged classes, a 1907 *Saturday Evening Post* article referred to such "goal-lessness" with respect to leisure travel: "Take an analogous case. Is aimless travel 'beneficial' or not? It is amusing, certainly; and therefore the aristocrats who could afford it have always traveled aimlessly. But now, says the Democratic Movement, the grand tour shall no longer be restricted to the aristocracy. Jump on the rural trolley-car, Mr. Workingman, and make a grand tour yourself. Don't care, Mr. Workingman, whether it is 'beneficial' or not. Do it because it is

amusing; just as the aristocrats do." Joseph Medill Patterson, "The Nickelodeons: The Poor Man's Elementary Course in the Drama," *Saturday Evening Post,* Nov. 23, 1907, 38. Patterson is reprinted in George C. Pratt, *Spellbound in Darkness: A History of the Silent Film* (1966; Greenwich, Conn.: New York Graphic Society, 1973), 46–51.

77   Gunning, "The Cinema of Attraction," 64–67; Gunning, "Non-Continuity, Continuity, Discontinuity, 101–112; Charles Musser, "The Nickelodeon Era Begins: Establishing the Framework for Hollywood's Mode of Representation," *Framework* 22 (Autumn 1983): 4–11; Hansen, *Babel and Babylon,* 44ff.; Gaudreault, "Les Détours du récit filmique (Sur la naissance du montage parallèle," 88–107; and Noel Burch, "Porter, or Ambivalence," *In and Out of Synch: The Awakening of a Cine-Dreamer,* trans. Ben Brewster (Aldershot: Scolar Press, 1991, 138–156. Burch's essay was originally published in *Screen* 19 (Winter 1978–79): 91–105.

78   See, in particular, Musser, "The Nickelodeon Era Begins," 5–6; Burch, "Porter, or Ambivalence," 151–153; Gunning, "The Cinema of Attraction," 64–65; and Gaudreault, " 'Théâtralité' et 'narrativité,' " 199–220.

79   See Gunning, *D. W. Griffith and the Origins of American Narrative Film,* 6–7, for a summary of these arguments and trends.

80   Gunning, "The Cinema of Attraction," 65–66; Musser, "The Nickelodeon Era Begins," 4; Robert C. Allen, *Vaudeville and Film,* 75ff.; Bowser, *The Transformation of Cinema, 1907–1915,* 1–8; and Thompson, "The Formulation of the Classical Style," 159–161.

81   André Gaudreault, *Du littéraire au filmique: système du récit* (Paris: Meridiens Klincksieck, 1988), 95–116. See n. 66, above. See also Noel Burch, "How We Got Into Pictures," 28–32.

82   In relation to Hale's Tours, Gunning, "The Cinema of Attraction," 65, notes that "such viewing experiences relate more to the attractions of the fairground than to the traditions of the legitimate theater," adding: "The relation between films and the emergence of the great amusement parks, such as Coney Island, at the turn of the century, provides rich ground for rethinking the roots of early cinema." He also describes early cinema as "a cinema of instants, rather than developing situations" ("An Aesthetic of Astonishment," 38).

83   Gunning, "The Cinema of Attraction," 66.

84   Hansen, *Babel and Babylon,* 40.

85   Hansen, *Babel and Babylon,* 23.

86   David Bordwell, "The Classical Hollywood Style, 1917–1960," in Bordwell et al., *The Classical Hollywood Cinema,* 12–23.

87   See Musser, "The Nickelodeon Era Begins," 5.

88   Burch, "How We Got Into Pictures," 25–26; Musser, "The Nickelodeon Era Begins," 6–9; Musser, *The Emergence of Cinema,* 2–4.

89   The state of audience understanding was characterized in an article Musser quotes from a 1908 issue of *Moving Picture World:* " 'Why do many people remain in the moving picture theatre and look at the same pictures two or even three times? Simply because they do not understand it the first time; and this is by no means a reflection of their intelligence. Once it is made plain to them, their curiosity is gratified and they are pleased to go' " (Musser, "The Nickelodeon Era Begins," 7). In terms of directing the spectator's attention, Musser sees the institutionalization of narrative film as in part a response to the increasing lack of clarity to spectators, as filmmakers began to run out of "stories, hit songs, successful plays and crazes familiar to most Americans" and already exploited in films. See Musser, "The Nickelodeon Era Begins," 6–9; Musser, *The Emergence of Cinema,* 2–3; Hansen, *Babel and Babylon,* 42–46.

90   Musser, "The Nickelodeon Era Begins," 10.

91 Thus, as Gunning makes clear, cutting in to a close-up was made to serve a narrative purpose, versus the display function of close-ups in films like *The Gay Shoe Clerk* (Edison/Porter, 1903), in which a sudden close-up of a woman's ankle was meant only to allow the spectator a closer voyeuristic leer at the exhibited foot ("The Cinema of Attraction," 66). See Bordwell, "The Classical Hollywood Style, 1917–1960," 1–84, for a veritable encyclopedia of the foregoing techniques and characteristics.

92 Thompson, "The Formulation of the Classical Style, 1909–1928," 163.

93 Hansen, *Babel and Babylon*, 83–84.

94 See Musser, "The Nickelodeon Era Begins," 10; Merritt 73; Tom Gunning, "Weaving a Narrative: Style and Economic Background in Griffith's Biograph Films," *Quarterly Review of Film Studies* (Winter 1981): 11–25; Burch, "How We Got Into Pictures," 30–31. Bowser emphasizes with respect to the radical changes occurring in 1908–9 in film form that in addition to new audiences and their demand for the story film, along with the need to standardize the film product, we must take into account the influence of the uplift movement and the fact that most new directors were coming from legitimate theater. Bowser, *The Transformation of Cinema, 1907–1915*, 53–65.

95 Noting early discourses on the moral and physical danger of the cinema for young women, Lauren Rabinovitz 72 writes: "Women moviegoers were thus positioned on and off the screen as both the subject and object of 'the gaze.' But these were not necessarily equivalent positions because women's sense of their own pleasure was legitimated only through their simultaneous desire to please a man."

96 Although uplifters wanted comedy suppressed because of its vulgarity (they saw it as amoral and antiestablishment), audience demand made comedies a standard feature of film programming in 1910. Bowser, *The Transformation of Cinema, 1907–1915*, 57, 179–180.

97 See Hansen, *Babel and Babylon*, 116.

98 See Musser, "The Nickelodeon Era Begins," 10; and Bowser, *The Transformation of Cinema, 1907–1915*, chap. 3, "The Recruiting Stations of Vice," 37–52, and chap. 4, "The Films: Alternate Scenes," 53–72.

99 Thompson claims that "one of the main causes in the shift from primitive to classical cinema involves a change in influences from the other arts, from an initial close imitation of vaudeville, to a greater dependence on short fiction, novels, and legitimate drama." "The Formulation of the Classical Style, 1909–1928," 161–162.

100 See Gunning, *D. W. Griffith and the Origins of American Narrative Film*; Gunning, "Weaving a Narrative: Style and Economic Background in Griffith's Biograph Films," 11–25; Robert M. Henderson, *D. W. Griffith: The Years at Biograph* (New York: Farrar, 1970), 158–177; and Harry M. Geduld, "Introduction," *Focus on D. W. Griffith*, ed. Geduld (Englewood Cliffs, N.J.: Prentice-Hall, 1971), 1–9.

101 Bellour, "Alterner/Raconter," 69–80.

102 Bellour, "Alterner/Raconter," 70–75.

103 See, for example, Gunning, *D. W. Griffith and the Origins of American Narrative Film*; and Bowser on the integration of the tracking shots in *The Girl and Her Trust* into a system of alternation (*The Transformation of Cinema, 1907–1915*, 250).

104 See Gunning, *D. W. Griffith and the Origins of American Narrative Film*, 204–205.

105 On Lubin's remake, see Musser, *The Emergence of Cinema*, 478.

106 Gunning, "The Cinema of Attraction," 64.

107 Bowser, *The Transformation of Cinema, 1907–1915*, 183.

108 Bowser, *The Transformation of Cinema, 1907–1915*, 183.

109 See Koszarski 174–175.

110 The quotes by Edison's production manager, Horace Plimpton, are from 1915 (Koszarski, 163). See also Koszarski 176 on Lloyd; and Musser, "Work, Ideology, and Chaplin's Tramp," 48–49, 53–54, on how Chaplin's films consistently offended polite, middle-class culture from the 1910s through the 1920s and beyond.

111 The identification of the Bathing Belles was made by John Huntley (20).

112 See *Teddy at the Throttle*, 1917 (Triangle-Keystone), supervised by Mack Sennett, directed by Clarence Badger, with Gloria Swanson, Bobby Vernon, and Wallace Beery. See *Film-Notes*, ed. Eileen Bowser (New York: MOMA, 1969), 25.

113 Bowser, *The Transformation of Cinema, 1907–1915*, 178.

114 See Huntley 17–19.

115 On the relation of serials to the development of the multireel and feature film, see Bowser, *The Transformation of Cinema, 1907–1915*, 206–210, and multireel film; and Koszarski 164–166.

116 Koszarski 164. Koszarski also notes that serials, at their peak in the teens, continued to be produced into the twenties, when they came to be associated with the children's audience (Koszarski 166).

117 Bowser, *The Transformation of Cinema, 1907–1915*, 206.

118 Huntley 19. See Ben Singer's excellent article on serial queens, "Female Power in the Serial-Queen Melodrama: The Etiology of an Anomoly," *Camera Obscura* 22 (Jan. 1990): 90–129. Unfortunately for me, his article appeared after my own research on the topic had been conducted and incorporated into this chapter. In addition to providing an overview of the genre and its spectatorship, Singer revises the conventional view of the genre by relating it to melodrama and women's popular fiction.

119 Singer 100–104; Bowser, *The Transformation of Cinema, 1907–1915*, 186–187.

120 One of them at least gives a woman an active role: *Between Orton Junction and Fallonville*, 1913 (see Huntley 17). The Edison boy films include *The Dude Operator* and *One Kind of Wireless* (both 1917).

121 Holmes and McGowan form one of the not uncommon husband-wife teams responsible for much silent film production, only with Holmes apparently not ever directing. See Bruno 109–121 on Elvira Notari and her husband and other such teams.

122 See Huntley 19–20 and Singer 102–104 for additional plot summaries of *Helen* episodes.

123 Information derived from the print of the film in the Library of Congress.

124 Singer 103 writes of *The Girl and the Game*: "At its most assertive, this fantasy of female prowess gravitates toward a reversal of gender positions." Bowser finds a direct link between feminism and serials in episode 13 of Helen (Feb. 1915), in which Helen loses her job as a telegrapher, but ultimately gets it back from the man who replaced her (*The Transformation of Cinema, 1907–1915*, 187).

125 On the legend, see Botkin and Harlow 35ff. Kate Shelley also provided the prototype for *Asleep at the Switch*'s table-cloth-waving heroine, as well as for Vitagraph's 1911 *A Mother's Devotion*, in which a mother ignites and waves her painstakingly sewn quilt to save her train engineer son, and everyone else aboard his train, from crossing a broken trestle hit by lightning in a storm.

126 See Singer 99–100 on women's sources; and Bowser, *The Transformation of Cinema, 1907–1915*, 206, on cross-promotional strategies linking film serials with serial literature in magazines and newspapers.

127 "Helen Holmes' extraordinary daredevil stunt work in *The Hazards of Helen*, for example,

may have less to do with an earnest stake in a progressive ideology of female emancipation than with the utter novelty and curiosity-value of a spectacle based on the 'category mistake' of a woman taking death-defying physical risks, getting filthy, brawling with crooks in muddy riverbanks — in short, of a woman acting like a man" (Singer 115).

128   Of course, the spectacle of a woman engaging with a large machine demanded some ideologically compensatory mechanisms: Helen must be rescued from time to time, be interested in marriage, and never desire to be an engineer or a manager, i.e., a man with power. Her expressions of power are bracketed as such, and there is no expectation of movement beyond the specified bounds. "The female spectator was thus offered the best of both worlds: a representational structure that indulged conventionally 'feminine' forms of vanity and exhibitionism while it refused the constraints of decorative femininity through an action-packed depiction of female prowess" (Singer 100).

129   Nancy Cott, *The Grounding of Modern Feminism* (New Haven, Conn.: Yale UP, 1987), 23–50; Peiss, *Cheap Amusements*, 3–55; Robert H. Wiebe, *The Search for Order, 1877–1920* (New York: Hill and Wang, 1967), 112ff.; and May 79. See Singer 104–115 on the relation of the serial queen genre to feminism and the New Woman of the late nineteenth and early twentieth centuries: the workingwoman.

130   See James Alan MacPherson and Miller Williams, eds., *Railroad: Trains and Train People in American Culture* (New York: Random House, 1976), 90.

131   Wiebe 122; Cott 22–24, 27–35, 40–41. See also Bruno, who details the participation of women working in the Neopolitan film industry as "sweatshop" workers doing invisible work (processing and editing film) (105–109).

132   On similar social-sexual trends in Germany and their relation to female point of view in German film ca. 1910–1912, see Heide Schlüpmann, "Early German Cinema — Melodrama: Social Drama," in *Popular European Cinema*, ed. Richard Dyer and Ginette Vincendeau (London: RKP, 1992), 206–219.

133   Wiebe 122.

134   Cott 23–24.

135   Cott 29–30. On the extremely vibrant New York radical feminist group founded in 1912, see Cott 38ff.; see also Judith Schwarz, Kathy Peiss, and Christina Simmons, " 'We Were a Little Band of Willful Women': The Heterodoxy Club of Greenwich Village," *Passion and Power: Sexuality in History*, ed. Kathy Peiss and Christina Simmons (Philadelphia: Temple UP, 1989), 118–137.

136   Ironically, this was a decade in which voter turnout among both men and women reached a new low in American electoral politics, and women's suffrage was put on the defensive by a combination of the media and a rash of "scientific" studies investigating the "failure" of the women's vote. (Cott 100ff.) Suffragettes (or suffragists, as they were known in the United States) appeared as a theme in American film as early as 1913, with the pro-suffragette *Eighty Million Women Want — ?* (Unique Film Co.), which featured two well-known English suffragettes, Emmeline Pankhurst and Harriet Stanton Blatch, as heroines who expose political fraud and save a young male lawyer wrongly accused of a crime. See Patricia King Hanson, ed., *The American Film Institute Catalog of Feature Films, 1911–1920, Film Entries* (Berkeley: U of California P, 1988), 238. The great Danish actress Asta Nielsen played a suffragette in *Die Suffragette* (PAGU/Urban Gad, 1913). Of course, the negative references to suffragettes in European and American culture far exceeded the positive.

137   T. J. Jackson Lears, "From Salvation to Self-Realization: Advertising and the Therapeutic Roots of the Consumer Culture, 1880–1930," *The Culture of Consumption: Critical Essays in*

American History, 1880–1980, ed. Richard Wrightman Fox and T. J. Jackson Lears (New York: Pantheon, 1983), 26. Chap. 3 of this book expands significantly on this area. As women were assumed to control household purchasing and to be particularly vulnerable to advertising's emotional pitches, the advertising industry stressed in its own journals how important it was to reach them. Lears, "From Salvation to Self-Realization," 26–27.

138   Lears, "From Salvation to Self-Realization," 27.

139   Christopher P. Wilson, "The Rhetoric of Consumption: Mass-Market Magazines and the Demise of the Gentle Reader, 1880–1920," *The Culture of Consumption*, 54–55.

140   Wilson 62. Friedberg, however, ascribes a greater and unprecedented agency to women beginning in the last half of the nineteenth century in relation to shopping, an activity in which women had "freedom to roam," shop—and look (36ff.).

141   May 122–126, 142–146. Significantly, Pickford lent her name vocally to the feminist cause, supporting women's right to vote (May 134).

142   See May 125 on the growing "kid" audience of the time; and Stuart Ewen, *Captains of Consciousness: Advertising and the Roots of Consumer Culture* (New York: McGraw-Hill, 1976), 139ff.

143   Singer 123. On the "New Woman," see Singer 107–115.

144   Koszarski 181.

145   On Fairbanks as the quintessential, *active* male role model in the late 1910s and early 1920s, see May 109–118.

146   This is in part because Alma rejects her snooty guardian, the manager of the railroad company.

147   On the decline of the American railroad, see Stover 133–138.

148   Mulvey 11–12.

149   Heath, "Film and System," 7–77, 91–113.

150   Heath, part 1, 66. See Heath earlier: " 'We're wasting our time around here,' comments Quinlan in the strip-joint; in Tanya's, time—the narrative—peters out" (65).

151   Peter Brooks, *Reading for the Plot: Design and Intention in Narrative* (New York: Knopf, 1984), 45.

152   Brooks 44.

153   Gerard Genette, *Narrative Discourse*, trans. Jane E. Lewin (Ithaca, N.Y.: Cornell UP, 1980), 109–112.

154   Daniel Moews, *Keaton: The Silent Features Close Up* (Berkeley: U of California P, 1977), 232.

155   Moews remarks on the sense in which Johnnie gains control of the narrative and the train in the second half of the film, but considers Annabelle's role through a male-centered lens: "Annabelle's progression is slow enough so that on most occasions her ignorance comically points up Johnnie's skill. He is the expert, she the novice . . ." (Moews, 234).

156   See, for example, Moews 51–52, 212ff. Moews takes pains to note that as much as Keaton is mechanized, his machines are humanized, beloved objects (212). For a comprehensive, revisionist treatment of the Keaton scholarship, see Charles Wolfe's "Buster Keaton and the Historical Imagination of Silent Comedy," paper read at the conference "1895: The Culture That Made Cinema," held at Stanford University, April 29, 1995.

157   Moews, 245.

158   The French film analysis term *defilement* translates roughly as "unfolding" (as in the unfolding or literal passing of a chain of images through the film projector). See Thierry Kuntzel, "*Le Defilement*/A View in Close-up," *Camera Obscura* 2 (1977): 51–68.

159   Here I am thinking of the "desiring machines" described by Gilles Deleuze and Félix

Guattari in *Anti-Oedipus: Capitalism and Schizophrenia*, trans. Robert Hurley, Mark Seem, and Helen R. Lane (New York: Viking, 1977), 1–8.

160   See Jacques Derrida, "La Pharmacie de Platon," *La Dissemination* (Paris: Editions du Seuil, 1972), 189–190; and "*La Loi du genre*/The Law of Genre," *Glyph* 7 (Spring 1980): 176–232.

161   See Gilles Deleuze, *Logique du sens* (Paris: Editions de Minuit, 1969), on paradox and the logic of the law of noncontradiction.

162   Thierry Kuntzel, unpublished seminar on *Letter from an Unknown Woman* (1948).

Three. The Railroad in the City

1   See Robert C. Allen, "Motion Picture Exhibition in Manhattan, 1906–1912: Beyond the Nickelodeon," 162–175; and Gunning, "An Unseen Energy Swallows Space," 355–366. Giuliana Bruno notes in relation to the exhibition contexts of early Italian and in particular Neopolitan cinema — notably, the arcade — that as "film was implanted within the cityscape, the cityscape was implanted within film" (37).

2   See Peiss, *Cheap Amusements*, 11–12; and Ewen 24–30. See also Roy Rosenzweig and Elizabeth Blackmar, *The Park and the People: A History of Central Park* (Ithaca, N.Y.: Cornell UP, 1992), 308–339, 384–387, 401–406, on how these phenomena affected public use of Central Park toward the end of the nineteenth and beginning of the twentieth centuries.

3   Joel A. Tarr, "From City to Suburb: The 'Moral' Influence of Transportation Technology," *American Urban History*, ed. Alexander B. Callow, Jr. (New York: Oxford UP, 1973), 203.

4   Alexander B. Callow, Jr., "Commentary," *American Urban History*, 155. By contrast, England had reached this point by 1860. Leon Marshall, "The English and American Industrial City of the Nineteenth Century," *American Urban History*, 173.

5   Production also took place, of course, outside the city in, for example, Brighton, England, Ithaca, New York, and, of course, Hollywood. On Lubin, see Kowall 19–23.

6   A sampling of titles to this effect: *Street Scene, Tokio, Japan* (AM&B, 1903); *Market Street Before Parade* (AM&B, 1903); *An Englishman's Trip from London to Paris* (AM&B, 1904); *Crowd Entering Gates, Futurity Day* (AM&B, 1902); *Market Square, Harrisburg, Pa.* (Edison, 1897); *How They Rob Men in Chicago* (AM&B, 1900); *A Mighty Tumble* (AM&B, 1901); *The Strenuous Life, or, Anti-Race Suicide* (Edison/Porter, 1904); *Lower Broadway* (AM&B, 1903); *Union Square* (AM&B, 1903); *Panorama of the Flatiron Building* (AM&B, 1903). *Skyscrapers of New York City from the North River* (Edison, 1903) admired the city from the vantage point of a barge, while *The Skyscrapers of New York* (AM&B, 1906) took place atop a partially built skyscraper.

7   See *City Hall to Harlem in 15 Seconds via the Subway Route* (Edison/Porter, 1904); and *Excavation for Subway* (AM&B 1903).

8   *[On] a [Good Old] Five Cent Trolley Ride* (Edison/Porter, 1905); *How the Old Woman Caught the Omnibus* (Hepworth, 1903); and *Madison Square, New York* (AM&B 1903). Even Méliès's legendary discovery of stop-action editing might be termed an urban discovery: when his filming of the Paris Opera was interrupted, an omnibus that had been in the shot abruptly "disappeared" when shooting resumed, only to be "replaced" by a hearse. The Méliès legend is recounted in, among other texts, Georges Sadoul, *Georges Méliès* (Paris: Editions Seghers, 1961), 24. But, as Tom Gunning points out, Méliès may well have employed a splice here (" 'Primitive' Cinema — A Frame-up? or The Trick's On Us," 5–6).

9   *The American Film Institute Catalog of Feature Films, 1911–1920* lists a number of titles set in the city, most premised on a city-country contrast. For example, *The Iron Strain* (1915) ends with the couple happily returning to the city of San Francisco. Many films were set in New

York: *The Heart of a Painted Woman*, 1915; *New York Luck*, 1917; *Tarnished Reputations*, 1920; and *A Nine O'Clock Town*, 1918 — all include the hardness, the vices of the city as a frame, but they reconcile characters to staying in the city through love. See the headings "Lure of the City," "City-Country Contrast," and "New York City" in Patricia King Hanson, ed., *The American Film Institute Catalog of Feature Films, 1911–1920, Indexes* (Berkeley: U of California P, 1988).

10   Trachtenberg 57–59. Trachtenberg further notes: "The term 'metropolis' signified a commanding position within a region which included hinterland. New economic, social, and political relations between the center and its outlying districts manifest themselves in the [post-Civil War] decades as rise and fall, prosperity and impoverishment. . . . Cities expanded not by absolute increases in population alone but also by thickening regional networks of transport and communication." (113.) By 1900, nine-tenths of all manufacturing took place in cities (Trachtenberg 114).

11   Stilgoe 289–310.

12   The station was "not so much a distinctive 'place' as a place for movement, for transactions made against an infallible clock" (Trachtenberg 121). See also Stilgoe 36–44. Carl Condit divides the evolution of the city into three periods: the horse-and-pedestrian, the railroad, and the automotive. In his terms, "the railroad "was decisive for the growth of the industrial city, since it was then that technology, for good and ill, became the chief determinant of urban form, with the rail pattern playing a major role" (Condit x).

13   See Stilgoe 21–32; and Schivelbusch 170–179. Many early films take spectators on "panoramic" trips aboard the interurban railroads (e.g., *Panoramic View from Pittsburgh to Allegheny*, Edison, 1902; and *A Trip to Berkeley, Cal.*, AM&B, 1906).

14   Meanwhile, the Indian film genre — which overlapped with the Western — thrived between 1907 and 1915. A key feature was the "naked Indian hero," designed to appeal to female spectators. Defined as noble, the hero existed primarily to sacrifice himself for white people. Native Americans were used as actors in this genre. By 1913, with the genre fading, Indians were becoming more and more villainous in Westerns. (See Bowser, *The Transformation of Cinema, 1907–1915*, p. 173–176.)

15   See films like the 1913 *Caprice* (Famous Players), which starred Mary Pickford. In this story, a mountain girl must suffer a great deal to learn "grace and charm" — the cultured ways of the city — before the man she loves, a New Yorker, can accept her and be happy. By contrast, later films like *Are They Born or Made?* (Humanology Film Producing, 1915, dist., by United Film Service) privilege a rural point of view in representing the unfortunate life of a city gangster raised in the slums who is ultimately saved by a farmer's daughter. (See plot descriptions in Hanson 121.)

16   Stilgoe 25 notes that around the turn of the century "rapid transit appears again and again in magazine articles as the most visible manifestation of urban haste. . . . The riders of streetcars and subway trains ate quickly, dressed quickly, ran quickly, did business quickly. When streetcar snarls stopped high-speed ground travel, the throngs dashed for subway and elevated trains. The urban public demanded — and usually received — speed in every sort of transportation." *Rube and Mandy at Coney Island* (Edison/Porter, 1903) is film history's favorite early film in the "bumpkin-in-the-city" genre. Rube and Mandy, two popular vaudeville figures who appeared in several films together, are the quintessential ill-mannered country couple. At Coney Island we watch them tackle the various rides, including a miniature train, with ungainly enthusiasm.

17   Like a similar AM&B film, *2 A.M. in the Subway* (discussed below), *A Rube in the Subway* was shot in AM&B's New York studio. See Kemp Niver, *Early Motion Pictures: The Paper Prints*

Collection in the Library of Congress, ed. Bebe Bergsten (Washington, D.C.: Library of Congress, 1985), 280.

18   An English film that sounds suspiciously like *A Rube in the Subway* bears the title *A Romance of the Underground Electric Railway* (Gaumont, 1906), but is probably the same film. See "Gaumont 'Elge' Lists 1906–08," *Early Filmmakers' Catalogues*, ed. British Film Insitute (London: World Microfilms Publications, 1983).

19   See Trachtenberg, who quotes Horatio Alger's *Ragged Dick: Or, Street Life in New York* (1867) as follows: " 'In the street life of the metropolis, a boy needs to be on the alert, and have all his wits about him' " (Trachtenberg 105–107).

20   Hansen, *Babel and Babylon*, 12.

21   Hansen, *Babel and Babylon*, 48.

22   Munsterberg 95.

23   Hansen, *Babel and Babylon*, 38.

24   Hansen, *Babel and Babylon*, 39–40.

25   Munsterberg 93.

26   The "Weimar Film Theory" special issue of *New German Critique* 40 (Winter 1987) contains the translation of Kracauer's "The Cult of Distraction: On Berlin's Picture Palaces (1926)," 91–96, as well as a number of articles on Kracauer, many of which address the notion of "distraction." See in addition to articles referenced below Anton Kaes, "Literary Intellectuals and the Cinema: Charting a Controversy (1909–1929)," 7–34; and Heide Schlüpmann, "Phenomenology of Film: On Siegfried Kracauer's Writings of the 1920s," 97–114.

27   Thomas Elsaesser, "Cinema, The Irresponsible Signifier or, 'The Gamble with History': Film Theory or Cinema Theory," *New German Critique* 40 (Winter 1987): 65–90, 67.

28   Kracauer, "Cult of Distraction," 91–95.

29   See Elsaesser, "Cinema, The Irresponsible Signifier or, 'The Gamble with History': Film Theory or Cinema Theory," 84–87; and Miriam Hansen, "Benjamin, Cinema and Experience: 'The Blue Flower in the Land of Technology,' " *New German Critique* 40 (Winter 1987), 218–22, on Benjamin's parallel path.

30   Hansen, *Babel and Babylon*, 8–9.

31   See Munsterberg 36–37 on the urban mode of attention as analogous to classical film attention in focusing on a face in the crowd or an object in a shop window; the urban spectator's eyes function as a kind of camera, picking out details and concentrating on them such that the busy background loses its clarity and vividness.

32   Benjamin, "The Work of Art in the Age of Mechanical Reproduction," 240: "The distracted person, too, can form habits. More, the ability to master certain tasks in a state of distraction proves that their solution has become a matter of habit."

33   For critical perspectives on gender and distraction from a feminist point of view, see Patrice Petro, "Modernity and Mass Culture in Weimar: Contours of a Discourse on Sexuality in Early Theories of Perception and Representation," *New German Critique* 40 (Winter 1987): 136–146; and Hake, "Girls and Crisis: the Other Side of Diversion," 158–164. Petro's article is taken from and developed further in her excellent study of female spectatorship in Weimar culture, *Joyless Streets* (Princeton, N.J.: Princeton UP, 1989).

34   Miriam Hansen, "Benjamin, Cinema and Experience," 185. See Gunning, "The Cinema of Attraction," 63–70. Gunning's model is discussed in chap. 2 of this book. See Freidberg on Corbusier and the city as a machine for producing speed traffic: "The city itself was a machine for mobility, generating a newly mobilized gaze" (p. 65).

35   Callow 155. City designers who followed Frederick Law Olmsted's example emerged in the

1870s and 1880s to address these problems *within* the city. Olmsted's great approach to city design was the park, most notably Central Park (1859), the supreme order and wholesomeness of which were intended to resolve the tensions between commercial and residential districts of New York City (Trachtenberg 106–108). The park was designed to "eradicate the communal culture of working-class and immigrant streets, to erase that culture's offensive and disturbing foreignness, and replace it with middle-class norms of hearth and tea table" (Trachtenberg 111). Meanwhile, however, ghettoes continued to proliferate during the 1870s, 1880s, and 1890s (Trachtenberg 119ff.).

36 By 1920 more than three-fourths of the U.S. urban population was foreign or first-generation (Callow 289).

37 See Marshall 173.

38 Jacob A. Riis, *How the Other Half Lives* (1890; New York: Dover, 1971).

39 For fuller descriptions of these films, see Hanson 290 and 313.

40 Lears, *No Place of Grace*, 67.

41 Lears, *No Place of Grace*, 7.

42 Trachtenberg 117.

43 "Money economy and the domination of the intellect stand in the closest relationship to one another. They have in common a purely matter-of-fact attitude in the treatment of persons and things in which a formal justice is often combined with an unrelenting hardness. . . . Money is concerned only with what is common to all, i.e., with the exchange value which reduces all quality and individuality to a purely quantitative level." Georg Simmel, "The Metropolis and Mental Life," *Georg Simmel: On Individuality and Social Forms— Selected Writings*, ed. with intro. Donald N. Levine (Chicago: U of Chicago P, 1971), 326. See also Trachtenberg 21: "As the domestic making of goods receded, city dwellers became more and more dependent on buying and selling, selling their labor in order to buy their sustenance; the network of personal relations, of family, friends, neighbors, comes to count for less in the maintenance of life than the impersonal transactions and abstract structures of the marketplace."

44 Simmel, 333–338. See also Schivelbusch 157 and Bruno 53–55, who draws a comparison between Simmel's description of the metropolis and the situation of spectatorship in the cinema.

45 Drinka 190. Urban malaise was even seen as a New York malady: "The title of John Girdner's book of 1901, *Newyorkitis*, identified a new disease—a special kind of inflammation that results from living in the big city and includes, among its numerous symptoms, 'rapidity and nervousness and lack of deliberation in all movements' " (Kern 125). Kern goes on to discuss a number of works on the city by such authors as William Dean Howells and Robert Musil, who single out urban transportation in all its forms as causes of nervous breakdown.

46 See Drinka 122.

47 *L'Illustration*, May 30, 1896: 454. The article identifies attendant symptoms—insomnia, nervous twitchings in the face, extreme irritability—and notes that these indices of neurasthenia manifested themselves at least every other week in "nervous subjects," who are, of course, predisposed to acquire neurasthenia.

48 Drinka 190–191.

49 Lears, *No Place of Grace*, 47–58, 245–247.

50 Lears, *No Place of Grace*, 104.

51 Lears, *No Place of Grace*, 138, 202ff.

52 Lears, *No Place of Grace*, 4–58. The Arts and Crafts movement (in both England and the United States sought to restore a sense of self in working with one's hands, but, as Lears notes, the "Arts and Crafts ideologues . . . came usually from among the business and professional people who felt most cut off from 'real life' and most in need of moral regeneration" (Lears, *No Place of Grace*, 61). American mistrust of progress was older than its ambivalent embodiment in the "machine in the garden," but its late nineteenth-century Victorian version bore a heightened relation to the strain of modern culture.

53 Lears, "From Salvation to Self-Realization," 10–11. In some cases, the railroads were directly responsible for these urban escape valves, whether by carrying the moviegoing public to the nickelodeons located near trolley or subway stops, or by direct patronage. *Moving Picture World* noted in 1907, for example, that a new "amusement theater" opening in Portland, Maine, was being leased by the New York Amusement Company with the Portland Railroad Company (*Moving Picture World*, June 26, 1907, 278.) See also Robert C. Allen, "Motion Picture Exhibition in Manhattan," 174.

54 Peiss, *Cheap Amusements*, 34.

55 Peiss, *Cheap Amusements*, 12, 34, 41ff.

56 Peiss, *Cheap Amusements*, 35.

57 Lears, *No Place of Grace*, 104.

58 Lears, *No Place of Grace*, 104. Andreas Huyssen notes a similar paranoia at work in the split between high art and mass culture in nineteenth- and twentieth-century Europe; he analyzes "the notion which gained ground during the nineteenth century that mass culture is somehow associated with woman while real, authentic culture remains the prerogative of men." Huyssen points out that in an age when both socialism and feminism were "knocking at the gate" of male-dominated culture, both traditional and modern high culture gendered the masses as feminine in order to exclude them from their privileged, male preserve. Andreas Huyssen, "Mass Culture as Woman: Modernism's Other," *After the Great Divide: Modernism, Mass Culture and Postmodernism* (Bloomington: Indiana UP, 1986), 47.

59 See Lears, *No Place of Grace*, 52–53. On railroad companies' promotional strategies from 1880s on, see Boxes 81, 82, 84, 85, 88, and 91 in Warshaw Collection.

60 Rev. Dr. Bridgman, *The Vacation Gospel* (Hamline, Minn.: Great Northern Railroad, 1890). Box 88, Warshaw Collection.

61 Bridgman 1–2.

62 Bridgman 2–3.

63 *Winter Pleasure Tours* (Philadelphia: Pennsylvania Railroad, 1890), 5. Box 80, Warshaw Collection.

64 *From Brockville, Canada on the St. Lawrence River via the Brockville, Westport and North-Western Railway* (New York: Wynkoop, Hallenbeck, Crawford, n.d.) 1. Box 85, Warshaw Collection. Perhaps the most ludicrous claim in this genre was that put forth by the Ulster and Delaware Railroad's guide to the Catskill Mountains, published in 1904. On the subject of summer rest, the guide noted that the "vacation habit" had now spread to all classes, but that few understood "the real lesson of the doctrine of rest." *The Catskill Mountains* (Kingston, N.Y.: Ulster and Delaware Railroad, 1904), 8. Box 94, Warshaw Collection: "Men and women in every walk of life, rich and poor alike, hustle along day after day through the busy months of each year between store or office and the home or club, in quest of the elusive dollar and the happiness or pleasure it may bring. Few ever stop to estimate the pace or measure the speed of their activities. . . . It is an ambitious age in which we live. . . . The careful conservation of vital force is the imperative lesson of the hour. Greater economy in

the use and control of our bodies and brains is strictly enjoined. . . . There must be stated periods of relaxation, recreation and absolute rest. . . . A breath of Nature, uncontaminated by the dregs of city civilization, is the unfailing panacea" (9). The brochure goes on to juxtapose the glories of fresh, unpolluted country air, the importance of solitude and wandering, and the beauty of the countryside, all aspects of the "vacation gospel," which is also clearly a rhetoric of advertising and promotion. See also *Health and Pleasure on America's Greatest Railroad,* Four-Track Series 55 (N.p.: New York Central, 1893), Box 94, Warshaw Collection, and *The Summer Boarder,* Travel Series 17 (N.p.: New York Central, ca. 1900), Box 80, Warshaw Collection.

65   Patrick G. Loughney points out that the film was probably a double satire on both suburban life in general, and a magazine published by the New Jersey Central Railroad called *The Suburbanite.* Biograph technicians and players would have been familiar with it, since they often traveled on the New Jersey Central to get to different locations for exteriors near New York City. The magazine apparently "was filled with breezy articles extolling suburban life over the crowded, expensive and unhealthy conditions of apartment life in Manhattan." Loughney, *Before Hollywood: Turn-of-the-Century Film from American Archives,* exhibition catalog, ed. Jay Leyda and Charles Musser (New York: American Federation of Arts, 1986), 119.

66   Bobrick 14–16.

67   Trachtenberg 47.

68   Bobrick, 142–148, 158–160, 182–186, 205–207.

69   Bobrick 93–97, 154, 226.

70   *L'Illustration,* Christmas 1896, 27; Déthier 58.

71   Bobrick 241.

72   See Sumiko Higashi on DeMille's *Kindling* (1915), an ambivalent construction of the social consequences of urbanization and industrialization (74–84).

73   Robert Lang uses the phrase "mantle of patriarchal responsibility" in *American Film Melodrama* (Princeton, N.J.: Princeton UP, 1989) 119. Lang sees *The Crowd* as an abstract melodrama that seems to resist the Oedipal in its locating of cause and effect in mass society, but it is ultimately concerned with coming to terms with the Father in a very Oedipal sense (Lang 130).

74   "John Sims' experience in the big city makes him a modern man, in whom the gap between aspiration or life as it is meant to be, and life as it in fact is, registers in a lifelong pattern of self-alienation and sense of having or being 'never quite enough' " (Lang 119).

75   Lang 126 notes with respect to *The Crowd* that the modern urban crowd deprives the individual of community, of "a place within an order."

76   See Benjamin, "On Some Motifs in Baudelaire," 166–176.

77   Gustave Le Bon, *The Crowd: A Study of the Popular Mind,* intro. Robert K. Merton (1895; New York: Viking, 1960), 23.

78   Le Bon 31.

79   He found this particularly true of Latin crowds: "Crowds are everywhere distinguished by feminine characteristics, but Latin crowds are the most feminine of all" (Le Bon 31, 39). See also Le Bon 46 and 50. The aesthetic prototype is Baudelaire's poet-in-the-crowd. In *Baudelaire and Freud* (Berkeley: U of California P, 1977), Leo Bersani sees the poet as penetrated by or open to the crowd in both a neurological and sexual sense — Baudelaire as prostituting himself, "sacrificing a certain wholeness or integrity for the sake of those pleasurable nervous shocks which accompany the release of desiring energies by scenes

from external life" (Bersani 11). For Bersani, this shattering of the artist's integrity by the crowd is a momentous, ultimately feminizing sexual event, making it an exemplary experience of the loss of self in modernity.

80 Le Bon's analysis of how the crowd's thinking in images leads it to confuse the real and the unreal, the subjective and the objective — thus giving such imaginings the character of hallucinations — bears a more than passing resemblance to the conventional analysis of a female hysteric (Le Bon 41–43). Cf. Peiss, *Cheap Amusements*, 7–8, 98ff., on the newfound sexuality of urban women; Huyssen, "Mass Culture as Woman: Modernism's Other," 47; and Anson Rabinbach, "The Body without Fatigue: A Nineteenth-Century Utopia," *Political Symbolism in Modern Europe: Essays in Honor of George L. Mosse*, ed. Seymour Drescher, David Sabean, and Allan Sharlin (New Brunswick, N.J.: Transaction Books, 1982), 51–57, which outlines the nineteenth-century concept of the body as a field of energy and forces that needed to be controlled in order not to destroy the will of the male worker.

81 Sigmund Freud, *Group Psychology and the Analysis of the Ego*, trans. and ed. James Strachey (1923; New York: Norton, 1959).

82 What Freud calls the "Ego-ideal" (and later, the superego) sets itself up as a critical, superior agency that imposes moral censorship. In love, it is replaced by the love object, which the ego sets up as beyond criticism. This is the point at which the metaphor of hypnosis holds significance for Freud. *Group Psychology*, 35–40.

83 Freud, *Group Psychology*, 46.

84 Freud, *Group Psychology*, 47.

85 Freud, *Group Psychology*, 59.

86 Besides his seminars over the years at the *Centre americain* in Paris, Bellour's ideas on hypnosis are familiar to American students of film theory through *Camera Obscura* (see, in particular, Bergstrom "Alternation, Segmentation, Hypnosis," 71–103; and Raymond Bellour "Ideal Hadaly (on Villiers's *The Future Eve*)," *Camera Obscura* 15 (1986): 111–136).

87 "By the hypnotic apparatus I mean the therapeutic-scientific situation which began with Mesmer at the end of the 18th century and developed throughout the 19th century up to Charcot and Bernheim, which was first used and then conceptualized by Freud (especially in *Group Psychology*), and which since then has been the object of a certain number of historical, theoretical and experimental works, especially in France (Chertok, Rausky, Lacanians like Nassif and Miller) and in the United States (Kubie, Margolin, Gill, Brennan, etc.), not to mention the many Soviet works I haven't read." (Bellour, quoted in Bergstrom, "Alternation, Segmentation, Hypnosis," 100) It is important to note that Bellour's interest in the "hypnotized" spectator of cinema grew out of his work on Fritz Lang's Dr. Mabuse films and also the novels of Dumas and Villiers de l'Isle-Adam. In Lang's films, a direct connection is suggested between hypnosis and cinematic subjectivity in "the kind of power in the production of the narrative due to the hypnotic powers" Mabuse possesses. (Bergstrom, "Alternation, Segmentation, Hypnosis," 101.) The visual nature of this power is crucial, as Janet Bergstrom points out; the power of enunciation in narrative cinema is vested to a large extent in control over point of view, and insofar as hypnosis exercises its power visually in the Lang films, hypnosis and cinema come together through enunciation. Bergstrom, "Alternation, Segmentation, Hypnosis," 101.

88 Raymond Bellour, seminar, *Centre americain* (*Place de l'Odeon*), Paris, 1983–84; Lawrence S. Kubie and Sydney Margolis, "The Process of Hypnotism and the Nature of the Hypnotic State," *American Journal of Psychiatry* 100 (March 1944): 610–642; Bellour, "Ideal Hadaly," 122–123.

89   Bellour, seminar, *Centre americain.*

90   See Michael Walsh, "Slipping into Darkness: Figures of Waking in Cinema," *Wide Angle* 5, no. 4 (1984): 14–20. See also Bergstrom, "Alternation, Segmentation, Hypnosis: Interview with Raymond Bellour," 103, where Bellour links the power of narrativity in cinema to the power of the family romance, which is the story of psychoanalysis.

91   Metz 45.

92   Metz 45–53. Jean-Louis Baudry, who makes the link between an Imaginary "whole" subject and the bourgeois individual that is also meant to think of itself as whole and autonomous. Baudry 25–40 sees the situation of the spectator—immobile like an infant, all senses reduced to sight and hearing, the psychic frontiers of censorship relaxed, in a dream-like state of suspension of disbelief—as a regression to an even more fundamental state, that of the infant in the womb. His cinematic spectator is ready and willing to accept anything on the screen, given the flattered position of mastery into which she/he is put, and the "suggestibility" of the viewing situation.

93   "On the one hand, my work rejoins Metz's and especially Baudry's analyses of regression, whereby the film state comes very close to the dream state. . . . On the other hand, I establish the connection between the film state and hypnosis by referring to the psychoanalytic notion of the ego ideal as it is developed by Freud in *Group Psychology.* This allows us to understand more clearly how the cinema produces a deep identification, both subjective and social, which explains the very great fascination it exercises." Bergstrom, "Alternation, Segmentation, Hypnosis," 101.

94   Munsterberg 47. See also Hansen, *Babel and Babylon*, 83.

95   Munsterberg 95.

96   Kubie and Margolis 611.

97   Daumier took "Sleeping Travellers" (on the train) as a subject, a caricature that for Schivelbusch epitomizes the "Monotony of the railroad journey" (61). See Patrice Petro, "After Shock/Between Boredom and History," 77–99. Train travel's well-known narcotic effects, and their connection to hypnosis, are exploited in many films, most notably Alfred Hitchcock's *The Lady Vanishes* (1938).

98   Anyone who has ever felt or witnessed the contagion of group laughter, cheering or pathos during a movie—even and especially a bad melodrama or action picture—will recognize this effect. Vis-à-vis the herd, Freud wrote: "A primary group of this kind is a number of individuals who have put one and the same object in the place of their ego ideal and have consequently identified themselves with one another in ego" (Freud, *Group Psychology*, 48). Freud also wrote: "Hypnosis is not a good object for comparison with a group formation, because it is truer to say that it is identical with it" (*Group Psychology* 47; see also 10–12, 19–53).

99   Friedberg 90 notes with respect to amusement parks that "one of the thrills of these rides was to literally throw the interaction between men and women off balance or to whirl gender roles into a centripetal frenzy." John Kasson has written about the loosening of social convention permitted at Coney Island in relation to a broader shift in sexual codes of conduct occurring at the turn of the century. He connects the tunnel rides, as well as other physically aggressive rides that literally threw couples together, to this new change essentially brought about by the rise of urban culture. John F. Kasson, *Amusing the Million: Coney Island at the Turn of the Century* (New York: Hill and Wang, 1978), 41–43. In Kasson's words, "Coney Island in effect declared a moral holiday for all who entered its gates. Against the values of thrift, sobriety, industry, and ambition, it encouraged extravagance, gaiety, aban-

don, revelry. . . . It served as a Feast of Fools for an urban-industrial society" (50). Kasson 74 also notes the strong connection many of the mechanical rides bore to urban rail transport.

100   The sleepiness of the porter bears a strong relation to historical reality, as porters were barred from sleeping on the job until their union negotiated a minimum of three hours' sleep in 1928 (Santino 19–23). As to the docility of the porter, what white people failed to realize, with rare exceptions, was that porters often played a persona to avoid being intimidated and to garner as big a tip as possible, as porters had no rights with respect to the employer, and no recourse if a passenger or conductor complained about his performance. In 1928, however, being a porter was highly politicized, with Randolph publicly struggling to make gains on behalf of the BSCP, which still had to wage a difficult battle on behalf of fairness to blacks long after Pullman finally signed an historic agreement with the union in 1937. See Santino 71–107; Jervis Anderson, *A. Philip Randolph: A Biographical Portrait* (New York: Harcourt, 1973), 162–163.

101   The terrified-newlywed stereotype was well-established in popular understanding of the honeymoon train. Jensen reproduces a 1905 series of photographs used to publicize the Santa Fe's California Limited; one of the photographs shows a black porter snickering at a newlywed husband "reading" a *Collier's* upside-down. (Jensen 228)

102   Lang 122.

103   This notion is reflected in our time in the concept of "subliminal seduction." Wilson Bryan Key's *Subliminal Seduction* (1973), which comes out of an explicitly MacLuhanite background, made popular what advertisers had considered to be true of themselves for decades, namely, the idea that advertising is seduction that works at the consumer's unconscious level: "In the concept of subliminal phenomena are included all those techniques now known to the mass media by which tens of millions of humans are daily massaged and manipulated without their conscious awareness." While Key's notions may be criticized for being perhaps too reductionist, they are familiar to — indeed, accepted by — advertisers. Wilson Bryan Key, *Subliminal Seduction* (New York: New American Library, 1973) 1.

104   Trachtenberg 135; Ewen 23–30, 35.

105   Lears, *No Place of Grace;* and Lears, "From Salvation to Self-Realization," 3–38. See also Ewen's seminal work in this area (81–102).

106   Roland Marchand, *Advertising the American Dream* (Berkeley: U of California P, 1985), 9, 25, 29. Ewen also shows how advertisers were extremely conscious early on of manipulating the "will" of the masses (81–94). In *The Mirror Makers — A History of American Advertising and Its Creators* (New York: Vintage, 1984) 94, Stephen Fox quotes from *Printers' Ink*, the advertisers' trade publication, this note from the early 1920s on the testimonial ad:

> "It pays to be personal now,
>   It brings in the shekels — and how!
>   If you want to sell drugs,
>   Or Baluchistan rugs,
>   Or revolvers to thugs,
>   Or a spray to kill bugs —
>   You've got to be personal now."

107   Marchand 66. See also Marchand 11, 56ff., and Fox 81. Lears notes how advertising recognized the importance of women as consumers early on ("From Salvation to Self-Realization," 26–27). See also Friedberg 35ff. on women and the department store, and on the gender-codified relation between looking and buying.

108 See Marchand 347. See also Sumiko Higashi's excellent study of DeMille's sex comedies and melodramas, which notes how beginning in the 1910s and reaching an apogee in the 1920s "his spectacles provided the advertising industry with valuable intertexts to promote consumption" (3). Also see Higashi 142–144, 159–164, and 175–179 on how DeMille addressed females through style and fashion and actually influenced the culture of consumption as much as being influenced by it.

109 Marchand 67 and 356.

110 Marchand 13.

111 Marchand 341, 360, 17. See Lears, "From Salvation to Self-Realization" 19, 24.

112 Marchand 118, 123. As early as 1903, Lears notes, advertisers were thinking in terms of the "suggestibility" of consumers and theorizing that if they were persuasive enough, they "could influence a consumer to act reflexively, without thought or hesitation" ("From Salvation to Self-Realization," 19).

113 See, for example, Trachtenberg 135 on the "language" of advertising.

114 Marchand 347. Lears writes that "after the turn of the century, success manuals increasingly prescribed what the sociologist David Riesman has called 'modes of manipulating the self in order to manipulate others.' The successful man or woman had 'no clear core of self' (in Riesman's words), only a set of social masks" ("From Salvation to Self-Realization," 8).

115 "Americans of the 1920s and 1930s may have seen themselves . . . as living in an Age of Crowds" (Marchand 358).

116 May 203–236.

117 Higashi 3–4. See also Maria LaPlace's engaging article on discourses of consumerism and their impact on the woman's film of the 1940s. "Bette Davis and the Ideal of Consumption: A Look at *Now Voyager*," *Wide Angle* 6, no. 4 (1985): 34–43.

118 May 211–213; Higashi 142–144.

119 See May 200–204.

120 Quoted in Don Martindale and Gertrud Neuwirth, translators and editors of Max Weber's *The City* (New York: Free Press, 1958), 39.

121 Writing in the 1910s and 1920s, early film critic and theorist Vachel Lindsay saw a direct connection between advertising and cinema in their common appeal to a "visual-minded public." He noted: "American civilization grows more hieroglyphic every day. The cartoons of Darling, the advertisements in the back of the magazines and on the billboards and in the street-cars, the acres of photographs in the Sunday newspapers, make us into a hieroglyphic civilization far nearer to Egypt than to England" (Lindsay xxxvi–xxxvii).

122 Lang 123. See also a 1907 essay on New York by William Dean Howells: " 'People are born and married, and live and die in the midst of an uproar so frantic that you would think they would go mad of it; and I believe the physicians really attribute something of the growing prevalence of neurotic disorders to the wear and tear of the nerves from the rush of trains passing almost momently, and the perpetual jarring of the earth and air from their swift transit. . . . Imagine . . . a wife bending over the pillow of her husband to catch the last faint whisper of farewell, as a train of five or six cars goes roaring by the open window! What horror! What profanation!' " Quoted in Kern 126.

123 See Emile Durkheim, *Suicide: A Study in Sociology*, trans. John A. Spaulding and George Simpson, ed. and intro. Simpson (New York: Free Press, 1951), 357–358.

124 Lang 120. Lang 128 states that "One cannot help but read *The Crowd* as a critique of a system that undermines the masculinity of a good man like John Sims."

125 At the same time, it is tantamount to *women* having one's masculinity. As will be recalled

from chap. 2, above, the increasing visibility of women in the public sphere, especially the work sphere, was seen as a threat to male identity, and as in some sense an "unfeminizing" of women (although this is not suggested in *The Crowd*, which focuses on John's subjectivity vs. Mary's).

126 It is significant that Mary's father is completely absent, even as a reference, while John's mother is equally nonexistent; this seems to be the film's way of presenting a contrast between maternity and paternity in all its starkness, without having to deal with both good and bad mothers and fathers. See also Lang 125: "The death of John's father coincided with the advent of mass society, which diminishes the individual." I agree only partially with Lang's interpretation that "John's Father, in a broad, metaphorical sense, is History; it is the crowd" (130). The Father is History, but the crowd is precisely what replaces him.

127 Lears, "From Salvation to Self-Realization," 24. See Ewen 125 on the death of patriarchal authority as such in modern advertising culture.

128 As such, John is the heir in the 1920s to Edward Bellamy's *Looking Backward* (1888), which also recommended leisure and consumption as a recipe for happiness (see Trachtenberg 50). As Lang 131 notes, "By the 1920s America has effectively become a mass society, and . . . offers only consumerism to satiate the hungers of the ordinary man. . . ." See also Murnau's *Sunrise* (1927); even in this film, the early equation of the city with evil, as represented by the city woman, is tempered when the country couple experiences a rebirth in the context of a range of city entertainments and consumerist activities.

129 Hansen sees the ending as an ironic commentary on the reduction of the individual to a fragment of the mass ornament. While I would agree that the ending is not conventionally "happy," I feel that the film encourages — primarily through the melodramatic reunion of the family — a reading of redemption and resolution. Indeed, the fact that the clown advertisement/juggler is the only option available to John is humbling for him and offers him, within the context of the narrative, an opportunity — albeit an ironic one — to reclaim some of his dignity as a father, husband and individual. See Miriam Hansen, "Ambivalences of the 'Mass Ornament': King Vidor's *The Crowd*," *Qui Parle* 5 (Spring/Summer 1992): 102–119.

130 For Judith Mayne, "examination of the woman question in Soviet film suggests that political coherence is a problematic entity; the woman question forgrounds crucial tensions that inform the films on many levels. . . . In other words, the cinematic ways in which the woman question is posed exemplify the ambiguity characteristic of Soviet film narrative." *Kino and the Woman Question* (Columbus: Ohio State UP, 1989), 9–10. I would like to point out that Mayne's important study, which fills a gap in understanding Soviet cinema of the 1920s and covers some of the ground on women and *Man with a Movie Camera* in this chapter (especially concerning male and female work), appeared after my own work on the film had been published. Lynne Kirby, "From Marinetti to Vertov: Woman on the Track of Avant-Garde Representation, "*Quarterly Review of Film Studies* 10, no. 4 (1989): 309–323. In a reciprocal gesture to Mayne, who graciously informed me of her unawareness of my work while completing her book, I wish to state my regret at not having her work available to me when I was first studying the film.

131 See Renato Poggioli, "Technology and the Avant-Garde," *Theory of the Avant-Garde*, trans. Gerald Fitzgerald (New York: Harper, 1971) 131–142; John Berger, "The Moment of Cubism," *The Look of Things*, ed. and intro. Nikos Stangos (New York: Viking, 1974); and Meyer Schapiro, "The Nature of Abstract Art," *Modern Art: 19th and 20th Centuries* (New York: Braziller, 1978), 206–211.

132 See Milton Brown et al., *American Art* (New York: Abrams, 1979), 388–389.

133   Stilgoe 74–103; and *The Hand of Man: Railroads in American Prints and Photographs*, exhi-bition catalog (Baltimore: Baltimore Museum of Art, Nov. 21, 1978–Jan. 7, 1979), illus. 60–64.

134   See my discussion of antimodernism and Le Bon earlier in this chapter. See also Andreas Huyssen, "The Vamp and the Machine: Technology and Sexuality in Fritz Lang's *Metropo-lis*," *New German Critique* 24–25 (Fall/Winter 1981–82): 221–237.

135   See Paul Virilio, *Speed and Politics*, trans. Mark Polizzotti (New York: Semiotext(e), 1986), 46–57, 119–120, 133–151.

136   Charles Baudelaire, "L'Horloge," *Petits poèmes en prose (le spleen de Paris)* (1864; Paris: Garnier-Flammarion, 1967), 75–76.

137   In "Woman's Time," Kristeva explores the association of women with space (as opposed to time or history), and the link between two types of temporality — cyclical and monumen-tal — and traditional Western conceptions of female subjectivity. Julia Kristeva, "Woman's Time," *Feminist Theory: A Critique of Ideology*, ed. Nannerl O. Keohane, Michelle Z. Rosaldo and Barbara C. Gelpi (Chicago: U of Chicago P, 1982), 34–36.

138   See Giorgio De Chirico, "Meditations of a Painter," *Theories of Modern Art*, ed. Herschel B. Chipp (Berkeley: U of California P, 1968), 397–401.

139   See Tristan Tzara, "Lecture on Dada," *Seven Manifestos and Lampisteries*, trans. Barbara Wright (London: John Calder, 1977), 109. See also David Bathrick, "Affirmative and Nega-tive Culture: Technology and the Left Avant-Garde," *The Technological Imagination: Theories and Fictions*, ed. Teresa De Lauretis, Andreas Huyssen, and Kathleen Woodward (Madison, Wisc.: Coda Press, 1980), 107–122.

140   See Fernand Léger, "The Machine Aesthetic: Geometric Order and Truth" *Functions of Painting*, ed. and intro. Edward F. Fry, pref. George L. K. Morris, trans. Alexandra Ander-son (New York: Viking, 1965), 62: "In the search for vividness and intensity, I have made use of the machines as others have used the nude body or the still life . . . I try to create *a beautiful object* with mechanical elements."

141   See *Herbert Bayer — A Total Concept*, exhibition catalog (Denver: Denver Art Museum, Nov. 11–Dec. 23, 1973), 60.

142   See F. T. Marinetti, "L'Homme multiplié et le règne de la machine," *Le Futurisme* (Lau-sanne: Editions de l'Age d'Homme, 1980), 111–116.

143   F. T. Marinetti, "Le Mépris de la femme," *Le Futurisme* (Lausanne: Editions de l'Age d'Homme, 1980), 105–110. See also Marinetti, "L'Homme multiplié," 111, on the need to dissociate the two conceptions "woman" and "Beauty" in order to equate Beauty with the machine.

144   Marinetti, "L'Homme multiplié," 111–112.

145   Boccioni's *Materia* (1912), which represents his mother as a quasi-mechanical, simultaneist force, is a vivid pictorial example of such an imbrication of the female — indeed, the mater-nal — and the mechanical.

146   See F. T. Marinetti, " 'Nous renions nos maîtres les symbolistes, derniers amants de la lune," *Le Futurisme* (Lausanne: Editions de l'Age d'Homme, 1980), 120.

147   See Jacques Derrida, "White Mythology: Metaphor in the Text of Philosophy," *Margins of Philosophy*, trans. Alan Bass (Chicago: U of Chicago P, 1982); and Derrida, *Spurs: Nietzsche's Styles*, trans. Barbara Harlow (Chicago: U of Chicago P, 1978).

148   Huyssen, "The Vamp and the Machine," 226.

149   Marinetti, "Le Mépris de la femme," 106, 110.

150   See Annette Michelson, Introduction, *Kino-Eye: The Writings of Dziga Vertov*, ed. and intro. Annette Michelson, trans. Kevin O'Brien (Berkeley: U of California P, 1984), xv–lxi.

151 See Vladimir Markov, *Russian Futurism: A History* (Berkeley: U of California P, 1968). I thank Miriam Hansen for reemphasizing the importance of the political differences between the Italian Futurists and their Russian counterparts.

152 See Alexander Gerschenkron, *Economic Backwardness in Historical Perspective* (Cambridge, Mass.: Harvard UP, 1966).

153 See, e.g., Christina Lodder, "Constructivism and Productivism in the 1920s," in *Art into Life: Russian Constructivism, 1914–1932*, published in conjunction with the exhibition held: Henry Art Gallery, University of Washington, Seattle, July 4–Sept. 2, 1990; Walker Art Center, Oct. 7–Dec. 30, 1990, State Tretyakov Gallery, Moscow, Feb.–Aug., 1991; intro. Richard Andrews and Milena Kalinovska, pp. 99–116.

154 Markov 145.

155 See Markov 105ff.

156 Dziga Vertov, "A Young Woman Composer," *Kino-Eye: The Writings of Dziga Vertov*, ed. and intro. Annette Michelson, trans. Kevin O'Brien (Berkeley: U of California P, 1984) 297.

157 Vertov, "Lullaby," *Kino-Eye*, 200.

158 See Jay Leyda, *Kino: A History of the Russian and Soviet Film*, 3d ed. (Princeton, N.J.: Princeton UP, 1983), 132–148.

159 See Walsh 14–20.

160 Youri Tsyviane, "*L'Homme à la caméra* de Dziga Vertov en tant que texte constructiviste," *Revue de cinéma/Ecran* 351 (June 1980): 122–125.

161 "Not FEKS, not Eisenstein's 'factory of attractions,' not the factory of doves and kisses (directors of this sort have not yet died out), and not the factory of death, either. . . . Simply: the FACTORY OF FACTS. Filming facts. Sorting facts. Disseminating facts. Agitating with facts. Propaganda with facts. . . . " Vertov, "The Factory of Facts," *Kino-Eye*, 59. Vertov said of *Man with a Movie Camera* that it was "100 percent cinematography," and "a 'higher mathematics' of facts" (Vertov, "The Man with a Movie Camera," *Kino-Eye*, 84).

162 See Stephen Crofts and Olivia Rose, "An Essay Towards *Man with a Movie Camera*," *Screen* 18 (Spring 1977): 37.

163 Crofts and Rose 37.

164 Tsyviane 120.

165 Crofts and Rose 36–39. Vertov himself saw the film in terms of class struggle and the conflict between new and old: "All this — the factory rebuilt, and the lathe improved by a worker, the new public dining hall, and the newly opened village day-care center, the exam passed with honors, the new road or highway, the streetcar, the locomotive repaired on schedule — all are victories, great and small, in the struggle of the new with the old, the struggle of revolution with counterrevolution, the struggle of the cooperative against the private entrepreneur, of the club against the beer hall, of athletics against debauchery, dispensary against disease" (Vertov, "The Man with a Movie Camera (A Visual Symphony)" (1928), *Kino-Eye*, 288.

166 Vertov, "The Essence of Kino-eye," (1925), *Kino-Eye*, 49. Vertov made clear the class orientation of his fact-based cinema: "We are not tearing down artistic cinema in order to soothe and amuse the consciousness of the working masses with new rattles. We have come to serve a particular class, the workers and peasants not yet caught in the sweet web of art-dramas. We have come to show the world as it is, and to explain to the worker the bourgeois structure of the world." Vertov, "Provisional Instructions to Kino-Eye Groups" (1926) *Kino-Eye*, 73.

167 Jacques Aumont, "Vertov et la vue," *Cinémas et Réalités*, ed. Jean-Charles Lyant and Roger Odin (St. Etienne: Université St. Etienne, 1984), 41–42.

168   Vertov, "Artistic Drama and Kino-Eye" (1924), *Kino-Eye*, 47.

169   Donald Kuspit, "The Status of Style," *Art Express* 1 (May–June 1981): 32–36. The phrase "will to stylelessness" is Kuspit's.

170   Kuspit 32, who further notes: "The variety of movements that constitute the seminal period of 20th century art are consciously opposed to a museum destiny and mean to take to the street with a vengeance. None of these movements were truly socially successful in their day—another sign that they were not viewed as styles, i.e., institutionalized as continuous with tradition. By means of stylelessness, they meant to deinstitutionalize art, to make it humanly useful. They did not want to produce show pieces, they did not want to pretend there was meaning when there was none, hiding this emptiness with a style. That their art became the basis for a style, yet still seems to us far from 'past,' shows at once the tragedy of the fate of all truly styleless art and its continuing viability" (36).

171   Vertov, "Provisional Instructions to Kino-Eye Groups," *Kino-Eye*, 72. See also a Vertov text of 1923, which should be compared with Léger's essay on "Machine Aesthetics," quoted in note 10, above: "I am kino-eye, I create a man more perfect than Adam, I create thousands of different people in accordance with preliminary blue-prints and diagrams of different kinds. . . . [T]hrough montage I create a new, perfect man." "The Council of Three," *Kino-Eye*, 17.

172   Derrida, *Spurs*, 71.

173   Here, as we lose a sense of the distinction between metaphor and metonymy, we gain the sense both of Metz's "métaphore mise en syntagme," i.e., metaphor that is per force created metonymically, and of cinema's difficulty in making metaphors that are not also metonymies (Metz 192–193). There is no better example of this than the sequence discussed earlier, in which the editor animates the train/film *défilement*. Here, at its most metaphoric, the train is unavoidably metonymic because of the literalness of the figure.

174   Deleuze and Guattari, *Anti-Oedipus*, 12.

175   See Derrida on writing, woman, and style in Nietzsche: "Because woman is (her own) writing, style must return to her. In other words, it could be said that if style were a man (much as the penis, according to Freud is the 'normal prototype of fetishes'), then writing would be a woman" (*Spurs*, 57). The point I wish to make with this comparison is that in Vertov as well, the pact between style and writing sealed in the woman's relation to truth disturbs both sexual difference and the difference between truth and appearance.

176   Michelson xl.

177   See Crofts and Rose 50–51.

178   Benjamin, "On Some Motifs in Baudelaire," 175.

179   Vertov, "Notebook Entry, 1927," *Kino-Eye*, 167. In a sense, the city with its traffic and crowds forms a kind of filmmaking authority insofar as the cameraman is subject to its directives and not the other way around: "A little man, armed with a movie camera, leaves the little fake world of the film-factory and heads for life. Life tosses him to and fro like a straw. He's like a frail canoe on a stormy sea. He's continually swamped by the furious city traffic. The rushing, hurrying human crowd surges 'round him at every turn. . . . Life here does not wait for the film director or obey his instructions. Thousands, millions of people go about their business. Thunderstorms, rain, tempests, snow do not obey any script. Fires, weddings, funerals, anniversaries—all occur in their own time; they cannot be changed to fit a calendar invented by the author of the film." Vertov, "The Man with a Movie Camera," *Kino-Eye*, 286–287.

180   See Benjamin, "On Some Motifs in Baudelaire"; and Baudelaire, "Les Foules:" "Multitude,

solitude: equal and convertible terms for the active and fecund poet. He who does not know how to people his solitude, does not know how to be alone in a bustling crowd . . . " (Baudelaire 61–62). See n. 165, above.

181 Aumont 42.

182 Deleuze and Guattari, chap. 1, "The Desiring-Machines."

183 Jean-François Lyotard, *Discours, Figure* (Paris: Klincksieck, 1971), 14.

Four. National Identity in the Train Film

1 The quotation is from Jay Leyda, *Kino: A History of the Russian and Soviet Film* (New York: Collier, 1983), 272. Significantly, Trauberg worked as an assistant on Eisenstein's *October* before making his own film.

2 See E. J. Hobsbawm, *The Age of Capital, 1848–1875* (New York: New American Library, 1979), 89; Immanuel Wallerstein, *The Politics of the World Economy: The States, the Movements and the Civilizations* (Cambridge: Cambridge UP, 1984), 35; and Benedict Anderson, *Imagined Communities* (London: Verso, 1985), 78, 80ff.

3 Theodore Zeldin, *Intellect, Taste and Anxiety*, vol. 2 of *France: 1848–1945* (Oxford: Clarendon, 1977), 3 (both quotations).

4 Anderson, *Imagined Communities*, 15.

5 Roland Barthes, *Mythologies*, trans. Annette Lavers (New York: Hill and Wang, 1972), 129.

6 Barthes, *Mythologies*, 138, 140.

7 Anderson, *Imagined Communities*, 19.

8 Anderson, *Imagined Communities*, 41–49.

9 Philip Rosen, "History, Textuality, Nation: Kracauer, Burch, and Some Problems in the Study of National Cinema," *Iris* 2, no. 2 (1984): 70.

10 Rosen 72, 83.

11 Siegfried Kracauer, *From Caligari to Hitler* (1947; Princeton, N.J.: Princeton UP, 1974), 35–39.

12 Thomas Elsaesser, "Social Mobility and the Fantastic: German Silent Cinema," *Wide Angle* 5, no. 2 (1982): 14–25.

13 Moews notes that Keaton's fascination with and love of the train and other machines is an expression of a very American attitude: "Noticeably absent . . . from Keaton, is the longstanding European reaction, one given in films both a contemporary and a continuing expression, fear of the assembly line, of machines in a factory, where the worker is regimented, dehumanized, and made the mechanical slave of a demanding iron god. . . . So far are Keaton's machines from possessing any depersonalizing aspect that the three most impressive of them have names themselves: The Navigator, The General, and The Stonewall Jackson. . . . Keaton's choice of machines, then, is an American movie-maker's affirmative choice" (213–214).

14 Schivelbusch 93. "Previously untouched," that is, by Europeans.

15 Schivelbusch 94.

16 The differences also extend to the architecture of the train carriage on both continents. As noted, the European train car was divided into individual compartments, and the cars themselves were distinguished by class (first, second, third, or fourth). By contrast, the American train car was open, spacious, and theoretically accessible to all. Both crime and class resentment were given a narrower berth by virtue of this design. See Schivelbusch 84–92, 104.

17   Bowser, *The Transformation of Cinema, 1907–1915*, 22.

18   Bowser, *The Transformation of Cinema, 1907–1915*, 23. By 1909, however, Edison's efforts to freeze out Pathé in the United States had led to a reduction in foreign production on American screens — from 60 percent in 1907 to less than 50 percent in 1909. And by 1911, American films accounted for 80 percent of the domestic market. Bowser, *The Transformation of Cinema, 1907–1915*, 23, 85.

19   Frantz Schmitt, "Méliès et ses contemporains: Quelques rapprochements," *Méliès et la naissance du spectacle cinématographique*, ed. Madeleine Malthête-Méliès (Paris: Klincksieck, 1984), 100; and Kristin Thompson, *Exporting Entertainment* (London: British Film Institute, 1985), 4.

20   Abel, *The Ciné Goes to Town: French Cinema, 1896–1914*, 46. See Miriam Hansen, "Universal Language and Democratic Culture: Myths of Origin in Early American Cinema," 321–351, in which she details the history of the concept of film as a "universal language" and how early filmmakers appropriated the term for a variety of ideological and marketing purposes. She also charts the association of universality with "Americanness," and with reference to the battle of independent filmmakers against Edison *and* foreign competition to make a properly "American" movie, notes: "With 'Americanness' assuming a strategic function in the struggle for market control, the cheerful internationalism of the primitive period was doomed to extinction" (332).

21   Thompson, *Exporting Entertainment*, 1–60.

22   Sklar 35.

23   Sklar 37.

24   Hansen, "Early Silent Cinema: Whose Public Sphere?" 181.

25   Mitry 254ff.; Hansen, "Early Silent Cinema: Whose Public Sphere?" 167–177.

26   During the war, Kleine distributed several films specifically about indoctrinating immigrants. See *George Kleine Papers*, Special Collections, Library of Congress, Washington, D.C. It is important, however, to keep in mind that, as Gunning insists, "[t]here is a constant discourse in trade journals from 1908 on describing the need for uniquely American films and with often unfavorable descriptions of the national flavor of French and Italian films" (unpublished note to author).

27   Thompson, *Exporting Entertainment*, 49–60, 61ff.; Sklar.

28   See Thompson, *Exporting Entertainment*, ix, 106–107, 113ff.

29   Kracauer, *From Caligari to Hitler,* 35.

30   Kracauer, *From Caligari to Hitler,* 35ff.

31   Richard Abel, *French Cinema: The First Wave, 1915–1929* (Princeton, N.J.: Princeton UP, 1984), 11–25.

32   Paul Monaco, *Cinema and Society: France and Germany During the Twenties* (New York: Elsevier, 1976), 68–73.

33   Monaco 41–45.

34   On Gance, see Kevin Brownlow, *The Parade's Gone By* (New York: Ballantine, 1968), 623, 631; and Steven Philip Kramer and James Michael Welsh, *Abel Gance* (Boston: Twayne, 1978), 10–12. Program notes for a screening of *The Iron Horse* at the Museum of Modern Art, in reference to the film's popularity, state that it grossed over $2 million, while it cost $280,000 to make. "Program Notes for *The Iron Horse*," Museum of Modern Art, New York, 1980. Richard Koszarski, *An Evening's Entertainment*, 33, reports from an unpublished survey that *The Iron Horse* was the most popular film of 1924.

35   Monaco 72–73. But, as Miriam Hansen points out, Monaco's generalization is not air-

tight, according to box-office statistics. Hansen, "Early Silent Cinema: Whose Public Sphere?" 181.

36   Lejeune 76. The review was originally published on Nov. 14, 1925, in the *Manchester Guardian*.

37   Nash Smith 46ff.

38   Quoted in Nash Smith 46.

39   Ward 21. National unity metaphors abounded in the discourse of both literary and "practical" men. See Ward 26–38.

40   See Ward 28ff. "The most hideous metaphors [for the train] were always overwhelmed in the public prints by a swarm of homely metaphors that mitigated the more monstrous excesses" (Ward 37).

41   Ward 81–93.

42   Quoted in Botkin and Harlow 2.

43   Ward 28.

44   Ward 30. "Americans' identification with their engines was prodded in part because locomotives took on physical characteristics that marked them as peculiarly American; no other nation's locomotives looked quite like them . . . including the most arresting American gadget of all, the cowcatcher . . . " (Ward 30–31).

45   Charles McGovern, unpublished research, Department of History, Harvard U, 1987.

46   Stover 133–137.

47   See Nick Browne, "The Spectator of American Symbolic Forms: Rereading *Young Mr. Lincoln*," *Film Reader* 4 (1979): 180–188.

48   Editors of *Cahiers du cinema*, "John Ford's *Young Mr. Lincoln*," *Film Theory and Criticism*, ed. Gerald Mast and Marshall Cohen (New York: Oxford UP, 1979), 790. See also the special issue of *Wide Angle* 2, no. 4 (1978) devoted to Ford; Richard Abel, "Paradigmatic Structures in *Young Mr. Lincoln*," 20–26, and J. A. Place, "Young Mr. Lincoln, 1939," 28–35.

49   Editors of *Cahiers* 794.

50   Editors of *Cahiers* 795.

51   Barthes, *S/Z*, 40.

52   Ken Nolley, "John Ford and the Hollywood Indian," *Film and History* 23 nos. 1–4 (1993): 44–57, on images of Native Americans in ten Ford films beginning with *Stagecoach* (1939). Quote on 47.

53   Nolley 49.

54   See *Native America*, ed. John Gattuso (Boston: Houghton Mifflin, 1993), 43–55; and Weeks and Gidney 126.

55   See Brown, 68–69, 141, 179–186, 264–273.

56   In 1872, only three years after the transcontinental railroad was completed, the Northern Pacific Railroad decided to build a new leg of its line over a portion of the Great Sioux Reservation (the Big Horn Mountain region) in direct violation of the Fort Laramie Treaty of 1868. The treaty had guaranteed the leading Northern Plains nations autonomy and the right to hold certain lands in perpetuity, including the newly created Great Sioux Reservation (Weeks and Gidney 100–101). Before abandoning its project during the economic panic of 1873, the Northern Pacific sent a team of surveyors accompanied by 1,800 federal troops to set up shop for six months in 1873, despite objections by Native American leaders. Had they stayed and carried out construction, the army was preparing for a full-scale battle (Weeks and Gidney 102).

57   Quoted in Williams 121. Also quoted in Williams is a letter from General Sherman to

General Grenville Dodge, the chief engineer for the Union Pacific: " 'I regard this road of yours as the solution of the Indian affairs and the Mormon question, and therefore [will] give you all the aid I possibly can' " (149). The chilling connotations of the "final solution" are not far-fetched, as Sherman led a concerted campaign of extermination against the Plains Indians.

58   See Brown 117 on the 1866 Civil Rights Bill's exclusions, and 342–344 on the 1879 case of *Standing Bear* v. *Crook* that went to trial arguing whether Indians could be defined as persons within the meaning of the U.S. Constitution.

59   Ford's Irishness was a tremendous influence on his entire filmmaking career; see editors of *Cahiers* 789. Note also in *The Iron Horse:* "Drill ye Chineymen drill/Drill ye haythens drill . . . ;" this recurrent Irish work song is so altered in the film by the Irish to address the Chinese as "heathen" others.

60   Williams 90, 94–95.

61   Williams 94, 96–97.

62   Williams 95–97, 130. See Jensen 98.

63   Jensen 98; Williams 220.

64   Williams 98.

65   Williams 210.

66   See Williams 181 on an 1867 strike by 3,000 Chinese workers. Williams 99 notes that the Chinese earned a measure of respect from their white bosses for their diligence and hard work, while indulging in far less violent forms of intoxication (opium) than the whiskey consumed in huge quantities by the raucous white workers.

67   On the representation of "community" in Ford films, see Michael Budd, "Genre, Director and Stars in John Ford's Westerns: Fonda, Wayne, Stewart and Widmark," *Wide Angle* 2, no. 4 (1978): 52–61; and Abel, "Paradigmatic Structures in *Young Mr. Lincoln*," 24–26.

68   See Nick Browne, "The Spectator-in-the-Text: The Rhetoric of Stagecoach," *Narrative, Apparatus, Ideology,* ed. Philip Rosen (New York: Columbia UP, 1986), 102–119.

69   See Walter Licht, *Working for the Railroad* (Princeton, N.J.: Princeton UP, 1983), 78–101, 244ff.; Williams 155–157, 215–216, 220; and Jensen 98–99.

70   On techniques of condensation clustered toward the beginning of the text in film, see Thierry Kuntzel, "The Film Work, 2" *Camera Obscura* 5 (1980): 6–69; also Bordwell, "The classical Hollywood style, 1917–1960," 25–29.

71   In this scenario Freud observed an eighteen-month-old child symbolizing the presence and absence of his mother by means of a wooden spool with a string attached. The boy would throw the toy and utter "fort," meaning, in German, "gone"; he would then reel it in, pronouncing "da," or "there." Freud connected the repetition of this game with the assumption of an active role by the child, who was thought to assume a position of power by representing, and therefore controlling symbolically, the presence and absence of his mother. Freud, *Beyond the Pleasure Principle* 8–11.

72   On hallmark traits of the classical film, see Bordwell, "The classical Hollywood style, 1917–1960," 3ff.

73   Although the film's publicity made much of the use of the two original locomotives, according to Kevin Brownlow there is reason to doubt Ford's claim. See "Program Notes for *The Iron Horse.*

74   There is, of course, an ancient Western tradition privileging male bonding as ideal coupling that extends back at least as far as Plato's *Phaedrus,* the dialogue that defined higher values in

terms of male platonic love, and *The Banquet*, the dialogue that defined male-love-for-male as the highest love.

75 Janet Bergstrom, "Sexuality at a Loss: The Films of F. W. Murnau," *The Female Body in Western Culture*, ed. Susan Rubin Suleiman (Cambridge, Mass.: Harvard UP, 1986), 243–261.

76 On Griffith's excess, especially as exemplified by *Intolerance*, see Hansen, *Babel and Babylon: Part II: "D. W. Griffith's Intolerance* (1916)."

77 See Abel, *French Cinema*, 279–281, on Impressionism as a social and cultural movement; and Abel, *French Cinema*, 251–256, on the cine clubs and journals. See also David Bordwell, "French Impressionist Cinema: Film Culture, Film Theory and Film Style," unpub. Ph.D. diss., U of Iowa, 1974.

78 Abel, *French Cinema*, 290.

79 Kramer and Welsh 38.

80 Monaco 68.

81 See Alfred Cobban, *A History of Modern France*, vol. 3: *1871–1962* (New York: Penguin, 1965), 121–137; and Monaco 71.

82 Abel, *French Cinema*, 242.

83 Abel, *French Cinema*, 243.

84 Monaco 69.

85 Monaco 69.

86 Monaco 74.

87 Noel Burch and Jorge Dana, "Propositions," *Afterimage* 5 (Spring 1974): 40–66; quoted in Abel, *French Cinema*, 291.

88 Abel, *French Cinema*, 291.

89 Bordwell, "French Impressionist Cinema." See also Abel, *French Cinema*, 287.

90 Abel, *French Cinema*, 292–294.

91 Clear thematic similarities can be traced across a number of French films of the 1920s. Monaco notes, for example, that "half of the most popular French films of the 1920s handle, in one way or another, an orphan story" (Monaco 84). This includes La Roue (see below).

92 Gance is interviewed in Brownlow 46.

93 On critical response to *La Roue*, see Abel, *French Cinema*, 328.

94 Abel, *French Cinema*, 328.

95 On *La Roue* as inspiration to Soviet filmmakers, see Abel, *French Cinema*, 327; Brownlow 625; and Leyda 201.

96 See Abel, *French Cinema*, 328.

97 Blaise Cendrars, "La Prose du Transsibérien et de la Petite Jéhanne de France," *Blaise Cendrars*, ed. Louis Parrot (Paris: Pierre Seghers, 1953), 107.

98 René Clair, "*La Roue*," quoted in Norman King, *Abel Gance: A Politics of Spectacle* (London: British Film Institute, 1984), 23.

99 Germaine Dulac, "*La Roue:* The Song of the Rails," quoted in King 26.

100 Dulac 26–27.

101 Jean Epstein, "*La Roue*" (1927), quoted in King 28.

102 Epstein 29.

103 Emile Vuillermoz, "*La Roue*," quoted in *French Film Theory and Criticism: A History/Anthology, 1907–1939*, ed., Richard Abel, vol. I: *1907–1929* (Princeton, N.J.: Princeton UP, 1988), 278.

104 King 21.

105 Quoted in King 21.

106 Abel, *French Cinema*, 256.

107 I screened two different prints of *La Roue* for this study — one from MOMA and one from an unattributed source. Both were extremely truncated. Yet, though each supplied different parts of the story, much missing information had to be obtained from plot summaries given elsewhere. See Abel, *French Cinema*, 326–339; King 83–87; and Kramer and Welsh 79–91.

108 Abel, *French Cinema*, 329.

109 Abel, *French Cinema*, 339.

110 Abel, *French Cinema*, 339.

111 Abel, *French Cinema*, 339.

112 The long-standing social division between Paris and the provinces provided a common motif in French films of the 1930s.

113 Guy Chaumel, *Histoire des cheminots et de leurs syndicats* (Paris: Librairie Marcel Rivière, 1948) 4–5; Schivelbusch 94, 176–179; Zeldin, *Politics and Anger*, 189; and Henri Vincenot, *La Vie quotidienne dans les chemins de fer au XIXe siècle* (Paris: Hachette, 1975), 20–21, 34–35.

114 See Schivelbusch 94.

115 Zeldin, *Politics and Anger*, 41, 191.

116 Chaumel 118–130.

117 Abel, *French Cinema*, 337.

118 Abel, *French Cinema*, 339.

119 Abel, *French Cinema*, 337.

120 When Gance is most like Zola, the train is oppressive; when he is most like Léger, the train is an aesthetic marvel, much as in *Man with a Movie Camera*.

121 Jean Baudrillard, "Crash," *Simulacres et simulations* (Paris: Editions Galilée, 1981), 173.

122 Gance's sad face is a direct reference to his wife's death in a tuberculosis sanitorium in the Alps while the film was being completed. See Abel, *French Cinema*, 327–328.

123 Norma is here, fleetingly, a double for Gance's dead wife, whom he idealized in life and death. See Abel, *French Cinema*, 328.

124 This kind of montage recurs across the film in connection with, typically, disaster. Sisif's attempted train crash with Norma aboard, for example, is figured as a gradually accelerating alternation of train wheels, steam, Sisif, Norma, the gauges and the fireman Machefer.

125 Abel, *French Cinema*, 333.

126 Emile Zola, *La Bête humaine* (Paris: Garnier-Flammarion, 1972/1890), 349. Author's translation.

127 The clouds caressing Norma recall the Greek myth of Jupiter and Io, in which Jupiter (Zeus) appeared to Io in the form of a cloud in order to possess her sexually, as she was otherwise forbidden to him.

128 See L'Herbier's 1919 *Rose France*, a film that identifies its female protagonist, Rose, with her greatest love, her country — France.

129 Vuillermoz 275.

130 Abel, *French Cinema*, 337.

Conclusion

1 Quoted in Philip Weiss, "Hollywood at a Fever Pitch," *New York Times Magazine*, Dec. 26, 1993, 26.

2   This is not to say that the train has no nostalgic connotations for Europeans as well; it is just that the history tends to be more recent. A major historical referent is obviously World War II, when the train's overwhelming significance was as Nazi transport of Jews, gypsies, leftists, and others to the camps. See Lars von Trier's *Zentropa* (1992); Jiri Menzel's *Closely Watched Trains*; and Joseph Losey's *Mr. Klein* (1977). Wartime films that include the train also show it to be a contested figure of nationality, as seen in the great French film *The Battle of the Rail* made by René Clément in 1945. There is great significance in this film around resistance — the French Resistance to the Occupation — that recalls both *October* and *The General*: the literal sense of controlling the train as controlling national destiny.

Works Cited

Abel, Richard. *The Ciné Goes to Town: French Cinema, 1896–1914.* Berkeley: U of California P, 1994.

———. *French Cinema: The First Wave, 1915–1929.* Princeton, N.J.: Princeton UP, 1984.

———, ed. *French Film Theory and Criticism: A History/Anthology, 1907–1939,* Vol. 1: *1907–1929.* Princeton, N.J.: Princeton UP, 1988.

———. "Paradigmatic Structures in *Young Mr. Lincoln.*" *Wide Angle* 2, no. 4 (1978): 20–26.

"Accidents de chemin de fer en spectacle." *L'Illustration* 30 (May 1896): 454.

Aldcroft, Derek. *The Atlas of British Railway History.* London: Croom Helm, 1985.

Allen, Frederick Werner. "The Adoption of Standard Time 1883: An Attempt to Bring Order into a Changing World." Unpublished paper. American Studies Department, Yale U, 1969.

Allen, Jeanne Thomas. "The Decay of the Motion Picture Patents Company." In Tino Balio, ed., *The American Film Industry.* Madison: U of Wisconsin P, 1976. 119–134.

Allen, Robert C. "The Archeology of Film History." *Wide Angle* 5, no. 2 (1982): 4–13.

———. "Motion Picture Exhibition in Manhattan, 1906–1912: Beyond the Nickelodeon." *Film Before Griffith.* Ed. John Fell. Berkeley: U of California P, 1983. 162–175.

———. *Vaudeville and Film, 1895–1915: A Study in Media Interaction.* New York: Arno, 1980.

———. "Vitascope/Cinematographe: Initial Patterns of American Film Industrial Practice." *Film Before Griffith.* Ed. John Fell. Berkeley: U of California P, 1983.

Anderson, Benedict. *Imagined Communities.* London: Verso, 1985.

Anderson, Jervis. *A. Philip Randolph: A Biographical Portrait.* New York: Harcourt, 1973.

"Artists Excursion on the B.&O.R.R." *Book of the Royal Blue* (Nov. 1900): 1–10.

Aumont, Jacques. "Vertov et la vue." *Cinémas et Réalités.* St. Etienne: Université St. Etienne, 1984. 23–44.

Baroli, Marc, ed. *Lignes et lettres.* Paris: Hachette Réalités/SNCF, 1978.

Barthes, Roland. *Mythologies.* Trans. Annette Lavers. New York: Hill and Wang, 1972.

——. *S/Z.* Trans. Richard Miller. New York: Hill and Wang, 1974.

Bathrick, David. "Affirmative and Negative Culture: Technology and the Left Avant-Garde." *The Technological Imagination: Theories and Fictions.* Ed. Teresa De Lauretis, Andreas Huyssen, and Kathleen Woodward. Madison, Wisc.: Coda, 1980. 107–122.

Baudelaire, Charles. *Petits poèmes en prose (le spleen de Paris),* 1864. Paris: Garnier-Flammarion, 1967.

Baudrillard, Jean. *Simulacres et simulations.* Paris: Editions Galilée, 1981.

Baudry, Jean. "Ideological Effects of the Basic Cinematographic Apparatus." *Apparatus.* Ed. Theresa Hak Kyung Cha. New York: Tanam, 1980. 25–40.

Beaupré, Lee. "How to Distribute a Film." *The Hollywood Film Industry.* Ed. Paul Kerr. London: Routledge, 1986. 185–203.

Bellour, Raymond. "Alterner/Raconter." *Le Cinéma américain: Analyses de films.* Ed. Raymond Bellour. Paris: Flammarion, 1980. 68–88.

——. "Ideal Hadaly (on Villiers's *The Future Eve*)." *Camera Obscura* 15 (1986): 111–136.

——, ed. *Le Cinéma américain.* Vol. 1. Paris: Flammarion, 1980.

——, Seminar. Centre américain. Place de l'Odéon, Paris, France, 1983–1984.

Benjamin, Walter. "On Some Motifs in Baudelaire." *Illuminations.* Ed. and intro. Hannah Arendt. Trans. Harry Zohn. New York: Schocken Books, 1969. 155–200.

——. "The Work of Art in the Age of Mechanical Reproduction." *Illuminations.* Ed. and intro. Hannah Arendt. Trans. Harry Zohn. New York: Schocken Books, 1969. 217–252.

Berger, John. "The Moment of Cubism." *The Look of Things.* Ed. and intro. Nikos Stangos. New York: Viking, 1974. 123–166.

Bergstrom, Janet. "Alternation, Segmentation, Hypnosis: Interview with Raymond Bellour." *Camera Obscura* 3–4 (1979): 71–103.

——. "Sexuality at a Loss: The Films of F. W. Murnau." *The Female Body in Western Culture.* Ed. Susan Rubin Suleiman. Cambridge, Mass.: Harvard UP, 1986. 243–261.

Bernheimer, Charles, and Claire Kahane, eds. *In Dora's Case.* New York: Columbia UP, 1985.

Bersani, Leo. *Baudelaire and Freud.* Berkeley: U of California P, 1977.

Bitzer, G. W. *Billy Bitzer — His Story.* New York: Farrar, 1973.

Bobrick, Benson. *Labyrinths of Iron: A History of the World's Subways.* New York: Newsweek, 1982.

Bordwell, David. "The Classical Hollywood Style, 1917–1960." *The Classical Hollywood Cinema: Film, Style and Mode of Production to 1960.* Ed. David Bordwell, Kristin Thompson, and Janet Staiger. New York: Columbia UP, 1985. 1–84.

——. "French Impressionist Cinema: Film Culture, Film Theory and Film Style." Ph.D. diss., U of Iowa, 1974.

Bordwell, David, Kristin Thompson, and Janet Staiger, eds. *The Classical Hollywood Cinema: Film, Style and Mode of Production to 1960.* New York: Columbia UP, 1985.

Botkin, B. A. and Alvin Harlow, eds. *A Treasury of Railroad Folklore.* New York: Crown, 1953.

Bowser, Eileen. "Before Hollywood: Turn-of-the-Century Film from American Archives." Symposium. Whitney Museum, New York, Jan. 31, 1987.

——. *The Transformation of Cinema, 1907–1915.* Vol. 2 of *History of the American Cinema.* General Editor, Charles Harpole. New York: Scribner's, 1990.

Bridgman, Rev. Dr. *The Vacation Gospel.* Hamline, Minn.: Great Northern Railroad, 1890.

British Film Institute. *Early Filmmakers' Catalogues.* London: World Microfilm Publications, 1983.

Brommel, Bernard J. *Eugene V. Debs: Spokesman for Labor and Socialism.* Chicago: Charles H. Kerr, 1978.

Brooks, Peter. *Reading for the Plot: Design and Intention in Narrative.* New York: Knopf, 1984.

Brown, Dee. *Bury My Heart at Wounded Knee: An Indian History of the American West.* New York: Bantam, 1972.

Brown, Milton, et al. *American Art.* New York: Abrams, 1979.

Browne, Nick. "The Spectator-in-the-Text: The Rhetoric of *Stagecoach.*" *Narrative, Apparatus, Ideology.* Ed. Philip Rosen. 1975. New York: Columbia UP, 1986. 102–119.

——. "The Spectator of American Symbolic Forms: Rereading *Young Mr. Lincoln.*" *Film Reader* 4 (1979): 180–188.

Brownlow, Kevin. *The Parade's Gone By.* New York: Ballantine Books, 1968.

Bruno, Giuliana. *Streetwalking on a Ruined Map: Cultural Theory and the City Films of Elvira Notari.* Princeton, N.J.: Princeton UP, 1993.

Buck-Morss, Susan. "Aesthetics and Anaesthetics: Walter Benjamin's Artwork Essay Reconsidered." *October* 62 (1992): 3–41.

Budd, Michael. "Genre, Director and Stars in John Ford's Westerns: Fonda, Wayne, Stewart and Widmark." *Wide Angle* 2, no. 4 (1978): 52–61.

Burch, Noel. "How We Got into Pictures." *Afterimage* 8/9 (Spring 1981): 24–38.

——. "Porter, or Ambivalence." *In and Out of Synch — The Awakening of a Cine-Dreamer.* Trans. Ben Brewster. Aldershot, England: Scolar Press, 1991. 138–156. Originally published in *Screen* 19, no. 4 (Winter 1978–79): 91–105.

Burch, Noel, and Jorge Dana. "Propositions." *Afterimage* 5 (Spring 1974): 40–66.

Callow, Alexander B., Jr., ed. *American Urban History.* New York: Oxford UP, 1973.

——, ed. "Commentary." *American Urban History.* Ed. Callow. New York: Oxford UP, 1973. 155–159.

Carbine, Mary. " 'The Finest Outside the Loop': Motion Picture Exhibition in Chicago's Black Metropolis, 1905–1928."

Camera Obscura 23 (May 1990): 9–41.

Cendrars, Blaise. "La Prose du Transsibérien et de la Petite Jehanne de France." *Blaise Cendrars.* Ed. Louis Parrot. Paris: Pierre Seghers, 1953. 90–109.

Cha, Theresa Hak Kyung, ed. *Apparatus.* New York: Tanam, 1980.

Chanan, Michael. *The Dream That Kicks: The Prehistory and Early Years of Cinema in Britain.* London: Routledge and Kegan Paul, 1980.

Charcot. *Leçons sur l'hystérie virile.* Introd. Michèle Ouerd. Paris: Le Sycamore, 1984.

Chaumel, Guy. *Histoire des cheminots et de leurs syndicats.* Paris: Librairie Marcel Rivière, 1948.

Chirico, Giorgio de. "Meditations of a Painter" (1912). *Theories of Modern Art.* Ed. Herschel B. Chipp. Berkeley: U of California P, 1968. 397–401.

"Le Cinématographe." *L'Illustration,* May 30, 1896, 446–447.

Clark, Christopher. "Time Consciousness and Social Change in Nineteenth-Century America." Unpublished paper, Department of History, York U, 1975.

Cobban, Alfred. *A History of Modern France.* Vol. 2: *1799–1871.* 1961. Harmondsworth: Penguin, 1977.

Cohen, Norm. *Long Steel Rail: The Railroad in American Folksong.* Urbana: U of Illinois P, 1981.

Complete Catalogue — Edison Films Orange, N.J.: Edison Manufacturing, 1901.

Condit, Carl. *The Railroad and the City: A Technological and Urbanistic History of Cincinnati.* Columbus: Ohio State UP, 1977.

Conot, Robert. *A Streak of Luck.* New York, Seaview, 1979.

Cott, Nancy. *The Grounding of Modern Feminism.* New Haven, Conn: Yale UP, 1987.

Crafton, Donald. "Audienceship in Early Cinema." *Iris,* No. 11 (Summer 1990): 1–12.

——. *Emile Cohl, Caricature and Film.* Princeton, N.J.: Princeton UP, 1990.

Crary, Jonathan. *Techniques of the Observer.* Cambridge, Mass.: MIT P, 1991.

Cripps, Thomas. *Slow Fade to Black: The Negro in American Film, 1900–1942.* New York: Oxford UP, 1993.

Crofts, Stephen, and Olivia Rose. "An Essay Towards *Man with a Movie Camera.*" *Screen* 18 (Spring 1977): 9–58.

Darrah, William C. *Cartes de Visites in 19th Century Photography.* Gettysburg, Pa.: W. C. Darrah, 1981.

——. *The World of Stereographs.* Gettysburg, Pa.: W. C. Darrah, 1977.

Daumier, Honoré. *Les Transports en commun.* Pref. Max Gallo. Paris: Editions Vilo, 1976.

Davis, Clarence B. "Railway Imperialism in China, 1895–1939." *Railway Imperialism.* Ed. Clarence B. Davis and Kenneth E. Wilburn. New York: Greenwood, 1991. 155–174.

Debo, Angie. *A History of the Indians of the United States.* Norman: U of Oklahoma P, 1983/1970.

De Dainville, Père François. "Cartographie industrielle de l'Europe au 19e siècle." *Traverses* 13: Le Modèle férroviaire (Dec. 1978): 120–127.

De Lauretis, Teresa, Andreas Huyssen, and Kathleen Woodward, eds. *The Technological Imagination: Theories and Fictions.* Madison, Wisc.: Coda, 1980. 107–122.

Deleuze, Gilles. *Logique du sens.* Paris: Editions de Minuit, 1969.

Deleuze, Gilles, and Félix Guattari. *L'Anti-Oedipe.* Paris: Editions de Minuit, 1972.

——. *Anti-Oedipus.* Trans. Robert Hurley et al. New York: Viking, 1977.

De Musset, Alfred. "Dupont et Durand." *Lignes et Lettres.* Ed. Marc Baroli. Paris: Hachettes/ SNCF, 1978. 79.

Derrida, Jacques. *Dissemination.* Trans. Barbara Johnson. Chicago: U of Chicago P, 1981.

——. "La Pharmacie de Platon." *La Dissemination.* Paris: Editions du Seuil, 1972. 69–198.

——. "*La Loi du genre/* The Law of Genre." *Glyph* 7 (Spring 1980): 176–232.

——. *Spurs: Nietzsche's Styles.* Trans. Barbara Harlow. Chicago: U of Chicago P, 1978.

——. "White Mythology: Metaphor in the Text of Philosophy." *Margins of Philosophy.* Trans. Alan Bass. Chicago: U of Chicago P, 1982. 78–199.

Deslandes, Jacques et Jacques Richard. *Histoire Comparée du Cinéma*, vol. 2: *Du cinématographe au cinéma, 1896–1906.* Paris: Casterman, 1968.

Déthier, Jean, ed. *Le Temps des gares.* Exhibition Catalog. Paris: Centre national d'art et de culture Georges Pompidou, Dec. 13, 1978–April 8, 1979.

De Vigny, Alfred. "La Maison du berger." *Lignes et lettres,* Ed. Marc Baroli Paris: Hachette/ SNCF, 1978. 84–85.

Dickson, William K., Laurie Dickson, and Antonia Dickson. *The Life and Inventions of Thomas Alva Edison.* New York: Thomas Y. Crowell, 1894.

Doane, Mary Anne. *The Desire to Desire.* Bloomington: Indiana UP, 1987.

——. " 'when the direction of the force acting on the body is changed.': The Moving Image." *Wide Angle* 7, nos. 1–2 (1985): 42–58.

Donzelot, Jacques. *The Policing of Families.* Trans. Robert Hurley. New York: Pantheon, 1979.

Drescher, Seymour, David Sabean, and Allan Sharlin, eds. *Political Symbolism in Modern Europe: Essays in Honor of George L. Mosse.* New Brunswick, N.J.: Transaction Books, 1982.

Drinka, George. *The Birth of Neurosis: Myth, Malady and the Victorians.* New York: Simon and Schuster, 1984.

Durkheim, Emile. *Suicide: A Study in Sociology.* Ed. and introd. George Simpson. Trans. John A. Spaulding and George Simpson. New York: Free Press, 1951.

Editors of *Cahiers du cinéma*. "John Ford's *Young Mr. Lincoln*." *Film Theory and Criticism*. Eds. Gerald Mast and Marshall Cohen. New York: Oxford UP, 1979. 778–831.

Eggert, Gerald G. *Railroad Labor Disputes: The Beginnings of Federal Strike Policy*. Ann Arbor: U of Michigan P, 1967.

Eisenstein, Sergei. "Dickens, Griffith and the Film Today." *Film Form*. Ed. and trans. Jay Leyda. 1949. New York: Harcourt, 1975. 195–255.

Ellis, C. Hamilton. *Railway Art*. Boston: New York Graphic Society, 1977.

Elsaesser, Thomas. "Cinema, The Irresponsible Signifier or, 'The Gamble with History': Film Theory or Cinema Theory." *New German Critique* 40 (Winter 1987): 91–96.

———. "Social Mobility and the Fantastic: German Silent Cinema." *Wide Angle* 5.2 (1982): 14–25.

Evard, Jean-Luc. "Ferry Dick." *Traverses* 13: Le Modèle férroviaire (Dec. 1978): 59–71.

Ewen, Stuart. *Captains of Consciousness: Advertising and the Roots of Consumer Culture*. New York: McGraw-Hill, 1976.

Fell, John, ed. *Film Before Griffith*. Berkeley: U of California P, 1983.

Feldstein, Richard and Judith Roof, eds. *Feminism and Psychoanalysis*. Ithaca, N.Y.: Cornell UP, 1989.

Ferro, Marc. "Images de l'histoire." *Traverses* 13: Le Modèle férroviaire (Dec. 1978): 52–53.

Fielding, Raymond. "Hale's Tours: Ultrarealism in the Pre-1910 Motion Picture." *Film Before Griffith*. Ed. John Fell. Berkeley: U of California P, 1983. 116–130.

Fisher, Lucy. "The Lady Vanishes: Women, Magic and the Movies." *Film Before Griffith*. Ed. John Fell. Berkeley: U of California P, 1983. 339–354.

Fleming, William J. "Profits and Visions: British Capital and Railway Construction in Argentina, 1854–1886." *Railway Imperialism*. Ed. Clarence B. Davis and Kenneth E. Wilburn. New York: Greenwood, 1991. 71–84.

Foucault, Michel. *The Archaeology of Knowledge*. Trans. A. M. Sheridan. New York: Harper Torchbooks, 1972.

———. *Discipline and Punish*. Trans. Alan Sheridan. New York: Vintage Books, 1979.

———. "Of Other Spaces." *Diacritics* 16.1 (Spring 1986): 22–27.

Fox, Richard Wrightman and T. J. Jackson Lears, eds. *The Culture of Consumption: Critical Essays in American History, 1880–1980*. New York: Pantheon, 1983.

Fox, Stephen. *The Mirror Makers: A History of American Advertising and Its Creators*. New York: Vintage Books, 1984.

Freeman, Michael and Derek Aldcroft. *The Atlas of British Railway History*. London: Croom Helm, 1985.

French, William E. "In the Path of Progress: Railroads and Moral Reform in Porfirian Mexico." *Railway Imperialism*. Ed. Clarence B. Davis and Kenneth E. Wilburn. New York: Greenwood, 1991. 85–102.

Freud, Sigmund. *Beyond the Pleasure Principle*. Trans. James Strachey. 1920. New York: Norton, 1961.

———. *Group Psychology and the Analysis of the Ego*. Ed. and trans. James Strachey. 1923. New York: Norton, 1959.

———. *The Interpretation of Dreams*. Trans. James Strachey. 1900. New York: Norton, 1963.

———. *Jokes and Their Relation to the Unconscious*. Ed. and trans. James Strachey. 1905. New York: Norton, 1963.

———. *The Pelican Freud Library*. Vol. 8: *Case Histories 1: "Dora" and "Little Hans."* Harmondsworth: Penguin, 1977.

Freud, Sigmund and Breuer, Josef. *The Pelican Freud Library*. Vol. 3: *Studies on Hysteria*. Harmondsworth: Penguin, 1974.

Friedberg, Anne. *Window Shopping: Cinema and the Postmodern*. Berkeley: U California P, 1993.

From Brockville, Canada on the St. Lawrence River via the Brockville, Westport and North-Western Railway. New York: Wynkoop, Hallenbeck, Crawford, n.d.

Fruitema, Evelyn J. and Paul A. Zoetmulder, eds. *The Panorama Phenomenon*. The Hague: Foundation for the Preservation of the Centenarian Mesdag Panorama, 1981.

Gattuso, John, ed. *Native America*. Singapore: Apa Publications, 1993. Dist. Houghton Mifflin/Boston.

Gaudreault, André. "Les Détours du récit filmique (Sur la naissance du montage parallèle)." *Les Cahiers de la Cinémathèque: Le Cinéma des premiers temps (1900–1906)* 29 (Winter 1979): 88–107.

——. "Film, récit, narration: le cinéma des frères Lumière." *Iris* 2.1 (1984): 61–70.

——. *Du littéraire au filmique: système du récit*. Paris: Méridiens Klincksieck, 1988.

——. "Temporality and Narrativity in Early Cinema, 1895–1908." *Film Before Griffith*. Ed. John Fell. Berkeley: U of California P, 1983. 311–329.

——. " 'Théâtralité' et 'narrativité' dan l'oeuvre de Georges Méliès." *Méliès et la naissance du spectacle cinématographique*. Ed. Madeleine Malthête-Méliès. Paris: Klincksieck, 1984. 199–220.

Geduld, Harry M. Introduction. *Focus on D. W. Griffith*. Ed. Harry M. Geduld. Englewood Cliffs, N.J.: Prentice-Hall, 1971. 1–9.

Genette, Gerard. *Narrative Discourse*. Trans. Jane E. Lewin. Ithaca, N.Y.: Cornell UP, 1980.

Gernsheim, Helmut and Alison Gernsheim. *L. J. M. Daguerre: The History of the Diorama and the Daguerreotype*. New York: Dover, 1968.

Gerschenkron, Alexander. *Economic Backwardness in Historical Perspective*. Cambridge, Mass.: Harvard UP, 1966.

Glatfelter, Edward. "Russia, the Soviet Union and the Chinese Eastern Railway." *Railway Imperialism*. Clarence B. Davis and Kenneth E. Wilburn, eds. New York: Greenwood, 1991. 137–154.

Gomery, Douglas. *Movie History: A Survey*. Belmont, California: Wadsworth, 1991.

Gunning, Tom. "An Aesthetic of Astonishment: Early Film and the (In)credulous Spectator." *Art & Text* 34 (Spring 1989): 31–45.

——. "The Cinema of Attraction: Early Film, Its Spectator and the Avant-Garde." *Wide Angle* 8, nos. 3–4 (1986): 63–70.

——. *D. W. Griffith and the Origins of American Narrative Film: The Early Years at Biograph*. Urbana: U of Illinois P, 1991.

——. "Heard over the phone: The Lonely Villa and the de Lorde tradition of the terrors of technology." *Screen* 32:2 (Summer 1991): 184–196.

——. "Non-Continuity, Continuity, Discontinuity: A Theory of Genres in Early Film." *Iris* 2.1 (1984): 101–112.

——. " 'Primitive' Cinema—A Frame-up? or The Trick's On Us," *Cinema Journal* 28 (Winter 1989): 3–12.

——. "An Unseen Energy Swallows Space: The Space in Early Film and Its Relation to American Avant-Garde Film." *Film Before Griffith*. Ed. John Fell. Berkeley: U of California P, 1983. 355–366.

——. "Weaving a Narrative: Style and Economic Background in Griffith's Biograph Films." *Quarterly Review of Film Studies* (Winter 1981): 11–25.

——. " 'The Whole World Within Reach': Travel Images Without Borders." Unpublished paper presented to the Second International Domitor Conference, "Images Across Borders/Images sans frontières." Lausanne, Switzerland, June 1992.

Habermas, Jürgen. *Legitimation Crisis.* Trans. Thomas McCarthy. Boston: Beacon, 1975.

Hake, Sabine. "Girls and Crisis: the Other Side of Diversion." *New German Critique* 40 (Winter 1987): 147–166.

——. *The Cinema's Third Machine: Writing on Film in Germany 1907–1933.* Lincoln and London: U of Nebraska, 1993.

Hampton, Benjamin. *A History of the Movies.* London: Noel Douglas, 1932.

The Hand of Man. Exhibition catalog. Baltimore: Baltimore Museum of Art, Nov. 21, 1978–Jan. 7, 1979.

Hansen, Miriam. "Adventures of Goldilocks: Spectatorship, Consumerism and Public Life," *Camera Obscura* 22 (Jan. 1990): 51–71.

——. "Ambivalences of the 'Mass Ornament': King Vidor's *The Crowd.*" *Qui Parle* 5, no. 2 (Spring/Summer 1992): 102–119.

——. *Babel and Babylon: Spectatorship in American Silent Film.* Cambridge, Mass.: Harvard UP, 1991.

——. "Benjamin, Cinema and Experience: 'The Blue Flower in the Land of Technology.' " *New German Critique* 40 (Winter 1987): 179–224.

——. "Early Silent Cinema: Whose Public Sphere?" *New German Critique* 29 (Spring/Summer 1983): 147–184.

——. "Of Mice and Ducks: Benjamin and Adorno on Disney." *South Atlantic Quarterly* 92 (Winter 1993): 27–61.

——. "Universal Language and Democratic Culture: Myths of Origin in Early American Cinema." *Myth and Enlightenment in American Literature* (In Honor of Hans-Joachim Lang). Ed. Dieter Meindl and Friederich W. Horlacher in collaboration with Martin Christadler. Erlangen: Erlanger Forschungen, 1985. 321–342.

Hanson, Patricia King, ed. *The American Film Institute Catalog of Feature Films, 1911–1920.* 2 vols. Berkeley: U of California P, 1988.

Harris, William H. *Keeping the Faith: A. Philip Randolph, Milton P. Webster, and the Brotherhood of Sleeping Car Porters, 1925–1937.* Urbana: U of Illinois P, 1991.

Harvey, David. *Consciousness and the Urban Experience: Studies in the History and Theory of Capitalist Urbanization.* Baltimore: Johns Hopkins UP, 1985.

Hastings, Paul. *Railroads: An International History.* New York: Praeger, 1972.

Health and Pleasure on 'America's Greatest Railroad.' Four-Track Series 55. New York: New York Central Railroad, 1893.

Heath, Stephen. "Film and System: Terms of Analysis." Parts I and II. *Screen* 16 (Spring and Summer 1975): 7–77, 91–113.

——. "Narrative Space." *Questions of Cinema.* Bloomington: Indiana UP, 1981. 19–75.

Henderson, Robert M. *D. W. Griffith: The Years at Biograph.* New York: Farrar, 1970.

Hendricks, Gordon. *The Edison Motion Picture Myth.* Berkeley: U of California P, 1961.

Herbert Bayer — A Total Concept. Exhibition catalog. Denver: Denver Art Museum, Nov. 11–Dec. 23, 1973.

Hertz, Neil. "Medusa's Head: Male Hysteria Under Political Pressure." *Representations* 4 (Fall 1983): 27–54.

Higashi, Sumiko. *Cecil B. DeMille and American Culture: The Silent Era.* Berkeley: U of California P, 1994.

Hobsbawm, E. J. *The Age of Capital, 1848–1875.* New York: New American Library, 1979.

Holm, David F. "Thailand's Railways and Informal Imperialism." *Railway Imperialism.* Clarence B. Davis and Kenneth E. Wilburn, eds. New York: Greenwood, 1991. 121–136.

Holmes, Burton. *The Burton Holmes Lectures — Illustrated in Color, Accompanied by a Series of Original Motion Pictures Projected by the Chronomatographe.* Chicago: E. Burton Holmes, 1897–1898.

———. *The Burton Holmes Travelogues.* Vol. 1. New York: MacClure, 1908.

———. *The World Is Mine.* Culver City, Calif.: Murray & Gee, 1953.

Huntley, John. *Railways in the Cinema.* London: Ian Allan, 1969.

Huyssen, Andreas. *After the Great Divide: Modernism, Mass Culture and Postmodernism.* Bloomington: Indiana UP, 1986.

———. "Mass Culture as Woman: Modernism's Other." *After the Great Divide: Modernism, Mass Culture and Postmodernism.* Bloomington: Indiana UP, 1986. 44–62.

———. "The Vamp and the Machine: Technology and Sexuality in Fritz Lang's *Metropolis.*" *New German Critique* 24–25 (Fall/Winter 1981–82): 221–237.

L'Illustration. May 30, 1896: 454.

———. Christmas 1896: 27.

Jacobs, Lewis. *The Rise of the American Cinema.* 1939. New York: Teachers College Press, 1968.

Jakle, John A. *The Tourist: Travel in Twentieth-Century North America.* Lincoln: U of Nebraska P, 1985.

Jensen, Oliver. *Railroads in America.* New York: American Heritage, 1975.

Johnson, William. "Early Griffith: A Wider View." *Film Quarterly* (Spring 1976): 2–31.

Josephson, Matthew. *The Robber Barons: The Great American Capitalists, 1861–1901.* 1934. New York: Harcourt, 1962.

Jowett, Garth. *Film: The Democratic Art.* Boston: Little, Brown, 1976.

Kaes, Anton. "Literary Intellectuals and the Cinema: Charting a Controversy (1909–1929)." *New German Critique* 40 (Winter 1987): 7–34.

Kasson, John F. *Amusing the Million: Coney Island at the Turn of the Century.* New York: Hill and Wang, 1978.

Keil, Charlie. "Steel Engines and Cardboard Rockets: The Status of Fiction and Nonfiction in Early Cinema." *Persistence of Vision* 9 (1991): 37–45.

Keohane, Nannerl O., Michelle Z. Rosaldo, and Barbara C. Gelpi, eds. *Feminist Theory: A Critique of Ideology.* Chicago: U of Chicago P, 1982.

Kern, Stephen. *The Culture of Time and Space.* Cambridge, Mass.: Harvard UP, 1983.

Kessler, Frank and Gabriele Jutz. "Panoradigmes." Unpublished paper. Seminar of Jacques Aumont. Université de Paris III, Paris, France, 1982–83.

Key, Wilson Bryan. *Subliminal Seduction.* New York: New American Library, 1973.

King, Norman. *Abel Gance: A Politics of Spectacle.* London: British Film Institute, 1984.

Kirby, Lynne. "From Marinetti to Vertov: Woman on the Track of Avant-Garde Representation." *Quarterly Review of Film Studies* 10, no. 4 (1989): 309–323.

———. "Gender and Advertising in American Silent Film: From Early Cinema to *The Crowd,*" *Discourse* 13.2 (Spring/Summer 1991): 3–20.

———. "Male Hysteria and Early Cinema." *Camera Obscura,* no. 17 (December 1988): 113–131.

———. "Temporality, Sexuality and Narrative in *The General.*" *Wide Angle* 9, no. 1 (1987): 32–40.

———. "The Urban Spectator and the Crowd in Early American Train Films." *Iris,* no. 11 (Summer 1990): 49–62.

Kofman, Sarah. *Le Respect des femmes.* Paris: Editions Galilée, 1984.

Kowall, Linda. "Siegmund Lubin, The Forgotton Filmmaker." *Pennsylvania Heritage* (Winter 1986): 18–27.

Koszarski, Richard. *An Evening's Entertainment: The Age of the Silent Feature Picture, 1915–1928.* Vol. 3 of *History of the American Cinema.* General Editor, Charles Harpole. New York: Scribner's, 1990.

Kracauer, Siegfried. "The Cult of Distraction: On Berlin's Picture Palaces (1926)." *New German Critique* 40 (Winter 1987): 91–96.

———. *From Caligari to Hitler.* 1947. Princeton, N.J.: Princeton UP, 1974.

Kramer, Steven Philip, and James Michael Welsh. *Abel Gance.* Boston: Twayne, 1978.

Kristeva, Julia. *La Révolution du langage poétique: l'avant-garde à la fin du XIXe siècle, Lautréamont et Mallarmé.* Paris: Seuil, 1974.

———. "Woman's Time." *Feminist Theory: A Critique of Ideology.* Ed. Nannerl O. Keohane, Michelle Z. Rosaldo, and Barbara C. Gelpi. Chicago: U of Chicago P, 1982. 32–45.

Krutch, Joseph Wood, ed. *Walden and Other Writings.* By Henry David Thoreau. New York: Bantam, 1982.

Kubie, Lawrence S. and Sydney Margolis. "The Process of Hypnotism and the Nature of the Hypnotic State." *American Journal of Psychiatry* 100 (March 1944): 610–642.

Kuisel, Richard F. *Capitalism and the State in Modern France.* Cambridge: Cambridge UP, 1983.

Kuntzel, Thierry. "*Le Défilement*/A View in Close-up." *Camera Obscura* 2 (1977): 51–68.

———. "The Film Work, 2." *Camera Obscura* 5 (1980): 6–69.

———. Unpublished seminar on *Letter from an Unknown Woman.* Paris, 1977.

Kuspit, Donald. "The Status of Style." *Art Express* 1 (May–June 1981): 32–36.

Lacan, Jacques. "The Agency of the Letter in the Unconscious or Reason Since Freud." *Ecrits: A Selection.* Trans. Alan Sheridan. New York: Norton, 1977. 146–178.

———. "The Function and Field of Speech in Psychoanalysis." *Ecrits: A Selection.* Trans. Alan Sheridan. New York: Norton, 1977. 30–113.

Lackawanna Railroad. New York: American Bank Note, 1906.

Lambert, Anthony J. *Nineteenth-Century Railway History Through the* Illustrated London News. London: Newton Abbot, 1984.

Lang, Robert. *American Film Melodrama.* Princeton, N.J.: Princeton UP, 1989.

LaPlace, Maria. "Bette Davis and the Ideal of Consumption: A Look at *Now Voyager.*" *Wide Angle* 6, no. 4 (1985): 34–43.

Lears, T. J. Jackson. "From Salvation to Self-Realization: Advertising and the Therapeutic Roots of the Consumer Culture, 1880–1930." *The Culture of Consumption: Critical Essays in American History, 1880–1980.* Eds. Richard Wrightman Fox and T. J. Jackson Lears. New York: Pantheon, 1983. 1–38.

———. *No Place of Grace: Antimodernism and the Transformation of American Culture, 1880–1920.* New York: Pantheon, 1981.

Lears, T. J. Jackson, and Richard Wrightman Fox, eds. *The Culture of Consumption: Critical Essays in American History, 1880–1980.* New York: Pantheon, 1983.

Le Bon, Gustave. *The Crowd: A Study of the Popular Mind* (1895). Intro. Robert K. Merton. New York: Viking, 1960.

Léger, Fernand. "The Machine Aesthetic: Geometric Order and Truth." *Functions of Painting.* Ed. and introd. Edward F. Fry. Pref. George L. K. Morris. Trans. Alexandra Anderson. New York: Viking, 1965.

Lejeune, Anthony, ed. *The C. A. Lejeune Film Reader.* Manchester, U.K.: Carcanet, 1991.

Leyda, Jay. *Kino: A History of the Russian and Soviet Film.* 3d ed. New York: Collier, 1983.

Leyda, Jay, and Charles Musser, eds. *Before Hollywood: Turn-of-the-Century Film from American Archives*. Exhibition catalog. New York: American Federation of the Arts, 1986.

Licht, Walter. *Working for the Railroad*. Princeton, N.J.: Princeton UP, 1983.

Liggett, Barbara. "A History of the Adoption of Standard Time in the United States, 1869–1883." Master's thesis, U of Texas, 1960.

Lindsay, Vachel. *The Art of the Moving Picture*. 1915. New York: Macmillan, 1922.

Lodder, Christina. "Constructivism and Productivism in the 1920s." *Art into Life: Russian Constructivism, 1914–1932*. Exhibition catalog. Intro. Richard Andrews and Milena Kalinovska. Henry Art Gallery, U of Washington, Seattle; Walker Art Center, Minneapolis; State Tretyakov Gallery, Moscow. New York: Rizzoli, 1990. 99–116.

Loughney, Patrick G. "The Suburbanite." *Before Hollywood: Turn-of-the-Century Film from American Archives*. Exhibition catalog. Eds. Jay Leyda and Charles Musser. New York: American Federation of the Arts, 1986. 119.

Lyotard, Jean-François. *Discours, figure*. Paris: Klincksieck, 1971.

MacGowan, Kenneth. *Behind the Screen: The History and Techniques of the Motion Picture*. New York: Delta, 1965.

Maddox, Kenneth W. "The Railroad in the Eastern Landscape: 1850–1900." *The Railroad in the American Landscape: 1850–1900*. Exhibition catalog. Wellesley, Mass.: The Wellesley College Museum, April 15,–June 8, 1981.

Malthête-Méliès, Madeleine, ed. *Méliès et la naissance du spectacle cinématographique*. Paris: Klincksieck, 1984.

Marchand, Roland. *Advertising the American Dream*. Berkeley: U of California P, 1985.

Marinetti, F. T. *Le Futurisme*. Lausanne: Editions de l'Age d'Homme, 1980.

Markov, Vladimir. *Russian Futurism: A History*. Berkeley: U of California P, 1968.

Marshall, Leon. "The English and American Industrial City of the Nineteenth Century." *American Urban History*. Ed. Alexander B. Callow, Jr. New York: Oxford UP, 1973. 172–179.

Martin, Edward Winslow. *History of the Grange Movement, or The Farmer's War Against Monopolies*. 1873. New York: Burt Franklin, 1967.

Martindale, Don, and Gertrud Neuwirth. Intro. *The City*. By Max Weber. Ed. and trans. Don Martindale and Gertrud Neuwirth. New York: Free Press, 1958.

Marx, Leo. *The Machine in the Garden: Technology and the Pastoral Ideal in America*. 1964. London: Oxford UP, 1981.

———. "The Railroad-in-the-Landscape: An Iconological Reading of a Theme in American Art." Ed. Jack Salzman. *Prospects* 10 (1985): 15–64.

Mason, J. M. "The Right to Regulate Railway Charges." New York: National Anti-Monopoly League, 1881–1882.

Mast, Gerald. *A Short History of the Movies*. Indianapolis: Bobbs-Merrill, 1977.

Mast, Gerald, and Marshall Cohen, eds. *Film Theory and Criticism*. New York: Oxford UP, 1979.

May, Lary. *Screening Out the Past: The Birth of Mass Culture and the Motion Picture Industry*. Chicago: U of Chicago P, 1983.

Mayne, Judith. "Immigrants and Spectators." *Wide Angle* 5, no. 2 (1982): 32–41.

———. *Kino and the Woman Question*. Columbus: Ohio State UP, 1989.

———. "Uncovering the Female Body." *Before Hollywood: Turn-of-the-Century Film from American Archives*. Exhibition catalog. Ed. Jay Leyda and Charles Musser. New York: American Federation of the Arts, 1986. 63–68.

McGovern, Charles. Unpublished dissertation research. Department of History, Harvard U, 1987.

McKisick, L. D. "Addressed to the Lawyers in Congress—In the Matter of Funding the Debt which the Central Pacific Railroad Company owes to the United States." *San Francisco Examiner,* Jan. 1896.

McPherson, James Alan and Miller Williams, eds. *Railroad: Trains and Train People in American Culture.* New York: Random House, 1976.

Mercer, Lloyd J. *Railroads and Land Grant Policy: A Study in Government Intervention.* New York: Academic Press, 1982.

Merritt, Russell. "Nickelodeon Theaters: Building an Audience for the Movies." *Wide Angle* 1, no. 1 (1979): 4–9.

Metz, Christian. *The Imaginary Signifier: Psychoanalysis and the Cinema.* Trans. Celia Britton et al. Bloomington: Indiana UP, 1982.

Michelson, Annette. Intro. *Kino-Eye: The Writings of Dziga Vertov.* Ed. and intro. Annette Michelson. Trans. Kevin O'Brien. Berkeley: U of California P, 1984. xv–lxi.

———, ed. *Kino-Eye: The Writings of Dziga Vertov.* Trans. Kevin O'Brien. Berkeley: U of California P, 1984.

Mitry, Jean. *Histoire du cinéma. Art et industrie.* Vol. 1: *1895–1914.* Paris: Editions Universitaires, 1967.

Moews, Daniel. *Keaton: The Silent Features Close Up.* Berkeley: U of California P, 1977.

Moi, Toril. "Representation of Patriarchy: Sexuality and Epistemology in Freud's Dora." *In Dora's Case.* Ed. Charles Bernheimer and Claire Kahane. New York: Columbia UP, 1985. 181–199.

Monaco, Paul. *Cinema and Society: France and Germany During the Twenties.* New York: Elsevier, 1976.

Morris, Peter. "Images of Canada." *Film Before Griffith.* Ed. John Fell. Berkeley: U of California P, 1983. 67–74.

Moving Picture World 18 May 1907: 166.

———. 22 June 1907: 249–250.

———. 26 June 1907: 278.

Mulvey, Laura. "Visual Pleasure and Narrative Cinema." *Screen* 16 (Autumn 1975): 6–13.

Mumford, Lewis. *Technics and Civilization.* 1934. New York: Harcourt, 1963.

Munsterberg, Hugo. *The Film: A Psychological Study of the Silent Photoplay in 1916.* 1916. New York: Dover, 1970.

Musser, Charles. "The American Vitagraph, 1897–1901: Survival and Success in a Competitive Industry." *Film Before Griffith.* Ed. John Fell. Berkeley: U of California P, 1983. 22–66.

———. *Before the Nickelodeon: Edward S. Porter and the Edison Manufacturing Company.* Berkeley: U of California P, 1991.

———. *The Emergence of Cinema: The American Screen to 1907.* Vol. 1 of *History of the American Cinema,* Charles Harpole, general editor. New York: Scribner's, 1990.

———. *High-Class Moving Pictures: Lyman H. Howe and the Forgotten Era of Traveling Exhibition, 1880–1920.* In collaboration with Carol Nelson. Princeton, N.J.: Princeton UP, 1991.

———. "The Nickelodeon Era Begins: Establishing the Framework for Hollywood's Mode of Representation." *Framework* 22/23 (Autumn 1983): 4–11.

———. "Toward a History of Screen Practice." *Quarterly Review of Film Studies* 3 (Winter 1984): 59–69.

———. The Travel Genre in 1903–04: Moving Toward Fictional Narrative." *Iris* 2, no. 1 (1984): 47–60.

———. "Work, Ideology and Chaplin's Tramp." *Resisting Images: Essays on Cinema and History.* Ed. Robert Sklar and Charles Musser. Philadelphia: Temple UP, 1990. 36–67.

My Canadian Sweetheart, or Aunt Tabby's Summer Boarders. N.p.: Connecticut Valley and Passumpsic Railroads, 1885.

Niver, Kemp. *Early Motion Pictures: The Paper Prints Collection in the Library of Congress.* Ed. Bebe Bergsten. Washington, D.C.: Library of Congress, 1985.

Noguez, Dominique. "Fantaisie férroviaire." *Traverses* 13: Le Modèle férroviaire (Dec. 1978): 95–102.

Nolley, Ken. "John Ford and the Hollywood Indian." *Film and History* 23, nos. 1–4 (1993): 44–57.

Northrup, Herbert R. *Organized Labor and the Negro.* New York: Harper, 1944.

Novak, Barbara. *Nature and Culture: American Landscape Painting, 1825–1875.* New York: Oxford UP, 1980.

O'Malley, Michael. *Keeping Watch: A History of American Time.* New York: Penguin, 1990.

Ortner, Sherry B. "Is Female to Male as Nature Is to Culture?" *Woman, Culture and Society.* Ed. Michelle Z. Rosaldo and Louise Lamphere. Stanford, Calif.: Stanford UP, 1974. 67–87.

Ouerd, Michèle. "Introduction." *Leçons sur l'hystérie virile, Charcot.* Paris: Le Sycamore, 1984. 11–31.

Patterson, Joseph Medill. "The Nickelodeons: The Poor Man's Elementary Course in the Drama." *Saturday Evening Post,* Nov. 23, 1907, 38. Reproduced in George C. Pratt. *Spellbound in Darkness: A History of the Silent Film.* 1966. Greenwich, Conn.: New York Graphic Society, 1973. 46–51.

Pecheux, Julien. *L'Age d'or du rail européen (1850–1900).* Paris: Berger-Levrault, 1975.

Peiss, Kathy. *Cheap Amusements: Working Women and Leisure in Turn-of-the-Century New York.* Philadelphia: Temple UP, 1986.

Peiss, Kathy, and Christina Simmons, eds. *Passion and Power: Sexuality in History.* Philadelphia: Temple UP, 1989.

Petro, Patrice. "After Shock/Between Boredom and History." *Discourse* 16 (Winter 1993–94): 77–99.

———. *Joyless Streets.* Princeton, N.J.: Princeton UP, 1989.

———. "Modernity and Mass Culture in Weimar: Contours of a Discourse on Sexuality in Early Theories of Perception and Representation." *New German Critique* 40 (Winter 1987): 115–146.

Pfeffer, Paula F. *A. Philip Randolph: Pioneer of the Civil Rights Movement.* Baton Rouge: Louisiana State UP, 1990.

Pinel, Vincent. "Petit guide chronologique du cinéma français (1895–1909)." *L'Avant-scène du cinéma* 334 (Nov. 1984): 7–16.

Place, J. A. "*Young Mr. Lincoln,* 1939." *Wide Angle* 2, no. 4 (1978): 28–35.

Poggioli, Renato. *Theory of the Avant-Garde.* Trans. Gerald Fitzgerald. New York: Harper, 1971.

Pratt, George C. *Spellbound in Darkness: A History of the Silent Film.* 1966. Greenwich, Conn.: New York Graphic Society, 1973.

Production Catalog of the American Mutoscope and Biograph Company (AM&B), 1896–1902. Museum of Modern Art Records. N.p., n.p.

"Program Notes for *The Iron Horse.*" Unattributed. Museum of Modern Art, New York, 1980.

Querrien, Anne. "Le petit train." *Traverses* 13: Le Modèle férroviaire (Dec. 1978): 95–102.

Rabinbach, Anson. "The Body without Fatigue: A Nineteenth-Century Utopia." *Political Symbolism in Modern Europe: Essays in Honor of George L. Mosse.* Ed. Seymour Drescher, David Sabean, and Allan Sharlin. New Brunswick, N.J.: Transaction Books, 1982. 51–63.

Rabinovitz, Lauren. "Temptations of Pleasure: Nickelodeons, Amusement Parks, and the Sights of Female Sexuality." *Camera Obscura* 23 (May 1990): 71–90.

The Railroad in the American Landscape: 1850–1900. Exhibition catalog. Wellesley, Mass.: Wellesley College Museum, April 15–June 8, 1981.

"Railway Accidents in the Third Quarter of 1904." *Railway Age*, Jan. 27, 1905, 105.

Railway Age Gazette, Feb. 13, 1914, 2.

Ramsaye, Terry. *A Million and One Nights*. New York: Simon and Schuster, 1926.

Rea, Samuel. "How the States Can Cooperate in the Efficient National Regulation of Railroads." N.p.: Pennsylvania Railroad, 1917.

Reed, Robert C. *Train Wrecks*. New York: Bonanza Books, 1968.

Reid, Mark A. *Redefining Black Film*. Berkeley: U of California P, 1993.

Richards, Jeffrey, and John H. MacKenzie. *The Railway Station: A Social History*. New York: Oxford UP, 1986.

Riesman, David, Nathan Glazer, and Reuel Denney. *The Lonely Crowd*. 1950. New York: Doubleday, 1955.

Riis, Jacob. *How the Other Half Lives*. 1890. New York: Dover, 1977.

Robinson, Ronald E. "Conclusion: Railways and Informal Empire." *Railway Imperialism*. Ed. Clarence B. Davis and Kenneth E. Wilburn. New York: Greenwood, 1991. 175–196.

———. "Introduction: Railway Imperialism." Ed. Clarence B. Davis and Kenneth E. Wilburn. *Railway Imperialism*. New York: Greenwood, 1991. 1–6.

Rosaldo, Michelle Z., and Louise Lamphere, eds. *Woman, Culture and Society*. Stanford, Calif.: Stanford UP, 1974.

Rosen, Philip. "History, Textuality, Nation: Kracauer, Burch, and Some Problems in the Study of National Cinema." *Iris* 2, no. 2 (1984): 69–84.

———. *Narrative, Apparatus, Ideology*. New York: Columbia UP, 1986.

Rosenzweig, Roy, and Elizabeth Blackmar. *The Park and the People: A History of Central Park*. Ithaca, N.Y.: Cornell UP, 1992.

Sadoul, Georges. *French Cinema*. London: Falcon Press, 1953.

———. *Georges Méliès*. Paris: Editions Seghers, 1961.

Sansot, Pierre. "Réseaux: Structures ou rêveries férroviaires." *Traverses* 13: Le modèle férroviaire (Dec. 1978): 36–48.

Santino, Jack. *Miles of Smiles, Years of Struggle: Stories of Black Pullman Porters*. Urbana: U of Illinois P, 1989.

Sayings and Writings About the Railway — By Those Who Have Managed Them and Those Who Have Studied Their Problems. New York: Railway Gazette, 1913.

Schapiro, Meyer. "The Nature of Abstract Art" (1937). *Modern Art: 19th and 20th Centuries*. By Meyer Schapiro. New York: Braziller, 1978. 206–211.

Schivelbusch, Wolfgang. *The Railway Journey: Trains and Travel in the 19th Century*. Trans. Anselm Hollo. New York: Urizen Books, 1979.

Schlüpmann, Heide. "Early German Cinema — Melodrama: Social Drama." *Popular European Cinema*. Ed. Richard Dyer and Ginette Vincendeau. London: Routledge and Kegan Paul, 1992. 206–219.

———. "Melodrama and Social Drama in the Early German Cinema." *Camera Obscura* 22 (Jan. 1990): 73–89.

———. "Phenomenology of Film: On Siegfried Kracauer's Writings of the 1920s." *New German Critique* 40 (Winter 1987): 97–114.

Schmitt, Frantz. "Méliès et ses contemporains: Quelques rapprochements." *Méliès et la naissance du spectacle cinématographique*. Ed. Madeleine Malthête-Méliès. Paris: Klincksieck, 1984. 99–106.

Schwarz, Judith, Kathy Peiss, and Christina Simmons. " 'We Were a Little Band of Willful Women': The Heterodoxy Club of Greenwich Village." *Passion and Power: Sexuality in History.* Ed. Kathy Peiss and Christina Simmons. Philadelphia: Temple UP, 1989. 118–137.

Simmel, Georg. "The Metropolis and Mental Life." *Georg Simmel: On Individuality and Social Forms — Selected Writings.* Ed. and intro. Donald N. Levine. Chicago: U Chicago Press, 1971. 324–339.

Simmons, Jack. *The Railways of Britain.* London: Routledge and Kegan Paul, 1972.

Singer, Ben. "Female Power in the Serial-Queen Melodrama: The Etiology of an Anomaly." *Camera Obscura* 22 (Jan. 1990): 90–129.

Sklar, Robert. *Movie-Made America: A Cultural History of American Movies.* New York: Vintage Books, 1975.

Smith, Henry Nash. *The Virgin Land: The American West as Symbol and Myth.* 1950. Cambridge, Mass.: Harvard UP, 1978.

Sontag, Susan. *Against Interpretation.* New York: Farrar, 1966.

———. *On Photography.* New York: Farrar, 1977.

Stephens, Carlene. " 'The Most Reliable Time': William Bond, the New England Railroads, and the Formation of Time Awareness in 19th-century America." *Technology and Culture* 30 (Jan. 1989): 1–24.

Stilgoe, John. *Metropolitan Corridor: Railroads and the American Scene.* New Haven, Conn.: Yale UP, 1983.

Stover, John. *The Life and Decline of the American Railroad.* New York: Oxford UP, 1970.

Suleiman, Susan Rubin, ed. *The Female Body in Western Culture.* Cambridge, Mass.: Harvard UP, 1986.

The Summer Boarder. Travel Series 17. N.p.: New York Central Railroad, ca. 1900.

Taft, Robert. *Photograph and the American Scene.* 1930. New York: Dover, 1964.

Tarr, Joel A. "From City to Suburb: The 'Moral' Influence of Transportation Technology." *American Urban History.* Ed. Alexander B. Callow, Jr. New York: Oxford UP, 1973. 202–212.

Theweleit, Klaus. *Männerphantasein.* Vol. 1: *Frauen, Flüten, Korper, Geschichte.* Frankfurt am Main: Verlag Roter Stern, 1977.

Thompson, E. P. "Time, Work-Discipline and Industrial Capitalism." *Past and Present* 38 (Dec. 1967): 56–97.

Thompson, Kristin. *Exporting Entertainment.* London: British Film Institute, 1985.

———. "The Formulation of the Classical Style, 1909–1928." *The Classical Hollywood Cinema: Film, Style and Mode of Production to 1960.* Ed. David Bordwell, Kristin Thompson, and Janet Staiger. New York: Columbia UP, 1985. 155–240.

Thoreau, Henry David. *Walden and Other Writings.* Ed. Joseph Wood Krutch. New York: Bantam, 1982.

Todorov, Tzvetan. *The Poetics of Prose.* Ithaca, N.Y.: Cornell UP, 1977.

Tours of Florida. Washington, D.C.: Pennsylvania Railroad, 1892.

Trachtenberg, Alan. *The Incorporation of America: Culture and Society in the Gilded Age.* New York: Hill and Wang, 1982.

Tsivian, Yuri. "*L'Homme à la caméra* de Dziga Vertov en tant que texte constructiviste." *Revue de cinéma/Ecran* 351 (June 1980): 122–125.

Tzara, Tristan. "Lecture on Dada." *Seven Manifestos and Lampisteries.* Trans. Barbara Wright. London: John Calder, 1977.

Uricchio, William and Roberta E. Pearson. *Reframing Culture: The Case of the Vitagraph Quality Films.* Princeton, N.J.: Princeton UP, 1993.

Vertov, Dziga. "Artistic Drama and Kino-Eye." (1924). *Kino-Eye: The Writings of Dziga Vertov.* Ed. and intro. Annette Michelson. Trans. Kevin O'Brien. Berkeley: U of California P, 1984.

———. "The Council of Three." *Kino-Eye* 17.

———. "The Essence of Kino-eye." *Kino-Eye* 49.

———. "The Factory of Facts." *Kino-Eye* 59.

———. "Lullaby." *Kino-Eye* 200.

———. "The Man with a Movie Camera," *Kino-Eye* 82–85.

———. "The Man with a Movie Camera (A Visual Symphony)," (1928) *Kino-Eye* 283–289.

———. "Notebook entry, 1927." *Kino-Eye* 167.

———. "Provisional Instructions to Kino-Eye Groups." *Kino-Eye* 73.

———. "A Young Woman Composer." *Kino-Eye* 297.

The Vestibule. Norfolk, Va.: Sam. W. Bowman, 1894/1895.

Vincenot, Henri. *La Vie quotidienne dans les chemins der fer au XIXe siècle.* Paris: Hachette, 1975.

Virilio, Paul. "L'Empire et l'emprise." *Traverses* 13: Le Modèle férroviaire (Dec. 1978): 3–27.

———. *Speed and Politics.* Trans. Mark Polizzotti. New York: Semiotext(e), 1986.

Vuillermoz, Emile. "*La Roue*" (1923). *French Film Theory and Criticism: A History/Anthology, 1907– 1939.* Vol. 1: 1907–1929. Princeton, N.J.: Princeton UP, 1988. 278.

Waller, Gregory A. "Another Audience: Black Moviegoing, 1907–16." *Cinema Journal* 31, no. 2 (Winter 1992): 3–25.

Wallerstein, Immanuel. *The Politics of the World Economy: The States, the Movements and the Civilizations.* Cambridge: Cambridge UP, 1984.

Walsh, Michael. "Slipping into Darkness: Figures of Waking in Cinema." *Wide Angle* 5, no. 4 (1984): 14–20.

Walther, Susan Danly. "The Railroad in the Western Landscape: 1865–1900." *The Railroad in the American Landscape: 1850–1950.* Exhibition catalog. Wellesley, Mass.: Wellesley College Museum, April 15–June 8, 1981.

Ward, James A. *Railroads and the Character of America, 1820–1887.* Knoxville: U of Tennessee P, 1986.

Warshaw Collection. National Museum of American History, Washington, D.C. Boxes 62, 76, 79, 80, 81, 82, 83, 84, 85, 88, 94, 95.

Weber, Max. *The City.* Trans. and ed. Don Martindale and Gertrud Neuwirth. New York: Free Press, 1958.

Weeks, Philip, and James B. Gidney. *Subjugation and Dishonor: A Brief History of the Travail of the Native Americans.* Huntington, N.Y.: Robert F. Krieger, 1981.

Weiss, Philip. "Hollywood at a Fever Pitch." *New York Times Magazine,* Dec. 26, 1993, 20–44.

Western Railways' Committee on Public Relations. *Railroad Facts, no. 4.* Chicago: Western Railways' Committee on Public Relations, 1926.

Whitman, Walt. *Leaves of Grass.* Intro. by Stuart P. Sherman. New York: Scribner's, 1922.

Wiebe, Robert H. *The Search for Order, 1877–1920.* New York: Hill and Wang, 1967.

Williams, Archibald. *The Romance of Modern Locomotion.* London: Seeley, Service, 1912.

Wilson, Christopher P. "The Rhetoric of Consumption: Mass-Market Magazines and the Demise of the Gentle Reader, 1880–1920." *The Culture of Consumption: Critical Essays in American History, 1880–1980.* Ed. Richard Wrightman Fox and T. J. Jackson Lears. New York: Pantheon, 1983. 39–64.

Winter Pleasure Tours. Philadelphia: Pennsylvania Railroad, 1890.

Wolfe, Charles. "Buster Keaton and the Historical Imagination of Silent Comedy." Unpublished paper presented at the conference "1895: The Culture That Made Cinema." Stanford U. April 29, 1995.

"The Wonder of the Age." *Book of the Royal Blue*, Oct. 1897: 2–3.

Zeldin, Theodore. *France, 1848–1945*. Vol. 1: *Politics and Anger*. Oxford: Oxford UP, 1977.

———. *France, 1848–1945*. Vol. 2: *Intellect, Taste and Anxiety*. Oxford: Clarendon, 1979.

Zerubavel, Eviatar. "The Standardization of Time: A Sociohistorical Perspective." *American Journal of Sociology* 88, no. 1 (1982): 1–23.

Zimmerman, Patricia R. "Filming Adventures in Beauty: Pictorialism, Amateur Cinematography, and the Filmic Pleasures of the Nuclear Family from 1897 to 1923." *Afterimage* 14 (Dec. 1986): 8–11.

Zola, Emile. *La Bête humaine*. 1890. Paris: Garnier-Flammarion, 1972.

JUL - - 2002

Lynne Kirby is a senior producer for the Courtroom Television
Network in New York.
Library of Congress Cataloging-in-Publication Data
Kirby, Lynne.
Parallel tracks : the railroad and silent cinema / by Lynne Kirby.
Includes bibliographical references and index.
ISBN 0-8223-1833-4 (cloth : alk. paper). — ISBN 0-8223-1839-3
(pbk. : alk. paper)
1. Railroads in motion pictures. 2. Silent films. I. Title.
PN1995.9.R25K57 1996   791.43'656 — dc20   96-26745 CIP